GU...
TO THE
GENEALOGICAL OFFICE
DUBLIN

COIMISIÚN LÁIMHSCRÍBHINNÍ NA HÉIREANN

GUIDE
TO THE
GENEALOGICAL OFFICE
DUBLIN

IRISH MANUSCRIPTS COMMISSION
1998

© 1998
Irish Manuscripts Commission

Reproduced from a facsimile of the 1949 edition *Analecta Hibernica* No 17
a facsimile of the 1970 edition *Analecta Hibernica* No 26
and an essay by John Grenham, 1998

Printed by ColourBooks, Dublin

Cover design by Dunbar Design

PAPERBACK 1 874280 23 1

CONTENTS

The Genealogical Office and its Records
      JOHN GRENHAM 1

Guide to Records of the Genealogical Office with a Commentary on Heraldry in Ireland and on the History of the Office
      JOHN BARRY 35

Index of Will Abstracts in the Genealogical Office, Dublin
      P. BERYL EUSTACE 79

THE
GENEALOGICAL OFFICE
AND ITS
RECORDS

JOHN GRENHAM

THE GENEALOGICAL OFFICE

THE GENEALOGICAL OFFICE is the successor to the office of Ulster King of Arms, also known simply as 'The Office of Arms', which was created in 1552 when Edward VI designated Bartholomew Butler the chief heraldic authority in Ireland, with the title of 'Ulster'. The reasons for the choice of 'Ulster' rather than 'Ireland' remain somewhat unclear; it seems likely that the older title of 'Ireland King of Arms' was already in use amongst the heralds at the College of Arms in London. Whatever the reason, Ulster King of Arms acquired full jurisdiction over arms in Ireland, and retained it for almost four hundred years until 1943, when the Office was renamed The Genealogical Office, and Ulster became 'Chief Herald of Ireland', with the same powers as his predecessor.

At the outset, the authority of Ulster was limited to those areas of the country under English authority; heraldry, as a feudal practice, was in any case quite alien to Gaelic culture. Up to the end of the seventeenth century, the functions of the Office remained purely heraldic, ascertaining and recording what arms were in use, and by what right families used them. From the late seventeenth century, Ulster began to acquire other duties, as an officer of the crown intimately linked to the government. These duties were largely ceremonial, deciding and arranging precedence on state occasions, as well as introducing new peers to the Irish House of lords, and recording peerage successions. In essence, these two areas, the heraldic and the ceremonial, remained the principal functions of the Office over the succeeding three centuries, with Ulster becoming registrar of the chivalric Order of St Patrick instituted in 1783, and continuing to have responsibility for the ceremonial aspects of state occasions at the court of the viceroy.

The functioning of the Office depended to an inordinate degree on the personal qualities of Ulster, and an unfortunate number of the holders of the position, in the eighteenth century especially, appear to have regarded it as a sinecure, paying little attention to the keeping of records and treating the manuscript collection as their personal property. It was only with the arrival of Sir William Betham in the early nineteenth century that the business of the Office was put on a sound footing, and serious attention paid to the collection and care of manuscripts. As a consequence, although a number of the official records are much earlier, the vast majority of the Office's holdings do not pre-date the nineteenth century.

In the course of carrying out its heraldic functions, the Office inevitably acquired a large amount of material of genealogical interest, since the right to bear arms is strictly hereditary. Nonetheless, the new title given to the Office in 1943, 'The Genealogical Office', was somewhat inaccurate. Its principal function continues to be heraldic, the granting and confirmation of official achievements to individuals and corporate bodies. Up to the 1980s, the Office also carried out commissioned research into family history. This service has been discontinued.

GENEALOGICAL OFFICE RECORDS

MANUSCRIPTS

The manuscripts of the Genealogical Office are numbered in a single series from 1 to 822. They are, however, of a very mixed nature, reflections of the Office's changing functions over the centuries, and are best dealt with in categories based on those functions. The following account divides them into (1) Official Records, (2) Administrative Records and Reference Works, and (3) Research Material.

(1) OFFICIAL RECORDS

A number of sets of manuscripts are direct products of the official functions of the Office, and may be termed official records. On the heraldic side, the principal records are the Visitations (GO 47–9), the Funeral Entries (GO 64–79), the official grants and confirmations of arms (GO 103–111g), and the Registered Pedigrees (GO 156–182). In addition to these, four other manuscript groups reflect duties which Ulster's Office acquired over the centuries. These are the Lords' Entries (GO 183–188), Royal Warrants for Changes of Name, (GO 26 & 149–154A), Baronets' Records (GO 112–4), and Gaelic Chieftains (GO 610 & 627).

The Visitations were an attempt to carry out in Ireland heraldic visitations along the lines of those which the College of Arms had been using in England for almost a century to control the bearing of arms. The results were meagre, confined to areas close to Dublin, and almost certainly incomplete even for those areas. The following places were covered: Dublin and parts of Co. Louth, 1568–70; Drogheda and Ardee, 1570; Swords, 1572; Cork, 1574; Limerick, 1574; Dublin city,

1607; Dublin county, 1610; Wexford, 1610. They are indexed in GO 117.

The Funeral Entries, covering the period 1588–1691, make up some of the deficiencies of the Visitations. Their aim was to record the name, wife and issue of deceased nobility and gentry, along with their arms. In addition, many of the Entries include very beautiful illustrations of the arms and armorial devices used at the funeral, as well as notes on the ordering of the funeral processions and ceremonies. An index to the Entries is found in GO 386.

One of the later effects of the lack of visitations was to make it difficult for Ulster to verify from his own records that a particular family had a right to its arms. This gave rise to the practice, peculiar to Ireland, of issuing 'confirmations' of arms, which were taken as official registrations, and were dependent on an applicant being able to show that the arms in question had been in use in his family for three generations or one hundred years. The records of these confirmations, and of actual grants of arms, are found in GO 103–111g, dating from 1698, and still current. Earlier grants and confirmations are scattered through the manuscript collection; a complete index to all arms officially recorded in the Office is to be found in GO 422–3. Hayes' *Manuscript Sources for the Study of Irish Civilization* reproduces this, and includes a summary of any genealogical information.

Since the right to bear arms is hereditary, the authentication of arms required the collection of a large amount of genealogical material. This is undoubtedly the origin of the Registered Pedigrees, GO 156–182, but the series very quickly acquired a life of its own, and the majority of entries are now purely genealogical. It is particularly important for the collection of 18th century pedigrees of Irish emigres to France, produced in response to their need to prove membership of the nobility; admission to such a position carried very substantial privileges, and the proofs required included the signature of Ulster. The series continues up to the present, and is indexed in GO 469, as well as Hayes' *Manuscript Sources*.

Partly as a result of difficulties concerning the status of lords who had supported James II, from 1698 one of the duties of Ulster became the keeping of an official list of Irish peers, 'Ulster's Roll'. In theory, all of those entitled to sit in the Irish House of Lords, whether by creation of a new peerage, or by succession, were obliged to inform Ulster before they could be officially introduced to the House. In practice, the vast bulk of information collected relates to successions, with the heirs supplying the date of death and place of burial, arms, marriages and issue. The series covers the period from 1698 to 1939, and is indexed in GO 470.

In order to regulate the assumption of arms and titles, after 1784 it became necessary to obtain a warrant from the king for a change of name and arms. From 1795, the Irish House of Lords made it obligatory to register such a warrant in Ulster's Office. The result is the manuscript series known officially as 'Royal Warrants for changes of name and licences for changes of name'. Most of the nineteenth century changes came about as a result of wills, with an inheritance made conditional on a change of name. Hayes' *Manuscript Sources* indexes the series.

A similar need to regulate the improper assumption of titles produced the Baronet's records, GO 112–4. A royal warrant of 1789 for 'correcting and preventing abuses in the order of baronets' made registration of their arms and pedigrees with Ulster obligatory. The volumes are indexed in GO 470.

The records of Gaelic Chieftains in GO 610 and 627 are the consequence of a revival instituted in the 1940s by Dr. Edward MacLysaght, the first Chief Herald of Ireland. He attempted to trace the senior lineal descendants in the male line of the last recorded Gaelic 'Chief of the Name', who was then officially designated as the contemporary holder of the title. The practice has met with mixed success, since the collapse of Gaelic culture in the seventeenth century left an enormous gulf to be bridged, and the chieftainships were not in any case originally passed on by primogeniture but by election within the extended kin-group. Nonetheless, more than twenty Chiefs have been designated, and the records of the research which went into establishing their right to the title are extremely interesting.

(2) ADMINISTRATIVE RECORDS AND REFERENCE WORKS

Many of the documents now part of the general manuscript series simply derive from the paperwork necessary to run an office. These include cash books, receipts, Ulster's Diaries, letter books, day books, and records of fees due for the various functions carried out by Ulster. Of these, the most interesting from a genealogical point of view are the letter books (GO 361–378), copies of all letters sent out from the Office between 1789 and 1853, and the Betham letters (GO 580–604), a collection of the letters received by Sir William Betham between c.1810 and 1830 and purchased by the Genealogical Office in 1943. The former are indexed volume by volume. The latter are of more potential value. The only index, however, comes in the original catalogue of the sale of the letters, dated 1936, a copy of which is to be found at the Office, though not numbered among the manuscripts. The catalogue lists the letters alphabetically by addressor, and a supplementary surnames index provides a guide to the families dealt with. Another eight volumes of the series, unindexed, are to be found in the National Archives (M.744–751).

As well as documents produced in the day-to-day running of the Office, a large number of manuscripts also relate to the ceremonial functions performed by Ulster. These include official orders relating to changes of insignia, papers dealing with precedence and protocol, records of official functions at the vice-regal court, and the records of the Order of St Patrick. There is little of genealogical interest in these.

In the course of their heraldic and genealogical work, Ulster and his officers accumulated over the years a large series of manuscripts for use as reference works. These include manuscript armories, ordinaries of arms, treatises on heraldry and precedence, a series of English Visitations, and blazons of arms of English and Scottish peers. The bulk of the material is heraldic, but there is a good deal of incidental genealogical information, particularly in the seventeenth century ordinaries of arms.

(3) RESEARCH MATERIAL

The most useful manuscripts in the Genealogical Office collection are those acquired and created to provide sources for genealogical research. The policy was begun in the early nineteenth century by Sir William Betham and continued by all of his successors, and has produced a wide range of material, much of it based on records which were destroyed in the Public Record Office in 1922. It may be divided into three broad categories: (i) Betham's own compilations; (ii) the collections of later genealogists; (iii) other records. The sheer diversity of these documents makes a complete account impractical here; what follows is a broad outline.

The greatest single work produced by Betham is the collection of abstracts of family information from prerogative wills. These are divided into a number of series: GO 223–226 ('Old Series' Vols I–IV) covers wills before 1700; GO 227–254 ('New Series' Vols 1–31) covers wills from 1700 to c.1800. The series are roughly alphabetical, with each volume containing its own index. Sir Arthur Vicars' *Index to the Prerogative Wills of Ireland 1536–1810* provides a guide to wills covered. Many of the sketch pedigrees include later amendments and additions from other sources. GO 255–6 provides an index of all of the marriage alliances recorded in the wills. Another series, GO 203–214

('Will Pedigrees' Vols I–XII) represents an unfinished attempt to rearrange all of these sketch pedigrees into strictly alphabetical order. Betham also produced a large number of sketch pedigrees based on other sources, collected as 'Ancient Anglo-Irish Families' Vols I–VI (GO 215–219), 'Milesian Families' Vols I–III (GO 220–222), and the '1st series' Vols I–XVI (GO 261–276) and 2nd series Vols I–VII (GO 292–298). All of these are indexed in GO 470.

As well as the sketch pedigrees and the letters (covered above under 'Administrative Records'), there are two other sources in the collection which owe their origin to Betham. The first of these, genealogical and historical excerpts from the plea rolls and patent rolls from Henry III to Edward VI (GO 189–193), constitute the single most important source of information on Anglo-Norman genealogy in Ireland. Betham's transcript of Roger O'Ferrall's 'Linea Antiqua', a collation of earlier genealogies compiled in 1709, is the Office's most extensive work on Gaelic, as opposed to Anglo-Irish, genealogy. This copy (in three volumes, GO 145–7, with an index to the complete work in 147) also contains Betham's interpolations and additions, unfortunately unsourced. It records the arms of many of the Gaelic families covered, without giving any authority for them, and is the source of most of the arms illustrated in Dr Edward MacLysaght's *Irish Families*.

Pedigrees and research notes produced by later amateur and professional genealogists make up a large part of the Office's manuscript collection. Among those who have contributed to these are Sir Edmund Bewley, Denis O'Callaghan Fisher, Tenison Groves, Alfred Moloney, T.U. Sadleir, Rev. H.B. Swanzy and many others, For the most part, their records concern either particular groups of families or particular geographical areas. Some of these have their own indexes, some are covered by GO 470 and 117, others have will abstracts only indexed in GO 429. The numerical listing at the end of this article provides a guide. As well as these, some of the results of Ulster's Office own research in the late nineteenth and early twentieth century are classed as manuscripts, GO 800–822. These constitute no more than a fraction of the total research information produced by the Office. They are indexed in Hayes' *Manuscript Sources*.

A final class of records consists of extremely diverse documents, having only their potential genealogical usefulness in common. It includes such items as freeholders' lists from different counties, extracts from parish registers, transcripts of the Dublin city roll of freemen, of returns from the 1766 census, of city directories from various periods, and much more. More detailed information will be found in the list at the end of this article.

ARCHIVES

As well as the manuscripts series, now closed, the Genealogical Office also has extremely extensive archive records of the commissioned research it carried out up to the 1980s. For the closing decades of the nineteenth century and the early decades of the twentieth century, these records are still largely concerned with the Anglo-Irish. Manuscripts 800–822 cover perhaps 5% of this material. The remainder is sorted in roughly alphabetical order in cardboard boxes along one whole wall of the Genealogical Office strong room. It is to be hoped that the Office can acquire the resources to sort and index it soon, since it contains a great deal of very valuable information.

After the creation of The Genealogical Office in 1943, the focus of the commissioned research shifted, with most work now carried out on behalf of the descendants of emigrants to Australia and North America. There are over 20,000 research files giving details of the results of this research. A continuing project to index the families concerned has so far covered over 6,000 of these; the results are on computer at the Office.

RESEARCH IN GENEALOGICAL OFFICE MANUSCRIPTS

The biggest single obstacle to research in GO manuscripts is the lack of a single, comprehensive index, though this has been mitigated to some extent by the recent work of Ms. V.W. McAnlis (see below) Many attempts have been made over the centuries of the Office's existence to produce a complete index; the result has been a proliferation of partial indexes, each covering some of the collection, none covering it all. These are dealt with below. In addition, the policy used in the creation of manuscripts appears to have become somewhat inconsistent from the 1940s. Before then only the earliest and most heterogeneous manuscripts had been numbered in a single series, with each of the other groups simply having its own volume numbers, 'Lords Entries Vol. II' or 'Registered Pedigrees Vol. 12', for example. The laudable attempt to produce a consistent numbering system, starting at GO 1 and moving through the collection, seems to have given rise to the piecemeal addition of material which was more properly the preserve of the National Library. The subsequent transfers to the Library, and renumbering of remaining material, produced a virtual collapse of the system in the upper numbers. No manuscripts exist for many of the numbers between 600 and 800. The numerical list of manuscripts at the end of this article reflects the current situation, with titles no longer in the Office given in brackets.

In recent years, Virginia Wade McAnlis has taken on the task of creating a consolidated index for Genealogical Office manuscripts, working from the microfilm copies available through the Family History Centres of the Church of Jesus Christ of the Latter-Day Saints, the Mormons. This work, in five volumes, is available from Ms McAnlis at 82 Gunn Road, Port Angeles, WA 98362–9108, USA. A copy is also available from the National Library of Ireland. It brings together the references from the indexes numbered as GO Mss 117, 148, 255–60, 386, 422–3, 470. Details of these are found below. In addition to the page references included in these indexes, Ms McAnlis also includes microfilm references for the Latter-Day Saints collection.

INDEXES

GO 59: This is a detailed calendar of manuscripts 1–58, particularly useful since many of these consist of very early heterogeneous material bound together for preservation.

GO 115: Indexes the following: Arms A–C; Grants & Confirmations, A & B; Visitations; British Families; Funeral Entries; Registered Pedigrees Vols 1–10. Only the Visitations (GO 47–49) and British Families (GO 44–46) are not indexed more fully elsewhere.

GO 116: An unfinished index

GO 117: Duplicates much of the material indexed in GO 422, GO 470 and Hayes' Manuscript Sources. Only the following are not covered elsewhere: Antrim Families (GO 213); Fisher Mss (GO 280–85); Irish Arms at the College of Heralds (GO 37); Irish Coats of Arms (Fota) (GO 526); Heraldic Sketches (GO 125); Betham Letter Books (GO 362–78); Ecclesiatical Visitations (GO 198–9); Reynell Mss (GO 445).

GO 148: Index to 'Linea Antiqua'. The version at the end of GO 147, 'Linea Antiqua' Vol. III is more complete.

GO 255–6: Index to Alliances in Prerogative Wills (Betham)

GO 386: Index to the Funeral Entries

GO 422–3: Index to arms registered at the Office

GO 429: Eustace Index to Will Abstracts at the Genealogical Office. The published version in 'Analecta Hibernica', Vol. 17, is less extensive than the manuscript copy.

GO 469: Index to Registered Pedigrees. This appears to be less complete than the version included in Hayes' *Manuscript Sources*. Attached to it is a typescript copy of the index to the Genealogical Office collection of pedigree rolls.

GO 470: Index to Unregistered Pedigrees. This is the single most useful index in the Office, covering the Lord's Entries, the Betham pedigrees and many of the genealogists' pedigree collections. It is

THE GENEALOGICAL OFFICE, DUBLIN

divided into three separate parts, and gives the descriptive titles in use before the adoption of the single GO numbering system. The flyleaf lists the manuscripts covered.

GO 476: Numerical listing of GO manuscripts. Dating from the 1950s, and now inaccurate for the higher numbers.

See also Hayes' *Manuscript Sources for the Study of Irish Civilisation.*

This indexes the following: Registered Pedigrees, GO 800–822, Fisher Mss (GO 280–5).

ACCESS

Access to the Genealogical Office Collection is through the manuscript reading Room of the National Library at 2 Kildare Street, the same building which houses the Office itself. For the most valuable manuscripts, in general those in the lower numbers, only microfilm copies are accessible, in the National Library microfilm reading room. The microfilms are as follows:

NL Pos. 8286:	GO Mss 47, 48, 49, 64, 65
NL Pos. 8287:	GO Mss 66, 67, 68, 69
NL Pos. 8288:	GO Mss 70, 71, 72, 73
NL Pos. 8289:	GO Mss 74, 75, 76, 77, 78
NL Pos. 8290:	GO Mss 79, 103, 104, 105, 106
NL Pos. 8290A:	GO Mss 93, 94, 95
NL Pos. 8291:	GO Mss 107, 108, 109
NL Pos. 8292:	GO Mss 110, 111, 111A to p.95
NL Pos. 8293:	GO Mss 111A from p.96, 111B, 111C
NL Pos. 8294:	GO Mss 111D, 111E, 111F
NL Pos. 8295:	GO Ms 112
NL Pos. 8295A:	GO Ms 113
NL Pos. 8295B:	GO Ms 141
NL Pos. 8296:	GO Mss 145, 146, 147 to p.42
NL Pos. 8297:	GO Mss 147 from p.43, 148, 149, 150 to p. 319
NL Pos. 8298:	GO Mss 150 from p.319, 151, 152
NL Pos. 8299:	GO Mss 153, 154
NL Pos. 8300:	GO Mss 154A, 155, 156, 157, 158, 159 to p.109
NL Pos. 8301:	GO Mss 159 from p.110, 160, 161, 162, 163, 164
NL Pos. 8302:	GO Mss 165, 166, 167, 168
NL Pos. 8303:	GO Mss 169, 170
NL Pos. 8304:	GO Mss 171, 172, 173
NL Pos. 8305:	GO Mss 174, 175
NL Pos. 8306:	GO Mss 176

NL Pos. 8307:   GO Mss 177, 178
NL Pos. 8308:   GO Mss 179, 180
NL Pos. 8309:   GO Mss 181, 182
NL Pos. 8310:   GO Mss 182A, 183, 184
NL Pos. 8311:   GO Mss 185, 186, 187
NL Pos. 8312:   GO Mss 188

LISTING OF GENEALOGICAL OFFICE MANUSCRIPTS

The following is a numerical list of Genealogical Office manuscripts, from 1 to 822. In the upper numbers especially, a significant proportion of the items have been moved. Where this is the case, the title is given in brackets and also, where possible, the destination of the manuscript.

GO MS	TITLE	INDEX
1	Case of Precedence. List of Peers 1634–89	
2	Royal Arms	
3	Letters Vol.1. Genealogical Scraps	
4	Exemption from Taxes etc. List of Baronets etc. Authority for Fees	
5	Funeral Arms temp. Preston, Ulster. Commissions for Visitations	
6	Forms of Processions etc.	
7	Treatise on Heraldry, 1347	
8	Fees of Office, Precedence, Royal Pedigrees, Order of Dignities, Irish Parliament	
9	Treatise on Nobility, Pedigrees of Ancient Baronies	
10	Ulster's Diaries 1698–1800 (numbered 10A)	Own Index
11	Ulster's Diaries 1800–37 (numbered 11A)	Own Index
12	Synopsis of Heraldry & Treatise on Funerals	
13	Honours conferred in Ireland	
14	Fees of Office Vol. 1 History of Ulster's Office	

15	Monumenta Eblana	
16	Miscellaneous Pedigrees & Letters	
17	Fees of Honour etc. Precedence	
18	Fees of Honour 1812	
19	Funeral Processions	
20	Fees of Honour	
21	Angl: Regn: Catg:	
22	Lodge's Memorials & Extracts from the Rolls etc.	No Index
23	Arms Paulet	
24	Coronation	
25	Receipts for Fees of Honour	
26	Assumed Names, Arms and Titles	
27	Papers on Change of Name	
28	Cling's Annuals	
30–35	Irish Nobility Volumes A to E	
36	Scottish Nobility E2	
37	Irish Arms A	
38–9	English Arms A & B	
40	English Arms, Funeral Processions etc.	
41–2	English Nobility A & B	
43	English Nobility No 19, Royal Arms and Badges	
44	British Families Vol 1, 1660/7	Indexed in 115
45	British Families Vol 2 1641–48	Indexed in 115
46	British Families Vol 3 Cromwell's Officers	Indexed in 115
47	Visitations Vol 1, Dublin 1568	Indexed in 117
48	Visitations Vol 2, Dublin 1607	Indexed in 117
49	Visitations Vol 3, Wexford	Indexed in 117
50	List of Peers, Baronets & Knights	

THE GENEALOGICAL OFFICE, DUBLIN

51	Knights Dubbed 1565–1616, Vol 1	
52	Knights Dubbed 1633–1687 etc. Vol 2	
53	Deering's Alphabet of English Knights, 1609	
54	Arms of Kingdom, Cities etc.	
55	Camden Grants	
56	Arms EI Part I, History of College of Arms	
57	Arms EI Part II, English and Scotch Nobility	
58	Arms EI Part III, Camden Grants & Molyneux Collection	
59	General Series, Ulster's Office Index	
60	Carney Sketches of Arms	
61	Arms B	
62	Smith's Ordinary of Arms, A No 2 Grants Carney and Hawkins	
63	Smith's Ordinary of Arms, B No 2	
64	Funeral Entries Vol 1 1588–1617	Indexed in 386
65	Funeral Entries Vol 2 1597–1603	Indexed in 386
66	Funeral Entries Vol 3 1604–1622	Indexed in 386
67	Funeral Entries Vol 4 1651–1682	Indexed in 386
68	Funeral Entries Vol 5 1622–1633	Indexed in 386
69	Funeral Entries Vol 6 1633–1652	Indexed in 386
70	Funeral Entries Vol 7 1636–1639	Indexed in 386
71	Funeral Entries Vol 8 1639–1641	Indexed in 386
72	Funeral Entries Vol 9 1640–1663	Indexed in 386
73	Funeral Entries Vol 10 1659–1689	Indexed in 386
74	Funeral Entries Vol 11 1672–1681 Arms of Irish Peers	Indexed in 386
75	Funeral Entries Vol 12 & 13 1683–1691	Indexed in 386
76	Funeral Entries Vol 14 1651–1669, 1787	Indexed in 386
77	Funeral Entries Vol 15 from 1861	Indexed in 386

THE GENEALOGICAL OFFICE, DUBLIN 15

78	Funeral Entries Vol 16 'A'	Indexed in 386
79	Funeral Entries Vol 17 1622–1729	Indexed in 386
80	Arms of English Baronets, Irish Grants	
81	Blazons of Arms	
82	Arms A	
83	Arms: Betham	
84	Draft Grants	Indexed in 422
85	Draft Grants	Indexed in 422
86	Funeral Certificates 1680 etc Draft Grants D	
87	Draft Grants E	Indexed in 422
88	Draft Grants Vol 1	Indexed in 422
89	Draft Grants Vol 2	Indexed in 422
90	Sketches of Arms	
91	Royal Genealogy of England	
92	English Arms B	
93	'Chaos' Vol 1	Indexed in 470
94	'Chaos' Vol 2	Indexed in 470
95	'Chaos' Vol 3	Indexed in 470
96	'Chaos' Vol 4	Indexed in 470
97	'Chaos' Vol 5	Indexed in 470
98	Irish Arms – Smith Rouge Dragon 1613	
99	Register of Arms, Ulster's Office. See 422	
100	Register of Knights Vol 3, 1800–1854	
101	Register of Knights Vol 4, 1853–1892	
102	Register of Knights Vol 5, 1893	
103	Grants and Confirmations of Arms A	Indexed in 422
104	Grants B	Indexed in 422

105	Grants and Confirmations of Arms C	Indexed in 422
106	Grants D	Indexed in 422
107	Grants and Confirmations of Arms E	Indexed in 422
108	Grants and Confirmations of Arms F	Indexed in 422
109	Grants and Confirmations of Arms G	Indexed in 422
110	Grants and Confirmations of Arms H	Indexed in 422
111	Grants and Confirmations of Arms J	Indexed in 422
111A	Grants and Confirmations of Arms K	Indexed in 423
111B	Grants and Confirmations of Arms L	Indexed in 423
111C	Grants and Confirmations of Arms M	Indexed in 423
111D	Grants and Confirmations of Arms N	Indexed in 423
111E	Grants and Confirmations of Arms O	Indexed in 423
111F	Grants and Confirmations of Arms P	Indexed in 423
111G	Grants and Confirmations of Arms Q	Indexed in 423
112	Baronets' Pedigrees – Brooke	Indexed in 470
113	Baronets of Ireland	
114	Baronets' entries Vol 1	
115	Index I	
116	Index II	
117	Index III	
118	Ulster's Office 3 (receipts & expenditure)	
119	Visitations of Norfolk and Suffolk, 1567	
120	Glover's Visitation of Yorkshire, 1685	
121	Yorkshire Families	
122	Peers of England – Pedigrees	
123	Glover's Visitation of Cheshire, 1580 St George's Visitation of Dorset and Devon, 1613 Siege of Karleeverock Dunfermline Glover's Ordinary	

124	Herald's Visitation, Lancashire, Cheshire, Yorkshire	
125	Heraldic Sketches	
126	English Barons	
127	Receipts for Fees of Honour	
128	Brooke's Precedency	
129	Arms of Cities of England	
130	Recent Grantees. College of Arms	
131	Marriages from Exshaw's & Hibernian Magazine Vol I 1741–1800	
132	Marriages from Exshaw's & Hibernian Magazine Vol II 1741–1800	
133	Marriages from Exshaw's & Hibernian Magazine Vol III 1743–1800	
134–8	Fisher Mss. Dublin Marriage Licence Bonds 1638–1800 These are all repeated and expanded in 473–5	
139	Fisher Mss. Will Notes A	Index: 117 & 429
140	Fisher Mss. Notes B	Indexed in 117
141	Fisher Mss. Will Notes C	Indexed in 429
142	Fisher Mss. Notes D	
143	Fisher Mss. Notes F	
145	O'Ferrall's Linea Antiqua I (Betham Collection)	Indexed in 147
146	O'Ferrall's Linea Antiqua II (Betham Collection)	Indexed in 147
147	O'Ferrall's Linea Antiqua III (Betham Collection)	Own Index
148	Index to O'Ferrall	
149	Royal Licences and Warrants I	
150	King's Letters & other entries II	
151	Royal Warrants 1820–45 III	
152	Royal Warrants 1845–68 IV	
153	Royal Warrants 1868–88 V	
154	Royal Warrants from 1889 VI	

155	Royal Warrants etc.	
156	Royal Warrants etc.	
157	Pedigrees, O'Ferrall's Linea Antiqua	see 147
156–82	Pedigrees, Vols I – XXVII	Indexed in 469
183–88	Lords Entries Vols I – VI	Indexed in 470
189	Excerpta R. Placit. Com. Banci Hiberniae Vol I, Henry III to Edward I	
190	Excerpta R. Placit. Com. Banci Hiberniae Vol II Edward II	
191	Excerpta R. Placit. Com. Banci Hiberniae Vol III Edward III	
192	Excerpta R. Placit. Com. Banci Hiberniae Vol IV Edward III to Henry VI	
193	Excerpt Rotulus Patenti Ban. Hiberniae Edward I to Edward VI	
194	Excerpta Rotulus Pipae Hiberniae Vol I Henry III, Edward II, Edward III	Now NL Ms 760
195	Excerpta Rotulus Pipae Hiberniae Vol II Edward II, Edward III	Now NL Ms 761
196	English Genealogy, Mss T.C.D. Vol I	
197	English Genealogy, Mss T.C.D. Vol II	
198	Ecclesiastical Visitations, 1607–1693	Indexed in 117
199	Ecclesiastical Visitations, 1607–1781	Indexed in 117
200	High Sheriffs, Constables etc.	
201	(Orders, Payments etc) (incl. Cromwellian State Accounts)	Now NL Ms 758
202	Gazette Notices, Changes of Name, 1864–76	
203–14	Will Pedigrees (Prerogative Wills)	see Vicars
215	Ancient Anglo-Irish Families Vol I, A–B	Indexed in 470
216	Ancient Anglo-Irish Families Vol II, C–F	Indexed in 470
217	Ancient Anglo-Irish Families Vol III, G–P	Indexed in 470
218	Ancient Anglo-Irish Families Vol IV, P–W	Indexed in 470
219	Ancient Anglo-Irish Families Vol V, A–W	Indexed in 470

THE GENEALOGICAL OFFICE, DUBLIN

220	Milesian Families Vol I, A–D	Indexed in 470
221	Milesian Families Vol II, B–M	Indexed in 470
222	Milesian Families Vol III, B–T	Indexed in 470
223	Wills, Old Series Vol I; Browne, Fitzgerald, Hamilton, Stewart, Walker, White, Wilson	See Vicars
224–6	Wills, Old Series (pre-1700), Vols II–IV A–Y	See Vicars
227–54	Wills, New Series, Vols 1–26, A–Z	See Vicars
255–6	Index to Alliances in Prerogative Wills Vol I, A–L, Vol II, M–Z	See Vicars
257–60	Prerogative Administrations Intestate Vols 1–4	Own Index
261–76	Betham Sketch Pedigrees, 1st Series, Vols I–XVI	Indexed in 470
277	Betham Peerage	
278	Ball	Indexed in 470
279	Stephens, Wexford Pedigrees Calendar of Dublin Wills	Indexed in 470
280–5	Fisher Mss, Vols 1–6 Wills in 429	Surnames in 117
286	Fisher. T.C.D. Matriculations 1637–1730	Own Index
287	High Sheriffs of Counties	
288	Fisher: King's Inns Admissions 1607–1771	
289	Fisher: Abstracts of Deeds & Wills 1	Wills in 429
290	Fisher: Abstracts of Deeds & Wills 2	Wills in 429
291	Index to Fisher Mss	
292–8	Betham Sketch Pedigrees, 2nd Series, Vols I–VII	Indexed in 470
299	Proclamations & Ceremonials	
300	Ulster Office (misc)	
301	Bath. Now in National Library	
302	Funeral Processions (from Add. Mss 1829, British Museum)	
303	Gentleman Ushers Book, 1842–64	

304	Funeral Viscount Nelson
305	Bath
306	Statutes of the Garter
307	Order of the Bath (Now at National Library)
308	Order of St Patrick (Receipts etc)
309	Precedents of Receptions
310	Order of St Patrick, Official Designs
311	Gentleman's Usher Book 1820–85
312	Order of St Patrick, Installation papers (Betham)
313	Order of St Patrick
314	Knights Dubbed, Ulster's Rolls
315	Order of St Patrick, Installation 1868
316	Order of St Patrick
317	Order of St Patrick papers
318	Ulster Office Forms
319	Official Orders
320	Order of St Patrick Investiture, Invitations
321	Book of the Vice-Regal Household 2
322–8	Official Entries & Letters 1854–1921, Vols 1–7
329	Renumbered 111E
330	Navan Uniforms
331	Uniform Book
332	Schedule of Civil Service Uniforms
333	Coronation of Edward VII
334	Note on Knighthoods of Ireland
335	Ceremonials, Order of St Patrick
336	Ceremonials, Order of St Patrick, 1872–1921
337–9	The Vice-Regal Court, Vols I–III

THE GENEALOGICAL OFFICE, DUBLIN

340	Lists of Knights	
340A	Lists of Knights	
341	Ulster's Rolls from 1660	
342	Peers' Pedigrees	
343	Official Orders, 1800	
344	Order of St Patrick: Certificates of Noblesse	
345	Funeral Entries 1797	
346	Dress Regulations	
347	Funeral Processions	
348–50	Ceremonial Books, Ulster's Office, Vols I–III	
351	Index (c. 1840?)	
352	Betham Address Book	
353	Day Book, Hawkins & Fortescue, 1777–1809	
354	Fortescue, 1788–1809	
355	Letter Book, 1814–16	
356	Day Book, 1812–18	
357	Ledger, 1812–46	
358	Ledger, 1809–25	
359	Day Book, 1824–39	
360	Cash Book, 1839–53	
361–78	Letter Books, 1789–1853	
380	Government Correspondence, 1827–36	
381	Government Correspondence, 1828–48	
382	The Coronation, 1902	
383	Arms C	
384	Donovan Ms	Indexed in 470
385	Bewley Ms	Indexed in 470
386	Index to Funeral Entries	

387	Knights dubbed in England	
388	Peers of Ireland, Ulster's Office Papers	
389–400	Davis Mss, Vols 9–20	Wills in 429
401	Copy of 295	
402	Fisher: Admissions to King's Inns, 1607–1771	
403	Royal Levees, 1821, 1824, 1849	
404	Davis Mss Vol I	Indexed in 470
405	Davis Mss Vol II	Indexed in 470
406	Carmichael Ms	Indexed in 470
407	Representative Peers, election lists	
408	Bewley family of Cumberland	
409–10	Warburton's Lexicon Armorum	
411	Arms of Foreign Royalties etc.	
412	Barry	Indexed in 470
413	Holland (tricks of arms)	Own Index
414	West	
415	Kelly: Wills	Wills in 429
416	Crosslé	Own Index Wills in 429
417–8	Drought	Wills in 429
419	Kemmis	
420	Swanzy Will Abstracts	Wills in 429
421	Prerogative Marriage Licences. See 605–7	
422	Arms Register I	
423	Arms Register II	
424–27a	Sadleir Will Abstracts Vols 1,2,3,4,4a	Wills in 429
428	Plunkett. Bantry Account Book, 1825	
429	Eustace Index of Will Abstracts at the G.O.	

430	1766 Religious Census Returns (photostat)	
431	'Extra Fisher'	
432–5	Irwin Mss	Wills in 429
435A	Irwin Mss. Bulteel and other families	Wills in 429
436–41	Irwin Mss	Wills in 429
442	Freeholders, Meath, Donegal, Fermanagh, Roscommon, Tipperary	
443	Freeholders, Clare, Kilkenny, Queen's, Westmeath. Armagh Poll Book 1753	
444	Printer registers of freeholders, Co. Longford 1800–35	
445–6a	Reynell Mss Partly in 117	Own Index
447	Chester Refugees 1688/9	
448	Newgate	
449	Burtchaell	
450	Molony and allied families	Wills in 429
451	Molony ms. Pedigrees etc. Principally families of Blood, Blout, Brereton	Wills in 429
452	Molony ms. Abstracts from the 'General Advertiser' and the 'Limerick Gazette', 1804–20	Alphabetical Order
453–55	Molony ms. Abstracts from the 'Clare Journal' and 'Ennis Chronicle', 1778–1810	Alphabetical Order
456	Molony mss. Misc. Pedigrees etc	Wills in 429
457	Molony mss. Misc. Pedigrees etc	Wills in 429
458	Molony mss. Misc. Pedigrees etc	Wills in 429
459	Molony mss. Misc. Pedigrees etc	Wills in 429
460	Molony mss. Pedigrees etc. Principally families of Brew, Adams, Chartres	Wills in 429
461	Molony mss. Will abstracts etc. Family of Chartres	Wills in 429
462	Pedigree of Chartres	

463	Molony mss. Notes on the families of Adams, Chartres, Tymens and England of Co. Clare.	Wills in 429
464	Molony mss. Misc. Pedigrees etc	Wills in 429
465	Notes on the Molony family	Wills in 429
467	Pedigree of O'Donnellan	
468	Traill	Indexed in 470
469	Index of Registered Pedigrees	
470	Index of Unregistered Pedigrees	
471	Cavanagh and allied families Wills in 429	Own Index
472	Calendar of Wills, Down Diocese	
473–5	Dublin Consistorial Marriage Licences	
476	List of Mss at the G.O.	
477	Search Book	
478/9	Now 111e & 111f	
480	Bewley family of Cumberland	
481	List of Claims, 1701	
482	Athenry Peerage Letters, 1821–5	
483	Fisher Marriage Licences (see 144a)	
484	Smyly and allied families	
485	O'Brien Pedigrees	
486	Ulster Office Form Book	
487	Abstracts from Charitable Wills	Wills in 429
488	Kelly of Clare	
489	Delafield of Dublin	
490–93	Roll of Freemen, Dublin City	
494	Concordatum Pedigrees (Sadleir), 1817–21	Not indexed
495	Castleknock Parish Register	

496	Crossly's Peerage	
497	Patent of precedency	
498	Montgomery pedigree	
499	Loftus Pedigree	
500	Burke-Ryan genealogy	
501	Walsh, Kelly & allied families	
502	(Betham Draft Book: now NL Ms 496)	
503	Donegan family	
504	Genealogy of family of Burgo French	
505	Pedigrees of Walker & allied families	
506	Stafford family history	
507	Loss of the Irish Crown Jewels	
508	Coachmakers blazons of arms	
509	Alphabet of Irish & English Arms	
510	1642 Field Officers	
511	Arms of Protestant Bishops of Ireland	
512	Bewley Notebooks (Box)	Wills in 429
513	Precedents	
514	Ash, Co. "Derry" c.1736	
515	Berkely Peerage: Pedigree, Correspondence & Notes	
516	Pedigree of O'Mangan 1709	
517	O'Hanlon of Orior, Co. Armagh	
518	Delamere Notes	
519	Shaw & Joyce pedigrees, Gun notes	
520–22	Blake and Butler Families of Tipperary and Clare	
523	Welply I, Chancery Bills, 1630–1785. Mainly Chinnery and Phair families	
524	Welply II, Exchequer Bills, 1675–1810. Mainly Chinnery family	

525	Eustace Miscellany	Own Index
526	Fota Ms (photostat) Irish Coats	Own Index
527	MacLysaght Miscellany	Own Index
528–34	Transcripts of Wills from the Society of Genealogists, London	Indexed in 429
535	Ainsworth Wills	Alphabetical Order
536	Religious Census Returns 1766, I	
537	Religious Census Returns 1766, II	
538	Hearth Money Rolls, Armagh, Donegal, 1664/5	
539	Protestant Housekeepers, Antrim, Derry, Donegal. 1740	
539A	Index to 539	
540	Bibliography of Irish Palatines	Own Index
541	Co. Louth, 17th century miscellany	
542	Directories, 1809: Belfast, Cork, Limerick, Waterford	
543	Field Officers, 1642 Wolfe and Shaw families Tipperary Attainders, 1688 Index to Book of Postings, 1700 Wives Certificates, Benevolent Annuity Co., 1771 Claims Before Commissioners, 1662	
544	Cook diary, Blain autobiography, Brett, Saunder, Freeman, Collis families	
545	Guerin	
546–51	Irish Obituaries A–Y	
552–3	High Sheriffs of Irish Counties, 1660–1900 I & II	
554–5	Students of King' Inns	
556	Smith Family History (Nuttall Smith)	
557	Sadleir: Marriages & Genealogical Notes	Own Index
558–61	Finucane & O'Brien Pedigrees	

562	Blennerhassett	
563	(Rental: Now NL Ms 5319)	
564	Gilles-Kelly notes	Own Index
565	(1) Extracts from the Pole-Hore Mss catalogue (2) Index to pedigrees in Howard and Crisp (ed.) Visitation of Ireland, Vols I–VI (3) Index to GO Ms 3 (4) Index to heraldic mss in GO 470 (5) Index to names and places in GO Ms 564 (6) Index to arms in GO 155–182 (7) Index to arms in IMA, Vols I–XIII (8) Index to arms in GO Mss 223–298 (9) Dublin Goldsmiths (10) Index to Peers' Pedigrees	
566	(Winder Papers. Now NL Ms 5229)	
567	(Thady O'Halloran's Commonplace Book Now NL Ms 5317)	
568	(Wolfe Rental. Now NL Ms 3908)	
569	Directories: Belfast, Cork, Waterford, 1805	
570	Magistrates & Grand Jurors in Co. Tipperary from 1658	
571	Grantees, Act of Settlement, Cos. Tipperary and Offaly	
572	1821 Census extracts, Cos. Tipperary and Offaly	
573–6	Sadleir Pedigree Notebooks 1–4 Mainly Tipperary and Offaly families	Indexed in 470
577	Dublin Parish Register extracts	
578	Parish Register Extracts	
579	Army List, Ireland, 1746	
580–604	Betham Letters Vols 1–25	
604A	Sherwood catalogue and Index to Betham letters	
605–7	Prerogative Marriage Licences, 1630–1858 A–Z	
608	Militia List 1761	
609	Irish Stockholders 1779	

THE GENEALOGICAL OFFICE, DUBLIN

610	Gaelic Chief's Authenticated Pedigrees I	
611	Lodge family	
612–7	Index to Ossory, Ferns & Leighlin Marriage Licence Bonds, 1691–1845	
618	Ossory Administration Bonds 1660–1857	
619	Ware: Bishops	
620	Miscellaneous Rentals	
621	Photostats: Taylor papers, Hegarty Papers, Inscriptions from St Bede's R.C. Church, New South Wales	
622	Ainsworth Miscellany	
623	Limerick Freeholders 1816–25	
624	Frost: Co Clare families	Own Index
625	Bozzetti d'arme	Own Index
626	Directory, Enniskillen, Ballyshannon, Donegal 1839	
627	Register of Gaelic Chiefs	
628	Sadleir: Miscellaneous Pedigrees	Indexed in 470
628A	Sadleir: Order of Malta	
629	O'Kelly Pedigrees	
630	Miscellaneous Pedigrees (1908–1943)	Own Index
631	Ainsworth Wills II	Not in 429
632	O'Malley	
633	Delafield and Butler families	
634	(O'Reilly Pedigrees)	
635	Warren & allied families	
636	Privy Councillors of Ireland	
637	Forbes Genealogy	
638	Nagle, White, Meekins, Madden, Vereker and Prendergast Pedigrees	

639	Dillon Patents	
640	(Betham Pedigrees. Now in NL)	
641	(Killaloe Catholic Parish Register Listing)	
642	Kilkenny College and its masters	
643	Material for Names Map	
644	(Stemmata Wyckhamiana: NL)	
645	Nangle (de Angulo) pediigree	
646	(Copies of GO Visitations, GO 46–8)	
647	Heard's Irish Pedigrees	Indexed in 470
648	Apothecaries, Dublin	
649	(Attainders 1689	
650	(Burke's Landed Gentry)	
651	(Burkes Armory)	
652	Smyly papers. Waller pedigree	
653	Davys family, Co. Roscommon	
654	Englefield & Gerrard Pedigrees	
655	Phillimore Irish Will Abstracts Index	
656	Fitzgerald Funeral Entries	
657	Genealogy of Fitzgeralds, Dukes of Leinster	
658	Maguire tabular pedigrees	
659–61	(Rentals of the Fitzpatrick estates, Co. Laois Now in NL)	
662	O'Hea notes	
663	(Madden. Now in NL)	
664	(Changes of Name: Now GO 26)	
665	Sadleir Miscellany	
666	Papers relating to Irish Families in France (Bound with GO 667)	
667	Co. Wicklow Hearth Money Roll	

668–70	Chancery & Exchequer Bills, Marriage Licence Bonds and other records, 1629–1747	
671	Register of Flags	
672	O'Brien Tabular Pedigrees	
673	Keating family	Own Index
674–81	(Malachy Moran Mss. Now NL Mss 1543–50)	
682	Lascelles Kelly (transcript of 564)	
683–4	Walsh-Kelly notebooks	
685	Walsh-Kelly notebook: Cork Wills of Galwey, Donovan, c.1728–1801	
686	Walsh-Kelly notebooks	
687	Graviana: Nugent, Barons Delvin	
688	(Killaloe Marriage Licences)	
689	Mackay/McGee Family History	
690	Rochfort & Ryland	
691–2	Hill I & II	
693	Hill III (O'Daly, Grey, Gerry, Whitcombe, etc.)	
694	Hill IV (Fox)	
695–7	Pogue I–III	
698	Coningsby Pedigree	
699	O'Malley history	
700	Seven wills (Crosslé)	Own Index
700A	(Lissan wills and marriage licences)	Own Index
701	C.of I. Parish Register extracts: Ballingarry, Co. Limerick, Whitechurch, Co Wexford, Eyrecourt, Co. Galway, St Patrick's, Dublin	
702	Gordon Ms (Crosslé)	
702a	Gordon Ms (Crosslé), newspaper cuttings	
703	(–)	
704	Carroll Wills	

THE GENEALOGICAL OFFICE, DUBLIN

705	(List of Priests & Sureties. Now NL Ms 5318)
706	Glenville Crests
707	Extracts from Tuam, Clonfert & Kilmacduagh C.of I. diocesan records
708	Kilkenny pedigrees (from Burtchaell)
709	(Grants Q. Now 111G)
710	(Parish register listing)
711	Memoir of the Butlers of Ormond
712	(Book of Arms: now NL Ms 472)
713	Irwin, Max, Butler, Crofts, McConnell, Herden
714–38	Loose Pedigrees A–W Indexed in 470
739	(Now GO 496)
742	Miscellaneous Pedigrees & Notes: Edwards & allied families
743	(Herbert Pedigrees)
744	(Fitzgerald of Derrineel)
745	(Notes for Irish Memorials Association)
746	Kennedy, Scotland & Ireland 1550–1820
747	(Bewley Miscellany)
749–50	(Knights Dubbed, 1590–1800)
751	(Sketches of Arms)
752	Admissions to freedom of Dublin, 1468
753	(Now GO 517)
754	(Now GO 514)
755	(Verner Family)
756	(Now GO 513)
757	(Now GO 503)
758	(Now GO 499)
759	(Now GO 509)

760	Miscellany: Brownrigg & Ronson
761	(Now GO 519)
762	(Now GO 698)
763	(Now GO 500)
764	(Now GO 511)
765	Grainger & allied families
766	(Now GO 519)
767	(Now GO 504)
768	(Now GO 502)
769	(Now GO 508)
770	(Now GO 505)
771	(Now GO 517)
772	(Now GO 497)
773	(Now GO 506)
774	Royal Warrants in Changes of Name
775	(McWillian Pedigrees)
776	(Now GO 516)
777	Braddyl papers
778	(Montgomery Pedigree)
779–787	(Chevalier O'Gorman papers. Now in NL)
788	(Register of Foreign Arms)
789	(Now GO 515)
790	(Photostat of Burgess Books)
791	(Extracts from Registered Pedigrees)
792	Pedigree & notes re Bushe
793	Lt-Col O'Hea
794	Lodge Family Histories
795	(–)

796	(–)	
797	(Hyde of Co. Cork)	
798	History of the Hickeys	
799	(–)	
800–822	Loose Pedigrees, Searches, Correspondence	Indexed in Hayes

GUIDE TO RECORDS
OF
THE GENEALOGICAL OFFICE, DUBLIN

WITH A COMMENTARY ON
HERALDRY IN IRELAND
AND ON THE
HISTORY OF THE OFFICE

JOHN BARRY Ph.D.

GUIDE TO RECORDS OF THE GENEALOGICAL OFFICE, DUBLIN, WITH A COMMENTARY ON HERALDRY IN IRELAND AND ON THE HISTORY OF THE OFFICE

The records of the Genealogical Office, formerly the office of the Ulster King of Arms, derive essentially from the functional nature of the office. They possess an organic unity and are not an arbitrary collection of manuscripts. They fall into a number of categories natural to the nature and scope of the duties of Ulster King of Arms and his officers. Before attempting to comment on them it is advisable to examine the historical circumstances that led to the establishment of an Office of Arms in Ireland in the mid-sixteenth century.

In order to find the genesis of the Office of Arms it is necessary to go back to the emergence of heraldry in western Europe during the first half of the twelfth century. True heraldry has been accurately defined as the systematic uses of hereditary devices centred on a shield.[1] In the first half of the twelfth century knights began to use devices on their shields to identify themselves in tournament and battle. Rarely if ever between the introduction of shields and the twelfth century is anything that looks like a personal shield device used.[2] When these devices were passed from father to son what we now call heraldry may be said to have evolved. In due course they became matters of family pride and indications of social importance. They underwent much change and, spreading from martial to civil use, their form and type were eventually reduced to a system. Historically the most continuous use of personal marks is on seals used to authenticate documents. The Frankish kings preserved this custom of classical times and in England, Edward the Confessor (1042–66) fastened his seal to a document by a cord instead of impressing it on the surface of the document, and made it two-sided like the leaden bulla of the popes. William the Conqueror and his successors followed this example, but showing on one side the king on his throne, and armed and mounted on the other, instead of two identical sides.

The normal seal device of the secular lord showed his mounted figure. When a device begins to appear on a knight's shield or on the flag of his lance point, and when this becomes hereditary, then it may be styled a heraldic device. No seal with a heraldic device is proved earlier than 1136.[3] Between 1136 and 1155 evidence from seals shows

---

[1] A. Wagner, *Heralds and Heraldry* (Oxford, 1956), p. 1.
[2] *Ibid.*
[3] Wagner, *Heraldry in England* (London, 1946). p. 6.

the simultaneous emergence of heraldry in France, England, Germany and Italy. While it is not possible to put forward any precise explanation for this, there are a number of possible explanations, all or some of which may have in part contributed to the evolution of heraldry.

Shield devices were undoubtedly used as a means of recognition as the term 'conoisance' in use from 1150 to 1200 suggests. Wace, writing circa 1160, attributes their use to the Normans at Hastings and to an earlier legendary past. The contemporary evidence from the Bayeux tapestry does not in fact bear out this assertion.[4] The first crusade at the end of the eleventh century is an obvious occasion for the necessity of 'conoisance' and the rise in popularity of the tournament at about the same period would provide a similar necessity. Since the first crusade was a mass European movement and the tournament was universally popular in feudal Europe, they both fulfil the condition of universality that would explain this simultaneous emergence of heraldry throughout Europe.

It must also be remembered that the twelfth century witnessed the development of feudalism into what has been styled its classical hereditary form. The association of these devices with the feudal knight, for whom hereditary right was all-important in the matter of succession to a fief, must undoubtedly have contributed to the distinctive hereditary character of heraldry. The contractual obligation of lord and vassal was the very cement of civil and military affairs, and if identification marks were invented they would tend to stay and become hereditary. Since the knight was the most important element in the feudal host, the devices he used became by association symbols of knightly status. Heraldry is part of the essence of feudal society. This factor must be borne in mind when we come to deal with the question of the development of heraldry in Gaelic Ireland.

The evolution of heraldry from a rudimentary type of military recognition to an elaborate form reduced to system with a technical vocabulary was a gradual process. Round suggests that the reign of Stephen (1135-54) was the period in which heraldic devices in England were assuming a definite form.[5] The first development from the device on the shield was the fashion of painting a device in front of the helm, not necessarily repeating all or part of the shield device. From this the next step, in the thirteenth century, was to fix a fan-shaped metal crest to the top of the helm. The final stage was an actual modelled figure of the device in leather or parchment. This was known as the crest. Crests, however, were not usual until the fourteenth century.[6] In the first half of the thirteenth century arms began to be painted on the linen surcoats over armour—hence coat of arms.[7]

---

[4] Ivan Arnold, ed., 'Le Roman de Brut de Wace', *Soc. des Anc. Textes francaises*, I (1938), 4963-64.
[5] J. H. Round, *Geoffrey de Mandville: A Study of the Anarchy* (London, 1892), p. 392.
[6] Wagner, *Heraldry in England*, p. 10.
[7] *Ibid.*

Meanwhile the peaceful uses of heraldry developed. Arms appeared first on seals as part of the owner's picture. They can be seen on the shield or on the flag at the lance-point, but towards 1200 they appear as the sole device. At first the shield appears alone, and the next development is when it is surmounted by the crested helmet. Together they are styled the coat of arms. On the great baronial seals, spaces might still remain between the flanks of the shield and the circle of the seal. In order to decorate and fill the background the seal engravers filled the spaces with birds or dragons on either side holding up the shield. These came to be styled supporters, and in course of time were regarded, by association, as part of the arms of peers. The chief civil use of arms was on seals. The distinctiveness and precision of the coat of arms was of considerable practical and legal use in authenticating documents. Then they begin to be used on tombs as part of the owner's picture. Finally they began to be applied to works of art and objects of use.

It is only natural to expect that contemporaneously with this development a technical vocabulary would evolve to meet the needs of description. The earliest verbal descriptions of arms occur in early French romances. Count de Marsy, who has analysed much of the evidence, found that the first recognizable descriptions are of devices painted on the helms, i.e., the crest; a little later, in the second half of the twelfth century, the principal changes on the shield begin to be specified; by 1200 the indications are fairly full, and by 1250 they are sufficient to reconstruct the arms. By 1270 a technical terminology is fully formed and regularly used.[8]

Since these distinctive marks were used in both military and civil affairs they must have been copyright by custom if not by law in order to serve their purpose. Yet for the first two hundred years of its existence heraldry appears to have done without legal control. Nevertheless, the strength of customary sanction is shown by the rarity of infringement. By the year 1300 there were about fifteen hundred different coats of arms in use in England, but at the siege of Carlaverock in 1300 it excited general surprise when two knights, Sir Brian Fitzalan and Sir Hugh Poyntz, were both found using the same arms *barry or and gules*.[9] Three German charters of the second half of the thirteenth century record concessions or agreements between private persons touching the bearing of their arms.[10] By the fourteenth century it is clear that arms were considered as property in both Germany and England.[11] Men grant their arms to another. A lord grants to his tenant all or part of his own arms sometimes as an augmentation to already existing coats of his

---

[8] M. Alexander Charles Count de Marsy, 'Le Langage heraldique au XII siecle dans les poemes d'Adenet le Roi', *Memoires de la Société Nationale des Antiquaries de France*, II, 169–212. Cited in Wagner, *Heralds and Heraldry*.
[9] Wagner, *Heraldry in England*, p. 11.
[10] G. A. Seyler, *Geschichte der Heraldik* (Nuremburg, 1885), p. 11.
[11] Wagner, *Heralds and Heraldry*, p. 20.

own.[12] To take an Irish example, the indented chief of Ranulf Glanville, Justiciar of Henry II, was taken by his wife's kinsmen, the Butlers of Ireland.[13] The custom also arose of cadet branches of a family bearing differenced versions of the ancestral coat borne by the head of the family. Towards 1500 this was systematized into fixed cadency marks by John Writhe, Garter King of Arms.[14]

Since it is clear that property in arms acquired legal recognition, the question of the exercise of control of arms other than by customary sanction arises. Contrary to what might be expected, the first connexion of heralds with heraldry is casual and incidental, and they are not initially associated with the control of arms. The civil usage of arms was a derived function, and the origins of heraldry lie in the feudal warfare of the mailed knight. In consequence, it is not surprising to find that jurisdiction in armorial affairs fell to the court which tried military offences, presided over by two officers, the constable and the marshall. Both offices go back to the reign of Henry I. In England Henry VIII abolished the office of constable, but the office of marshall survived and is represented today by the Duke of Norfolk, Earl Marshall of England and titular head of the College of Arms.[15] Surviving records of the preceedings of this court in England are few. The first heraldic case for which we have any evidence dates from 1345.[16] This was at the siege of Calais when a dispute concerning armorial bearings arose between Nicholas Lord Burnell and Robert Lord Morley. Disputes of this nature were, of course, most likely to occur at a siege or tournament, when knights from different places were gathered together for any length of time. Judgment was said to have been given by a herald called Lancaster at the command of the two military officers, the constable and the marshall. There is no suggestion that the herald took part in the trial itself.[17] The approximate date at which heralds begin to acquire official standing in relation to this court appears to be some time in the fifteenth century.[18]

Heralds do not seem to occur in English records before the reign of Edward I, but for a century earlier mention of them in French romances gives us a fair idea of their status. Almost all references in the romances associate them with the tournament.[19] In regions where the tournament was not in use there is, according to Paul Meyer, no mention of heralds.[20] Their official standing in relation to the control of arms evolved from this early casual connexion with heraldry.

---

[12] Wagner, *Heraldry in England*, p. 14.
[13] *Ibid.*, p. 13.
[14] *Ibid.*
[15] Wagner, *Heraldry in England*, p. 15.
[16] *Ibid.*
[17] Wagner, *Heralds and Heraldry*, p. 23.
[18] *Ibid.*, p. 24.
[19] Edmond Faval, *Les Jongleurs en France au Moyen Age* (Paris, 1910), pp. 270–271.
[20] *Romania*, X (1882), 36.

GUIDE TO RECORDS OF GENEALOGICAL OFFICE 41

Heralds, like minstrels, often led a wandering life to wherever tournaments might be held. An indication that Norman Ireland formed part of general European feudal chivalry is contained in a late thirteenth-century poem which describes how heralds used roam from Holland, Flanders or Brabant to wherever tournaments might be held in Denmark, Scotland or Ireland.[21] At this stage, in fact, heralds appear to trespass on minstrels' prerogatives. In 1338 a wardrobe account in England records a payment to Master Conrad, king of the heralds in Germany, and two other minstrels of divers great lords in Germany for making minstrelsy before the king at Christmas.[22]

From the reign of Edward III in England we find heralds entrusted with military and diplomatic duties. The earliest references in the accounts to the heralds of the king of England are in 1290.[23] The first recorded instance of a herald as messenger of war is the account of the opening of the Hundred Years' War, in Froissart's chronicle, where a herald called Carlisle arrives with messages announcing war from the king's vassals in Saxony. This is an account that one would associate more with the classical Greek *kerux* than with what is now styled heraldry. In the fourteenth century also names of heralds begin to appear. In 1338 payments were made to Andrew Norreys or Noirois, king of heralds.[24] Earlier there is an account of a Scottish herald called Dundee, who came before the English at Alnwick and announced that he was sent for parley.[25] Lancaster Herald who proclaims the decision in the case of Lovel versus Morley has already been cited.

It is in the fourteenth century too that the office of King of Heralds or King of Arms evolved throughout most of Europe, in kingdoms and in provinces within kingdoms. A further refinement was the development of Principal King of Arms in a kingdom. In England there are references to Falcon King of Arms in the fourteenth century, and Froissart has the oldest reference to the creation of a King of Arms when Chandos Herald, author of the political life of the Black Prince, was so created by Richard II in 1377.[26] The first mention of Montjoye King of Arms in France is when Charlot, who had been Anjou King of Arms in Cyprus and then in Artois, was crowned 'Montjoye roi d'armes de France' by Charles V (1364–80).[27] The answers of Anjou King of Arms, written within a few years of 1400, provide much information on the creation and duties of kings of arms, heralds and pursuivants. The account goes into great detail, which may be summarised as developing

---

[21] Aug. Scheler, ed., *Dits et Comte de Baudoin de Condè et de son fils Jean de Condè . . . et accompagnes de notes explications* (Brussels, 1886), I, 153–57.
[22] Quoted in Wagner, *Heralds and Heraldry*, p. 27.
[23] John Anstis, *Officers of Arms*, p. 40. Manuscript cited in Wagner, *Heralds and Heraldry*.
[24] Anstis, *ibid.*, p. 75 (citing wardrobe account and issue roll). Cited in Wagner, *Heralds and Heraldry*.
[25] Wagner, *ibid.*, p. 35.
[26] Simeon Luce, ed., *Froissart Chroniques* (Paris, 1869), p. 216.
[27] Wagner, *Heralds and Heraldry*, p. 35.

from the conduct of the tournament to include embassies of war and peace with, as Wagner puts it, a king of general professorship of the science of chivalry. The little captains of fortresses might have their pursuivants, the greater nobles their heralds; the great kings of arms were favoured servants of the kings of France and England. There is one omission: the connexion with what we now call heraldry is not as much as mentioned.[28] Nevertheless, from the beginning the heralds had a close practical connexion with heraldry through the tournament, where it was necessary for them to identify the arms of the knights.

The tournament itself predated heraldry. It appears to have originated in the eleventh century. As I have already indicated, by gathering knights unknown to one another in one place, in circumstances which required that they be readily distinguishable, it would in itself make some kind of conoisance almost necessary. The rule of devolution and inheritance to which the bearing of these cognizances conformed followed the prevailing feudal pattern.

The heralds were, from the first, expected to recognize arms, although in a poem of Chretien de Troyes, written between 1164 and 1174, a herald fails to identify the arms of Lancelot, but it is clear that he is expected to do so.[29] As Wagner observes, it is ironic that the first recorded act of the first recorded herald should be his failure to recognize arms.

By the end of the thirteenth century a knowledge of heraldry was an essential part of the herald's qualifications. At the same time this knowledge was shared by others. Walter of Heminburgh tells us that at the battle of Eversham in 1265 it was Earl Simon's barber 'qui homo expertus erat in cognitione armorum' who identified the arms of the approaching army, and was misled by them to the destruction of his master.[30]

Wagner has traced the connexion of the heralds with the great medieval rolls of arms, the great source of medieval heraldry both in England and on the Continent. It is clear that by the end of the fourteenth century the most natural possessor of a roll of arms was a herald. Three great continental armorials, that compiled c. 1369–1400 by Heyner, herald of the Duke of Gelderl, that armorial linked with Navarre, dated by Professor Prinet 1368–75, and the armorial by Giles le Bouvier 'Roi d'Armes de France' c. 1400, have two significant characteristics in common. Each is compiled by a king of arms, and each is arranged on a regional basis. In Wagner's well-documented opinion this was not fortuitous but an indication that it was the duty of a king of arms to have knowledge of arms within his sphere of office, and that it would be natural for him to fulfil this duty by making written and illustrated records on a systematic basis.[31]

---

[28] Cited in Wagner, *ibid.*, p. 45.
[29] Wendelen Förster, ed., *Der Karrenritter von Christian von Troyes* (Halle, 1889), II, 5535–65.
[30] H. C. Hamilton, ed., *Chronicon Walteri de Hemenburgh* (London, 1848), I, 323.
[31] Wagner, *Heralds and Heraldry*, pp. 47–55.

As yet there is no indication that a knowledge of heraldry was considered as anything more than a necessary auxiliary or tool of the heralds in carrying out their duties at the tournament. There is no suggestion that the heralds have any function in the control of arms. In this connexion it is important to remember the answers of Anjou King of Arms already mentioned.

As in so many aspects of European affairs, France led the way in developing control of arms through the heralds. Between 1430 and 1468 explicit instructions were given to the provincial kings of arms for the making of visitations, March by March, every three years. They are to produce returns of noble tenures and of the names, arms, crests and 'cries de guerre' of the tenants. These instructions are as explicit as those of Henry VIII in 1530 which initiated the English visitations.[32]

We need not go into the disputed enactments of 1417, purported to be made by Thomas, Duke of Clarence. If these are genuine they show that a developed system of provincial jurisdiction and visitation and a disciplined organization of the officers of arms under the jurisdiction of the constable, together with a transformation of the authority of the king of arms into a sovereignty over armorial bearings can be definitely attributed to England in the first quarter of the fifteenth century. Their authenticity is discussed by Anstis.[33]

Two years previously Henry V had created the new office of Garter Principal King of Arms who enjoyed pre-eminence, if not authority, as Montjoye had long enjoyed in France, and as King of Arms of the Order of the Garter he held an unparalleled position.[34] The details of his position were not, however, carefully worked out, and Garter had to fight for three centuries before the disputed limits of his jurisdiction were fixed.

The development of the control of arms inevitably took different turns in different countries, although the herald's association with arms was always close. In this study, however, we are concerned with the question of this control under the English crown first in England and later in Ireland. Before considering this it is necessary to deal with the question of the grant of arms. Originally, arms had simply been assumed by members of the knightly class. Since, however, only knights had occasion to bear arms, in course of time arms inevitably came to be regarded as evidence of privilege, dignity or nobility, and worthy of being granted by imperial or royal authority. By letters patent 31 May 1338, the Emperor Lewis made what is possibly the first recorded grant of arms to an individual.[35] This was in fact a cession by the emperor of part of his own coat. D. L. Galbreath believed that all grants before

---

[32] *Ibid.*, p. 57.
[33] John Anstis, *Register of the Order of the Garter*, II, 323–24. Cited in Wagner, *Heralds and Heraldry*.
[34] Wagner, *Heralds and Heraldry*, p. 63.
[35] Seyler, *Geschichte der Heraldik*, p. 814.

c. 1390 were 'cessions of part of his own coat'.[36] Therefore, arms were looked on as property and on the continent in the fourteenth century it is implied that the bearing of arms is a privilege of noblemen. The earliest grant of arms by an English king, dated 1 July 1389, recites that since the French king has challenged one of his knights to perform certain deeds of arms with him, 'We, in order that our liege may be received honourably, and may be able to perform the said deeds, have received him into the estate of gentleman, and have made him esquire, and will that he be known by arms, and bear them henceforth as follows, *argent a chapeau with an ostrich feather gules.*'[37]

All early grants by the English crown, as Sir George Sitwell remarked, are in essence grants of ennoblement, and a distinction is drawn in them between the principal object, which is usually 'nobilitare nobilemque facere', and the addition of arms 'in signo hujus nobilitatis'.[38] In contrast, the German *Wappenrief* or grant of arms from the emperor or other sovereign is common from the fifteenth century onwards.

The rarity of English crown grants is due to their replacement by grants from the king of arms. Within thirty years of the foundation of Garter Principal King of Arms, arms were being granted by the kings of arms, although they initially appear to have been more in the nature of certificates that the arms devised belong to no one else. The practice seems to have grown from the duty of the kings of arms to know and register the arms of gentlemen within their marches. From this grew the practice of certifying arms and the later practice, peculiar initially to England, of the granting of arms by the kings of arms.[39] Curiously, the course of events in France was to take a radically different turn. The heralds' authority over arms steadily faded, and in 1615 armorial authority was given to the new office of 'juge d'armes'.[40] Soon after 1460 Clarenceux King of Arms stated that he granted arms by virtue of 'the power and authority of the king's good grace to me in that behalf committed'.[41]

In the third quarter of the fifteenth century these heraldic surveys began to give particulars of pedigrees. The heralds must, inevitably, have long had an interest in proving gentility and the right to arms.[42]

In 1530 it was decided that Norroy and Clarenceux, the provincial kings of arms, should make visitations in their respective provinces and that pedigrees as well as arms should be registered.[43] The entry books of the English visitations contain a vast amount of heraldic and genealogical information, although descent is seldom carried back further

---

[36] Cited in Wagner, *Heralds and Heraldry*, p. 65.
[37] Thomas Rymer, *Foedera* (1743), VII, 65.
[38] *The Ancestor*, I, 80–81.
[39] Wagner, *Heraldry in England*, p. 20.
[40] Wagner, *Heralds and Heraldry*, p. 81.
[41] Wagner, *Heraldry in England*, p. 20.
[42] *Ibid.*
[43] *Ibid.*, p. 20 ff.

than the great-grandfather of a living descendant, and often not so far.[44] At this time also there was a substantial increase in the number of new grants of arms, primarily occasioned by those planted on monastery land who sought arms as a badge of their new standing. Wagner points out that in this light Henry's orders for heraldic visitations take on much significance.[45]

The English kings of arms and heralds who had a first charter of incorporation from Richard III in 1484 were the primary authority under the crown in the control of arms.[46] Arising out of this, since the right to bear arms depended primarily on antecedents, they became genealogists. This process was powerfully aided by the instructions for the visitations of 1530. The heralds did not cease to be ceremonial officers, but their duties in that direction gradually grew less and their genealogical duties increased. These were the developments which were to shape the records of the College of Arms and ultimately, by their application to Ireland, to shape the nature of the records in the office of Ulster King of Arms in Ireland.

Unfortunately very little in the way of a comprehensive study of the development of heraldry in Ireland has been attempted. A certain number of articles in the archaeological society journals deal with specific heraldic questions, such as Dr. McLysaght's article in the centenary issue of the *Journal of the Royal Society of Antiquaries of Ireland* on the arms of Ireland.[47]

There are only two contributions of any importance treating of the general question of the evolution of heraldry in Ireland: two articles in the *Journal of the Royal Society of Antiquaries of Ireland*, one by R. Canon ffrench,[48] and the other by E. C. Armstrong.[49] Canon ffrench's work leans on evidence from the Irish epics and bardic poetry. He concedes that the standards mentioned there cannot really be described as heraldic, but he does not at any stage define with any degree of scientific precision what he understands as heraldry. Armstrong's work, as one might expect from his expertise on Irish seals, leans heavily on the evidence from the seals and seal matrices available. This is the classical technique in the examination of the evolution of heraldry. Unfortunately the evidence available in Ireland is meagre but, such as it is, it enabled Armstrong to come to some conclusions scientifically based on the evidence. The conclusions have been in general substantiated by the

---

[44] Wagner, *Heralds and Heraldry*, p. 101.
[45] Wagner, *Heraldry in England*, p. 15.
[46] Mark Noble, *History of the College of Arms* (London, 1805).
[47] E. McLysaght, 'Some observations on the Arms of the four Provinces', *R.S.A.I. Jn.*, LXXIX (1949), 60–63.
[48] 'The Arms of Ireland and Celtic tribal Heraldry', *R.S.A.I. Jn.*, XXXV (1905), 234–48.
[49] 'A note as to the time Heraldry was adopted by the Irish Chiefs', *R.S.A.I. Jn.*, XLIII (1913), 66–72.

later work of Professor Curtis on the seals of the great collection of Ormond deeds.[50]

Heraldry, as we have seen, was in its formative stage at the time of the invasion of Ireland. It is not unreasonable to assume that heraldic development in Anglo-Norman Ireland did not differ in essence from the general development of heraldry in feudal Europe. A full investigation of this question would involve an examination of all the available evidence from seals and an immense amount of field work in a survey of monuments in churches and tombstones. It would also be necessary to examine the English rolls of arms; in particular, the occasional rolls of knights present at battle or siege for any evidence concerning the shields of Anglo-Irish lords who are known to have been present in large numbers, particularly during the Scottish wars.[51] It would also be advisable to examine the great continental rolls which purport to be universal armorials. Mr. Colin Campbell, for instance, points out that the late thirteenth-century French armorial blazons the arms of 'Le Roi d'Irlande' as *azure a harp or*.[52]

Regrettably, it is not feasible in a study of this nature to attempt a comprehensive study of Irish heraldry, but enough evidence exists to show that heraldry in Anglo-Norman Ireland was essentially similar to heraldry in feudal Europe. The same prerequisites for its development existed. The social and political system was based on the feudal law of devolution of property and the contractual obligation of lord and vassal. The military system was based on the feudal mailed knight. The early foundations of the military religious orders, the Knights Templars and Hospitallers, and the occasional effigy of a crusader in churches show the connexion with the crusades.[53] The thirteenth-century poem already cited (see page 71) indicates that the tournament was practised in medieval Ireland and was attended by heralds from the continent. Readily available evidence is, however, regrettably very scanty. Professor Curtis, in his examination of the seals of the Ormond deeds, states that the first seal which can be identified as a full armorial seal is that of the Calf or De Veel family of Norragh, Co. Kildare, dated 1347.[54] In view of the general paucity of evidence and of the very real difficulties of identification, too much should not be made of this. E. C. Armstrong describes an armorial seal of Laurentius Petyt with arms which can be identified as a *fess sable with mullet for difference*, although the field is unidentifiable.[55] The arms of Petyt are *or a fess sable*. As Armstrong points

---

[50] E. Curtis, 'Some Medieval Seals out of the Ormond Archives', *R.S.A.I. Jn.*, LXVI (1936), 1-8.
[51] See J. Lydon, 'An Irish Army in Scotland, 1296', *Irish Sword*, V (1962), 184-90, and 'Irish Levies in the Scottish Wars', *ibid.*, 207-17.
[52] Letter in *The Coat of Arms*, XXXVII (1959), 16.
[53] C. Litton Falkiner, 'The Hospital of St. John of Jerusalem in Ireland', *R.I.A. Proc.*, XVI, sect. C (1907), 275-317.
[54] Curtis, 1 ff.
[55] E. C. Armstrong, 'Some Matrices of Irish Seals', *R.I.A. Proc.*, XXX, sect. C (1912-13), 191 ff.

out, the family of Petyt or Petit is mentioned frequently in Sweetman's calendar.[56] Another shield in this collection of armorial seals can be blazoned fully as follows, *Ermine on a cross gules five escallops or*. Papworth's ordinary of arms, as again Armstrong points out, identifies this coat as the arms of Wayling or Weyland, a family who from the evidence in Sweetman's calendar, had settled in Ireland at an early period.[57]

A factor which must also be borne in mind is that many of the great Norman lords held property in both Ireland and England. The arms on an armorial pendant in the Royal Irish Academy have been identified by Armstrong as *or a flaunch gules*, arms of the family of Hastings, Earls of Pembroke.[58] Laurence Hastings, Earl of Pembroke (1318–48), also held the lordship of Wexford in Ireland. The senior house of the Butlers were also great English noblemen and, as we have seen, took their arms from their kinsman Ranulf Glanville, the English judiciar (see page 6). Amongst eighteen shields in the heraldic glass of Ockewell Manor House in the parish of Bray in Berkshire, there is an illustration of the arms and crest of Sir James Butler, knighted by Henry VI in 1426, who succeeded his father as fifth Earl of Ormond and was beheaded after his capture at Towton Field in 1461.[59]

Heraldic evidence from the churches and cemeteries in Irish towns shows that heraldry developed in much the same fashion as it did in England. The late Thomas Westropp's examination of St. Mary's Cathedral in Limerick may be taken as an example. The three slabs in the Galwey tomb reveal the shield of Richard Baltingford (1357–90), *a fess engrailed and a label of five points*. To the right is the tablet of his grandson, Edmund Galwey, bearing a shield with a cross and a bend over it; this can readily enough be identified as Galwey Arms impaling for Artur *a chevron between three clarions*.[60] To the left is a tablet of Geoffrey Galwey, with the arms of Galwey impaling for Stritch *a double-headed eagle*. Geoffrey Galwey died 4 January 1444/45, and his will was proved eight days later. The north and south external buttresses display respectively shields with *a chevron between three escallops*, and *a chevron between three clarions*. Above the second shield is the name Johannis Artur. Westropp cites the Arthur manuscripts as stating that 'Thomas Arthur, bailiff of the city, 1407–09, and mayor 1421–26, and his wife Johannah, daughter and heiress of David Muryagh, alderman of Cork, re-edified the elaborate facade of the choir, putting their respective arms over the north and south doors, not through a spirit of vainglory, but in order that others hereinafter should initiate the memorials of their piety.'[61]

---

[56] H. S. Sweetman, ed., *Calendar of Documents relating to Ireland* (London, 1877), I, 292, 474; II, 46, 84, 259.
[57] *Ibid.*
[58] E. C. Armstrong, 'A Note on four armorial Pendants', *R.I.A. Proc.*, XXX, sect. C (1912–13), 191 ff.
[59] *Archaeologia* (1773–1838), VI, 322.
[60] T. Westropp, 'Carvings in St. Mary's Cathedral, Limerick', *R.S.A.I. Jn.*, XXII (1892), 70.
[61] *Ibid.*

Except for the Christian name this would substantiate the evidence on the shields. Westropp suggests that the slabs were removed from the doors to the buttresses and that a Christian name above the genitive Johannis was removed. Similar examples of fairly elaborate heraldry are to be found in other Irish towns, such as Youghal, Galway and, of course, Dublin.

It is clear, therefore, that the inherent probability of identical development of heraldry in Ireland and England is confirmed by the evidence. The question of the adoption of heraldry by the Gaelic aristocracy is a much more difficult and complex one.

Geoffrey Keating and other seventeenth-century Irish scholars believed that the ancient Irish did use heraldry.[62] All these assertions really prove is that heraldry was well established amongst the native Irish in the seventeenth century. Since its social implications were by then predominant, Keating and other apologists would naturally be anxious to emphasize the antiquity and dignity of the native Irish. Keating, in fact, suggests that the origin of bearing arms amongst the Irish is to be found in Egypt, when the ancestors of the Irish living in Egypt observed the Israelites bearing arms for their respective tribes.[63]

That the Irish carried standards to identify them in battle is quite evident from the accounts of battles. The *meirge* or standard was in use from a very early time.[64] These standards cannot, however, be identified as being identical with armorial bearings as defined in the heraldic sense. The elaborate description of Donogh MacNamara harnessing himself for battle in *Caithreim Toirdealbhaigh,* written as late as 1459, does not mention anything which can be definitely identified as armorial bearings. 'The soldiers closely sewing their ensigns to the vast poles and fastening their colours by their borders to the lofty poles of their spears.'[65] There is no suggestion of anything in the nature of a personal shield device being used. Even Keating implicitly suggests that the standards were collective, adapted from the alleged standards of the tribes of Israel, and not from individuals. Further, they are not explicitly stated to be shield devices.

In dealing with the native Irish aspect of heraldry, it cannot be too strongly emphasized that heraldry evolved from the feudal system and is intimately associated with feudalism in its social, legal and military manifestations, in particular with its laws of hereditary devolution. While symbolic devices of one kind or another have always attracted humanity, it is not too much to say that the form taken in this particular type of symbolic device, which we style heraldry, was shaped by the feudal system. Such refinements as the bearing of the arms of an heiress

---

[62] See John O'Donovan, ed., *The Banquet of Dun na n-Gedh and the Battle of Mag Rath* (Dublin, 1842), pp. 348 ff., where this question is fully discussed.
[63] John O'Daly, ed., 'Poem from Keating's Foras Feasa ar Erinn', *Kilkenny Arch. Society Jn.*, I (1851–53).
[64] O'Donovan, p. 347.
[65] *Ibid.*, p. xiii.

in an *escutcheon of pretence* by the husband, that is, bearing his wife's arms in a small shield in the centre of his own shield, rather than the ordinary impalement, and the right of the issue of the marriage to quarter their mother's arms, seem to be a reflection of the feudal law of property devolution in the high Middle Ages. An heiress was entitled to succeed to a fief, but it became the property of her husband on marriage and passed normally to the eldest son of the marriage. The succession of Strongbow to the kingdom of Leinster through his marriage to Eva McMorrough and the subsequent transmission to William the Marshall through his marriage to Isabella, the daughter and heiress of Strongbow, was perfectly normal legal feudal practice. If heraldry had fully evolved at the time this hereditary succession could and would be indicated in a fully quartered shield.

Feudalism did not, however, operate in Gaelic Ireland; the Irish system of succession to office and property was radically different from feudal succession. It was based on membership of a *derbhfine* or family group of four generations. This question has been treated fully by Professor Eoin MacNeill,[66] and further investigated brilliantly by MacNeill's student, Professor James Hogan.[67] It is sufficient for us to appreciate that the feudal law of primogeniture in succession to office or property did not prevail in the legal system of Gaelic Ireland. Neither did the custom of the succession of property to a female in the absence of a male heir, and the subsequent assumption of these responsibilities by her husband *ob imbecillatum sexus,* as the feudal lawyers so bluntly put it. Similarly, warfare in Ireland did not evolve around the mailed knight with his personal and hereditary obligation to lead his vassals and to follow his lord. In consequence, the tournament as it developed in western Europe was not known in pre-Norman Ireland. Therefore, the factors which together contributed to the appearance of heraldry, as we know it, did not exist in Gaelic Ireland.

It is a truism to say that Gaelic Ireland was profoundly affected by the Norman invasion. Before examining the regrettable scanty evidence available for the use or non-use of heraldry amongst the native Irish aristocracy, it might be well to discuss when they began to be influenced by the military, social and legal customs of the invaders in so far as this influence may have led to the adoption of heraldry. We have fairly clear evidence that the Irish were using armour by the time of the battle of Athenry in 1316.[68] A more significant development, however, is the fact that, under Norman influence, there appears to have been a deliberate, but in the long run unsuccessful, attempt to repudiate the traditional system of elective kingship, with its bias towards a collateral succession. Professor Hogan has pointed out that in the case of the

---

[66] *Celtic Ireland* (Dublin, 1921), pp. 114–43.
[67] 'The Irish Law of Kingship', *R.I.A. Proc.*, XL, sect. C (1931–32), 187–254.
[68] E. Curtis, *Med. Ire.*, 2nd ed. (London, 1938).

kingship of McCarthy Mór, a lineal succession was successfully introduced in 1302, in place of the previous succession of collaterals.[69] Similarly, the northern Uí Neill appear to have established a lineal succession in 1325 after the death of Domhnall Ua Neill.[70]

Turning to the evidence available from seals, we find that the Irish princes were using seals at least as early as the thirteenth century.[71] One seal in the British Museum catalogue is attributed to 'Brian, King of Ceneoleogain' (ob. c. 1276). The seal contains an effigy. The king is described as being 'in armour with flat helmet, sword and shield with uncertain charge riding to right on a pacing horse'.[72] There is no discernable heraldic charge in the illustration that appears in Armstrong's paper. In the Royal Irish Academy collection there is a shield of Donal McCarthy, King of Desmond (ob. c. 1302), showing an effigy of the king on horseback galloping to the right with a sword in hand.[73] He does not carry a shield, and there is not any trace of armorial bearings. It was, in fact, after his death that the McCarthy Mór family adopted lineal succession. In the Ormond deeds there is a seal of Roderic, son of Alan Kennedy, attached to a deed of 1337. The device on the shield appears to be a lion, or perhaps as Curtis suggests, the mysterious *onchú*.[74] In any event they are not what later came to be accepted as the traditional Kennedy arms, and the issue is further confused by the use of miscellaneous devices on later Kennedy seals. In one sixteenth-century deed, Cornelius O'Kennedy of Parke in Tipperary appears to have borrowed a Rothe seal with Rothe arms. The borrowing of seals was not, of course, uncommon.[75]

The earliest armorial seal of an Irish prince for which we have any evidence, appears to be that of Aodh O'Neill, son of Donal, who died in 1325. It is clear from Professor Hogan that this Aodh initiated the lineal succession, although he himself did not directly succeed his father.[76] A collateral Henry intervened. He did, however, initiate a lineal succession that was to last without a break until the end of the fifteenth century.[77] It is also worthy of note that he is named in a summons of Edward III in 1335 to the magnates of Ireland to attend the king in his war against the Scots.[78]

The seal is stated to bear a shield with a dexter hand and the inscription 'S. Odonis O'Neill Regis Hibernycorum Ultonie'. Unfortunately its provenance is unknown until it came from the neighbourhood of Belfast into the hands of Horace Walpole c. 1784. Walpole describes the

---

[69] Hogan, 189.
[70] *Ibid.*, 249.
[71] E. C. Armstrong, *R.S.A.I. Jn.*, XLIII, 66–72.
[72] *British Museum Catalogue of Seals* (London, 1895), IV, 695.
[73] Armstrong, *R.S.A.I. Jn.*, XLIII, 69.
[74] Curtis, *R.S.A.I. Jn.*, LXVI, 1 ff.
[75] *Ibid.*
[76] Hogan, *R.I.A. Proc.*, XL, sect. C, 189.
[77] *Ibid.*
[78] Rymer, *Foedera* (1745), 9th Edw. III.

seal as 'a silver seal, extremely ancient, of Hugh O'Neill, King of Ulster, brought out of Ireland by Mr. William Brestow'.[79] The seal then came into the possession of a William Cave, who was said to own it in 1853. Reeves himself, in fact, only saw an electrotype copy in the cabinet of a collector. It has, however, been accepted as being authentic by both Reeves and Armstrong. Professor Hogan's chart shows no later Hugh until the great Elizabethan, Hugh, Earl of Tyrone, who in any event would not have described himself precisely in the terms of the inscription.

Hugh O'Neill eventually succeeded his father, and Professor Hogan comments that his 'usurpation of the kingdom in defiance of the custom by which a collateral was to be preferred to a descendant ... would seem to inaugurate a deliberate policy ... to establish a lineal succession'.[80] He had the support of the Deputy, Sir Ralph d'Ufford, and he may also have accompanied the king against the Scots. His relatively close association with Anglo-Norman Ireland would have made him acquainted with heraldry, and he apparently adopted the ancient symbol of the red hand, which much predated heraldry, as the principal charge on the shield. This, with various refinements, became the O'Neill arms. The first evidence we have of the adoption of the hereditary personal device on a shield, which we call heraldry, so peculiarly in harmony with feudal lineal succession, is its adoption by the O'Neill who succeeded in initiating a lineal succession for his descendants in Ulster.

The most that can be claimed for this evidence is that an inherent probability in the nature of heraldry has been confirmed in the case of one of the great Irish families, the quasi-royal house of the O'Neills. The way would have been prepared by the previous adoption of the use of armour and seals amongst the Irish princes, and the general tendency towards fusion which had been proceeding between the two races, despite the legislation arrived at preventing it. The conversion into heraldic form of pre-existing royal or tribal emblems has continental parallels. The fleur-de-lis as a decorative form is of immense antiquity and came to be used as an ensign of the royal house, but the flory shield of France is not found until 1239.[81] The heraldic use of the imperial eagle has a similar history.[82] The next evidence we have of the use of armorial bearings amongst the native Irish is an account by J. Scott Porter of a tomb said to be that of 'Cooey na-nGall Ó Catháin', who was captured by the English in 1376, according to the Four Masters. There is a tomb on the shield with the arms, *party per pale on dexter a stag passing under a tree, sinister party per fess in chief an ox and in base a salmon.*[83]

---

[79] William Reeves, 'The Seal of Hugh O'Neill', *U.J.A.*, 1st ser., I (1853), 255–59.
[80] Hogan, *R.I.A. Proc.*, XL, sect. C, 189.
[81] G. Dernay, 'Le Blason d'apres le sceaux du Moyen-Age', *Société Nationale des Antiquaries de France*, Mémoires XXX, VIII, 39–89.
[82] Oswald Barron, 'Art Heraldry', *Encycl. Brit.*, 11th ed.
[83] J. Scott Porter, 'Some Account of the Sept of Ó Catháin of Ciannachta Gluine-Geimhin', *U.J.A.*, 1st ser., III (1855), 1–9, 261–71.

The recently published *Shell Guide* states that, according to local tradition the effigy beside the arms on the tomb is that of Cooey na-nGall.[84]

What tends to make me have some doubts about this is an observation of John O'Donovan's to the effect that he had probably examined more tombstones in Ireland than any other scholar and did not observe 'any escutcheon of a Milesian family older than Elizabeth's time'.[85] In the absence of a personal examination of the monument, it is not possible to be more definitive, but the recent work of the editors of the *Shell Guide* bears out Scott Porter's evidence.

These two representations appear to be the only instances indicating the use of armorial bearings amongst the Irish aristocracy in the fourteenth century. It is, perhaps, not without significance that the two individuals in question had exceptionally close relations with the English. Further extensive searches might reveal more, but the bulk of the seals used bear miscellaneous devices such as griffons, wyverns, galleys, etc.[86] It must, however, be remembered that the bulk in question is very small; it would be dangerous to infer too much from this, especially as Armstrong did not deal with evidence from tombstones or other monuments. Armstrong's statement that the available heraldry does not appear to have been generally adopted by the Irish chiefs until the fifteenth century, or even later, can be accepted, with reservations, until more information is available. Indeed the first extant armorial seal of an Irish prince is to be found in the Ormond collection of deeds, now in the National Library of Ireland. It is a seal of Donal Reagh McMurrough Kavanagh. The arms are a lion passant on the shield with supporters of lions on either side. The identical arms are used on seal in a treaty between Donal Reagh's grandson, Murrough McMurrough Kavanagh, and Piers Butler in 1525.[87] This is heraldry, according to Wagner's precise definition: the use of identical marks on a shield transmitted in the male line. It would be fallacious to deduce firmly from this that the Irish princes did not generally adopt heraldry until the turn of the fifteenth century. It must be remembered that, in fact, the first full armorial seal of a Norman family in the whole Ormond collection is as late as 1347.[88] This late date of the use of armorial seals suggests that it might be advisable to revise the accepted view of equating the general adoption of heraldry with evidence from seals, at least as far as Ireland is concerned.

In the sixteenth century evidence gained from fiants, seals and monuments shows a much wider use of heraldry amongst the native Irish than in previous centuries, although by no means do all of the

---

[84] Lord Killanin and Michael V. Duignan, *Shell Guide to Ireland* (London, 1962), p. 262.
[85] O'Donovan, introd.
[86] E. C. Armstrong, *Irish Seal Matrices and Seals* (Dublin, 1913), p. 16.
[87] Curtis, *R.S.A.I. Jn.*, LXVI, 72–76. I have verified Professor Curtis' observations by examining the originals.
[88] Armstrong, *R.I.A. Proc.*, XXX, sect. C.

seals display heraldic devices. There is a seal matrix in the Royal Irish Academy with the inscription, Johannes O'Reli, Myles, that has for device a hand between two wheel-like figures. The matrix is attributed by Armstrong to the sixteenth century.[89] The Annals of the Four Masters refer to a John Roe O'Reilly who was knighted together with Turlough O'Donnell in 1583. The date of the matrix, in Armstrong's opinion, coincides approximately with the date of the knighting. The significance of this is that one would conclude from the evidence of the seal that armorial bearings were not then in use amongst the O'Reillys. In this instance there is clear proof that such an inference would be wrong. There is a monument of 1581 in Clonabreany church, Co. Meath, where the arms of Plunkett are impaled with the arms of O'Reilly, *two lions counter rampant holding a hand appaumee*. It is not possible, of course, to identify the tinctures, but these are clearly O'Reilly arms.[90] This is a salutary warning against drawing too definitive conclusions from any one source.

There are two other matrices displaying shields of arms in the collection described by Armstrong, one bearing the name John MacArt, and the other, Godfrey O'Dougherty. Armstrong also examined the fiants of Elizabeth, now unfortunately lost. Amongst these he found the surrenders of twenty-nine Irish and Norman chiefs. The seals of twenty-three of these had disappeared; two were sealed with blobs of plain wax, and four had armorial seals attached. One seal was that of Sir Lucas Dillon; two of the others, those of Connell O'Molloy and Feahan O'Ferrall Boy, bear the arms of O'Molloy and O'Ferrall respectively, and the fourth, the seal of Sir Turlagh O'Brien, has a quarterly coat, *1st and 4th three lions passant in pale 2nd three pheons meeting in point and 3rd a pheon*.[91] These arms, as described by Armstrong, are the arms of O'Brien, Lord Inchiquin, who quartered what may be termed the basic O'Brien arms in this manner. The Inchiquin O'Brien arms are illustrated in Genealogical Office Manuscript 32, compiled c. 1595–97 under the direction of Christopher Ussher, Ulster.

There is an entry in T. C. D. Manuscript 582 which refers to the capture by Sir John Travers in 1542 of two heraldic guidons, one from the MacDonnells, which appears from the description to be MacDonnell arms, and one from O'Cahan's Castle on the Bann, which in fact, seems to be Maguire arms. How this and other heraldic manuscripts came into the Library of Trinity College must be dealt with later (see page 27). Du Noyer noted Brady arms in Ardbracken churchyard, Co. Meath, in 1585.[92]

Towards the end of the sixteenth century, the Ulster Kings of Arms,

---

[89] *Ibid.*, 451.
[90] George du Noyer, 'Catalogue of 103 Drawings of Coats of Arms from original Sketches from Tombstones', *R.I.A. Proc.*, X, sect. C (1866–69), 402–12.
[91] Armstrong, *R.I.A. Proc.*. XXX, sect. C, 451.
[92] Du Noyer, 402.

first Christopher Ussher and subsequently Daniel Molyneux, began to compile the arms of the Irish peers, including the peers of Gaelic Irish stock. Manuscript 32 in the Genealogical Office, already mentioned, includes illustrations of the arms of O'Brien, Earl of Thomond, O'Brien, Lord Inchiquin and O'Neill, Earl of Tyrone. The next list, Genealogical Office Manuscript 34, includes illustrations of the arms of O'Neill, Baron of Dungannon, and of O'Donnell, Earl of Tyrconnell. It must be emphasized that these records are not grants of arms; they are records of arms already in use, noted by the Ulster King of Arms.

In this study it is not possible to do more than to attempt to draw a picture, from readily available evidence, of the heraldic practice in the dual society that was Ireland prior to the end of the Gaelic world as a legal and political entity at the beginning of the seventeenth century. The question is relatively easy to define as far as feudal Anglo-Norman Ireland is concerned. It is clear that the place of heraldry in this society did not differ radically from its place in feudal England, although as might be expected the evidence for Ireland is not by any means as full.

The position is more complex where Gaelic Ireland is concerned. The adoption of a personal hereditary device on a shield and the subsequent wider use of that device, known as heraldry, evolved naturally out of the feudal system and was in harmony with its military, legal and social concepts. Neither the Irish system of devolution of property and office nor the Irish military system favoured symbolism taking this form. The gradual part-fusion between the two races brought about a change in the situation. Readily available evidence does not exist in sufficient quantity to enable us to say with certainty when the Gaelic aristocracy first began to adopt heraldry. It does seem that it was associated with the attempt at adopting the English feudal principle of lineal descent in the male line for succession to office. Heraldry must have become familiar to the Irish magnates in their constant traffic with their Norman neighbours and in their adoption of armour and other feudal methods of warfare. The capture of the heraldic guidons in 1542 is particularly interesting in relation to this. Unfortunately, seal evidence is scanty, and even where Norman heraldry is concerned can be misleading if relied on too heavily, as exemplified in a study of the seals of the Ormond collection of deeds. The seal matrix of O'Reilly is a further indication of the dangers of drawing too definite conclusions from seal evidence alone.

It is clear that by the sixteenth century the great Irish families, O'Neill, O'Donnell, McCarthy, O'Brien—in particular those who in the course of the policy of 'surrender and regrant' were induced to accept peerages—were using what can clearly be recognized as hereditary armorial devices. Since there is no evidence that they applied for grants of arms at this time, and since the records in the Ulster Office indicate that these were the arms in use by them, it seems reasonable to conclude that these families had been using arms for some time prior to this. Unfortunately, it is not possible to be more precise than this except in the case of the O'Neills, who were shown to be using arms as early as the fourteenth century. It is clear also that by the sixteenth century some families who did not receive 'honours' from the English crown were using arms, and in the case of one family, the Ó Catháins, there is evidence that this usage also went back to the fourteenth century. Conversely it appears that some of the families who did receive knighthood, but not any of those who received peerages, were not using arms even as late as the sixteenth century. Whether the great bulk of the native Irish families, whose arms are illustrated in Dr. McLysaght's work, were using arms in the sixteenth century, is not certain, and is not immediately relevant to an introduction of this nature.[93] It must be borne in mind that Dr. McLysaght's work makes it clear that quite prominent native Irish families never used arms; in view of the nature of hereditary devolution and military practice in Ireland this is not altogether surprising, as we have seen. Nevertheless the practice of heraldry was not uncommon amongst the native Irish at the time of the establishment of the Office of Ulster King of Arms in 1552. Even if the greater proportion of the armorial bearings enumerated by Dr. McLysaght did come into existence later, the difference is one of degree rather than of kind.

Heraldry was associated in practice with Anglo-Norman Ireland. It is of significance that the early references we have to the use of arms by the Irish chiefs show that the individuals in question had close associations with the Anglo-Normans or with the English administration; Aodh O'Neill was in alliance with the justiciar and may have served with the king in Scotland; the O'Cahan arms are associated with a Cahan styled 'Cooey na nGall'; the McMurrough Kavanagh family was closely associated with the Normans in Leinster, particularly with the Butlers, and the first O'Reilly arms are found impaled, i.e., indicating a marriage with the Pale family of Plunkett. Lord Justice FitzWilliam explicitly associates heraldry with anglicization; when writing to Cecil in 1562 he refers 'to the discountenance of heraldry and the prevalence of rhymers who set forth the most beastliest and odious of men's doings'.[94] The observations of Keating and other seventeenth-century commentators, when they attribute a long ancestry to the use of armorial bearings amongst the native Irish, show that the practice of heraldry was widely established in the seventeenth century. Late seventeenth-century Irish manuscripts occasionally have blazons of arms in the English manner with varying degrees of accuracy.[95] There is a degree of consistency in rendering heraldic terms into Irish when the blazons are in Irish: thus *armas* for 'arms', and *ar mhachaire* for 'on a field'.[96]

---

[93] Edward McLysaght, *Irish Families, their names, arms and origins* (Dublin, 1957).
[94] *Cal. S.P. Ire.*, 1509–73, V, 191.
[95] See R.I.A. MSS 23 G. 4, p. 480; 23 E. 16, p. 249; 23 M. 46, p. 23.
[96] *Ibid.* See also A. McLoughlin, 'A Gaelic Armory', *R.S.A.I. Jn.*, LXXXIV (1954), 68–71.

After the Treaty of Limerick in 1691, the dispossessed Irish on the continent found themselves part of a social system, particularly in France, in which status and consequent professional advancement depended to a large extent on the possession of a coat of arms and an attested pedigree. This circumstance probably explains the interest of scholars such as Diarmuid O'Conor, Charles Lynegar, Hugh McCurtin and Roger O'Feral (a group of scholars centred in Dublin in the early eighteenth century) in heraldry. O'Conor, for instance, made a certificate of arms in 1724 for Mathew Quilty of Malaga in which he describes himself as 'Antiquarius pro regno Hiberniae electus et juratus'.[97] James Terry, Athlone Pursuivant of Arms, fled to France with James II, taking with him the seal of the office and some of the records.[98] He subsequently issued pedigrees and certificates of arms from the court of St. Germain to many of the Jacobite exiles.[99] Hugh McCurtin, Aaron Crossly informs us, gave a pedigree to Ulster out of old Irish books in his possession.[100]

Probably the most difficult problem in Irish heraldry is the question of the earliest usage of the great bulk of the arms collated first by Roger O'Feral in his *Linea Antiqua* in 1708, now preserved in the Genealogical Office.[101] This collection comprises the great majority of the arms of native Irish families. These have been supplemented to some extent by records of arms in, largely, French archives and by arms certified by Terry and other Irish scholars. These are the sources drawn upon by Dr. McLysaght for blazons of arms by native Irish families in his work.

From the beginning of the seventeenth century the whole of Ireland was brought within the social and political framework of English society. The bulk of the Irish nobility and gentry initially attempted to adapt themselves to this society, but by the end of the century the great majority of them had been dispossessed and had followed the example of the northern Gaelic princes at the beginning of the century by going or being forced into exile after the Cromwellian and Williamite confiscations. The Irish exiles in Europe entered into continental society. Within this society, the demise of heraldry as a utilitarian military device meant in fact an increase in its value as a status symbol. In this context the preoccupation of some Irish scholars with heraldry takes on a new significance, although one would hesitate to say that they simply invented arms for families as they needed them. Keating's observations in the first half of the century show clearly that heraldry was widespread among the native Irish even then, and he was writing at a period when the

---

[97] Photostat in Genealogical Office from family papers.
[98] William Betham, 'Records of the Office of Arms', G.O. MS 11. Printed in abbreviated form in *Ir. rec. comm. rep.*, I, 2nd rep. (1811), app. 8, 65.
[99] C. E. Lart, *The Pedigrees and Papers of James Terry, Athlone Herald at the Court of James II in France (1690–1725)* (n.p., 1938), p. 65.
[100] A. Crossly, *Peerage* (1724), p. 102, n.
[101] G.O. MS 155.

majority of the Gaelic landed proprietors outside Ulster were still, if rather insecurely, on their lands.

There is not any direct evidence that the Office of Arms was established partly or wholly as a means of extending English influence over the country. We can only speculate as to the reasons which led to its establishment at this time in the mid-sixteenth century. It is desirable to consider the establishment of the Office in the historical environment of the time rather than in isolation.

There were two important historical factors in Ireland at this time which may have contributed to the establishment of the Office. One was the adoption by Henry VIII, in the previous reign, of the style King of Ireland, instead of the previous title, Lord of Ireland. This followed from Henry's breach with Rome, and was obviously intended as a manifestation of Henry's repudiation of the concept, dating from the invasion, that the kings of England held Ireland as a papal fief. The sensitivity of Henry to papal symbolism can be deduced from the fact that it appears to be at this time that the arms *azure a harp or* were definitely adopted as the arms of Ireland, rather than the arms *azure three crowns or*, too reminiscent of the papal tiara.[102] The establishment of a Kingdom of Ireland would be further emphasized by setting up a King of Arms for the realm. It may also be observed that it was during the reign of Edward VI that the Protestant policy of the English crown was firmly established. The second factor is the expansionist self-confident policy in Ireland of successive Tudor administrations. By 1552 the English government was well on the way to curbing the power of the 'overmighty subjects'. The quasi-royal house of Kildare had been crushed; the turn of their southern kinsmen, the house of Desmond, was to come; the native Irish magnates were being forced to accept titles from the crown in the course of the policy of 'surrender and regrant', and the new policy of plantation was soon to be initiated in Leix and Offaly. Set in this historical background the lasting establishment of the Office of the Ulster King of Arms can be seen as a symbol of the new vigorous Tudor administration in Ireland.

There is some scattered evidence of the existence of previous kings of arms in Ireland prior to the establishment of Ulster. A well-documented account of this by T. Blake Butler is to be found in the *Irish Genealogist*.[103] There is a mention in Froissart's Chronicle as early as 1392 of 'Chandos le Roi d'Irland'. As Butler points out, Froissart is often inaccurate, and Sir John Chandos, who was slain at Leusac in 1369, had no connexion with Ireland. He had, in any event, his own personal herald.[104] The next reference to Ireland King of Arms is when James Butler, fourth Earl of Ormond, obtained from Henry V the appointment of John

---

[102] J. Barry, 'The Arms of Ireland and Munster', *R.S.A.I. Jn.*, XCII (1962), 79–81.
[103] 'The Officers of Arms of Ireland', *Ir. Geneal.*, XI (October 1943–44), nos. 1, 2.
[104] *Ibid.*, no. 1.

Kitley as Ireland King of Arms.[105] The ordinances of Rouen made 5 January 1419/20 by the kings of arms and heralds in chapter, record the kings of arms as being 'Garter, Clarenceux, Noirey, Aquitaine and Ireland'. All these officers are described as being 'de obedience Angleterre'.[106] Ireland attended the coronation of Catherine, Henry's queen, at Westminster, 22 February 1420/21.[107] In the following reign Thomas Collyer held the office both of Ireland and Clarenceux King of Arms, although whether or not he held the two offices simultaneously is uncertain.[108] It must be pointed out that there is not any positive evidence to connect the office of Ireland King of Arms with the lordship of Ireland other than the title, except for the association of the Earl of Ormond with the first creation. We find for the first time a specific association of the office with Ireland in the reign of Edward IV. The ninth of Edward IV has an entry stating that the King has 'created and ordained out trusty and well beloved Walter Ireland to be king of arms of our land of Ireland and for the sustentation of the same granted him ... £20 yearly'.[109] This Walter Ireland was, in fact, Walter Bellenger. There is a manuscript extant in the College of Arms in London written at the request of 'Walter Bellenger, native of Dieppe ... by Johann Pelessier, scholar of the University of Paris, and servant of the said Ireland King of Arms'. It is stated that the office of Ireland is older than Garter but Bellenger never challenged Garter for precedence.[110]

Between 1477 and 1485 he was apparently involved in a dispute with Sir Thomas Holme, Clarenceux, as the following extracts shows. 'Grant of Arms by Sir T. Holmes Clarenceux, to the confraternity founded in the chapel of the Guild Hall, within the city of London ... dated July 1482 cancelling a previous grant of the said arms made ultra vires by Walter Bellenger, otherwise called Ireland king of arms of the land of Ireland.'[111] This supports the evidence of the financial document already quoted that Bellenger as Ireland King of Arms exercised jurisdiction over the lordship of Ireland. It would also appear that he was incorporated in the chapter over which Garter was recognized as principal king of arms.[112] Bellenger was deprived of his office with the accession of Henry VII, August 1485, and there appears to be no further record of a king of arms connected with Ireland until the appointment of Ulster in 1552.

King Edward VI recorded the appointment of Ulster King of Arms in his diary for February 2nd, 1551/52. 'There was a king of arms made for Ireland whose name was Ulster, and whose province was all Ireland;

---

[105] John Lodge, ed., Archdall *Peerage* (1784), IV, 11.
[106] Butler, *Ir. Geneal.*, XI, no. 1.
[107] *Ibid.*
[108] *Ibid.*
[109] D. Quinn, ed., 'Guide to English financial Records for Irish History', *Anal. Hib.*, 10 (1941), p. 44.
[110] Butler, *Ir. Geneal.*, XI, no. 1.
[111] *Catalogue of Heralds' commemorative Exhibition, 1484–1934* (London, 1935), p. clxiii.
[112] Wagner, *Heralds and Heraldry*, p. 63.

and he was the fourth king of arms, and the first herald of Ireland.[113] Here again there is not any direct evidence as to why the title 'Ulster' was assumed in preference to the older title 'Ireland'. Butler points out that there was an apparent connexion between the offices of Clarenceux King of Arms in England and that of Ireland King of Arms, or that they were at least held for a time by the same individual, and that the title Clarenceux was conferred initially in honour of Lionel, Duke of Clarence. Lionel married Elizabeth de Burgo, heiress of William de Burgo, Earl of Ulster; his daughter Philippa married the third Earl of March, and the title became merged in the crown through the marriage of her grand-daughter Lady Anne Mortimer with Richard Plantagenet, Earl of Cambridge. Butler sees the derivation of the title Ulster in this extremely tenuous thread of titles and connexions. The explanation perhaps gives more plausibility if we remember that the origins of most of the titles of the English heraldic officials derive from equally casual and haphazard connexions.[114]

Whatever the origin of the title, Bartholomew Butler was created Ulster King of Arms by patent dated 1 June 1552, and he was the sole authority by royal letters patent for issuing patents of arms and recording family pedigrees of persons of Irish descent.[115] He was created Ulster in the presence of most of the other members of the college. 'In the partition fees 6th Edward VI he had 8d when each of the other kings for their attendance 12d . . .' but at the creation of the earl of Kildare he had an equal share of the partition money with the other kings of arms.[116] This indicates that at this time Ulster was in some way connected with the College of Arms in London, but that his special connexion with Ireland was recognized. After the appointment of Nicholas Narbonne, 7 July 1556, Ulster was never regarded as an office belonging to the English College of Arms. Both the office of Ulster and that of Athlone Pursuivant of Arms are solely appropriated to Ireland.[117] The position is obscured to some extent by the fact that Ulster's office had not a clear charter of incorporation and, in consequence, its relationship with the College of Arms is often puzzling and contradictory. This confusion is as much due to the close relationship between the two kingdoms and the regrettable laziness and incompetence of many of the Ulster Kings of Arms as to any inherent difficulty. According to the opinion of the law officers, 23 April 1810, Ulster King of Arms was not in any way under the control or subject to Garter King of Arms or the English College of Arms. Nor was he under the authority of the Earl Marshall of England.[118]

When dealing with the records of the office it must be borne in mind

---

[113] M. Noble, *History of the College of Arms* (London, 1805), p. 143.
[114] 'Members of the College of Arms', G. E. C., *Peerage*, II, appendix E.
[115] 'The Genealogical Office, Dublin Castle', Burke's *Peerage* (London), 1953.
[116] Noble, p. 173.
[117] *Ibid.*
[118] Burke's *Peerage*.

60 GUIDE TO RECORDS OF GENEALOGICAL OFFICE

that Ulster, in addition to his armorial and genealogical duties was also an important officer of the crown and closely connected with the administration, particularly with the Irish House of Lords. He has been described as 'at one time the senior and only permanent member of the staff of the Lord Lieutenant, and responsible for arrangement connected with the state visits of the sovereign etc.'[119] In the records of the office there is a diary of the state duties of Ulster King of Arms, compiled by William Hawkins, Ulster, 1698–1736, which gives a fairly complete insight into the duties of Ulster as an officer of the crown.[120] Another manuscript in the office contains a memorial from Hawkins to the Lord Lieutenant setting out celebrations for the birthday of the Prince of Wales in which Ulster is to play a prominent part. This memorial is endorsed by the lords justice.[121] Clearly he regards these ceremonial duties, and his duties in connexion with the House of Lords, as most important. His diary, in fact, deals only with these duties. In his account of his investiture in May 1698 in the council chamber by one of the commissioners of the great seal under warrant from the lords justices, he says that the 'clerk of the council administered the oaths required by the act of Parliament, and I subscribed to the declaration'.[122] His duties, in his capacity as a state official, appeared to coincide with those of the Earl Marshall in England, part of whose duties was the regulation of all state ceremonies.[123]

Ulster also attended on the House of Lords, as already stated, where 'he assists in the introduction of a new peer, which is the only time he attends in this house unless when . . . the Government comes to parliament.'[124] He exercised another function in connexion with the House of Lords; this was the keeping of the list of lords or 'Ulster's list'. In a 1698 memorandum of Hawkins 'to be observed by the clerk of the house' he states that 'all the lords are called by a list of them delivered by me to the clerk'.[125] The function derived indirectly from his heraldic and genealogical duties. Hawkins further informs us that 'the lords who have not may enter their patents [or arms] with me and pay my fees, without which neither he nor his successors would be summoned or enrolled [on Ulster's list] but be passed by as the other lords who have not entered their lists with me.'[126]

The fact that this was a very real duty may be judged from an entry for the year 1707: 'Lord Grandinson's introduction was deferred for want of his patent, but the roll being produced I introduced him.'[127]

---

[119] *Ibid.*
[120] G.O. MS 17, pp. 77–85.
[121] G.O. MS 4, p. 157.
[122] G.O. MS 17, p. 32.
[123] F. Nicholas, *Irish Compendium or Rudiments of Honour* (London, 1745). Chapter iv has an account of the duties of the Earl Marshall, but does not discuss the nature of Ulster's office.
[124] *Lords' jn. Ire.*, II, p. 476.
[125] G.O. MS 17, p. 17.
[126] G.O. MS 388, p. 84.
[127] G.O. MS 17, p. 40.

As a result of many difficulties, it was finally decided in this year by the Irish House of Lords that 'after the decease of any nobleman . . . their heirs or executors should enter in the king of arms office the death of such lords with arms and matches and issues of their family . . . the date of death and place of burial'.[128] This order gave rise to the books of 'lords entries' in the office. It also led indirectly to a considerable mass of material being accumulated in the nineteenth century when Betham and Burke coped with claims to peerage.[129] This is an indication of how what appeared to be a relatively simple function of the office can have a considerable effect on the nature of the material accumulated in its archives.

It is advisable at this stage to take note of previous published descriptions of the office of arms. There is a report on the records of the office by Sir William Betham in 1811 before he became Ulster.[130] He states that many books were carried off by James Terry, Athlone Pursuivant, who fled to France with James II. Terry also brought with him the official seal of the office. Betham adds that there are manuscripts belonging to the office in the library of Trinity College, Dublin. James Terry, a Limerick man, was Athlone Pursuivant at the exiled court of St. Germain after he fled from Dublin. After his death in 1725 his papers passed to Charles d'Hozier, the French juge d'armes.[131] They remained in d'Hozier's family until 1793, when they are said to have been deposited in the Archives Nationales. Some of his papers found their way into the Bibliothèque Nationale.[132] Others were edited and published by C. E. Lart in 1938.[133] In this publication the problem of the dispersal of Terry's manuscripts is not discussed. Neither is there any attempt made to differentiate between the papers accumulated by Terry in the course of his long professional career as a genealogist, and the manuscripts that he is said to have taken to France from the records of the office. A further examination of this would be an interesting and valuable piece of work, but it is sufficient in this study to know that the problem exists.

Betham also refers to 'the books' belonging to the office in the library of Trinity College. Professor Curtis relates how three manuscripts found their way into Trinity, through the Ussher connexion.[134] This very full account of the dispersal of the manuscripts of a king of arms was not by any means an isolated instance. We find a reference to a 'book of arms',

---

[128] *Lords' jn. Ire.*, pp. 168, 169, 189.
[129] Official minutes of evidence, Committee of Claims to Peerage . . . (1882), in J. Foster, *Collectanea genealogica* (n.d.), pp. 77–84.
[130] 'Records of the Office of Arms', answers to queries given by W. Betham, *Ir. rec. comm. rep.*, 1811–15.
[131] Butler,*Ir. Geneal.*, XI, no. 1, 44.
[132] See N.L.I. microfilm, positive 132, 'Terry papers and correspondence'.
[133] Lart, *Pedigrees and Papers of James Terry*.
[134] E. Curtis, 'Extracts out of heralds' Books in Trinity College, Dublin, relating to Ireland in the 16th Century', *R.S.A.I., Jn.*, LXII (1932), 28–49.

which was in the possession of Richard Carney, Ulster, in 1681 being sold by public auction in 1733.[135] This tendency towards dispersal must have been accentuated by the fact that there appears to have been no permanent address for the office, unlike the College of Arms in London. It seems apparent also that successive Ulsters regarded heraldic and genealogical manuscripts, apart from the official records of the office which they were obliged to keep, as being their personal property.

Under these circumstances it is not surprising that the records of the office suffered. Even in the beginning of the nineteenth century, apart from the official series, they were very meagre in quantity. A collection of letters of G. F. Beltz, Lancaster Herald at the College of Arms, illustrates the situation as late as 1802. Beltz was trying to compile a pedigree of a Richard Sullivan living in England. He visited various public offices of records where 'a want of systematic arrangement appears to pervade the whole'.[136] He spent some time at Ulster's Office but he informs us that 'from the limited collection of genealogical evidence it contains, my object has not been materially promoted'.[137]

Sir William Betham's tenure of office in particular radically improved the situation. Betham had been Deputy Ulster since 1807 before he succeeded Fortescue in 1820. During his term of office from 1820 until 1853 he laboured indefatigably at increasing the amount of genealogical and heraldic material in the office. He is perhaps best known by genealogists for the abstracts of Irish prerogative wills that he compiled and left in the office, but he accumulated and compiled many other documents from material now lost, and vastly improved the inadequate records of the office. The value of his work was immeasurably enhanced by the subsequent destruction of so much of the primary sources from which he worked. This accumulation was continued by his successors, in particular by the letters and papers of Sir John Bernard Burke, who succeeded Betham in 1853, by G. D. Burtchaell, Athlone Pursuivant, T. U. Sadleir, Deputy Ulster, and by Chief Herald Dr. Edward McLysaght and his successor Mr. Gerard Slevin. The papers of many private genealogists also found their way into the office in the nineteenth and twentieth centuries.

In more modern times, T. U. Sadleir wrote a brief account of the records of the office in the *Genealogists' Magazine*.[138] In his *Guide to Irish Genealogy*, Father Wallace Clare adverts to the more important genealogical sources to be found there. Mrs. Margaret Falley in her recent work also deals briefly with its records.[139] There is a handlist of bound manuscripts in the office, numbered 1–700A, and in addition there are

---

[135] *Anal. Hib.*, 1 (1930), p. 118.
[136] Gilbert Coll. Letters from George F. Beltz, Lancaster Herald, to Isaac Heard, Garter, and to R. J. O'Sullivan (Letter no. 18, MS 211).
[137] *Ibid.*, Letter no. 10.
[138] T. U. Sadleir, 'Ulster Office Records', *Genealogists' Magazine*, VI, no. 10 (1934), pp. 434–48.
[139] Margaret Dickson Falley, *Irish and Scotch-Irish ancestral Research*, 2 vols. (pr. pr., 1962).

GUIDE TO RECORDS OF GENEALOGICAL OFFICE 63

sixteen cartons, the contents of which largely consist of rolls, some vellum, containing pedigrees. A number of the pedigrees includes emblazons of arms.

Many of the bound manuscripts, such as the prerogative will abstracts, the registers of grants and confirmations of arms from 1698 and others, are in numerical series. Conversely, many more manuscripts appear to be arranged arbitrarily, and some individual manuscripts are collections of heterogenous material bound together. The following description from the handlist of Manuscript 4 illustrates this: 'Papers relating to the duties of the officers of arms [e.g., appointments, fees and exemptions from taxes of officers of arms]; paper on the foundation of certain monasteries in Ireland; list of knights of the Bath made at coronation of Charles I; names of the nobility and officers of France, 1598; affidavit by Denis Hughes as to the rescue from him of William MacKeigue, a prisoner, 1741; articles of peace between Charles I and his Roman Catholic subjects in Ireland, 1646 [see Gilbert, *History of the Irish Confederation*, V, 286–310]; lists of baronets of Ireland, 1620–1780; lists of baronets of England, various dates, mainly seventeenth century, 247 pp. [2 ff. vellum], various sizes, mainly 13 × 8'. This is not an untypical description of many manuscripts. Although the series of grants and confirmations of arms commences as an unbroken series in 1698 under Hawkins, many earlier grants or drafts and copies of grants are to be found scattered through the collection. The same state of affairs appertains with relation to the funeral entries.

It follows therefore that to describe the manuscripts as they are numbered would be an unsatisfactory method of procedure. In any attempt at describing the records of the office it is essential to bear in mind that they derive essentially from its functional nature; they are not an arbitrary collection, but possess an organic unity. They fall into a number of categories natural to the nature and scope of the duties of the Ulster King of Arms and his assistants. These duties have already been generally indicated.

Sir William Betham recognized this in 1811. G. O. Manuscript 11[140] contains a substantially fuller account of his 'Answer to the queries proposed by the record commissioners respecting the state of the office of the Ulster king of arms' than that contained in the printed report.[141] The records were then, apparently, kept at Betham's private house, No. 7, North Cope Street, Dublin, although Betham was at the time only Deputy Ulster. The Government allowed £40 p.a. as a rent for this service. In his answer to the first enquiry Betham described fairly completely the records of the office. He first listed the documents that 'may be considered as the records of the office'. These were the visitations, funeral entries, registered pedigrees, registrations of arms, volumes of

---

[140] G.O. MS 11, fol. 19.
[141] See footnote 130.

the pedigrees and arms of the peers of Ireland, i.e., lords entries, pursuant to an order of the House of Lords of 12 August 1707; a book of the pedigrees and arms of the baronets of Ireland under a royal warrant of 30 September 1789 'correcting and preventing abuses in the order of baronets'; books containing lists of the peers as they sat in parliament at various times, and of the creations of peers, baronets and knights from the time of Queen Elizabeth to Betham's own time; a book of royal licences for changes of name and arms. Betham then describes what he called 'many manuscript books . . . copies and abstracts relative to genealogical and antiquarian research' and other heterogeneous material.

It is clear from this document that Betham recognized that the records of the office fell into clearly defined categories even in his time. It must also be remembered that the records have expanded substantially in the intervening 150 years, and the categorization may now be carried a stage further. This account is also important as it informs us of the extent of the records in 1811.

The first category into which the records of the office fall is that which Betham styled the manuscripts that 'may be described as the records of the office', that is, documents essential to the purpose for which the office was established. As we have seen, Ulster was the sole authority in Ireland for issuing patents of arms and recording pedigrees for persons of Irish descent. Heraldic visitations taking note of the arms and issue of armigenous persons were carried out regularly in England from 1530. They were a consequence of the control of arms acquired by the College of Arms under the Earl Marshall, and thenceforward in England they provided the main acceptable evidence at any particular time that an individual had acquired arms by hereditary right that had been ratified by the competent authority, i.e., the heralds on visitation. The heralds' competence in genealogy, as a necessary auxiliary, arose out of these.

The same scheme was envisaged for Ireland. Manuscript 5, p. 1, contains a copy of a warrant of 1567, by Sir Henry Sydney, Lord Deputy, stating that 'Nicholas Narbon, Ulster, king of arms of the realm of Ireland intendeth to repair unto all parts of the same to visit and observe the arms . . . of all noblemen . . . and to correct all false armour and all such as without his consent do presume to bear arms . . . except they be lineally descended of blood and name from such their ancestors as by the law of arms they may of right bear and use, also upon true certificate to have made to register all their arms, descents, marriages of all nobles and gentlemen of the realm of Ireland . . . ' This warrant was repeated in February 1607, when the then Ulster, Daniel Molyneux, was directed to enquire into the 'arms, pedigrees and genealogies . . . of all noblemen and gentlemen whether English or Irish'. This instruction was necessary because it was apparently 'a common practise of many . . . to usurp and encroach upon the names and coats of arms of many ancient and noble

GUIDE TO RECORDS OF GENEALOGICAL OFFICE 65

families of the realm'.[142] The result of these instructions was disappointing. In all there are accounts for seven visitations in the office; the first four under Nicholas Narbon, 1568–74, and the others under Daniel Molyneux, 1607–10. There are records of visitations for the following places: Dublin and part of Louth, 1568–70; Drogheda and Ardee, 1570; Swords, 1572; Cork, 1574; Limerick, 1574; Dublin, 1607 and 1610; and Wexford, 1610. They are contained in G. O. Manuscripts 47–49. There may have been other visitations made which do not survive.

The visitations were carried out in a leisurely manner, sometimes ranging over a period of years, and some of the accounts contain very few entries. They are all for areas of the Pale, or for areas which had formerly been in it, or for municipal districts familiar with the English administrative system. The paucity of the entries prior to 1603 is not surprising, but it is difficult to ascertain why the visitations were not carried out more extensively when the country as a whole had been brought under the English administration in Dublin.

The immediate effect of the relative absence of visitations in Ireland meant that little evidence was available to prove that arms claimed by any individual did, in fact, descend to him by hereditary right from an ancestor who had them properly certified by the heralds on visitation. This gave rise to the custom peculiar to Ireland of the 'confirmation of arms', as a variant of the grant of arms. Ulster King of Arms, in addition to grants, conferred confirmations of arms, and registered the confirmation in the office if the applicant could show that the arms in question had been used by his family for one hundred years or for three generations.

This brings us to the next series of official records in the office, the entries of patents of arms, that is of grants and confirmations of arms issued by Ulster, the sole authority in Ireland for the issuing of patents of arms.

There are records of grants and confirmations of arms dating from Bartholomew Butler, the first Ulster, to contemporary grants and confirmations made by the present Chief Herald. The series was made in methodical chronological order from 1698, commencing with William Hawkins, and is contained in a numerical series of manuscripts in the office. A number of earlier drafts of ratifications of arms is bound together in a series styled draft grants, and others are scattered miscellaneously through the collection. Many of the earlier grants are lost; some are to be found in the library of Trinity College, Dublin, manuscripts previously mentioned. The text of the patent of confirmation normally gives more genealogical information than the text of the grant. This, in view of its nature, is understandable. A complete index of all certificates of arms from 1552 is to be found in G. O. MS 422–23.

---

[142] G.O. MS 5, pp. 2–4.

Another series that is regarded as being a record of official certificates of arms is that known as 'Funeral Entries'. The following extract from a document in the office casts a light on the nature of this series: 'By virtue of an act of state or decree bearing date the fourth of August, Anno Domini 1627 . . . for the better preservation of the memory of the nobility and gentry their marriages, posterity, and arms. The king of arms here is straightly charged to make a true and fair entry of certificates of the matches, issues, times of decease and of arms of all such of the nobility and gentry of this realm as shall happen to die, which certificates are by the said act of state or decree to be returned unto the office of the king of arms for the time being by the heirs and executors of such of the nobility and gentry as shall so die for which entry there is appointed certain fees to be payed to the said king of arms.'[143] This document dated 12 February 1633/34 instructs Darby Morris, yeoman, to 'repair unto the several heirs and executors or administrators of those whose names be under written . . . to intimate unto them the effect of the said act of state or decree, and to require them to send unto me under their hands the certificates above mentioned . . . together with the fees due for the same . . . I shall carefully enter and record in my office according to the charge to me by the said act of state'.[144]

Although this is the first reference I have been able to trace referring to a formal decree instructing Ulster to keep funeral entries, it is probable that there were earlier decrees. In any event there are records of funeral entries in the office from 1588. As the instruction to Morris states, the entries include the name, wife and issue of the deceased. It also normally shows either an illustration in colour, or a trick of the arms, and it frequently shows the armorial devices displayed at the funeral, with notes on the ordering of the funeral ceremonies.

There are altogether fifteen volumes of funeral entries covering the period 1588–1691. There is also a transcript of one volume which was detached from the others and deposited in the British Museum; it comprises funeral entries of various dates between 1622 and 1729.[145] There was apparently a nineteenth-century revival of this practice, as another volume covers the period 1862–98. Other funeral entries are to be found scattered throughout the collection. Manuscript 345, for example, is an elaborate funeral entry on vellum, one of the relatively few vellum manuscripts in the collection. It is the funeral entry of Charles Manners, Duke of Rutland. The entries, however, relate mainly to the seventeenth century. The nineteenth-century entries seem to have been in the nature of a romantic revival.

I have not been able to trace any formal repeal of the decree instructing Ulster to record these certificates, which give such valuable genealogical information about so many of the seventeenth-century Irish gentry. It

---

[143] G.O. MS 2, fol. 7.
[144] *Ibid.*
[145] B.M. Add. MS 4820.

appears to have been a difficult duty to administer on occasion; particularly in connexion with the collection of fees. We have an account by Thomas Preston, Ulster, of a Thomas Clark of Dublin refusing to return the entry of his father, Simon, saying that although Simon had in his lifetime written himself gentleman, he was not one in fact. In consequence, Ulster instructs Alban Leverett, Athlone Pursuivant, to ask Clark by what authority he bears the arms which he has carved impaled with his wife's arms of the ancient family of Usher, and in default of a satisfactory reply that would, of course, commit Clark to paying the fee, Athlone Pursuivant is to see to it that the arms are defaced.[146] An incident of this kind was not an isolated one. Nevertheless, a large collection of these entries was made throughout the seventeenth century.

The practical discontinuance of this series does, in fact, coincide with circumstances that arose in the course of Ulster's duties in connexion with the Irish House of Lords, which eventually gave rise to the collection of manuscripts known as Lords Entries. It is advisable now to examine the circumstances leading to this evolution.

Among the duties of state exercised by Ulster was the keeping of the list of peers or Ulster's Roll. William Hawkins, Ulster, 1698–1736, states in 1698 in a memorandum 'to be observed by the clerk of the house' that 'all the lords are called by a list of them delivered by me to the clerk'.[147] At this period, it was frequently found that the list contained names that should be omitted, and further that it omitted names that should be included. The main problem appeared to have been the difficulty of determining whether outlawries passed on lords for their part in rebellion had been reversed or not. Lords committees in 1692, 1695 and 1697 had tried to determine these facts in individual cases, in particular in the case of Edmund, Lord Mountgarrett.[148] Conversely, peers were sometimes omitted from the list because they neglected to inform Ulster of the creation. Hawkins specifically refers to a resolution of the Lords committees 'that the lords who have not may enter their patents [i.e., of arms] with me and pay my fees, without which neither he nor his successors would be or enrolled [i.e., on the list] but be passed by, as the other lords who have not entered their patents with me'.[149] Hawkins acted on this principle; writing in 1707 he informs us that 'Lord Grandison's introduction was deferred for want of his patent, but the roll being produced I introduced him.'[150]

There was still difficulty with the roll. In July 1707, in reply to an order 'that he should make and return a perfect list of all the lords of the kingdom', Hawkins petitioned the house 'setting forth his reasons for not making the list complete', and praying for an order 'to enable him

---

[146] G.O. MS 2, fol. 9.
[147] G.O. MS 17, p. 37.
[148] Lords' jn., 2, 481–83.
[149] G.O. MS 388, p. 84.
[150] G.O. MS 17, p. 40.

to do it for the future'. The result of this was the Lords' resolution of August 1707 'that for the service of the peerage of this kingdom immediately after the decease of any nobleman . . . their heirs or executors should enter in the king of arms office the death of such lords with arms and matches and issues of their family, the date of death, and the place of burial'.[151] This order gave rise to the series known as Lords Entries in the office. The information given is identical with that in the funeral entries, except that the entries are limited to peers.

The entries are in six volumes covering the period 1698–1939. The practice had apparently been initiated prior to the instruction of 1707. It survived the abolition of the Irish House of Lords in 1800, presumably because of the right of the Irish peers to elect representatives to the British House of Lords.

There is not any immediate practical reason why the appearance of the lords entries should almost coincide with the termination of the funeral entries. The series was initiated, as we have seen, to solve an immediate practical administrative problem.

In the absence of any positive evidence, we can only speculate as to the reason for the termination of the funeral entries. It must be borne in mind that the eighteenth century was the age of reason in English and and Anglo-Irish society. The sceptical cultured oligarchs who ruled England since the revolution of 1688 had little interest in the regulation of pedigrees and arms, a social asset which they shared with the poorest gentry. On the other hand, membership of the House of Lords, even of the Irish one, implied and conferred power, and it was in consequence essential that entry be properly regulated.

Another official series in the office is the series styled 'Registered Pedigrees'. There is a large number of pedigrees made in the office and authenticated under the hand and seal of the Ulster King of Arms of the day. The practice appears to have been initiated as early as 1687, and pedigrees are still being registered by the Chief Herald. This series is, of course, more genealogical than heraldic. In some cases, however, arms are emblazoned or illustrated on the pedigrees, and these are accepted as an official ratification by Ulster. Unlike the lords entries and funeral entries, there is not any record of an official statute or administrative order directing Ulster to keep these records.

Perhaps the most interesting of the registered pedigrees are those of the Irish émigrés in Europe in the eighteenth century. This followed from the necessity for the descendants of those who followed James II into exile to integrate themselves into European society. In order to acquire the social standing necessary for responsible positions in the state or for commissions in the army they needed certificates of noblesse supported by genealogical proof.[152] The pedigrees and certificates of

---

[151] *Lords' jn. Ire.*, pp. 168, 169, 189.
[152] Lart, p. xvi.

arms of James Terry, Athlone Pursuivant, at the Stuart court in exile, provided genealogical and heraldic information in support of claims of noblesse.

The dispersal of the St. Germain Court in 1718, the death of Terry in 1725 and the further decline in the prestige of the Stuarts after 1745 deprived the Irish émigrés of an acceptable source of proofs for their status as gentry. At the same time, the descendants of the émigrés, by reason of their long service to continental crowns, particularly the French, were by the middle of the eighteenth century becoming eligible for the highest honours in their new environment. For this further step in the absorption of the Irish, particularly in France, more was needed than for naturalizations and commissions in the army, for which apparently a certificate of the type that 'Matthew Crone is a gentleman descended from a good family in Ireland', appeared to be inadequate.

By the late eighteenth century the French degrees of nobility had become rigidly fixed, and all but the highest ranks were excluded from court circles.[153] In order to be admitted, it was necessary to prove that the candidate's family had ranked among his country's nobility for at least three hundred years.[154] General Daniel O'Connell, brother of Maurice of Derrynane, found it impossible in his early career to secure the promotion that his abilities would normally have deserved, because of his inability to secure admission. Writing to Maurice in 1780 he explains that 'There's a matter of the greatest consequence to promoting my fortune and expectations. I mean that of my genealogy. This is a point so much looked to in this country that without it a man, whatever his merit or capacity, will scarce ever rank among the great. It is indispensably necessary to be present at court to roll with the nobility, and to be admitted to that honour a genealogy must be produced.'[155] The eighteenth century was the age of reason in France no less than in England, but the French monarchy paradoxically and blindly swam against the current intellectual tide, and even accentuated its emphasis on antecedents in the second half of the century. The wider implications of this do not immediately concern us, but these political realities in eighteenth-century France are reflected in the records of the Ulster Office of Arms.

The community of aristocracy in Europe was such that the descendants of the dispossessed Irish looked to Ulster's office to supply these proofs of nobility. The number of registered pedigrees issued to Irish émigrés increased steadily throughout the eighteenth century; from 1740 onwards they are very numerous indeed. The standards that prevailed in the preparation of these pedigrees fall far short of modern standards of scholarship. Indeed they were not always accepted even in their own time. We have at least one well-documented account of a pedigree

---

[153] Stuart Papers I, 122 (1967).
[154] Richard J. Hayes, 'A forgotten Irish Antiquary', *Studies*, XXX (1941), 593.
[155] Cited in Hayes, *ibid.*, from a MS in private possession.

certified by Ulster in the second half of the eighteenth century that did not satisfy the French authorities. The guardian of these privileges in France was juge d'armes, and for much of the second half of the eighteenth century the genealogist, Bernard Cherin, scrutinized the proofs for final authorization by the juge d'armes, at this time Antoine D'Hazier.[156]

Three pedigrees had been sent by Sir William Hawkins, Ulster, 1765-87, to a member of the Allen family of St. Wolstan, Co. Kildare, residing in France. None of the pedigrees was correct. They simply assert a descent from a Norman duke who came over with the Conqueror without giving evidence in support.[157] Allen reports Cherin as saying that no such duke existed.[158] The pedigrees do not give the qualifications of the attestors.[159] In this account of Allen's attempt to obtain a proper pedigree there is a mémoire on 'The getting of proofs of noblesse of an Irish house'. This may be compared with another account relating to the Roche family, to be found in the Royal Irish Academy.[160] Both accounts refer to the need for the signature and seal of the king of arms of the country in which the proofs mentioned are to be found, and the need for attestation by two notaries. Significantly the Roche mémoire also mentions the necessity for a certificate by the 'king's heralds and pursuivants of arms of the heraldic college, London'.[161] From this it is regrettably clear that a certificate from Ulster's office alone was not regarded as sufficient to ensure a correct genealogy. Nevertheless the value of these pedigrees for their own period, at least, must not be underestimated.

In the nineteenth century Sir William Betham, in addition to improving the inadequate records of the office, carried out genealogical research of a much higher standard than that of his predecessors, although his work and that of his successor, Sir John Bernard Burke, was not above reproach and was severely criticised by Horace Round.[162]

In the eighteenth century the improper assumption of titles and arms was particularly prevalent in English and Anglo-Irish society. In order to deal with the situation in Ireland, the Irish House of Lords published 'Rules and Orders' in 1784.[163] Royal warrants for changes of name and arms are more frequent after this, although initially warrants of this kind referring to Irish persons might be addressed to the Earl Marshall in

---

[156] *Biographie Universelle*, XI, 286.
[157] The material is contained in R.I.A. MSS 24, D. 2, pp. 87 ff., and 24, G. 20, pp. 139 ff.
[158] R.I.A. MS D. 2, p. 89.
[159] R.I.A. MS 24, G. 20, pp. 139 ff.
[160] R.I.A. MS D. 9, pp. 49-50. Mémoire on the method of obtaining Royal Rank in France.
[161] *Ibid.*
[162] See H. G. F. E. de Montmorency, *A Memorandum explaining the Claim of the Morres Family to bear the Name of de Montmorency* (n.p., 1938). This is a defence of Round's criticisms of Betham. See Anthony Wagner, *English Genealogy* (London, 1960), pp. 342-44, on Round as a genealogist.
[163] *Rules and Orders to be observed by the Upper House* (London, 1784), p. 62.

England.[164] In 1795, however, the Irish House of Lords resolved that whenever his majesty grants changes of name and arms 'he should order the licence to be addressed to the Ulster King of Arms to be exemplified and entered in the Irish Office of Arms'. It was further stated that such fees were to be paid as are usually paid in England.[165] This order gave rise to the series known as 'Royal warrants for changes of name and licences for changes of names'. This practice was also continued when the office was taken over by the Irish government.

Another series which arose out of the improper assumption of titles are the pedigrees and arms of baronets, made under a royal warrant of 1789 'for correcting and preventing abuses in the order of baronets'.[166] A record similar in kind to this is a modern one initiated by Dr. Edward McLysaght, the first Chief Herald. This is a list of duly authenticated senior lineal descendants in the male line from the last duly elected 'Chief of the Name' of Irish families. This list is published in Thom's Directory.[167]

These are the main records of the office that came into being because of heraldic and genealogical duties of Ulster. There were other duties appertaining to Ulster that did not imply the keeping of a series of records, but to which there are references in the archives of the office.

There is one interesting document entitled the oath of the king of arms when he shall be crowned.[168] It is undated but would appear to be in an early seventeenth-century hand. There are altogether five 'articles' in the oath. Articles three to five inclusive deal with the King of Arms' duties concerning heraldry, and by implication genealogy. The King of Arms is enjoined to have knowledge of all 'the noble gentlemen . . . which should bear coats' [of arms] and he 'shall promise truly to register all acts of honor'. The second article is simply a promise to devote himself to the skill and techniques of his profession so that 'he may be better furnished to teach others in the Office of Arms under you and execute with more wisdom and eloquence such charges as the Sovereign Lord . . . shall say unto you'. The first article of the oath, however, deals with an aspect of Ulster's duties with which we have not yet concerned ourselves: 'First when the king shall command you to do any message to any other king, prince or estate, or any other person out of this realm or any person of what state, degree, or condition he be within the kingdom that you shall do it honourably and truly as your wit and reason serve you.' The role of the King of Arms as ambassador, king's messenger, or herald in the classical sense fell into disuse with the rise of permanent resident ambassadors in the sixteenth century, and in England and consequently

---

[164] A warrant for 1790 referring to Carleton in Donegal is addressed to the Earl Marshall (N.L.I. microfilm, neg. 72, 'Royal Warrant for change of name and arms').
[165] Lords' jn. Ire., VII, p. 368.
[166] G.O. MS 11, fol. 18.
[167] It is published officially in Iris Oifigiúil from time to time and taken by Thom's Directory from that source.
[168] G.O. MS 2, p. 5.

in Ireland the genealogical and heraldic duties of the heralds became the principal ones. Nevertheless vestiges of the earlier duties remain.

It was Ulster's duty to proclaim a state of war or peace. On 11 December 1655, Richard Carney, principal herald,[169] was ordered to proclaim peace between the Commonwealth and Spain. It was 'to be done with sounds of trumpet and other usual ceremonies'.[170] Similarly, 29 March 1714, the Lord Lieutenant instructed William Hawkins, Ulster, that since her majesty had concluded a truce with the king of Spain, 'We hereby authorize and require you . . . to publish the said peace at the usual places, and in the accustomed manner within the city of Dublin, according to the tenor of the proclamation herewith sent you, which is to be done tomorrow the 30th day of March between the hours of eleven and twelve of the clock on the forenoon, when the lord mayor, recorder, alderman, and sheriffs of Dublin are to be present as in like cases hath been accustomed.'[171]

Ulster has been described as 'at one time the senior and only permanent member of the staff of the Lord Lieutenant, and responsible for arrangements connected with state visits of the sovereign'.[172]

William Hawkins, Ulster, 1698–1736, has left a diary of state duties, 1698–1713.[173] Ulster keeps a record of the lords justices' progress through towns and garrisons in 1698, and lays down ceremonial for their giving audience to the 'city and college of Dublin'.[174] A memorial from Hawkins to the Lord Lieutenant arranging celebrations for the birthday of the Prince of Wales, in which Ulster is to play a prominent part, is endorsed by the lords justices: 'We approve of what is proposed and require all persons concerned to confirm thereto.'[175] From Hawkins' diary one gets the clear impression that he regarded the ceremonial duties, together with his duties to the House of Lords as being the most important responsibilities of his office. Indeed the routine of the office seems to have been left to subordinates.

Ulster's duties in his capacity as a state official appear to coincide with those of the Earl Marshall in England, a part of whose duties was the regulation of all state ceremonies. This aspect of Ulster's work, of its nature, did not lead to the keeping of a series of manuscripts such as the visitations, funeral entries and the like. Nevertheless there are many manuscripts dealing with these duties in the office. They include manuscripts relating to state ceremonials, functions held by the vice-regal court, documents relating to precedence and protocol, official orders relating to changes in insignia and styles consequent upon the Act of

---

[169] Appointed Principal Herald by Oliver Cromwell 19 February 1655; the style assumed under the Commonwealth.
[170] G.O. MS 6, p. 10.
[171] Ibid., p. 35.
[172] Burke's *Peerage* (1953), p. clxiv.
[173] G.O. MS 17.
[174] Ibid., pp. 77–83.
[175] G.O. MS 4, p. 157.

Union, lists of persons presented and bodies presenting addresses at royal levees in Dublin and so on. There are also papers relating to the installation of the Order of St. Patrick in Dublin, of which Ulster was registrar, just as Garter King of Arms in London is registrar of the Order of the Garter.

They are the main documents essential to the duties of the King of Arms. The next category into which the archives may be divided consists of those manuscripts which have been drawn upon already to demonstrate as far as possible the circumstances that led to the first series being preserved. These are documents relating to the administration of the office. Some of them have been mentioned already: warrants for the making of visitations and funeral entries, the oath of the King of Arms, Hawkins' diary of state duties, Betham's account of the records in 1810, etc. Other manuscripts relating to the duties of Ulster and his associates include papers relating to the conduct of funeral processions, to the fees due in connexion with various duties such as changes of name, grants of arms, creation of peers, investiture of knights, promotion of peers and on the appointment of bishops and archbishops. There is material of this kind dating from the late sixteenth century to the twentieth.

Administrative documents of another kind are those that came into being to expedite the day-to-day business of the office. There is, for instance, the 'diary of business done in Ulster's office 1797–99'. There is also a day book of business and of expenses, 1809–18. With the accession of Sir William Betham the office appears to have been much more efficiently administered, and there is a corresponding increase in documents of this kind. Betham did not become Ulster until 1820, but he had been Athlone Pursuivant and Deputy Ulster from 1807. There are eighteen bound volumes of 'letter-books', i.e., copies of letters sent from Ulster's office covering the period 1810–50. There is also a collection of letters received by Betham, 1810–30. There is one 'letter-book' for the period immediately prior to Betham, covering the years 1789–1812. Betham seems to have been a methodical man about his expenses as 'cash-books' of his survive.

Calendars and indexes may also be styled administrative documents, since they are aids to the efficient working of the office. The collection is well indexed. There are indexes to all the principal collections, grants and confirmations of arms, funeral entries, registered pedigrees, unofficial pedigrees. There is a calendar of manuscripts 1–58, by Sir Bernard Burke. This is particularly useful as these manuscripts comprise many of the earlier manuscripts containing much heterogenous material bound together. Another valuable manuscript, if only because it illustrates the inadequate state of the records at the time, is the description of the records given by Betham in 1811 (see page 29) in answer to the queries of the record commissioners in 1810. A compilation which may also be included here is a compilation of material relating to the loss of the Irish crown jewels. This includes a collection of letters dealing with the incident, many in the hand of Sir Arthur Vicars, the Ulster King of Arms concerned.

There is a large category of documents deriving from the functions of the office. They are accidental to the office but, as it were, naturally accidental. They are diverse in themselves: their unity consists in the fact that they are manuscripts of different kinds accumulated by the officers of arms or their associates, as tools to assist them in their heraldic and genealogical duties.

These include many manuscript armories and ordinaries of arms, such as an alphabet of arms of English families settled in Ireland, prepared in the later sixteenth century. There is an ordinary of arms compiled c. 1605 by William Smith, Rouge Dragon Pursuivant in the College of Arms. There are also many more specialized heraldic manuscripts. Some of the more interesting are emblazons in colour of the arms of Irish peers between 1595 and 1597 and emblazons of the arms of knights dubbed by the Lord Deputy, 1566–1617. Since these recipients of honour include some of the native Irish aristocracy, these manuscripts are a valuable source of evidence for the extent of the use of heraldry in Gaelic Ireland. While these manuscripts are predominantly of heraldic interest, some of them contain genealogical information as well. There is an emblazon in colour of the armorial achievements of the Lord Deputy and the Council, together with notes on their pedigrees compiled by Daniel Molyneux, Ulster, c. 1606. William Roberts, Ulster, 1643–55, under a commission from the Marquis of Ormond, prepared emblazons of the armorial achievements and notes on the pedigrees of the officers of the regiments of Castell and Hungerford, sent to Ireland by the Parliament in 1647. Alban Leverett, Athlone Pursuivant, compiled a similar document for officers of the regiments of Sothill, Venables, Sankey and Laurence, which were sent to Ireland by the Parliament in 1649. There are many manuscript ordinaries of this specialized kind.

Another type of document is that concerned directly with the science of heraldry. The earliest manuscript in the office[176] is a composite manuscript in Latin and English, part of an early fifteenth-century treatise on heraldry. This is one of the relatively few vellum manuscripts in the office. It is a relatively late acquisition, as it is not mentioned by Betham in his account of the records in the office in 1810. Its provenance is, however, unknown. Another vellum manuscript of this kind is 'a treatise on precedence' by Ralph Brooke, York herald, c. 1595. Another vellum manuscript is a rather bizarre piece of genealogical expertise purporting to be a genealogy of the English royal family from Adam through Cymbeline to Henry VIII.

Copies of English visitations for Lancashire, Cheshire, Devon and Dorset also found their way into the office. There are also emblazons of arms of English and Scottish peers compiled at different times. A

---

[176] G.O. MS 7

manuscript compiled c. 1660 gives arms of English and Welsh cities and towns.

The particular value of many of the genealogical manuscripts is that they are frequently abstracts from now lost sources formerly in the Public Record Office. In this connexion the office and, because of the destruction of the Public Record Office, Irish scholarship in general is heavily indebted to the work of Sir William Betham. Betham's compilations are very large indeed. There are five volumes of historical and genealogical abstracts from the plea rolls from Henry III to Henry VI. It must be remembered that the plea rolls are probably the most important single source for what may be styled Anglo-Norman feudal genealogy. The Norman interest in genealogy was practical. The ties cementing feudal society together were those of law and service, but they were hereditary; in consequence, genealogical information is found particularly in the plea rolls. There are in addition two volumes of similar information abstracted from the pipe rolls, from Henry III to Edward III. His greatest single work, however, is the abstracts in tabulated pedigree form of the wills proved at the prerogative court of the Archbishop of Armagh, 1536–1810.[177] There are many more collections of genealogies compiled by Betham over the years in the course of his career as a genealogist. There are many collections of abstracts of diocesan wills in the office. A guide to these has been published by Miss P. B. Eustace in *Analecta Hibernica*, 17. These abstracts were compiled by different genealogists at various times. Other manuscripts of this kind are abstracts of prerogative marriage licences and of prerogative administrations intestate. There are many pedigrees in the office compiled from various sources by different genealogists such as Sir Edmund Bewley, J. Atkins Davis, Alfred Molony, Denis O'Callaghan Fisher, T. U. Sadleir, W. H. Welply and others.

Perhaps the most important manuscripts relating to Gaelic families are the 'Linea antiqua', compiled by Roger O'Feral in 1709, a collection of pedigrees of Irish families, with black and white sketches of arms. This is a particularly interesting manuscript. Dubhaltach Mac Firbhisigh, writing in 1650, undertakes to give the 'Branches of kinship and genealogy of every generation that took possession of Ireland from now to Adam, except Formorians, Norsemen and Saxon foreigners'.[178] Another manuscript is entitled 'A table of the names of the mere Irish septs'; there are pedigrees of Irish families in Irish and English, and there are further illuminated pedigrees with arms of the families of O'Brien, Earl of Thomond, O'Donnell, Earl of Tyrconnell and O'Neill, Earl of Tyrone.

This category may be extended to include manuscripts that are not pedigrees but that were obviously acquired by the office as sources of

---

[177] Vicars, *Prerog. wills*, is a guide to this collection.
[178] *Geneal. tracts*, p. 1.

genealogical research. These are documents of a very diverse nature. They include 'Ecclesiastical Visitations of Protestant dioceses between 1607 and 1781'; a list of high sheriffs of the counties of Ireland (except Derry) to the year 1772 compiled by John Lodge; lists of freeholders of Irish counties at various dates, poll books of counties, extracts from Protestant parochial registers and from a few Catholic registers; a typed roll of freemen of the city of Dublin, 1468–85 and 1575–1774, prepared by Miss Gertrude Thrift; 'A list of the field officers chosen and appointed for the Irish expedition . . . under the command of Philip Lord Wharton . . . 1642'; transcripts made by T. U. Sadleir and others of the parliamentary returns as to religion made by Protestant rectors, by order of the Irish House of Lords in 1766, covering forty-one parishes; names of Protestant housekeepers relating to counties Donegal, Derry and Antrim; copies and abstracts of letters and papers relating to the Palatine settlements in Ireland, c. 1710–1805, collected by Tenison Groves; list of the Tipperary gentlemen attainted by King James; fragments of 1821 census returns; extracts from hearth money rolls from different counties; lists of officers of regiments reviewed in Ireland at various dates from 1757 to 1787. For more detailed information about these and other similar manuscripts, it is essential to consult the handlist of manuscripts available in the office.

Some manuscripts whose connexion with the functions of the office is tenuous are interspersed in the collection. There is, for instance, a seventeenth-century manuscript copy of the Annals of Friar John Clyn. There is also a manuscript autobiography of the Rev. Adam Blair (1718–90) copied from the original by his great-great-grandson, Tenison Groves. Since Groves was an active genealogist and much of his genealogical work was acquired by the office, one can understand how this manuscript found its way into the collection.

We can now summarize the result of this investigation into the records of the Genealogical Office. They are not an arbitary collection of manuscripts; they possess an organic unity deriving from the nature and function of the Ulster Office of Arms. There are many lacunae in the earlier records. There are a variety of reasons for this. Two of the principal causes would appear to be that apparently successive Ulsters regarded the records as being their own private property, and because of the flight to France of James Terry, Athlone Pursuivant, with some of the records. In consequence, many of the earlier records have been lost; some have been traced to other archives, particularly to the library of Trinity College, Dublin, and to the British Museum. Nevertheless an extensive series of records survives in the office. Their origins can be attributed to the official duties of the kings of arms. Due to the rather dilatory manner in which most of the Ulster Kings of Arms attended to their heraldic and genealogical duties, there were very few compilations of pedigrees or heraldic manuscripts acquired for the office to assist the officers of arms in carrying out their duties. This situation

GUIDE TO RECORDS OF GENEALOGICAL OFFICE

changed radically during the tenure of office of Sir William Betham, first as Deputy Ulster and Athlone Pursuivant, and then for thirty-three years as Ulster King at Arms. During this period, Betham enormously expanded the source of material in the office, and his work was continued by his successors. By now the office has acquired a collection of unique value to the historian as well as to the herald and genealogist.

INDEX OF WILL ABSTRACTS
IN THE
GENEALOGICAL OFFICE
DUBLIN

P. BERYL EUSTACE

FOREWORD

As Wills are of the first importance in the compiling of pedigrees a few facts about Irish Wills may help the amateur genealogist. Between 1536 and 1858 Wills in Ireland consisted of two classes, Prerogative and Diocesan. Diocesan Wills were those proved in the Consistorial Court of the Protestant Bishop within whose Diocese the testator was domiciled, but the Will of any testator who had effects worth more than £5 (called *bona notabilia*) in more than one Diocese had to be proved in the Prerogative Court of the Archbishop of Armagh. Both series of Wills were eventually deposited in the Record Office, Dublin. In 1895 and 1899 an Index of the Dublin Diocesan Wills appeared in the Reports of the Deputy Keeper of the Records[1] for those years, while in 1897 Sir Arthur Vicars edited the *Index to the Prerogative Wills of Ireland* 1536–1810. The publishing, by Messrs. Phillimore & Co.[2] of a series of Indexes of Irish Wills was proceeding when, in June 1922, all the original Wills with the exception of eleven Prerogative and one Consistorial were destroyed. To-day the genealogist, having detected an entry in an index of Wills, has to try to find a copy or an abstract of it made before 1922. The following are the most useful reference books:

1. *The 55th, 56th and 57th Report of the Deputy Keeper of the Records in Ireland* (Dublin, 1928, 1931, 1936), listing copies of Wills salved, Wills presented, etc.
2. *Reports of the Deputy Keeper of the Records, Government of Northern Ireland* (Belfast, from 1925).
3. Sir Arthur Vicars: *Index to the Prerogative Wills of Ireland*, 1536–1810. Sir William Betham compiled what he called his " genealogical analysis " of all these Wills up to the year 1800. His notebooks are now at the Record Office, Dublin, while his Will Pedigrees drawn up from these notes fill 31 vols. at the Genealogical Office. A copy of the series is at the Record Office, Belfast, but lacks the countless annotations of successive Officers of Arms which have added greatly to the value of the volumes at the Genealogical Office.
4. Rev. Wallace Clare: *Guide to Copies and Abstracts of Irish Wills*, (1930).

It must also be remembered that Wills made by the principal residents are often to be found in local histories. Printed family histories are another source and Irish Wills or abstracts from them

---

[1] Appendix to the *Twenty-Sixth Report of the Deputy Keeper of the Public Records* (Dublin, 1895): " Index to the Act or Grant Books and to Original Wills of the Diocese of Dublin to the year 1800." Appendix to the *Thirtieth Report of the Deputy Keeper of the Records* (Dublin, 1899): " Index to the Act or Grant Books and to Original Wills of the Diocese of Dublin, 1800–1858."

[2] Phillimore & Co. have printed *Calendars of Irish Wills* for the following Dioceses (London, 1909–21): *Vol. I*: Ossory, 1536–1800; Ferns, 1601–1800; Leighlin, 1652–1800; Kildare, 1661–1800. *Vol. II*: Cork and Ross, 1548–1800; Cloyne, 1621–1800. *Vol. III*: Cashel and Emly, 1618–1800; Waterford and Lismore, 1645–1800; Killaloe and Kilfenora, 1653–1800; Limerick, 1615–1800; Ardfert and Aghadoe, 1690–1800. *Vol. IV*: Dromore, 1678–1800; Peculiar of Newry and Mourne, 1727–1858. *Vol. V*: Derry, 1615–1858; Raphoe, 1684–1858.

can be traced in such varied publications as *Notes and Queries, The Irish Genealogist, Brown's Cases,* etc.

Wills of many Irish Members of the Society of Friends are to be found at the Friends' Meeting House, 6 Eustace Street, Dublin.[1] A list, compiled by Edward Phelps, Esq., M.A., of the Wills in the Stewart Kennedy Notebooks in the Library, Trinity College, is kept at the Record Office, Dublin and Belfast. Also in Trinity Library are early Dublin Wills and Inventories.[2] Details of charitable bequests, published in the *Dublin Gazette* from circa 1825 ("To the Commissioners of Charitable Donations and Bequests;' and all whom it may concern") seldom supply genealogical information, but from these notices the date of a Will, the names of the executors and the date of probate can generally be learnt.[3]

The Irish Manuscripts Commission is helping to locate many other Wills. Its Inspector includes in his reports, published in *Analecta Hibernica,* mention of Wills to be found in private collections of MSS. in Eire. The Commission is also having abstracts made of the Wills at the Registry of Deeds, Dublin, for the period 1708–1785. Over two thousand Wills were registered there, primarily because they concerned real estate in Ireland. Some, it is true, deal solely with the clauses about the testator's lands, but many others were registered in full.

The Will "abstracts" at the Genealogical Office (formerly Office of Arms), Dublin Castle, vary in length from a few words to complete copies of Wills (the letters N.F.P. for "no further particulars" indicating the shortest). It will be noted that some of the collections include administrations or "admons." Amongst the more useful collections those of Dublin and Cork Wills compiled by D. O'Callaghan Fisher deserve special attention. In this collection of Dublin Wills, additional information not given in the MSS. has been taken from the Appendix to the *26th Report of the Deputy Keeper of the Records* (1895) and is shewn within square brackets.

This index does not include two of Sir William Betham's valuable compilations which now form part of the official records of the Genealogical Office : (1) Betham's Will Pedigree series to 1800 which, as had been already explained, are listed in Vicars, *Index to the Prerogative Wills of Ireland,* 1536–1810, and (2) Betham's Abstracts from the Prerogative Administrations Intestate. Since this Index was compiled some unclassified material, which contains, *inter alia,* will abstracts, has come to light and will be indexed by the Office in due course together with some recent acquisitions.

Thanks are due to Mr. T. U. Sadleir, Deputy Ulster King of Arms to March, 1943, and to Dr. E. McLysaght, Chief Herald and Genealogical Officer, for permission to compile this index ; to Dr. A. J. Otway-Ruthven and Mrs. V. E. Clarke for their help in correcting proofs ; and also to the many genealogists known and unknown, whose painstaking work in the past forms the basis of this index.

P. BERYL EUSTACE

March, 1948.

---

[1] The following volumes are in the care of the Registrar: Carlow Monthly Meeting, Book of Wills and Inventories, 1675–1740 ; Edenderry do., 1728–1763 ; Mountmellick do., 1755–1795 ; Co. Wexford do., 1680–1760 ; Dublin do., 2 vols. 1683–1772.

[2] MSS. 552 (E. 3. 32), in Latin. See H. F. Berry: *Register of Wills and Inventories of the Diocese of Dublin* 1457–1483 (Royal Society of Antiquaries of Ireland, Extra Volume, 1898). In addition to the Latin text a translation in English is given in this book, while the Introduction contains useful information about early Wills.

[3] See also p. vii *supra*.

MSS. EXAMINED FOR WILL ABSTRACTS

                                                                                              ABBREVIATIONS

BEWLEY. Compiled by Sir Edmund Bewley   B.

CAVENAGH. Presented by Col. W. O. Cavenagh   Cav.

CHARITABLE DONATIONS AND BEQUESTS. Short abstracts made by T. U. Sadleir, from the Report of the Commissioners, 1805 and 1814   C.D.B.

CROSSLÉ. Abstracts made by Philip Crosslé   Cr.

DAVIS. Abstracts made by J. N. C. Atkins Davis   Davis.

DROUGHT. Drought Will abstracts made by Philip Crosslé   Dr.

EUSTACE. Compiled by P. B. Eustace   Eu.

FISHER. Over 2,000 abstracts found in the collections of MSS. compiled by D. O'Callaghan Fisher. "Dub." vol., surnames A–E only, contains abstracts of 16th, 17th and early 18th century Dublin Diocesan Wills. In Vol. "F," the majority of the abstracts are from Cork and Cloyne Diocesan Wills.   Dub. F., F. 2. F.A., F.B., F.D., F.E., F.F.

IRWIN. Compiled by Sir Alfred Irwin   Ir.

KELLY. Presented by Edmund Festus Kelly   Ky.

MEMORIALS. Wills printed in Journals of the Irish Memorials Association   M.

MOLONY. Compiled by Alfred Molony   Mol.

SADLEIR. Compiled by T. U. Sadleir, Registrar and Deputy Ulster King of Arms, 1913 to March, 1943. In Sadleir 4 are included abstracts made by Major V. C. T. Hodson   S. 1., S. 2., S. 3., S. 4.

    Irish Wills in India Office   S. 4. (H. I.)
    Irish Wills, Bombay and Madras Establishments   S. 4. (H. BM.)
    Officers in Bengal Army (not many wills in H.O.)   S. 4. (H.O.)

SWANZY. 863 abstracts, the majority being of Down, Connor and Dromore wills, made by the late Very Rev. H. B. Swanzy, Dean of

MSS. EXAMINED FOR WILL ABSTRACTS

ABBREVIATIONS

Dromore. Presented by Rev. Chancellor J. B. Leslie, who compiled the collection from the Swanzy MSS. now in his possession — Swan.

WELPLY. Abstracts from the Society of Genealogists, London, collected by W. H. Welply and others — W.

Other MS. sources are named in full, *e. g.*, Sullivan MSS.

N.B.—The year given is that of the grant of Probate unless the word "Dated" or "D" (died) is prefixed.

The name of the Diocese, where known, is added after the name of the collection, *e.g.*, S. 2. Tuam. An abstract from a Prerogative Will is indicated by the letter "P," *e.g.*, Swan. P.

Variations or alternatives in the abstracts themselves are shewn in round brackets. Square brackets enclose information which is not in the abstracts but is taken from printed sources, such as the index volumes mentioned in the Foreword.

INDEX OF WILL ABSTRACTS IN THE GENEALOGICAL OFFICE, DUBLIN

Abbott, Jane, Kinsale, widow   1750. F.A.
"   John, Ballyloskey, Co. Tipperary
                 Dated 1767. S.1. Killaloe
"   Richard, Kinsale, gent.   1743. F.A.
"   Samuel, Fort, Co. Limerick   1701. S.1.P.
"   Thomas, Charleville, Co. Cork,
        innkeeper   1717. W. Cloyne
"   [Abbot], William, [Agherime] Dated 1635. Dub.
Abell, Abraham, Cork, merchant   1778. F.A.
"   Richard, Cork, merchant   1802. F.A.
Ablayne, Isaac   Dated 1656. Dub.
Accourt, Henry, Dublin, merchant   Dated 1695. Dub.
Acheson, Alexander, Tonnybeague, Co.
       Fermanagh   1710/11. Swan.
"   née Chaigneau, Jane   1787. Swan.
"   Robert, Dublin   1776. Swan. P.
Achmuty, Arthur   1793. S.4. (H.I.)
"   Arthur Forbes   Dated 1780. S.4. (H.I.)
Acton, Edward   Dated 1654. Dub.
"   John, Dublin   1717. F.P.
Adair, Alex., Killughe, Co. Down, gent. Admon. 1720. F.A.
"   Capt. Alexander, Carrickfergus Admon. 1797. F.A.
"   Archibald, Dublin, shipwright Admon. 1753. F.A.
"   Arthur, Park Gate, par. of Donegore   1787. S.4.P.
"   Benjamin, Loughanmore, Co.
       Antrim, gent.   Admon. 1730. F.A.
"   Blarney, Ballymena, Co. Antrim Admon. 1734. F.A.
"   Cornet Charles, Pearce's Dragoons   1711. F.A.
"   Foster, Hollybrook, Co. Wicklow, Esq. 1786. F.A.
"   Gilbert, Tobergill, par. of Donegore   1738. S.4. Connor
"   James, Donegore   1686. S.4. Connor
"   James, Kilbride   1733. S.4. Connor
"   James, Crow Street, Dublin   1751. F.A.
"   Jane, Hollybrook, Co. Wicklow, widow 1747. F.A.
"   Dame Jane, widow of Hugh Murphy,
       late of Dublin, Esq., decd.   1800. F.A.
"   John, Dublin, Esq.   Admon. 1760. F.A.
"   John [? Arthur], Park Gate, par. of
       Donegore, Co. Antrim, gent.   1787. F.A.

Adair, John, Dublin, shopkeeper   Admon. 1797. F.A.
  ,, John, Rath, Queen's Co., Esq.   1809. F.A.
  ,, Mabella, Dublin, widow   Admon. 1780. F.A.
  ,, Michael, Dublin, merchant   Dated 1699. F.A.
  ,, Sir Robert, Ballymenagh   Dated 1655. S.4.P. and F.A.
  ,, Robert, Belfast   Admon. 1684. F.A.
  ,, Robert, Dublin, Esq.   1737. F.A.
  ,, Sir Robert   1764. F.A.
  ,, Robert, Dublin, Esq.   Admon. 1790. F.A.
  ,, Robert, St. Marylebone, formerly of St. James, surgeon   Admon. 1791. F.A.
  ,, Thomas Benjamin, Loughanmore, Co. Antrim   1768. S.4. Connor
  ,, William, Litter, King's Co.   1715. F.A.
  ,, William, Ahoghill, Ballyministragh   1729. S.4. Connor
  ,, William, Ballyminister, par. of Aughahill, Dio. of Connor   1799. F.A.
Adaire, als. Espie, Jane. *See* Getty
  ,, Thomas, Clonterry, Queen's Co., gent.   1755. F.A.
  ,, Thomas, Stradbally, Queen's Co.   1792. F.A.
  ,, William, Ballymanagh, Co. Antrim, Esq.   1666. F.A.
  ,, William, Rath, Queen's Co., gent.   1774. F.A.
  ,, William, Gardiner Street, Dublin   1796. F.A.
Adale, Edward [alias O'Dale, Corduff]   Dated 1623. Dub.
Adam, Thomas, Esker   Dated 1556. Dub.
Adams, Anthony, Aclare, Co. Meath, gent.   1766. F.A.
  ,, Abigail, Ennis, Co. Clare, widow   1790. Mol. P.
  ,, Catherine, City of Cork, widow   1799. Mol. P.
  ,, Daniel, Knockmoneybeg, Co. Cork   1716. Mol. P. and F.A.
  ,, Daniel, Youghal, Co. Cork, merchant   1797. Mol. Cloyne
  ,, Edward, Doneraile   1656. Mol. P. and F.A.
  ,, Elenor, Carlow   1773. Mol. Leighlin
  ,, Elizabeth   1749. Mol. P.
  ,, George, Hoathstown, Co. Meath, Esq.   1775. F.A.
  ,, Henry, the Cross of Killinick, Co. Wexford   1707. Mol. Ferns
  ,, Henry, Cloonee, Co. Limerick   1796. Mol. Limerick
  ,, Humphry, Waterford, saddler   1703. Mol. Waterford
  ,, John, Parish of Carrigrohan, Cork   1637. Mol. Cork
  ,, John, Dublin, baker   Dated 1639. Dub.
  ,, Joseph, Moyrhee, Co. Clare, gent.   1743. Mol. Killaloe
  ,, Joseph, Ennis, Co. Clare, gent.   1773. Mol. P.
  ,, Margaret, Cork, widow   1734. Mol. Cork
  ,, Mary, Waterford   1819. Mol. Waterford

Adams, Michael, Ballycullane, Co. Limerick,
        now of Charleville, Co. Cork   1802. Mol. P. and F.A.
„   Prudence, Milltown, Co. Cork, widow 1778. Mol. P. and F.A.
„   Richard, Knockmonelea, Co. Cork   1766. Mol. Cloyne
„   Richard, City of Cork, Esq.   1789. Mol. P. and F.A.
„   Robert, The Combe, Dublin   [1664]. Dub.
„   Robert, Waterford, saddler   1714. Mol. Waterford.
„   Robert, Hoathstown, Co. Meath, gent. 1729. F.A.
„   Roger, Shandrum, Co. Cork, gent.   1762. Mol. P. and F.A.
„   Roger, Jones's Square, City of Cork 1789. Mol. P. and F.A.
„   Samuel, Cork, Esq.   1791. Mol. P. and F.A.
„   Tayler, Highmount, Co. Limerick,
        gent.   1770. Mol. Limerick
„   Tayler, Prospect Lodge, Co. Limerick 1818. Mol. Limerick
„   Thomas, Read Cross, Co. Wicklow
                                Dated 1682. Dub.
„   Thomas, Knockmoneleagh, Co. Cork 1774. Mol. Cloyne
„   Rev. Tobias, Rector and Vicar of
        Britway and Vicar of Ahern   1805. Mol. Cloyne
„   William, Killue   1752. Mol. P.
„   William, Royal Hospital in Dublin 1758. Mol. P.
„   William, Glinlary, Co. Limerick
                                Dated 1774. Mol. Limerick
„   William, Limerick, cooper   1778. Mol. Limerick
„   William, Laurencetown, Co. Limerick,
        gent.   1801. Mol. Limerick
„   William, Ashfield, Co. Cork   1819. Swan. P.
„   William, Willbrook, Co. Clare, gent. 1819. Mol. P.
Adamson. *See* Addamson.
Adayre, Archibald, Litter, King's Co., Esq.
                                Admon. 1698. F. 2 and F.A.
„   Charles, Clonbrony, Co. Longford, Esq.
                       Admons. June and Sept. 1688. F.2.
„   Elinor, Clonbrony, Co. Longford,
        widow   Admon. 1688. F.2.
Addams, Edward, Corporal in Dillon's Horse 1666. Mol. Cashel.
Addamson [Adamson], Thomas, Shrewland,
        Co. Kildare, yeoman   Dated 1710. Dub.
Adderley, Francis, Drumkeen, Co. Cork   1719. W.P.
„   George, Rathdown, Co. Wicklow
                                Dated 1686. Dub.
„   Thomas, senr., Ballyneboy Dated 1644 W. Cork
„   Thomas, Innishannon, Esq.   1658 F.2. and W.P.
„   Thomas, Innishannon, Co. Cork,
        Esq.   1691/2. F.2. and W.P.
„   Thomas   1786. S.4. (H.I.)

Adderley, Thomas, Innishannon, Co. Cork 1791. F.A.
Adderly, Francis, Drumkeen 1719. F.P.
Addis, Ann, Maynooth, widow Dated 1649. Dub.
„ Fenton, Summerhill, Co. Cork, Esq. 1773. F.A.
„ John, Cork, merchant 1742. W.P.
„ William, Athy, Co. Kildare,
 innkeeper Dated 1682. Dub.
Addison, John, Thomas St., brewer Dated 1674. Dub.
Adlecron, Mary [als.] de St. Julien, [Dublin],
 widow Dated 1706. Dub.
Aentwyssyll or Antwise, [Entwistle], Joseph
 Dated 1601. Dub.
Agharen (Agherne), Capt. Owen, Rochestown
 Dated 1668. F.A.
Agnew, Ann, Cross, par. of Ballymoney, 1686. S.4. Connor
 widow
„ Francis, Mabuy 1681. S.4. Connor
„ James, Ballymoney 1709. S.4. Connor
„ James, Donegore, carpenter 1771. S.4. Connor
„ James, Tobergall, par. of Donegore 1791. S.4. Connor
„ John, Lisneshanker, par. of Maralin 1768. S.4. Dromore
„ John, Co. Longford 1781. S.4. P.
„ Patrick, Kilwaghter, Co. Antrim 1725. S.4. P.
„ William, Killwaughter, Co. Antrim,
 Esq. 1776. S.4. P.
Aikin, David, Dublin Dated 1654 .Dub.
Akie, William, Lisselong, Co. Monaghan
 Dated 1765. Swan. Clogher
„ William, Feagh 1734. Swan. P.
Alcock, Catherine, Athlone, Co. Westmeath,
 widow Admon. 1699. F.A.
„ George, Lisserlogh, Co. Sligo
 Admon. 1697. F.A.
„ Jane, widow 1713. F.P.
„ Maskelyne, Rough Grove, Co. Cork,
 Esq. 1798. F.A.
„ William, Dublin 1705. F.E.
Alderdice, James, Belfast 1812. C.D.B.
Aldersey, Randall, Dublin, Esq. Dated 1637. Dub.
„ Thomas Dated 1616. Dub.
Aldborough, Martha, Countess Dowager of 1802. C.D.B.
Aldworth, Boyle, Newmarket, Co. Cork 1789. F.A.
„ Mary, Little Island, Co. Cork,
 spinster 1805. F.A.
„ Richard, Bonoghatrasnah, Co. Cork 1705. F. Cloyne
„ Sir Richard, Newmarket, Knt.
 Admons. 1691, 1729 F.A.

Aldworth, Richard, Newmarket, Co. Cork
　　　　　Esq.　　　　　　　　　　　1776. F.A.
　,,　　　William, Newmarket, Co. Cork　1737. F. Cloyne
Alexander, George　　　　　Dated 1585. Dub.
　,,　　　Sir Jerome, Dublin, Knt.　　1670. F.A.
　,,　　　John, New Ross, merchant　　1771. F.A.
　,,　　　William Ferguson　　Died 1833. S.4. (H.O.)
Alkin, Thomas, [New Street], Dublin, gent.
　　　　　　　　　　　　　　　Dated 1702. Dub.
Allat, Thomas　　　　　　　Dated 1664. Dub.
Allen,　Abraham, Fermoyle, Co. Cork
　　　　　　　　　　　　　　　Dated 1721. F. Cloyne
　,,　　Aylmer, Cork, burgess　　　　1792. F.A.
　,,　　Christopher, Dublin　　Dated 1577. Dub.
　,,　　Christopher, Cork, burgess　　1804. F.A.
　,,　　Francis, Ballymount, Clondalkin,
　　　　　yeoman　　　　　　　Dated 1650. Dub.
　,,　　George, Bettyville, Co. Cork, gent.　1787. F.A.
　,,　　Giles, Dublin, alderman　Dated 1599. Dub.
　,,　　Kyrle, Clashnure, Co. Cork, gent.　1809. F.A.
　,,　　John, St. Wolstan　　　　　　1609. Dub.
　,,　　John, St. Wolstan, Co. Kildare, Esq.　1662. Dub.
　,,　　John, Wicklow, gent.　Dated 1705. Dub.
　,,　　Joshua, Viscount　　　　　　1816. S.1.P.
　,,　　Stephen [a soldier]　Dated 1654. Dub.
　,,　　Stephen, Killowning, Co. Tipperary,
　　　　　Esq.　　　　　　　　　　　1678. F.2.
　,,　　William, Shandrum, Co. Cork, gent.　1799. F.A.
　,,　　William, Castleton of Kyldroght, Co.
　　　　　Kildare　　　　　　Dated 1558. Dub.
Alley, Mary, Cork, widow　　　1728. F.A. and W.P.
　,,　　Thomas, Rathcormuck　　　　1693. W.P.
Alleyn, Lt.-Col. Edward　　　　1664. F.P.
Allibond, George, St. James, Co. Dublin
　　　　　gent.　　　　　　　Dated 1654. Dub.
Allin, Anne. *See* Buchanan.
　,,　　Elizabeth, Cork, widow　　　1767. F.A. and Swan.
　,,　　als. Hawkins, Jane, wife of John A., of
　　　　　Cork, merchant　　　　　　1716. F.
　,,　　John, Cork, clothier　　　　　1761. F.A.
　,,　　John, Youghal, merchant　　1786. F.A.
　,,　　Robert, Dublin, carpenter　Dated 1662. Dub.
　,,　　Samuel, Youghal　　　　　　1789. Swan. and F.A.
　,,　　Susannah, Youghal　Not dated　Swan.
　,,　　William, Cork, shipwright　　1806. Swan. and F.A.
Alsop, als. Mee, Grace, Upper Combe, Dublin　1683. W.P.

Alwin, Marian, Cork, widow Dated 1692. F.
„ Thomas, Cork, merchant 1693. F.
„ William, Cork 1661. F.
„ William, Cork 1704. F.
Alwyn, Thomas, Dublin, tanner Dated 1666. Dub.
Ambrose, Henry, St. John's Lane, par. of St.
   Catherine's, Dublin, yeoman
          Dated 1634. Dub.
„ Thomas, par. of St. Michael in
   Oxmantown, near Dublin Dated 1664. Dub.
Ames, Thomas [a soldier] Dated 1656. Dub.
Amirald, als. Bindon, Eleanor, Burraskeyne,
   Co. Tipperary   1714. S.1.
„ Rev. Joseph, Archdeacon of Killaloe
        Not dated — S.1.
Amirant, Mary, Killeneife, Co. Tipperary 1769. S.1.
Amos, John, Dublin, gent. Dated 1689. Dub.
Anby, William, St. Michan's, Dublin Dated 1639. Dub.
Anderson, David, Dublin, chirurgeon Dated 1650. Dub.
„ George, Dublin, merchant Dated 1659. Dub.
„ Henry, Dunbell, Co. Kilkenny, Esq. 1790. S.4.P.
„ John, Dublin, gent. Dated 1633. Dub.
„ Rev. Paris, Carrick, Co. Tipperary,
   clerk   Dated 1772. S.4. P.
„ William, The Combe [Dublin],
   joiner   Dated 1671. Dub.
Anderton, George, Dublin, barber surgeon
          Dated 1622. Dub.
Andoe, William, Little Hollywood, Co.
   Dublin, farmer Dated 1671. Dub.
Andowe, Richard, Darreston, Co. Dublin,
   farmer   Dated 1626. Dub.
Andrew, Patrick, Corduff Dated 1606. Dub.
„ Patrick, [Braghan] Dated 1688. Dub.
„ William, Castleknock Dated 1568. Dub.
Andrewes, Eliz., Bride St., Dublin Dated 1665. Dub.
„ James, Newtowne, par. of St. Mar-
   garet's   Dated 1693. Dub.
„ als. Dungan, als. Holiwood, Margaret,
   Dublin, widow Dated 1672. Dub.
„ Nathaniel, Dublin, gent. Dated 1678. Dub.
„ William, The Combe, [Dublin]
          Dated 1667. Dub.
Andrews, Edward, Park, Co. Cork, Esq. 1801. F.A.
„ Edward, Bridgefield, Co. Cork, Lt.,
   R.N.   1826. Swan. P.

Andrews, Elizabeth, widow of Rev. John A.,
Kilkenny 1749. Ir.
,, John, Rath, King's Co. 1733. S.1.Killaloe
,, Peter, Ballybreedy, Co. Cork, gent. 1702. F.A.
,, Richard, Effelstown, par. of Lusk,
[Co. Dublin], farmer Dated 1626. Dub.
,, Richard, Tallow, Co. Waterford 1724 or 1725. F.A.
,, Thomas, Dublin Dated 1678. Dub.
Andris, Thomas, a soldier Dated 1656. Dub.
Andwarpe, John, Dublin, goldsmith Dated 1564. Dub.
Anesloe, Thomas, Ballicaine, Co. Wicklow,
farmer Dated 1699. Dub.
Anglesey, Sir Arthur Annesley, Earl of, Visct.
Valentia and Baron Mountnorris 1686. W.P.
,, Arthur, Earl of 1737. W.P.
,, Elizabeth, Countess Dowager of 1698. W.P.
,, James, Earl of 1711. W.P.
,, John, Earl of 1711. W.P.
Anster, Ellinor, Charleville, Co. Cork, widow 1726. F. Cloyne
,, John, Charleville, Co. Cork 1795. F.A.
,, Martin, Charleville, Co. Cork
merchant 1726. F.A.
Anthony, John, [Co. Wicklow] Dated 1667. Dub.
,, Robert Dated 1693. Dub.
,, Thomas, College Green, Dublin 1801. C.D.B.
Antwise, or Aentwyssyll, Joseph Dated 1601. Dub.
Ap Howell, Lewis, Dreshiog, Co. Dublin
Dated 1659. Dub.
Ap John, Edward, Ballyneclough, Co.
Limerick 1733. S.2. Cashel
,, John, a soldier Dated 1654. Dub.
,, John, a soldier 1655. S.2.P.
,, Michael Marshall, Linfield, Co.
Limerick 1817. S.2.P.
,, Thomas, Trienmana, Co. Limerck 1737. S.2. Cashel
Arbuckle, Rev. Alexander, Dublin 1801. S.2.
,, James, Belfast, merchant 1736. S.1.P.
,, James, Dublin, M.D. 1747. Swan.
,, James, Donaghadee, Co. Down 1811. S.1.P.
Arbuthnot, John, Rock Fleet Castle, Co.
Mayo 1798. S.2. P
,, Richard, Co. Mayo Dated 1777. S.2.
Archbold, Breane [Barnaby], Balleycuanbery,
Co. Wicklow Dated 1631. Dub.
,, Edmond, Lissenhall Dated 1617. Dub.

Archbold, Edmond, Downe, Co. Wicklow,
    gent.   Dated 1624. Dub.
,,   Edward, Templecargy, Co. Wicklow
                                  Dated 1623. Dub.
,,   Gerrald, Kenlestown, Co. Dublin
                                  Dated 1623. Dub.
,,   John, Killincargy, [Co. Wicklow]
                                  Dated 1651. Dub.
,,   Laurence, Castledermot, Co. Kildare
                                  Dated 1684. Dub.
,,   als. Galbalie, Maude, Dublin, widow
                                  Dated 1628. Dub.
,,   Nicholas, Palmerstown, [Co. Dublin]
                                  Dated 1629. Dub.
,,   Patrick, Dublin, chirurgeon
                                  Dated 1694. Dub.
,,   Pierce, Knocklyne   Dated 1644. Dub.
,,   Redmond, Glancormucke, Co. Wic-
    low   Dated 1628. Dub.
,,   Richard, Dublin, merchant
                                  Dated 1617. Dub.
,,   Richard, Killmachud, Co. Dublin,
    gent.   Dated 1677. Dub.
,,   Thomas, Ragenny   Dated 1596. Dub.
,,   William   Dated 1609. Dub.
,,   *See* Aspoll.
Archbould, Thomas, New Street, Dublin
                                  Dated 1639. Dub.
Archdall, Elizabeth   Dated 1696. Dub.
Archdeacon, Henry, BallymcDaniel, Co. Kerry
                                  Dated 1685. F.2. and F.A.
,,   Henry, Cork, gent.   1774. F.A.
,,   James, Callan, late of Dublin,
    glover   1744. Cav. Dublin
,,   James, Kildromin, Co. Limerick 1796. F.A.
,,   John   Dated 1790. S.4. (H.I.)
,,   Thomas, Dorset Street, Dublin 1804. C.D.B.
,,   Richard, New Ross   1771. Cav. Ferns
,,   William, New Ross, innkeeper 1745. Cav. Ferns
Archdekin, Catherine, Killjames, Co. Kilkenny
                                  Dated 1721. Cav. Ossory
,,   Mathias   Dated 1768. Cav. P.
Archer, Alicia [Elisha], corporal, Redmond's
    Troop   Dated 1651. Dub.
,,   Clement, Enniscorthy, Co. Wexford,
    Esq.   1733. W. Ferns

IN THE GENEALOGICAL OFFICE, DUBLIN 93

Archer, Henry, Enniscorthy, Co. Wexford,
    merchant   1730. W.P.
"   John, Ballyean, Co. Wexford, gent. 1663. F.2
"   Robert, Dublin, gent.   1733. W.P.
Arday [Ardan], Patrick, [Ballyfermot]
     Dated 1558. Dub.
Arisken (Erskine), James, Ballinanny   1739/40. Swan. Armagh
Armantier, David, Dublin, coffee house keeper
     Dated 1708. Dub.
Armstead, Elizabeth, Cork, spinster   1790. F.A.
"   Jane, Cork, spinster   1785. F.A.
"   John, Cork, merchant   1771. F.A.
"   Sarah, widow of John A., of Cork,
     merchant   1783. F.A.
"   Sarah, Cork, spinster   1792. F.A.
Armstrong, Alexander, Co. Cavan   Admon. 1703. Ir.
"   Alexander, Carrickmakiggen, Co.
     Leitrim   1721. Ir. and S.4.
"   Alexander, Carrickmakeggan
     Dated 1720. Swan.
"   Alexander, Fegenny, Co.
     Monaghan   Admon. 1745. S.4. Clogher
"   Alexander   1817. S.4. (H.O.)
"   Andrew, Drunmury   Admon. 1698. Ir.
"   Andrew, Ballycumber, King's Co. 1717. B.
"   Arthur, now of Dublin   1817. Swan. P.
"   Benjamin, Baillieborow   1756. S. 4. Kilmore
"   Christopher, Gortaramore, Co.
     Leitrim   1755. Swan, and S.4.
       Kilmore
"   Christopher, Fosbery, Co. Leitrim 1799. Swan. P.
"   Dorothy, Swanlinbar   1812. Swan. P.
"   Edmund, Killilee, Vicar of Kilcol-
     gan   1747. S.4.P.
"   Edmund, Capt.   1811. S.4. (H.BM.)
"   Francis, Rakeevan, Co. Cavan   1740. S.3. and S.4.
       Kilmore
"   Hugh, Derrycheely, Co. Fermanagh
     1781. Swan. P.
"   Isabella, Killely, Co. Galway   1748. S.4.P.
"   Isabella, Glencoran, widow
     Dated 1763. S.4. Kilmore
"   James, Cootehill, Co. Cavan, gent. 1753. Swan. P.
"   James, Kilmakirel, Co. Leitrim   1766. S.4. Kilmore
"   James, Lesgool, Co. Fermanagh   1781. Swan. P.
"   Jane, May Bawn, Co. Fermanagh 1829. Swan. **Clogher**

INDEX OF WILL ABSTRACTS

Armstrong, Jane, Maguiresbridge, widow   1859. Swan. P.
„   John, Derreboy   1685. S.4. Clogher
„   John   1701. S.4. Kilmore
„   John, Castlepolls, Co. Cavan, gent. Admon. 1701/2. Ir.
„   John, late of Co. Cavan   Admon. 1703. Ir.
„   Lieut. John, Earl of Donegal's Foot   1705. S.4. P.
„   John, Rakeevan, Killan Parish   Admon. 1729. S.4. Kilmore
„   John, Mullnagolman, Co. Cavan   1764. S.4. Kilmore
„   John, Bumper Lodge   1830. Swan. P.
„   John, Ross, nr. Manorhamilton, Co. Leitrim   1859. Swan. P.
„   Joseph, Woodfort, Co. Meath   Not dated   Swan. P.
„   Lancelot, Crulan, Templecarne Parish   Admons. 1700, 1723. S.4. Clogher
„   Margaret, Dublin, widow   1808. Swan. P.
„   Martin, Killaconkill, Co. Leitrim   Admon. 1693. S.4.
„   Martin, Jamaica   1779. S.3. Jamaica
„   Nenon, Chapelizod   1790. Swan. P.
„   Richard   D. 1859. S.4. (H.O.)
„   Robert, Largindarrock, Cleenish Parish, Co. Fermanagh   1680. S.4. Clogher
„   Robert, Legewell, Co. Cavan   1725. S.4. Kilmore
„   Robert, Legewell, Co. Cavan   Admon. 1725. S.4. Kilmore
„   Robert, Cornet in Wolseley's Horse   Admon. 1732. S.4.
„   Robert, Aughamacue   1734. S.4. Clogher
„   Robert, Carrigallen, Co. Leitrim   1764. Swan. and S.4. Kilmore
„   Simon, Aghamore, Co. Leitrim   1721. Swan., Ir., and S.4.
„   Simon, Aghmore, Co. Leitrim, gent.   Admon. 1721. Ir.
„   Simon, Moybane, Co. Fermanagh   1813. Swan. Clogher
„   Simon, Hollymount, Co. Leitrim   1859. Swan. P.
„   Thomas, Longfield, Co. Leitrim   Admon. 1699. S.4.
„   Thomas, Aghavore, Co. Leitrim   1735. Swan., Ir., and S.4. Kilmore
„   Thomas   1763. S.4. Kilmore

Armstrong, Warnford, Ballycumber, King's
         Co.   1767. B.
„   William, Pullakiel, Co. Cavan   1758. S.4. Kilmore
„   William, Kilbrackin, Co. Leitrim 1778. Swan. P.
„   William, Cherrybrook, Leitrim   1790. Swan. P.
Arnold, Clement, Captain in Sankey's Regt.
                                  Dated 1649. Dub.
„   Rev. Edward, Dromore   1765. Swan. Dromore
Arsticken, Katherine, als. Katherine ny Lodge
                                  Dated 1589. Dub.
Arthur, George, Dublin, gent.   Dated 1678. Dub.
Arundel, Christopher, Essex Street, Dublin
                                  Dated 1685. Dub.
Arundell, Charles, Dublin, skinner   Dated 1561. Dub.
„   Lucretia, Dublin, widow   Dated 1678. Dub.
Ash, Cairns, Kinsale, Co. Cork, Esq.   1744. F.A.
„   Edward, Waterford, gent.   1761. F.A.
„   Henry, Dublin   [1630]. Dub.
„   Jonathan, Killoquirk, Co. Tipperary
                                 Dated 1674. Dub.
„   John, Corneren, Libs. of Derry, gent 1684. F.A.
„   Sarah, Kinsale, widow   1750. F.A.
„   *See* Aysh.
Ashe, als. Hallisy, Elizabeth, Cork, widow   1810. F.A.
„   Jonathan, Cork, merchant   1781. F.A.
„   Jonathan, Asheville, near Limerick,
      Esq.   1803. F.A.
„   Richard, Ashefield, Co. Meath, Esq. 1727. W.P.
„   Richard, Sandyhill, Co. Cork, Esq.   1805. F.A.
„   St. George, Bp. of Derry   1718. W.P.
„   Thomas, Dublin, late of Barlborough, Co.
      Derby, Esq.   1708. F.A.
„   Thomas, St. John's, Co. Meath, Esq.
                                 Dated 1722. W.P.
Ashbourne, Henry, Dublin, gent   Dated 1641. Dub.
Asheney, James, Glasnyvin   Dated 1607. Dub.
Ashley, George, Dublin   Not dated   Dub.
Ashton, Peter, Dublin, gardener   Dated 1703. Dub.
Ashwood, Bridget, Dublin, widow   Dated 1699. Dub.
Askew, John, Oxmantown, yeoman   Dated 1699. Dub.
„   *See* Askue.
Askin, Robert, Strabane, merchant   Dated 1724. Swan. Derry
Askue [or Askew], John, Dublin, glazier
                                  Dated 1668. Dub.
Aspoll [als. Archbold], John   Dated 1575. Dub.

Aston, Major Henry, Dublin, merchant
　　　　　　　　　　　　　　　　Dated 1706. Dub.
　,,　Sir William, Richardstown, Co. Louth　1671. W.P.
Atcheson, William, Skeagh, Parish of Cleenish
　　　　　　　　　　　　　　　　Dated 1656. Swan.
Atherton, Ruth, Liverpool, widow　Dated 1692. Dub.
Atkin, John, Youghal, alderman　　　1708. F.A.
　,,　John Thomas, Cork, clk.　　　　1765. F.A.
　,,　John Thomas, Leadentown, Co. Cork,
　　　　Esq.　　　　　　　　　　　　1786. F.A.
　,,　Walter, Ballinleaden als. Leadington,
　　　　Co. Cork, clk.　　　　　　　1741. F.A.
　,,　Walter, Windsor, Co. Cork, late of Lea-
　　　　denton　　　　　　　　　　　1795. F.A.
　,,　William, Coolnacloughfinny, Co. Cork,
　　　　gent.　　　　　　　　　　　1730. F.P. and F.A.
Atkins, Anne, Dublin, widow　　Dated 1673. Dub.
　,,　Augustine　　　　　　　　　　　1682. W. Cork.
　,,　Sir. Thomas, Dublin.　　　　　　1695. F.P.
　,,　William, Youghal, merchant　　　1657. F.A.
　,,　William, Lt.-Col., and Bt. M. Gen.　1822. S.4. (H.BM.)
Atkinson, Anthony, Cangort, King's Co.　1744. S.1.P.
　,,　Michael, Lr. Coombe, Dublin,
　　　　clothier　　　　　　　　Dated 1678. Dub.
Atkison, William　　　　　　　　　　1663. Dub.
Atkisson, William, Kilteel　　　Dated 1700. Dub.
Auchenleck, Rev. James, Ballyvelan, R. of
　　　　Cleenish, Co. Fermanagh　　1685. F.2.
　,,　William, Cultagh, Co. Fermanagh 1803. C.D.B.
Auchinleck, William, Lieut.　　　　　1799. S.4. (H.BM.)
Austen, Elen　　　　　　　　　　　　1808. F.A.
　,,　Elizabeth, Dublin, widow　　　　1794. F.A.
　,,　Elizabeth, widow of Rev. Robt. A.,
　　　　D.D., Archdeacon of Cork　　1807. F.A.
　,,　Jane, Dublin, spinster　　　　　1807. F.A.
　,,　Robert, D.D., Archdeacon of Cork　1792. F.A.
　,,　Thomas, Inskinny, Co. Cork　　　1766. F.P.
　,,　William, Inkenny, South Liberties of
　　　　Cork, Esq.　　　　　　　　　1798. F.A.
Austin, Elizabeth, Cork, widow　　　1762. F.A.
　,,　Joseph, Cork, alderman　　　　　1761. F.A.
　,,　Thomas, South Liberties of Cork, Esq. 1762. F.A.
Axtell, Joseph, Dublin, soap boiler　Dated 1638. Dub.
Aylett, Richard, Killencroft, Co. Cavan
　　　　　　　　　　　　　　　　Dated 1660. Dub.
Aylmer, Alexander　　　　　　　Dated 1650. Dub.

Aylmer, Alexander　　　　　　　Admon. 1664. Dub.
　„　　als. Barnewall, Mabell, widow
　　　　　　　　　　　　　　　Dated 1654. Dub.
Aylworth, Sir Richard, Newmarket, Co. Cork,
　　　Knt.　　　　　　　　　Admon. 1629. F.A.
Aysh, George, Dublin, merchant　Dated 1678. Dub.

Babe, Andrew　　　　　　　　Dated 1652. Dub.
Babington, David, Nth. Gt. George's St.,
　　　Dublin, solicitor　　　　Dated 1834. Swan.
　„　　als. Wray, Rebecca. *See* Dunkin.
　„　　Rev. Thomas, Billy, Co. Antrim
　　　　　　　　　　　　　　　Dated 1823. Swan. Connor
Bacon, Edward, Doulin, par. of Aughanloe, Co.
　　　Londonderry　　　　　　1709. W. Derry
　„　　Robert, Dublin　　　　Dated 1610. Dub. and W.
　　　　　　　　　　　　　　　　　　　　Dublin
　„　　Robert, parish of Tamlaghtfinlagan, Co.
　　　Derry　　　　　　　　　1746. W.P.
　„　　William, Ballycartan, par. of Tam-
　　　lathard, Co. Derry　　　1705. W. Derry
Badcock, Thomas, carpenter　　1707. Dub.
Badger, Roger, Knockvicar, Co. Roscommon,
　　　gent.　　　　　　　　　Dated 1652. Dub.
Badham, Brettridge, Rockfield, Co. Cork, Esq. 1744. B. and F.A.
Badhams, William　　　　　　Dated 1655. Dub.
Bagaley (or Bayley), [Bayly], John, Corbally,
　　　Co. Kildare　　　　　　Dated 1685. Dub.
Bagenal, Ann, Dunleckny, Co. Carlow　1731. B.
　„　　Beauchamp, Bagenalstown, Co. Car-
　　　low　　　　　　　　　　1802. B.
　„　　George, Dunleckny　　　1625. B.
　„　　Nicholas, Ballymoney　　1607. B.
　„　　Nicholas, Plas Newydd, Anglesey　1713. B.
Bagge, William, Gortnecross, als. Crossfield,
　　　Co. Cork　　　　　　　1709. F.A.
Bagot, Edward, Walterstown, Co. Kildare　1711. S.4. Kildare
　„　　Rev. Walter, Monasterevan, Co. Kildare 1815. S.4. Kildare
Bagwell, Anne, widow of John B., junr., of Kil-
　　　more, Co. Tipperary　　1739. F.A.
　„　　John, Clonmell, Co. Tipperary, mer-
　　　chant　　　　　　　　　1754. F.A.
　„　　John, Kilmore, Co. Tipperary, Esq. 1785. F.A.
　„　　Mary, Cork, widow　　　1765. F.A.
　„　　Phineas, Cork, merchant　1760. F.A.
　„　　William, Clonmel, Esq.　1756. F.A.

Bailey, John, Westpanstowne, par. of Lucan,
    yeoman   1669. Dub.
Baily, Catherine, Dorset St., Dublin, widow   1802. C.D.B.
  ,,   Jane, widow   1723. W.P.
Baiteson, John   Dated 1684. Dub.
Baker, Catherine, Shanagarry, Co. Cork   1694. F.P. and W.P.
  ,,   Clement, soldier, late of Golden Meade,
        Co. Cambridge   Dated 1654. Dub.
  ,,   Elizabeth, Cork, widow   1792. F.A.
  ,,   George, Dublin, gent.   Dated 1638. F.2.
  ,,   George, [Patrick St.], Dublin, gent.   1638. Dub.
  ,,   George, Cork, cooper   1797. F.2.
  ,,   Godfrey, Cork, Esq.   Dated 1786. F.2.
  ,,   Grace, Dublin, widow   Dated 1708. Dub.
  ,,   John, Cork, gent.   1795. F.A.
  ,,   John, Ashgrove, Co. Cavan   1798. Swan. Kilmore
  ,,   Paul, Cork, merchant   1789. F.2.
  ,,   Peter, Cork, gent.   1797. F.2.
  ,,   Richard, Dublin, paver   Dated 1693. Dub.
Baldock, Rutland, Ensign   Dated 1703. Dub.
Baldwen, Margery, par. of Templemartin,
      widow   1627. W. Cork.
Baldwin, Alice, Summerhill, Queen's Co.   1767. S.1. Leighlin
  ,,   als. Warren, Alice, [Cork, widow]   1795. F.2. and F.A.
  ,,   Anne, [Dublin], spinster   1668. Dub.
  ,,   Charles, Dublin, Esq.   1730. F.2.
  ,,   Rev. Charles   1749. F.2.
  ,,   Elinor, Dublin   Dated 1668. Dub.
  ,,   Elizabeth, Dublin, spinster   1751/2 F.2.
  ,,   Henry, Garraneaghovny, als. Moss-
      grove, par. of Templemartin, Co.
      Cork   1750. W. Cork
  ,,   Henry, Mountmellick, Queen's Co.   1756. F.2.
  ,,   Henry, Curravodey, Co. Cork, Esq.   1770. F.2. and F.D.
  ,,   Herbert, Currinordy, Co. Cork   1696. W. Cork
  ,,   James, Pollericke, par. of Kilmory,
      Co. Cork   1688. W. Cork
  ,,   James, Macroom, Co. Cork, Esq.   1809. F.A.
  ,,   John, Corolanty, King's Co.   1699. S.1.P.
  ,,   John, Shinrone, King's Co.   1698. S.1.P. and F.2.
  ,,   John, Dysart, Queen's Co.   Dated 1797. F.2.
  ,,   Jonathan, Summerhill, Queen's Co. 1748/9. F.2.
  ,,   Jonathan, Maryborough, Queen's Co.
                                    Dated 1795. S.1.
  ,,   Joseph, Desart, Queen's Co.   1758. F.2.
  ,,   Lucy, Dublin, spinster   1768. S.1.P.

Baldwin, Mary, Dublin 1712. F.
" Richard, Dublin, gent. 1666. F.2.
" Rev. Richard, Prebendary of Kilbrittain 1743. F.2.
" Richard, Dublin, Esq. 1768. F.2.
" Richard, Dublin, Esq. 1795. F.2.
" Richard, Doone, Queen's Co. 1805. S.1.
" Walter, Garrancoonig, Co. Cork 1677. W. Cork
Balfe, John, Kilmartin Dated 1587. Dub.
" Walter, Heathfield, Co. Roscommon 1804. C.D.B.
Balfore, James, Lord Baron of Clonawley [1634]. Dub.
Balfour, Sir William, Westminster, Middlesex, Knt. 1721. W.P.
Ball, Anne. *See* Dillon
" Charity, Dublin, widow 1671. Dub.
" Daniel, Dublin, tanner 1666. Dub.
" Edmond, Dublin, butcher Dated 1605. Dub.
" als. Curteis, Jane, Baldrumyn, widow Dated 1647. Dub.
" John, Dublin, gent. Dated 1584. Dub.
" Michael, Dublin, gent. Dated 1703. Dub.
" Richard, Capt. Lieut. [1665]. Dub.
" Thomas, soldier, Clarke's Regt. Dated 1654. Dub.
" Walter, Dublin, alderman Dated 1598. Dub.
Ballard, Benjamin, gent. 1715. F.A.
" Benjamin, Cork City Admon. 1724. Ir.
" John 1705. Dub.
Balowne, William, Athy, merchant 1633. Dub.
Bamber, Capt. James, Dean Hill, East Meath Dated 1703. Dub.
Bancons, Isaac, Cork, merchant 1733. F.A.
Bane, Pryce, Cowll Kyle, Co. Wicklow, yeoman Dated 1629. Dub.
Banfield, Francis, Carrane, Co. Cork, gent. 1762. F.A.
" William, [Ballyecooley, Castlemacadam] 1700. Dub.
Bankes, Joseph, Dublin, gent. Dated 1672. Dub. and W. Dublin
" Rev. Richard, R. of Delgany, Co. Wicklow 1682. W.P.
" Rev. Richard, Eyre Court, Co. Galway, clk. 1730. W.P.
Banks, Anne, Rathcoole Dated 1619. Dub.
" als. Bayley, Elinor, Westpanstowne, Dio. Dublin Dated 1672. Dub. and W. Dublin

Banks, Ralph, Kilkenny, pewterer Dated 1656. Dub.
  „   Ralph, Kilkenny 1658. Dub.
Bannister, John, gent. Dated 1650. Dub.
  „   See Barrister.
Barber, Thomas Dated 1619. Dub.
Barcklaye, Joan, Towie Dated 1675. Dub.
Barclay, Rev. Andrew, Newmarket, Co. Clare
  Dated 1755. F. Killaloe
  „   David, Killaloe, clk. Dated 1715. F. Killaloe
  „   Gavin, Chanter of [St. Patrick's],
     Cashel 1664. F.2.
Bardan, Anne. See Birne.
Bardon, William, Ringsend, brewer 1689. Dub.
Bargett, Swithin, [St. Thomas' Court], Dublin,
     tailor 1675. Dub.
Barker, Francis, City of Waterford, Esq. 1773. Swan. P.
  „   Rainsford, William St., Dublin 1801. C.D.B.
  „   William, Dublin, Esq. Dated 1629. Dub.
Barkly, Matthew, Chester, ironmonger
  Dated 1660. Dub.
Barlow, James, Dublin Dated 1667. Dub.
  „   John, Aghnamallagh, Co. Monaghan,
     Esq. Dated 1742. Swan. P.
  „   Henry, Newgrove, Co. Monaghan 1736. Swan. Clogher
  „   Mary, Newgrove 1753. Swan. P.
  „   Ralph, Aghnamallogh, Co. Monaghan 1746. W.P.
  „   Robert, [Bride's Ally], Dublin, gent.
  Dated 1700. Dub.
Barnaby, Francis, Dublin, gent. Dated 1684. Dub.
Barnard (Bernard), Francis, Castlemachouse
     [Castlemaghoun], Co. Cork, gent.
  Dated 1657. Dub.
  „   William, Dublin 1682. M.
Barne, Hugh Bane. See O'Barne.
  „   Thomas, parish of Erit[h], Co. Kent,
     gent. Dated 1659. F.2.
Barns, Diana, Grange, Co. Kilkenny 1730. B.
  „   Thomas, Grange, Co. Kilkenny 1684. B.
  „   Thomas, Grange, Co. Kilkenny 1710. B.
  „   Thomas, Kilculleheen, Co. Waterford 1722. B.
  „   Thomas, Monasteroris, King's Co. 1741. B.
Barnesley, Henry, Dublin, tanner Dated 1699. Dub.
Barnett, Edmond, Towermore, Co. Cork, gent. 1763. F.A.
  „   Elizabeth, Butterfield, widow 1710. Dub.
  „   William, Dublin, clothier 1670. Dub.
Barnewall, Alicia. See Nugent.

Barnewall, Christopher, Dublin, tanner
                                Dated 1627. Dub.
„   Mabell. *See* Aylmer.
„   Marcus, Drimnagh, Esq.   Dated 1597. Dub.
„   Oliver, Dublin, shoemaker   Dated 1690. Dub.
„   Richard, Dublin, alderman Dated 1653. Dub.
„   Richard, Dublin, formerly of Edin-
        boro', in Scotland   1697. Dub.
„   Robert, Shankill   Dated 1590. Dub.
„   Robert, Donbroe, Esq.   1635. Dub.
„   Robert, Dublin, Esq.   1700. Dub.
Barnewell, John, Lispopell, gent.   Dated 1567. Dub.
Barney, or Deberney [Debernay], James
        [Jaque], pensioner   Dated 1706. Dub.
Barnsby, Ralph, Chapelizod, coachman
                                Dated 1640. Dub.
Barr, Charles, Cork, skinner   1743. F.A.
Barre, Thos. *See* Beare.
Barrelly, David, Kanturk, Co. Cork   1802. C.D.B.
Barrett, Alice, Dublin, widow   Dated 1629. Dub.
„   David   Dated 1650. Dub.
„   Edmond, Curlogh, Co. Cork, farmer 1783. F.A.
„   Edward, Cork, merchant   1760. F.A.
„   John, Knockaveagh, otherwise Brick
        Hill, Co. Cork, farmer   1764. F.A.
„   John, City of Cork, late of Coolowen
        North Libs. of Cork   1774. F.A.
„   Richard, Dublin, vintner   1702. Dub.
„   Robert, Mallow   1772. F. Cloyne
„   Thomas, Curbah, Co. Cork, farmer 1766. F.A.
Barrington, Alexander, Castletown, Co. Cork,
        Esq.   1708. W. Ferns
„   Benjamin, Limerick, alderman   1733. W.P.
„   Benjamin, Gt. Ship Street, Dublin,
        Esq.   1748. W.P.
„   Benjamin, Limerick, burgess   1769. W. Limerick
„   Catherine, Dublin, spinster   1749. W.P.
„   Christopher, Loghteoge, Queen's
        Co.   1687. W.P.
„   John, the younger, Ballyrone,
        Queen's Co.   Admon. 1740. W.
„   Joshua, Lib. of St. Patrick's Close,
        Dublin   1743. W.
„   Margaret, the elder, Dublin, widow 1753. W.
„   Mark, Bristol, England, formerly of
        Ballycogly, Co. Wexford, gent. 1747. W.

Barrington, Nicholas, Capt., Killome, Queen's
Co.   Dated 1667. F.2. and W
„   Nicholas, Ballycogly, Co. Wexford,
gent.   1747. W. Ferns.
„   Nicholas, Lambstown, Co. Wexford   1770. F.2.
„   Randolph, Lib. of St. Patrick, clerk   1746. W.
„   Sarah, Lib. of St. Patrick's Close, widow   1749. W.
„   Susanna. *See* Chambers.
„   Susanna, Ballymakene, Co. Wexford, widow   1735. W. Ferns
„   Thomas, Ballymackane, Co. Wexford   Dated 1719. W. Ferns
„   William, Ballenepierce, Co. Wexford, gent.   1732. W. Ferns
„   William, Raheenlusk, Co. Wexford 1753. W. Ferns

Barrister [Bannister], John, Dublin, carpenter
Dated 1647. Dub.

Barron, Alice, Waterford, spinster   1813. C.D.B.
„   Nicholas, Cork, priest   1784. F.A.

Barrowe, Lieut. Thomas, Carlingford Dated 1651. Dub.

Barry, Edward, Cork, M.D.   1710. F. and Davis
„   Francis, Tinegaragh, Co. Cork   1770. F.2.
„   Garrett oge, Ballymaeslyny   1691. W. Cloyne
„   Henry, Lord Santry   1736. W.P.
„   Henry, Lord Santry   1751. W.P.
„   James, Santry, Esq.   Dated 1675. Dub. and W. Dublin
„   James, Dublin, Esq.   1727. W.P.
„   James, Carrigleigh   1752. F.P.
„   James, Rockstown, Co. Limerick   1828. Mol. P.
„   John, Ballyshonin, Co. Cork   1782. F.2.
„   John, Ballyglisson, Co. Cork   Dated 1772. F.2.
„   Joseph, Dublin, gent.   1683. F.2.
„   Michael, Farnan, Co. Limerick, gent. 1748. F.2.
„   Michael, Donnybrook, Co. Dublin   1751. F.2.
„   Rebecca, Rath, Co. Limerick, widow   1774. F.2.
„   Redmond FitzJames, Pollencurry   1614. W. Cork
„   Redmond, Rathcormick, Co. Cork   1690. F.P.
„   Redmond, Ballyclogh, Co. Cork   1739. F. and W.P.
„   Redmond, Ballyclogh, Co. Cork   1741. W.P.
„   Redmond, Rathcormack, Co. Cork, Esq.   1750. F.P.
„   Richard, Condonstown, Co. Cork, gent.   1639. F.Cork.

IN THE GENEALOGICAL OFFICE, DUBLIN 103

Barry, Richard, Robertstowne, Co. Cork, gent.
                                      Dated 1661. F. and W. Cork
  „   Richard, Dublin, Esq.   1678. F.E.
  „   Richard, Dublin, gent.   1699. W.P.
  „   Richard, sometime of Ireland, now of
        London, gent.   Dated 1706. Dub.
  „   Lieut. Thomas   1660. Dub.
  „   Thomas, Cork, gent.   Dated 1761. F.2.
  „   Samuel, Ballycreggane, Co. Tipperary 1740. S.1.P.
Barter, Benjamin, Annagh, Co. Cork, Esq. 1807. F.A.
  „   Francis, Templemichael   1710. W. Cork
  „   John, Cooldaniel, Co. Cork   1742. F.A. and W.
                                                  Cork
  „   Mary, spinster   1794. F.A.
  „   Thomas, Killeene, Co. Cork, gent. 1682. F. A. and W.
                                                  Cork
  „   Thomas, Annaghmore   1750. F.A. and W.
                                                  Cork
  „   Thomas, Innishannon, [Co. Cork] 1765. F.A.
  „   Thomas, Dublin, gent.   1787. F.A.
  „   William, Temple Michael   1692/3. F.A. and W.
                                                  Cork
  „   William, Affoland   1770. F.A.
Barton, als. Hill, Anne, [Dublin]   1650. Dub.
  „   Edward, Springhill, Co. Tyrone 1801. Swan. P.
  „   Henry, Ringsend, Co. Dublin   1665. Dub.
  „   Symon, Dublin, shoemaker Dated 1650. Dub.
  „   Thomas, Dublin   1695. Dub.
  „   Thomas, Newmarket, Co. Dublin 1702. Dub.
Bartram, Henry, Mallow, clothier   1780. F.A.
Barwick, Edward, Cork, merchant   1747. F.A.
Baskevile [Baskerville], Mary, [Dublin]
                                        Dated 1564. Dub.
Basnett, George, [Kildare, gent.]   1653. Dub.
Basse, Susanna, Gurtenlehard, Queen's Co.
                                        Dated 1643. Dub.
Bastable, Arthur, Castlemagner, Co. Cork 1728. F.2.
  „   Arthur, Castlemagner   1773. F.2.
  „   Charles, junr., Castlebrett, Co. Cork 1710. W. Cloyne
Bate, Anne, Dublin, widow   Dated 1672. Dub.
  „   George, Charlesfort, Ireland   1725/6. F.A.
  „   Mary, Kinsale, widow   1728. F.A.
  „   Peter, Dublin, gent.   1665. Dub.
Bateman, Catherine, Shanagarry, Co. Cork 1694. F.
  „   George Brooke, Altavilla, Co.
        Limerick   1809. S.1.P.

Bateman, John, Killeen, Co. Kerry, Esq. 1719. F., F.A. and S.I.
Bates, Alexander, Dublin, merchant 1801. F.A.
„ Thomas 1805. F.A.
„ or Bathe, William, [St. Patrick's Close],
    Dublin, gent. Dated 1640. Dub.
Bateson, Thomas, Organist, of Blessed Trinity,
    [Christ Church], Dublin Dated 1629. Dub.
Bath, Bartholomew, [Lawndeston] Dated 1577. Dub.
„ Bartholomew, Lawdeston, gent. Dated 1578. Dub.
„ Dorothy, Killincarrig, Co. Wicklow,
    widow 1729. Ir.
„ Henry, Ballinegeragh, Co. Dublin, gent. 1617. Dub.
„ Patrick, Smithfield, Dublin, chirurgeon 1688. Dub.
„ Thomas, Church Street, maltster Admon. 1717. Ir.
„ Walter, Rogerstown, par. Lusk, farmer
    Dated 1598. Dub.
Bathe, Sir Peter, Athcarne, Co. Meath, Bart.
    Dated 1685. Ir.
„ Richard, Dublin, merchant Dated 1615. Dub.
„ Richard, Dublin Admon. 1720. Ir.
Bathurst, Henry, gent., Recorder of Cork and
    Kinsale 1676. F.A.
„ Joseph, Stoneybatter, gent. 1700. Dub.
Bawne, Thomas, [St. Katherine's], Dublin,
    skinner Dated 1641. Dub.
Bayley, als. Banks, Elinor, Westpanstown,
    Dublin Dated 1672. Dub. and W.
                                                       Dublin
„ alias Bagaley, John, Corbally, Co. Kil-
    dare 1685. Dub.
„ (Bayly), John, Castlemore, Esq. 1698. W. Cork
„ John, Castlemore Dated 1716. F.
„ (Bayly), John, Castlemore, Co. Cork 1724. W. Cork
„ Roger, Dublin, coachman Dated 1676. Dub.
„ John, Dublin, carpenter Dated 1699. Dub.
„ John, Debsboro, Co. Tipperary 1733. S.I.P.
„ Robert, Dublin, yeoman 1702. Dub.
Bayly, Jno., Cork, alderman Dated 1707. Sullivan MSS.
Bayneham, Joseph, Athy, Co. Kildare, maltster,
    formerly of Worcestershire
    Dated 1634. Dub.
Baynes, Edward, [Dublin], clerk Dated 1670. Dub.
Beachan, Edmund, Dublin, maltster 1667. Dub.
Beaden, Samuel, [St. Thomas' Court], Dublin 1704. Dub.
Beaghan, Edmund, Dublin, maltster Dated 1666. Dub.
„ John, Dublin, maltster Dated 1650. Dub.

IN THE GENEALOGICAL OFFICE, DUBLIN 105

Beaghane, Edward, Donabate Dated 1589. Dub.
Bealinge, Ismay, Newhall, Tawlagh, Co. Dublin,
   widow 1639. Dub.
„ Walter Dated 1632. Dub.
Beamish, Catherine, parish of Ballymoddan,
   Co. Cork, widow Dated 1642. F.2.
„ George, Mount Beamish, Co. Cork,
   gent. 1765. F.2.
„ Francis, Curraghvaraban 1679. F.
„ Francis, [? Carravarahane], parish of
   Ballymodan Dated 1679. F.2. and Davis
„ Francis, Kilmalody, [Co. Cork]
    Dated 1681. F.2.
„ Francis, Killmaloda, widower
    [? proved] 1750. F.2.
„ Francis, Kilmaloda, gent.
    Not dated [? 1763]. F.2.
„ John, West Gully, parish of Bally-
   modan, Co. Cork, gent Dated 1668. F.2.
„ Mary, Bandon Not dated [? 1777]. F.2.
„ Richard, Ballinard, farmer 1734. F.2.
„ Richard, Ballyva 1777. F.2.
„ Richard, Raharoon, Esq. Dated 1788. F.2.
„ Thomas, Bandonbridge Dated 1681. F.2.
„ Thomas, Raharoon, Co. Cork 1729. F.2.
„ Thomas, Cork, gent. Dated 1772. F.2.
Beanman, John, Hyde Park, Co. Wexford 1803. C.D.B.
Beardley [Beardsley], Thomas, [Dublin]
    Dated 1684. Dub.
Beare (or Barre), Thomas, Dublin, merchant,
    Dated 1580. Dub.
„ Richard, Moyalloe, Co. Cork 1701. W.
„ Richard, Mallow, gent. 1719. W.
„ William, Lisbon and Bath 1771. F.
Beasley, Edmund, Dolphin's Barn, Co. Dublin,
   clothier Dated 1707. Dub.
Beatty, Arthur, Faranveer, Co. Cavan 1741. Swan. Kilmore
„ als. Dudghen, Barbara, Drumhaldry,
   Co. Leitrim Dated 1701. Swan.
„ Charles, Farrinvear, Co. Cavan 1704. Swan. Kilmore
„ Claud, Lieut., Coolaherty, Co. Long-
   ford 1729/30. Swan. P.
, Daniel McNeale, Hillmount, Co.
   Antrim Dated 1876. Swan.
„ David, Raheenduff, Co. Wexford 1855. Swan. P.
„ Edward, Dublin 1794. F.

Beatty, Eliz., Lyle, Co. Armagh   1790. Swan. P.
„   George, Lismoy, Co. Longford   1806. Swan. Ardagh
„   James, Dublin, Barrister-at-Law   1807. Swan. P.
„   James, Enniskillen   1856. Swan. P.
„   John, par. of Killeshandra, Co. Cavan   1681. Swan.
„   John, Corr, Co. Cavan   1726/7. Swan and S.4. Kilmore
„   John, Monaghan   1759. Swan. P.
„   John, Spring Park, Co. Longford   1815. Swan. P.
„   John, Clones   1824. Swan. Clogher
„   Robert, Mullinahinch, Co. Fermanagh   1780. Swan.
„   Robert, Springtown, Co. Longford   1769. Swan. P.
„   Rosa, Clones   1796. Swan. P.
„   Vincent, Lt.-Col., R.A.   1856. Swan. P.
Beaty, David, Cuortenan, Co. Down   1733. S.4. Dromore
Beaven, Jenkin, Capt. in Axtell's Regt.   [1660]. Dub.
Becher, Edward   1617. W. Cork
„   Elizabeth, Aghadown, Co. Cork   1721. W. Cork
„   John, Dublin, gent.   1721. F.A.
„   John, Bristol, merchant   1742. W. Cork
„   Michael, Aghadown, Co. Cork   1726. F.A. and W.P.
„   Phane, Quarter Master Gen. of all the Forces under command of the Lord Lieut.   1656. W.P.
„   Thos., Sherkin, Co. Cork   Dated 1705. F.
„   Thomas, Sherkin, Co. Cork, Esq.   1709. F.A.
Beck, Anthony, Dublin, gent.   1690. Dub.
„   Gabriel, Dublin   Dated 1705. Dub.
„   Sarah, Dublin, spinster   1801. C.D.B.
Becke, Henry, Dublin, mason   Dated 1698. Dub.
Beckett, Randal, Dublin, gent.   1672. F.2.
Beckford, Peter, Loggaghdordin, parish of Ballimore Eustace, yeoman   Dated 1684. Dub.
Beckwith, Thomas, Dublin, yeoman   Dated 1672. Dub.
Bee, Edward, Dublin, apothecary   Dated 1618. Dub.
„   James, Dublin, tanner   Dated 1617. Dub.
„   als. Dixon, Maude, Dublin, widow.   Dated 1618. Dub.
„   Patrick, Wicklow   Dated 1617. Dub.
Beech, Hugh, Dublin, distiller   1679. Dub.
„   Richard, Uttoxeter, Stafford, gent., trooper, Cromwell's Horse   Dated 1653. Dub.
Beevans [Beevens], Dorothy   Dated 1694. Dub.
Beg[g], Nicholas, Boraneston, gent.   Dated 1621. Dub.
Begg, John, Dublin, brewer   1708. Dub.
„   Margaret, Boranston, Co. Dublin   Dated 1599. Dub.

Begg, William, Dublin, shoemaker   Dated 1605. Dub.
Begge, Walter, Bertonstown [Boranston], Co.
      Dublin, gent.   Dated 1635. Dub.
Beinbrig, Hugh, Smithstown, Co. Kildare
         Dated 1637. Dub.
  ,,   Thomas, Smithstown, [Co. Kildare]   1636. Dub.
Belcher, Robert, par. of St. Mary, Shandon,
      Cork, carpenter   1642. W. Cork
  ,,   Thomas, St. Finbarry's, Cork   1694. W. Cork
Bell, Andrew, Ardleny, Co. Cavan   1756. Swan.
  ,,   Edward, Kilteele, Co. Kildare   Dated 1675. Dub.
  ,,   Gamaliel, Bellbrook, Queen's Co.   1799. B.
  ,,   George, Creighton's Grove, Co. Tipperary   1766. S.1.
  ,,   George, Douglas, Isle of Man   1802. C.D.B.
  ,,   Henry, Lisburn, Co. Antrim, linen draper   1786. Swan. P.
  ,,   John, Revernon, Co. Down   1703. Swan. Down
  ,,   John, Belfast   1714. B.
  ,,   Richard, [Dublin]   Dated 1650. Dub.
  ,,   Robert Thomas, Ashfield Glebe, Co. Cavan,
      clk.   1835. Swan. Kilmore
  ,,   Robert, Lisburn, Co. Antrim, merchant   1746. Swan.
  ,,   Susanna, widow of Robt. B., of Lisburn   1760. Swan. P.
  ,,   Thomas, Donore, Co. Dublin   1713. B.
  ,,   William, Tinnahinch, Queen's Co.   1743. B.
Bellew, James, Cavins Street   1708. Dub.
Bellewe, James, Dublin, merchant   Dated 1636. Dub.
Bellingham, Sir Daniel, Dublin, Knight and
      Bart.   1672. F.2.
  ,,   Sir Richard, Bart.   1699. F.2.
Benet [Bennett], Walter, Dublin   Dated 1650. Dub.
Benion, Richard, Rathfarnham   Dated 1629. Dub.
Benn, Frances, Dublin, widow   Dated 1703. Dub.
  ,,   William, Dublin, carpenter   Dated 1675. Dub.
Bennett, Anne, Cork, spinster   1806. F.A.
  ,,   Elizabeth, Cork, widow   1749/50. F.A.
  ,,   Elizabeth, Cork, widow of alderman
      George B.   1768. F.A.
  ,,   Francis, Cork, gent.   1722. F.A.
  ,,   Jane, Cork, widow   1695. F.2. and W.P.
  ,,   John, Athy, gent.   Dated 1710. Dub.
  ,,   John, Rockspring, N. Libs. of Cork,
      Esq.   1809. F.A.
  ,,   Joseph, Recorder of Cork   1767. F.A.
  ,,   Nicholas, Trooper in Col. Prittie's
      Regt.   Dated 1655. Dub.
  ,,   Philip, Kilbrook, Co. Cork, gent.   1752. F.A.

Bennett, Robert, Dublin, alderman Dated 1659 Dub.
„ Thomas, Ballyloughan, Co. Carlow 1778. B.
„ William, Dublin, gent. Dated 1666. Dub.
„ See Benet.
Bennis, Christopher, Dublin Dated 1624. Dub.
Benson, Christopher, Dublin Dated 1709. Dub.
„ Edward, Downpatrick, clk. 1741. Swan. Down
„ Mary, Downpatrick, widow 1782. Swan. Down
„ Trevor, clk., Minister of Hillsborough 1782. Swan. Down
„ William, Hillsborough, Co. Down 1811. Swan. Connor
Bentley, George, Dublin, gent. Dated 1650. Dub.
„ Robert 1629. F.A.
„ Robert, Major 1822. S.4. (H.BM.)
Bently, John, Leixlip, Co. Kildare Dated 1703. Dub.
„ Robert, Dublin, merchant 1735. F.A.
„ Nathan, Dublin, shearman Dated 1690. Dub.
Bercket, Thomas, [Dublin], basket-maker
  Dated 1663. Dub.
Beresford, John Claudius 1847. S.4.
„ William, Dublin, gent 1627. Dub.
Berkby, John, Kilmainham, miller 1707. Dub.
Berkeley, Rev. George Dated 1804. M.
Bermingham, John, Maynooth, gent. 1636. Dub.
„ John, Dublin, carpenter 1689. Dub.
„ William, Dublin Dated 1593. Dub.
„ See Bremenghane, Breminghame,
Bernard, Benjamin, Ferbane, King's Co. 1812. S.1. Meath
„ Charles, Drimsillick Dated 1728. S.1. Leighlin
„ Deborah, Carlow, widow 1732. S.1. Leighlin
    and B.
„ Frances, Dublin 1803. C.D.B.
„ Francis, Castlemagher 1690. W. Cork
„ Francis, Monard, North Libs. of Cork,
    gent. 1723. F.A.
„ Francis, Dublin, Justice of Common
    Pleas 1731. W.P.
„ Franks, Dublin 1791. S.1. Dublin
„ Franks, Clonmulsk, Co. Carlow 1760. S.1.Leighlin
    and B.
„ Franks, Clonmulsk, Co. Carlow 1782. B.
„ George, Dublin 1751. S.1.P.
„ Hudson, Carlow 1780. S.1.P.
„ Joseph, Carlow 1763. S.1.P. and B.
„ John White, Dublin 1734. S.1. Dublin
„ Mary, Rathrush 1737. S.1. Leighlin
„ Mary, Dublin 1791. S.1.P.

Bernard, Philip, Carlow					1760. S.1.P.
„		Philip, Carlow					1789. S.1. Leighlin
„		Thomas, Bernard's Grove, Queen's
			Co.						1744. S.1.P. and B.
„		Thomas, Roesboro', Co. Kildare			1798. S.1.P.
„		Thomas, Gayville, Co. Carlow			1807. S.1.P.
„		Thomas, Clonmulsk, Co. Carlow
							Dated 1720. S.1.P. and 1721. B.
„		Thomas, Birr, King's Co.			1788. S.1.P.
„		William, Newtown, Co. Carlow			1742. S.1. Leighlin
„		William, Carlow					1790. S.1.
„		William, Dublin					1790. S.1.
„		William T., Lr. Gardiner's St.,
			Dublin						1836. S.1.P.
,,		See Barnard.
Berrington, Ottywell, Oxmantown, smith
							Dated 1642. Dub.
Berry, Anne, Dove's Grove, King's Co., widow 1783. B. and S.1.P.
„		Charles, Dove's Grove, King's Co.		1824. B.
„		Elizabeth, Kilkenny, widow			1717. B.
„		Elizabeth, Dublin, spinster			1741. B.
„		Frederick, Birr, King's Co. (Lodged
			1845)						1830. B.
„		Henry, Clontarf, Co. Dublin			1717. B.
„		James Armstrong, Inchtown, King's
			Co.						1834. B.
„		Jane, Ballymoney, King's Co.			1723. B.
„		John, Dublin					1626. B.
„		John, Clonehane, King's Co.			1705. B.
„		John, Clonehane, King's Co.			1730. B.
„		John, Broadwood, Co. Westmeath			1767. B.
„		Jonathan, Dove Grove, King's Co.		1781. B.
„		Rev. Joseph, Arthurstown, Co. Louth 1661. F.2.
„		Letitia, Dublin, widow				1741. B.
„			 „		„	„	Dated 1741. F.
„		Margery, Dublin, widow				1764. B.
„		Mary, Dublin, widow			Dated 1699. Dub.
„		Mary, widow of Lt.-Col. Berry			1724. B.
„		Mary, Parsonstown, King's Co.			1830. B.
„		née Cox, Olivia, Dove Grove, King's
			Co.						1840. B.
„		Robert, Dublin					1728. B.
„		Thomas, Eglish Castle, King's Co.		1816. B.
„		Thomas, Dublin					1837. B.
„		Lieut. William					1703. B.
„		Lieut. William, Bellassy's Regt. Dated 1701 F. and Dub.

Berry, William, ex. Lieut-Col. 1717. B.
„ William, Dublin 1767. B.
Berstow, Jeremie, Dublin, merchant Dated 1693. Dub.
Best, Roger, Moy, Co. Tyrone 1803. C.D.B.
„ William, Parksgrove Co. Kilkenny,
  gent. 1640. Dub.
Betson [Betsow], Thomas, Grangegorman, Co.
  Kildare 1706. Dub.
Bettes, John, Dublin, gent. Dated 1580. Dub.
Bettesworth, Peter, Ballydulee, gent. 1707. F.2.
Betts, Thomas, Govr. of Duncannon [Fort], Co.
  Wexford Dated 1657. Dub.
Bettsworth, Elizabeth 1653. F.
„ Richard, Pallas, Co. Limerick 1647. F.
„ Richard, Ballydalen 1713. F.
Betty, Edward, Barconbury, Co. Cavan 1863. Swan. [? Kilmore]
„ Thomas, Ardregoul, Co. Fermanagh,
  farmer 1714. Swan.
„ Rev. Veaitch, Lakefield, Co. Cavan 1796. Swan. [? Kilmore]
Bevans, Maude, widow Dated 1649. Dub.
Bew, Thomas, Carheenerbull, Co. Clare 1745. Mol. Killaloe
Bewley, Daniel, Edenderry, King's Co. 1743. B.
„ Elizabeth, Edenderry, King's Co. 1745. B.
„ Elizabeth, Diocese of Kildare 1745. B.
„ George, Dublin 1782. B.
„ Mary, Dublin 1739. B.
„ Mungo, Edenderry, King's Co. 1783. B.
„ Thomas, Dublin 1730. B.
Bewsick, Edward, Corporal Dated 1656. Dub.
Beynon [Beymon], Michael, Dublin Dated 1688. Dub.
Bibby. See Bybbye.
Bible, Mary (wife or widow of Robert B., of
  Kilworth) Dated 1773. Davis
„ Robert, Kilworth, Co. Cork, gent.
    Dated 1772. Davis
Biddulph, John, Stradbally, Queen's Co. 1741. S.1.
Biggs, Edith 1760. W.
„ Jeremiah, Bandon, clothier 1772. F.A.
„ Joseph, Bandon, clothier 1772. F.A.
„ Richard, Castlebiggs, Co. Tipperary 1796. S.1.P.
„ Thomas, Bellvue, Co. Tipperary 1796. S.1.P.
„ William, Shannakiel, Co. Tipperary 1730. S.1. Killaloe
Bigland, Henry, London, citizen Dated 1689. Dub.
Bignell, Edward, Lr. Combe, brewer Dated 1709. Dub.

IN THE GENEALOGICAL OFFICE, DUBLIN 111

Billing, Oliver, Carlow, merchant   Dated 1656. Dub.
Billy, William, Dublin, Esq.   Dated 1627. Dub.
Bindon, Catherine, widow of Rev. Dean B.   1772. S.1.P.
   „   David, Cloony, Co. Clare   1733. S.1.P.
   „   Eleanor. *See* Amirald.
   „   Henry, Limerick   1664. F. and F.2.
   „   Henry, Ennis, Co. Clare   1740. S.1.P.
   „   Thomas, Dean of Limerick   1740. S.1.P.
Birch, John, soldier   Dated 1653. Dub.
   „   John, Kilmainham, tanner   Dated 1674. Dub.
   „   Rev. William, Roscrea, Co. Tipperary   1776. S.1.P.
   „   *See* Byrtch.
Birchensha, [Sir] Ralph, Knt., Comptroller of
           the Musters   Dated 1622. Dub.
Bird, Thomas, Dublin, merchant   Dated 1650. Dub.
   „   John Jenkins   1837. S.4. (H.I.)
Birkett, John, Dublin, clerk   Dated 1681. Dub.
Birmingham, William, Clonkerran, Co. Kildare,
           gent.   Dated 1604. Dub.
Birne, als. Bardan, Anne, Rathweade, Co.
           Carlow, [widow]   [1658]. Dub.
   „   Anthony, Kilpatrick, Co. Wicklow, gent.
                               Dated 1652. Dub.
   „   David, Dublin, chandler   1610. Dub.
   „   James, Dublin, cook   Dated 1620. Dub.
Bishop, Widow   1711. W. Cloyne
   „   Lieut. Benjamin Bowen   1784. S.4. (H.BM.)
Bisshopp, Robert, Dublin, barber chirurgeon
                               Dated 1685. Dub.
Bitchiner, Francis, Clonakilty, Co. Cork,
           yeoman   1813. C.D.B.
Blackall, Robt.   Died 1868. S.4. (H.O.)
Blackburn, Richard, Carrickena, Co. Roscom-
           mon   Admon. 1723. Ir. and F.A.
   „   Richard, Rathkenay, Dio. Meath,
           gent.   Admon. 1746. Ir.
Blackburne, Andrew, Carrickena, Co. Roscom-
           mon, Esq.   1708. Ir.
   „   John, Londonderry, merchant   1710. F.A.
   „   John, Raphoe, Co. Donegal, gent.
                            Admon. 1750. F.A.
   „   Rev. Richard, Carrickdrumruske,
           Co. Leitrim   1680. Ir. and F.
Blacke, Margaret, Dublin, widow   Dated 1685. Dub.
Blacker, Edward   1777. S.4. (H.BM.)
   „   William, Capt.   1787. S.4. (H.BM.)

Blackman, Symon, soldier, Clarke's Regt.
                                  Dated 1654. Dub.
Blacknall, Richard, Ballynekell   Dated 1634. Dub.
Blackney, Christopher, Dublin, merchant
                                  Dated 1617. Dub.
Blackwood, Christopher, Dublin, clerk
                                  Dated 1669. Dub.
    „   John, Bangor, Co. Down   1659. S.1.
    „   John, the elder, Bangor, Co. Down 1698. S.1. Down
    „   John, Ballydie, Co. Down   1726/27. S.1. Down
    „   Mary, Dublin, widow   Dated 1675. Dub.
Bladen, Ellenor, Dublin, widow   1667. Dub.
Blagrave, John, [Lt.-Col., Dublin]   1653. Dub.
Blake, John, [Dublin, sailor]   Dated 1650. Dub.
    „   Peter, Galway, gent.   1691. Cr. Tuam.
    „   Peter, Corbally, Co. Galway   1712. Cr.P.
    „   Robert, Dublin, innholder   Dated 1669. Dub.
    „   Sir Valentine, Galway   1653. Dub.
    „   Walter, Drum, County of town of Gal-
            way   1704. Cr. Tuam
Blakelyn, John, Dublin, merchant   Dated 1710. Dub.
Blakeney, Theophilus, Abbert, Co. Galway 1813. C.D.B.
    „   Simeon, Tuam   1780. Swan.
Blakeny, Robert, Major, Gallagh, Co. Galway
                                  Dated 1658. Dub.
Blan, or Bland, Richard, Athy, Capt. Hopkin's
       Troop   Dated 1662. Dub.
Bland, Nathaniel, LL.D., Judge of the Pre-
       rogative Court   1760. F.2.
Blaquire, James, Lt.-Col. 13th Regt. of Dra-
       goons   1803. C.D.B.
Blathwaite, Thomas, Dublin, joiner   Dated 1688. Dub.
Blayney, Richard, Carrick, Co. Monaghan, Esq.
                                  Dated 1641. Dub.
Bleakely, Mary, Tullyconaght, Co. Down 1813. C.D.B.
Bleathwaite, Elizabeth, Dublin, widow Dated 1693. Dub.
Blennerhassett, Edward, Belleek, Co. Ferman-
        agh, formerly of Parkthorp in
        Norfolk   1662. F.2.
    „   John, Ballyseedy, Co. Kerry 1709. F.
    „   John, Tralee, gent.   Dated 1743. W. Ardfert
    „   Leonard, Castle Hassett, Co.
            Fermanagh, Knt.   1639. F.2.
    „   Thomas, Tralee   1747. W. Ardfert
    „   Ursula, widow or wife of Sir
            John B.   1638. F.2.

IN THE GENEALOGICAL OFFICE, DUBLIN 113

Bligh, John 1667. F.
„ Robert, Dean of Elphin 1778. B.
Blood, Charles, Lady Castle, Co. Kildare.
    gent. 1749. F.2.
„ Elizabeth, Bohersalla, Co. Clare, widow 1750. Mol. P.
„ Elizabeth, widow of Thomas B. 1750. F.2.
„ Elizabeth, widow of Mathew B. 1779. F.2.
„ Elizabeth, Dublin 1798. F.2.
„ als. Gilbert, Jane, Baltiboys, Co. Wicklow 1791. F.2.
„ John, Ballykelly, Co. Clare, gent. 1799. F.2.
„ Mary, widow of Hugh B. 1773. F.2.
„ Mathew, Ballykincurra 1760. F.2.
„ Neptune, Bohersallah, Co. Clare, gent. 1741. F.2.
„ Thomas, Bohersallagh, Co. Clare, gent. 1731. F.2. and Mol. P.
„ Thomas, Corrofin, Co. Clare, gent. 1741. Mol. P.
„ Thomas, Corofin, Co. Clare
    Dated 23 Feb., 1736 [N.F.P.] F.2.
„ Thomas, Limerick, cordwainer Dated 1759. F.2.
„ Thomas, Ballybarney, Co. Kildare 1765. F.2.
„ Thomas, Dublin 1767. F.2.
„ William, Dublin, merchant 1727. F.2.
Bloomfield, Ben, Eyrecourt, Galway 1737. S.2. P.
„ als. Carroll, Clara, Eyrecourt, Galway 1824. S.2. P.
„ Jenny, Redwood, Co. Tipperary.
    Unproved   Not dated S.1.P.
„ John, Redwood, Co. Tipperary
    Dated 1770. S.1.P.
„ Richard, Meelick, Co. Galway 1809. S.1.P.
„ Stephen, Co. Galway 1814. S.1.
Blount, Charles, Dublin, gent. Dated 1682. Dub.
„ Samuel, Lismacue, Co. Tipperary 1699. S.1.P.
Blumfield, Benjamin, Shanless Grange, Co.
    Louth, farmer 1726. S.1.
„ als. Finey, Eliz., widow Dated 1765. S.2.
„ Mary, St. Andrew's Par., Dublin 1728. S.2.
Blunden, Overington, Clonmorency, Co. Kilkenny, gent. 1685. F.
Blundevile, Richard, Dublin, gent. Dated 1664. Dub.
Blunt, Charles, [Dublin] Dated 1677. Dub.
„ Thomas, Dublin, innkeeper Dated 1641. Dub.
Blyke, Dudley, Kilcurley, Co. Louth 1727. W.P.
Boardman, Robert, soldier, Morgan's Troop
    Dated 1653. Dub.
Boate, George, Duckspoole, Co. Waterford 1812. C.D.B.

INDEX OF WILL ABSTRACTS

Boate, Gerard, Clonekeny, Co. Tipperary   1696. S.1.P.
Bocham or Boxham, John, Ballyboughall
                             Dated 1614. Dub.
Boddell, Henry, Balreask, Co. Meath   1741. Swan. P.
Bodkin, John, Castletown, Co. Galway   1804. C.D.B.
    ,,   Thomas, Galway, merchant   1803. C.D.B.
    ,,   Valentine, R.C. Warden of Galway   1813. C.D.B.
Bogart, Lambart Vandam, Amsterdam, merchant   [1616]. Dub.
Bohilly, Tige, Blarney Lane   1749. W. Cork
Boileau, John Peter   D. 1818. S.4. (H.I.)
Bolan, Thos., Ennis, Co. Clare   1770. Mol. P.
Boland. See Bolland.
Boles, Francis, Ballinlawbegg, Co. Cork, gent.   1674. W. Cork
    ,,   Francis, Moyge, refiner   1738. W. Cloyne
    ,,   John, Woodhouse, als. Mogarbane, Co. Tipperary   1731. F.A., F.2., and S.1.P.
    ,,   John, Carrignashiny   1739. W. Cloyne
    ,,   Jonathan, Killibrahir, gent.   1704. W. Cloyne
    ,,   Nathaniel, Oxmantown   1659. Dub.
    ,,   Richard, Moyge, Co. Cork, Esq.   1751. F.2.
    ,,   Richard, Youghal, Co. Cork, gent.   1793. F.2.
    ,,   Samuel, Midleton, Esq.   1735. F.2.
    ,,   Thomas, Kilbracken, Co. Cork, Esq.   1749. F.2.
Bolger, Denis, [Tipperary, yeoman]   1667. Dub.
    ,,   Mary, Balharie, Co. Wexford, widow   1812. C.D.B.
Bolland [Boland], John, Dublin, gent.   1789. F.2.
    ,,   John, Cork, Esq.   1792. F.2.
Bolton, Cornelius, Waterford, Esq.   1699. F.2.
    ,,   George, Tralee, formerly of Youghal   1813. C.D.B.
Bomer (Bonier), Jeoffry, St. Mary's Abbey near Dublin, innkeeper   1640. Dub.
Bomford, Edward, Hightown, Co. Westmeath   1756. B.
    ,,   Jane, Dawson Street, Dublin, widow   1785. Ir.
    ,,   Laurence, Killeglan, Co. Meath   1721. Ir.
    ,,   Margaret, Hightown, Co. Westmeath   1763. B.
    ,,   Thomas, Clownstown, Co. Meath   1757. Ir.
Bonbonous, John, Cork, clothier   1731. W. Cork
Bonbounous, Joseph, Cork, merchant   1744. W. Cork
Bond, Christian, Wexford   1714. W. Ferns
    ,,   Edward, Tyra, Co. Armagh   1769. Swan.
    ,,   John, Wexford   1683. W. Ferns
    ,,   John, the elder, Knockmarra, Co. Wicklow   1701. Dub.
    ,,   John, Woodfort, Co. Cork   Dated 1745. F.

IN THE GENEALOGICAL OFFICE, DUBLIN 115

Bond, Thomas, senr., Dublin, weaver   1706. Dub.
  ,,   Thomas, Clownstown, [Co. Meath]   1757. Ir.
  ,,   Valentine, Dublin, mariner   1669. Dub.
Bonfield, Thomas, Limerick   1804. C.D.B.
Bonier, Jeoffry. *See* Bomer.
Bonny, George, Dublin, yeoman.   Dated 1686. Dub.
Boone, John, Dublin   Dated 1695. Dub.
Boothby, James Brownell, Twyford Abbey,
         Middlesex   Dated 1847. S.1.
Bor, als. Cusack, Begnet, Dublin, widow   1674. W.P.
  ,,   Christian, Dublin, merchant   Dated 1637. W.P.
  ,,   Jacob, Brigadier Genl.   1723. W. Dublin
  ,,   John, Dublin, merchant   1683. W.P.
  ,,   John, Dublin, Esq.   1741. W.P.
  ,,   Margaret, Dublin, widow   1694. W.P.
  ,,   William, Dublin, a minor   Admon. 1744. W.
Boran, Allson. *See* Kerdiff.
Borland, John, senr., Dublin, smith   1707. Dub.
Borr, Christian, Drynagh, Co. Wexford, Esq. 1686. W.P.
  ,,   Christian, Bigg Butter Lane, near Dublin,
         Esq.   1733. W.P.
  ,,   William, Dublin, Esq.   Admons. 1772, 1794. W.
Borran. *See* Borrow.
Borrelly, Melchier, Dublin   1802. C.D.B.
Borrow [Borran], John, Dublin   1651. Dub.
Bostocke, Mary, Dublin, spinster   1672. Dub.
Boston, Symon, soldier, Clarke's Regt.   Dated 1654. Dub.
Boswell, Dudley, Parson of St. John's, Dublin
         Dated 1650. Dub.
  ,,   Jane, Dublin, widow   Dated 1650. Dub.
Bouden [Bowden], Jeremy   Dated 1650. Dub.
Boughan, als. Kilkelly, Judy, Galway   1826. Cr. Tuam
Boulton, Anne, Stoneybatter, [Co. Dublin,
         widow]   1707. Dub.
  ,,   John, Blackhorse Lane, Co. Dublin,
         carman   1707. Dub.
Bourchell or Boursell [Burchell], Ingram, Bray   1635. Dub.
Bourgh, Miles, of Hamilton's Company   Dated 1703. Dub.
Bourke, David, Dublin, merchant   Dated 1630. Dub.
  ,,   David, Ballynagrana, Co. Limerick   1749. Mol. P.
  ,,   David, Bruff, Co. Limerick, gent   1794. Mol. P.
  ,,   Edmond, Cahanconneff, Co. Limerick   1750. Mol. P.
  ,,   Edmond, Kipishock, Co. Limerick
         gent.   1624. F.2.
  ,,   Ellis, Cool Lodge, Co. Mayo, late of
         Kinturk   1789. Cr. Tuam

INDEX OF WILL ABSTRACTS

Bourke, James, Limerick   Dated 1657. Dub.
"   John, Ballintubber, Co. Limerick   1773. Mol. Limerick
"   John, Gortnagroga, farmer   1787. Mol. Limerick
"   Thomas, Clogh, Co. Galway   Dated 1640. Dub.
"   Thomas, Limerick   1783. Mol. P.
"   William, Pollardstown, Co. Limerick, Esq.   [1657]. Dub.
"   William, Castle Bourke, Co. Mayo   1742. S.1.Tuam
"   William, Coolenee, Co. Limerick   1752. Mol. P.
Bourne, John, Clouncallow, Co. Cork, Esq.   1774. F.2.
Bourney, George   1686. Dub.
Bowden, William, [St. Nicholas Without], Dublin, tanner   Dated 1678. Dub.
     See Bouden.
Bowdler, John, Dublin, gent.   1662. F.2.
Bowe, Hugh, Dublin, founder   1707. Dub.
Bowen, Henry, Farahy, Co. Cork   1658. F.2.
"   John, Oak Grove, Co. Cork   1803. C.D.B.
"   Nicholls, Bowensford, Co. Cork   1729. F.
"   Oliver, Castle Karra, Co. Mayo   1653. Dub.
"   Richard, Lusk, yeoman   Dated 1681. Dub.
"   Richard, Dublin, vintner   Dated 1682. Dub.
"   Richard, Rathmines Rd., Co. Dublin 1842. S.4.P.
"   Robert, Ballyadams, Queen's Co., Esq. 1619. F.2.
"   Robert, Ballyadams, Queen's Co.   1624. F.2.
"   Capt. William, Castlekenny, Co. Mayo 1584. F.2.
"   William, Drung, Co. Cork   1703. F.
Bowerman, Alice, Moyne, Co. Clare   Dated 1764. W.
"   Henry, Cooline, Co. Cork, gent.   1700. W.
"   Henry, Cooline   1718. F.
Bowes, Catherine, Mountrath, Queen's Co. widow   1802. C.D.B.
"   Robert, Dublin, surgeon   Dated 1799. C.D.B.
Bowles, George, Mount Prospect, Co. Cork, Esq.   1803. F.A.
Boxham, or Bocham, John, Balleboughell, Dublin   Dated 1614. Dub.
Boxwell, Jane, Wexford, widow   1838. B.
"   John, Lingstown, Co. Wexford   1815. B.
"   John, Linziestown, Co. Wexford   1835. B.
"   William, Wexford   1810. B.
Boy, James, [Wood Quay], Dublin, shoemaker 1677. Dub.
Boyce, Catherine, Dublin, widow   1706. Dub.
"   Nathaniel, Dublin, merchant   1735. F.2.
Boyd, George, Dublin, ship carpenter   Dated 1654. Dub.

IN THE GENEALOGICAL OFFICE, DUBLIN

Boyd,	John, New Ross, gent.	1771. F.A.
„	Mary, Dublin, widow	Dated 1707. Dub.
„	William	Died 1804. S.4. (H.O.)
„	Sir William, Mt. Gordon, Co. Mayo, Knt.	1813. C.D.B.
Boyes,	Lieut. Geo.	1784. S.4. (H.BM.)
Boylan,	Patrick, Harristown, Co. Louth, farmer	1801. C.D.B.
Boyle,	Bellingham	1771. F.A.
„	als. Saunders, Elizabeth, Galway, widow	1801. C.D.B.
„	Richard	1711/12. F.
„	Richard, Dublin, Esq.	1711. W.P.
„	Sarah, Dublin, widow	Dated 1688. Dub.
„	William, Donore, [Dublin], brewer	Dated 1686. Dub.
Boys,	Lt.-Col. Comyn	1786. S.4. (H.BM.)
Boyse,	Rev. Nathaniel, V. of New Market, Co. Cork. Dated 18 July, 1788. [N.F.P.]	1792. F.2.
Braban,	Roger, [Ballina Banog, Co. Wexford]	Dated 1625. Dub.
Brackenbury,	John, [Dublin, gent.]	Dated 1652. Dub.
Braddell,	George, Bullingate, Co. Wicklow, Esq.	1772. F.A.
„	Henry, gent.	1760. F.A.
„	John, Ballyshane, Co. Carlow, gent.	1781. F.A.
„	Mary, Cronyhorn, Co. Wicklow, widow	1784. F.A.
„	Matthew, Mallow, Co. Cork, gent.	Dated 1800. F.A.
„	Michael, Carnew, Co. Wicklow	1764. F.A.
„	Michael, Croney Horn, Co. Wicklow gent.	Admon. 1788. F.A.
„	Thomas	1809. F.A.
„	William, Dublin, woolen draper	1782. F.A.
Bradford,	Frances	1803. C.D.B.
Bradlie	[Bradley], Alline	Dated 1652. Dub.
Bradly,	Francis, soldier	Dated 1654. Dub.
„	Richard, Dublin, merchant tailor	1709. Dub.
Bra[d]shaw,	Elizabeth, St. John's, Dublin.	Dated 1689. Dub.
Bradshaw,	Jasper, New Roe, Liberty of Donore, Co. Dublin	Dated 1665. Dub.
„	Sarah, Woodpark, Co. Meath	1814. C.D.B.
„	Thomas, Dublin, joiner	1705. Dub.
Bradstock,	Rowland, Dublin, gent.	1737. M.

Bradstreet, Dame Elizabeth — 1801. C.D.B.
Brady, Henry, Reinskea, Co. Galway — 1770. Mol. P.
   " Hugh, Kilkony, Co. Galway, gent. — 1748. Mol. P.
   " John D. — 1826. S.4. (H.O.)
   " William, Dublin, chaplain Dated 1569. Dub.
   " William, Williamstadt, Co. Galway, Esq. — 1791. Mol. P.
Braghall, Thomas, Tassagard — 1608. Dub.
Bramfield, Randle, Dublin Dated 1698. Dub.
Bramlo, Francis, Little Clanshagh, Co. Dublin, farmer — [1686]. Dub.
Brangan, John, Baltrassy, Co. Meath, farmer 1640. Dub.
   " William, Balrothery Dated 1621. Dub.
Brass, George, Kilbride, Co. Wicklow, gent. Dated 1704. Dub.
Braughall, Robert, Clonsillagh Dated 1669. Ir.
Bray, Robert, Portenure, Co. Longford, Esq. Dated 1747. F.E.
Brayrley, Abraham Dated 1655. Dub.
Brecknall, Nicholas, Thomas Court, Dublin Dated 1666. Dub.
Bredin, Christopher, Rue Hall, Co. Cavan 1809. Swan. P.
   " als. Hamilton, Clements. *See* Hassard.
   " James, Dorset St., Dublin, grocer. 1771. Swan. P.
   " Thomas, Cloncallow, Co. Longford, gent. 1763. Swan. P.
Bremenghane [Bermingham], Patrick, Corballes, Co. Meath, gent. Dated 1608. Dub.
Breminghame [Bermingham], Peter, The Pat, Dunboyne Dated 1633. Dub.
Brereton, John, Redwood, Co. Tipperary Dated 1770. S.1.
   " John, Ashgrove, King's Co. 1788. S.1.P.
   " John, senr., Clonbrock, King's Co. Dated 1818. Sadleir Deeds.
   " Mary, Dublin, widow 1704. Dub.
   " William, New Hall, King's Co., gent. Dated 1736. S.1.P.
   " William, Dublin, merchant 1753. S.1.
   " William, Kilmartin, Queen's Co. 1806. S.1.P.
Brerton, John, Newcastell, farmer Dated 1594. Dub.
Bressie, Francis, Drummore, Co. Donegal 1681. B.
Breton, John, Cork, gent. 1718. F.A. and W.P.
Brett, Benjamin, [Tawlagh, Dublin], Esq. Dated 1643. Dub.

Brettridge, Roger, Castlebrettridge, Co. Cork,
	Esq.	1683. F.2.
Brew, Jonathan, Trelig, Co. Clare	1778. Mol. Killaloe
„	Richard, Clonkerry, Co. Clare	1827. Mol. Killaloe
Brewster, Anne. *See* Evans.
„	Elizabeth, widow or wife of John B.
	of Ballycurran, Queen's Co.	1740. F.2.
„	Mathew, St. Mary's Abbey, inn-
	keeper	Dated 1631. Dub.
„	William, Shandon Park, Co. Cork
	Dated 29 April, 1731. Proved 18
	Nov. 1734 [N.F.P.]	F.2.
Brian, James, of The Skar, gent.	Dated 1598. Dub.
Brice, Mary, Balhary, widow	1690. Dub.
Bricher, John (soldier)	Dated 1656. Dub.
Brickley [Buckley], Richard, Killarny, Co.
	Wicklow, farmer	Dated 1691. Dub.
Brickly, Elizabeth, Donore, widow	1700. Dub.
Bridgeman, Elizabeth	1735. W. Limerick
„	Henry, Co. Clare	Dated 1722. W. Killaloe
Bridger, Richard, Well St., Westerham, Co.
	Kent, Esq.	1708. Dub.
Bridges, Robert, Finglas	Dated 1675. Dub.
„	William, Dublin, shoemaker	Dated 1637. Dub.
Brigges, Thomas	Dated 1649. Dub.
Briggs, John, Dunstable, Beds.	1695. S.1. and S.4. P.
Bright, Margaret Londonderry, widow
	Dated 1658. Dub.
Briglye, Thomas, Santry	Dated 1639. Dub.
Brisco, Edward, Dublin, brewer	Dated 1674. Dub.
Briscoe, Gabriel, Dublin, Esq.	Dated 1668. Dub.
„	Mary, Dublin, widow	1678. Dub.
Brise, Catherine, [Dublin]	Dated 1618. Dub.
Bristow, Susanna, Dublin, linen draper	1683. Dub.
Britten [Britton], Francis, Lord Protector's
	Own Troop of Horse	1658. Dub.
Britton, John	Dated 1726. Swan.
„	Winifred, Belvedere, par. of Wexford 1790. Swan.
Brock, Elnathan, Dublin	Dated 1659. Dub.
Brocklesby, Elizabeth. *See* Fendall.
Broderick, Rev. Geo. *See* Burdett.
„	(Brodrick), Sir John	1712. W.P.
„	St. John, Middletown, Co. Cork	1728. F.A.
Brodgen, William, Kilmeshogue, Co. Dublin,
	farmer	Dated 1685. Dub.
Broghall, William, Clonsilla, Co. Dublin	1677. Ir.

Broma or Broomer, [Broomer], John, Palmers-
　　　　town, [Co. Dublin]　　　Dated 1703. Dub.
Bromachan [Bromocum], William, Lazyhill,
　　　　Dublin　　　　　　　　Dated 1673. Dub.
Bromefield [Bromfeld], Joyce, [Carlow],
　　　　widow　　　　　　　　　　1644. Dub.
Bromidge, Thomas, Yardley, Co. Worcester,
　　　　gent.　　　　　　　　　　1648. Dub.
Brooke, [Dame] Lady Anne, Londonderry
　　　　　　　　　　　　　　Dated 1656. Dub.
Brookeing, Richard, Dublin, gent.　　1686. W.P.
Brooker, George, late of Clarke's Coy. [Hospital,
　　　　Dublin, yeoman]　　　Dated 1660. Dub.
Brookes, Charles, Dublin, cordwainer　1707. Dub.
Brooking, Ellinor, Dublin, widow　Dated 1677. Dub.
　,,　　　Joshua, Clonekilty　　　1685. W. Cork.
　,,　　　Richard, Dublin, barber chirurgeon
　　　　　　　　　　　　　　Dated 1677. Dub.
Brooks, Elizabeth, Mallow, Co. Cork　1729. F.
　,,　　　Ellinor, [Dublin, widow]　Dated 1641. Dub.
　,,　　　Walter, Kilcrowe, Parish Churchtown
　　　　　　　　　　　　　　Dated 1620. Dub.
Broome, Elizabeth. *See* Gregory.
　,,　　　Joshua, [Cork], merchant taylor　1711. W. Cork
　,,　　　Mathias, [St. Patrick St.], Dublin,
　　　　leather dresser　　　　Dated 1686. Dub.
　,,　　　William, Athy, skinner　Dated 1684. Dub.
Broomer, or Broma, John, Palmerstown, [Co.
　　　　Dublin]　　　　　　　Dated 1703. Dub.
Broomfield, William, Carlow　　　　1639. Dub.
Brothereppe, Walter, Dublin　Dated 1593. Dub.
Broughton, Amphillas, Dublin, widow
　　　　　　　　　　　　　　Dated 1682. Dub.
　,,　　　Charles, Dublin, Esq.　　1746. F.A.
　,,　　　John, Drogheda, alderman　1756. F.A.
　,,　　　John Richard, Dublin, gent.　1774. F.A.
　,,　　　Mary, St. Peter's St., Dublin,
　　　　widow　　　　　　　　　　1777. F.A.
　,,　　　Mary, relict of Robert B.　1777. F.A.
　,,　　　Richard, Scribblestown, Co. Dublin,
　　　　Esq.　　　　　　　　　　1678. F.A.
　,,　　　Robert, Galway　　　　1777. F.A.
　,,　　　Roger, Killognea, King's Co., gent　1738. F.A.
Brounfield. *See* Brunfield.
Browkes or Brookes, John, Trumpeter, Dublin
　　　　　　　　　　　　　　Dated 1632. Dub.

Brown, David, par. of Magheragall, Co. Antrim,
yeoman, 1687. Eu.
„ David 1698. Eu. Connor
„ George, Neale, Co. Mayo, Esq. 1737. F.A.
„ James, Aghohill Dated 1688/9. Eu.
„ James, Junr., Island Magee 1694. Eu.
„ James, parish of Connor, Co. Antrim
Dated 1711. S.3.
„ John, Island Magee Dated 1694. Eu.
„ John, Carnaglish, par. of Kilard, Co.
Antrim 1695. Eu.
„ John, Drumaquern, Co. Antrim
Dated 1700. S.3.
„ John, The Neale, Co. Mayo, Esq. 1712. F.A.
„ Julia, Dublin, widow of John B., Neal,
Co. Mayo, Esq. 1729. F.A.
„ Matthew, Dublin Dated 1652. Dub.
„ Samuel 1806. S.4. (H.I.)
„ Thomas, Carlow, gent. 1743. W.P.
„ William, Islandmagee, Co. Antrim 1738. S.3.
Browne, Alexander, Ballymore [1578]. Dub.
„ Alexander, Dublin 1699. Dub.
„ Ambrose, Grangegorman 1615. Dub.
„ Andrew, Waterford, merchant 1660. Dub.
„ Anne, Dublin, widow 1689. Dub.
„ Christopher, Dublin, baker Dated 1633. Dub.
„ Christopher, Dublin, baker Dated 1638. Dub.
„ Daniel, Jobstowne, Co. Dublin, gent.
Dated 1702. Dub.
„ David, Loughtowne, Co. Dublin,
farmer Dated 1631. Dub.
„ Francis Dated 1634. Dub.
„ Garthrit, Ballymore Eustace, Co.
Dublin, widow 1687. Dub.
„ George, D.D., Provost of Trin. Coll.
Dub. 1699. S.2.P.
„ James, Dublin, miller Dated 1638. Dub.
„ James, Dublin, bricklayer [1669]. Dub.
„ James, Limerick, merchant 1782. S.1.P.
„ John, Dublin, merchant D. 1616. Dub.
„ John, Dublin, yeoman Dated 1633. Dub.
„ John, Kirkirmane, parish of Carn-
castle 1639. Eu.
„ John, Bandonbridge, Co. Cork, mer-
chant 1669. W. Cork
„ John Dated 1683. Dub.

Browne, John, Dublin, sergeant in Charlemont's
　　　　Regt.　　　　　　　　　　　1704. Dub.
　,,　　Mabell, [Dublin, spinster]　　1668. Dub.
　,,　　Martin, Clonfad　　　　　　1790. Ky.
　,,　　als. Sedgrave, Mary, Dublin, widow
　　　　　　　　　　　　　　Dated 1649. Dub.
　,,　　Mary, widow of Rev. Richard B.　1722. F.
　,,　　Nicholas, senr., Dublin, baker
　　　　　　　　　　　　　　Dated 1620. Dub.
　,,　　Nicholas, Coolocke　　　Dated 1700. Dub.
　,,　　Patrick, Corduffe, par. of Lusk, inn-
　　　　keeper　　　　　　　　　　1681. Dub.
　,,　　Obadiah, Dublin, Doctor of Music　1715. F.A.
　,,　　Peter, Bishop of Cork and Ross　1735. F.A.
　,,　　Richard, Coolcower, Co. Cork　1712. F.
　,,　　Richard, Dublin, baker　　Dated 1607. Dub.
　,,　　Richard, Dublin, tailor　　Dated 1640. Dub.
　,,　　Richard, Kinsale, Co. Cork, burgess　1661. Dub.
　,,　　Robert　　　　　　　　　Dated 1598. Dub.
　,,　　"Sir Robert, Minister of the Petti-
　　　　comons." [Rev., Petty Canon St.
　　　　Patrick's]　　　　　　　Dated 1640. Dub.
　,,　　Robert, Magheraleave, par. of Derry-
　　　　aghy, Co. Antrim　　　　　1694. Eu.
　,,　　Roger, Dublin　　　　　　Dated 1654. Dub.
　,,　　Stephen, Dublin　　　　　Dated 1670. Dub.
　,,　　Symon, [Castleheny, Co. Dublin, far-
　　　　mer]　　　　　　　　　Dated 1652. Dub.
　,,　　Thomas, Kinsale, burgess　Dated 1659. Dub.
　,,　　Thomas, Dublin, glover　　　1700. Dub.
　,,　　Valentine, Dublin　　　　　1801. C.D.B.
　,,　　Walter, Dublin, shoemaker　1623. Dub.
　,,　　William, Cork, mariner　　　1614. F. and Davis
　,,　　William, [? of the Pill, St. Michan's],
　　　　yeoman　　　　　　　　Dated 1621. Dub.
　,,　　William, Dublin, smith　　　1648. Dub.
　,,　　William, Dublin, cornet　　1654. Dub.
　,,　　William, Coleraine　　　　　1691. Eu.
　,,　　William, Dublin, coachmaker Dated 1701. Dub.
Brownelow, James, senior, Dublin, gent.　1707. Dub.
Brownerigg, John, [Dublin]　　　Dated 1699. Dub.
Browning, John, Dublin　　　　　1703. Dub.
　,,　　William, Clanmorrishmeen, Co.
　　　　Waterford　　　　　Dated 1658. Dub. and F.2.
Brownloe, William, senr., Ballywilly, Co.
　　　　Armagh　　　　　　　　1703. W. Armagh

Brownlow, als. Chamberlain, Arthur, Brown-
        lowsderry, Co. Armagh, Esq.   1711. W. Armagh
,,   Jane, relict of Arthur B., of Lurgan,
        Esq.   1721. W.P.
,,   William, Brownlowsderry, Co Ar-
        magh, Esq.   1739. W.P.
Brownlowe, als. Chamberlain, John, Nislerath,
        Co. Louth   1716. W.P.
,,   Standish, Esq.   1716. W.P.
,,   Sir William, Brownlowsderry, Co.
        Armagh, Knt.   Dated 1660. W.P.
Brownly, Martin, Usher's Quay, Dublin   1803. C.D.B.
Brownrigg, Abraham, Rahenduff, Co. Wexford 1790. Swan. P.
,,   Henry John, Southampton, late of
        L'Orient, France   1847. Swan. P.
,,   John, York St., Dublin, barrister-
        at-law   1797. Swan. P.
,,   Thomas, Lagan, Co. Wexford   1696. F.2.
Bruce, John, Shandon, Co. Cork   1631. F. Cork
,,   Jonathan, Dean of Kilfinora and R. of
        Charleville, Co. Cork   Dated 1757. F.2.
Brudnell, Francis, Ballyguile, Co. Limerick,
        gent.   1772. F.A.
Bruen, Elenor Catherine, York Street, Dublin,
        spinster   1798. F.A.
,,   Henry, Dublin, gent.   Admon. 1700. F.A.
,,   Henry, Oak Park, Co. Carlow, Esq. 1796. F.A.
,,   Moses, Boyle   1757. F.A.
Brunfield or Brounfield, Adam, Dublin, turner 1674. Dub.
Bruninge, Robert, Co. Meath, clk.   Dated 1655. Dub.
Brunker, Brabazon, Rockcorry, Co. Monaghan
        Dated 1802. Swan. Clogher
,,   Catherine, Fairfield, Co. Monaghan 1812. Swan. Clogher
,,   Ralph, Dundalk, Co. Louth   Dated 1705. Swan. Drogheda
,,   Ralph, Cootehill, Co. Cavan   1799. Swan. P.
,,   Thomas, Dunleer, Co. Louth   1724. Swan. Drogheda
,,   Thomas, Carlingford   1754. Swan. Drogheda
,,   Thomas, Belgreen, Co. Cavan   1808. Swan. P.
Brunton, Anne, Dublin, widow   1706. Dub. and W.
        Dublin
,,   Anthony, Thomas Court, Dublin   1690. Dub. and W.
        Dublin
,,   Anthony, Dublin, merchant   1741. Swan. P.
,,   William, Cabra Lane, Co. Dublin,
        yeoman   1707. Dub. and W.
        Dublin

Brush, Francis, Dublin   Dated 1691. Dub.
Bruton, John, Newcastle, Diocese of Dublin
         Dated 1656. Dub.
Bryan, James, Capel St., Dublin   Admon. 1720. Ir.
  ,,   James, Ballintemple   1747. Ir.
  ,,   John, Ringsend, Co. Dublin, merchant
         Admon. 1715. Ir.
  ,,   Sir Lawrence, Dublin, [Rev.] chaplain
         Dated 1598. Dub.
       Margaret, Dublin, widow   Dated 1643. Dub.
       Patrick, Dublin, Esq.   Admon. 1661. Ir.
  ,,   Patrick   Admon. 1684. Ir.
  ,,   Patrick, Dublin, minor   Admon. 1720. Ir.
  ,,   Patrick, Ballinapark, Co. Wicklow   1783. Ir.
  ,,   Patrick, Harold's Cross, Dublin, farmer   1804. C.D.B.
  ,,   Peter, Wicklow, farmer   Admon. 1744. Ir.
  ,,   Pierse, Queen's Co., Esq.   1711. Ir.
  ,,   William, Davidstown   1807. Ir.
Bryce, Richard, Dublin, merchant   Dated 1616. Dub.
Brymingham, als. Kenedy, Jane, Dublin   1615. Dub.
Bryne [? Byrne], Charles, Dublin, merchant   [1680]. Dub.
Buchanan, née Allin, Anne   Dated 1800. Swan.
Buchmore, Richard, Miltowne, Co. Kildare,
         miller   Dated 1637. Dub.
Buchinger, Matthew, Dublin   1739. S.I.P.
Buckeley (Bulkeley), Richard, Dublin, brewer   1717. F.A.
Buckland, William, Chiddock, Co. Dorset,
         [Dublin]   Dated 1654. Dub.
Buckley. *See* Brickley.
Buckly, John, Kilkenny   1660. Dub.
Budds, William, Dolphin's Barn, Co. Dublin,
         yeoman   1669. Dub.
Buggell, Richard   [1659] Dub.
Bulkeley, Alice, [Oldbawne, Tallagh], widow
         Dated 1652. Dub.
  ,,   John, Bray   Dated 1685. Dub.
  ,,   Katherine, Balgady, widow   Dated 1574. Dub.
  ,,   Thomas, Dunkilt, clk.   1679. W. Ossory
  ,,   Thomas, Kilkenny, gent.   1720. W. Ossory
  ,,   *See* Buckeley.
Bulkelly, Rev. Darby, Prospect Hill, Co. Limerick, R.C. Priest [N.F.P.]   1813. C.D.B.
Bulkely, John, Mallow, clk.   1702. W. Cloyne.
Bulkley, John, Ballyfermott, [Co. Dublin]   1701. Dub.
Bull, Nathaniel, Grenanstown, Co. Meath,
         Esq.   1738. W.P.

Bullar, Edward, Loghanstown, Co. Dublin
	Dated 1691. Dub.
Bullen, Catherine, Kilroe, Co. Cork	1734. F.P. and F.B.
„	Edward, Loghanstowne, Tullah	1691. Dub.
„	Edward, Old Head, Co. Cork, gent.	1737. F.2.
Bullinbrooke, John	1698. Ir.
Bullock, Michael, Lernamoyle, Co. Fermanagh
	Dated 1723. Swan. Kilmore
Bullocke, John, Vicar-Choral, Christ Church,
	Dublin	Dated 1619. Dub.
Bulmore, Thomas, Dublin, gent.	Dated 1695. Dub.
Bulteel, Dominick, Vicar of Outragh, Co.
	Leitrim	Admon. 1743. Ir.
„	Isaac, Dublin, merchant	1724. Ir.
„	John, Derevackney, Co. Cavan	1804. Ir. and Swan.
		Kilmore
„	Sanford, Ballynamore, par. of Outragh,
	Co. Leitrim	Admon. 1745. Ir.
„	Susanna, Dublin, widow	1732. Ir.
Bunbury, Anne, Kilfeacle, Co. Tipperary,	1749. S.1. Cashel
	widow
„	Benjamin, Killerig, Co. Carlow	1716. B.
„	Benjamin, Carlow, Esq.	1747. F.2.
„	Benjamin, Kilfeacle, Co. Tipperary,
	Esq.	Dated 1765. F.2.
„	Benjamin	1792. F.2.
„	Elizabeth, widow of Sir [Gerard]
	Irvine	1735. F.2.
„	Henry, Dublin, merchant	1682. F.2.
„	John, Mallow	Dated 1766. F.2.
„	Joseph, Johnstown, Co. Carlow,	1730. F.2.
	Esq.
„	Joseph	1769. F.2.
„	Mary, Killerig, Co. Carlow	1711. B.
„	Mathew, Kilfeacle, Co. Tipperary,
	Esq.	1733. F.2.
„	Robert, Portarlington	Dated 1790. F.2.
„	Susanna Priscilla, widow of Thomas
	B. of Carlow	1797. F.2.
„	Rev. Thomas, Ballyseskin, Co. Wex-
	ford, clk.	1682. F.2.
„	Thomas, Tipperary, Esq.	1773. F.A.
„	Thomas, Kill, Co. Carlow, Esq.	1781. F.2.
„	Thomas, Dublin, Esq.	1781. F.2.
„	Thomas, Clontarf, Co. Dublin	1791. F.2.
„	Rev. Thomas, Castlemartyr, Co.
	Cork	1793. F.2.

Bunbury, Walter, Dublin, merchant. 1690. F.2.
„ William, Lisnavale, Co. Carlow, Esq. 1755. F.2.
„ William, Mount Temple, Co. Tipperary, Esq. 1772. F.2.
Bunn, Dorothy, Co. Wicklow, widow. Admon.
    Not dated   Ir.
„ Nicholas, Dublin, butcher   Dated 1699. Dub.
Bunting, Henry, Dublin, soldier   Dated 1669. Dub.
Bunworth, Rev. Peter, Newmarket   Dated 1750. F.
Burcham, John, [St. Nicholas Without], Dublin, weaver   1690. Dub.
„ John, Dublin, butcher   Dated 1691. Dub.
Burchell. *See* Bourchell.
Burdan, Anne. *See* Birne.
Burden, or Burney, James   Dated 1653. Dub.
Burder, Richard, Dublin, plumer   Dated 1654. Dub.
Burdett (or ? Broderick,) Rev. George, (? Burleigh)   1739. Swan.
„ Sir Thomas, Garrahill, Co. Carlow, Bart.   Dated 1724. F.2.
Burges, Jane, Dublin, widow   1674. Dub.
„ Robert, Dublin, gent.   Dated 1665. Dub.
Burgess, Thomas, senr., Labacally, Co. Cork, gent.   1713. W. Cork
Burke, als. Lynch, als. Garvey, Annabel. *See* Keaghry.
„ Mrs. Anne   Dated 1872. Mol.
„ Anne B.   Dated 1861. Mol.
„ als. Power, Cisly, Loughrea, widow   1770. S.1.
„ Sir David, Bart.   1661. F.2.
„ Edward, Tullery, Co. Galway, gent.   1753. Cr. Tuam
„ Ellis, Kinturk, now of Coole Lodge   1789. S.4. Tuam
„ Gerald, Dublin, Esq.   1741. Cr. P.
„ Herbert, Carrowe, Co. Galway   1748. Cr. Tuam
„ Father Hubert, P.P., of Arnaghdown, Co. Galway   1714. Cr. Tuam
„ John, Birr, King's Co.   1741. Cr. P.
„ als. Maughon, Hannah, Cregeene, Co. Galway   1768. S.1. Clonfert
„ Margery, Killskeagh, Co. Galway, widow   Dated 1761. Cr. P.
„ Mary, Birr, King's Co., widow   1767. Cr. P.
„ Mary, Dublin, spinster   1802. C.D.B.
„ Myles, Co. Galway   1698. Ir.
„ Nicholas, Prospect Hill, Galway   Not dated   S.2.

Burke, Sylvester, Loughrea, gent. 1767. S.1. Clonfert
„ Thomas, Pallice, Co. Galway, Esq. 1657. Dub.
„ Thomas, Creggeen, Co. Galway, gent. 1756. S.1. Clonfert.
„ Sir Thomas, Marble Hill, Co. Galway,
  Bart. 1813. S.1.P. and C.D.B.
„ Ulick, Clare, Galway 1670. Ir.
„ William, Lt. in Galway Regt. of Militia 1804. C.D.B.
Burn, Mathew, Dublin, saddler Dated 1705. Dub.
Burnell, Richard, [? Garranes], Barony
  Duhallow, Co. Cork 1664. F.2.
Burnett, Walter, Dublin, gent. Dated 1695. Dub.
Burney (or Burden), James Dated 1653. Dub.
Burridge, als. Moore, Frances, widow or wife
  of Rev. Ezekiel B. [? 1725]. F.2.
Burrowes, Ann, Butlerstown, Co. Cork, widow 1725. W. Cork
„ Ellen, Carn (Cavan) 1830. Swan. P.
„ Isaac Bredin, Shasbring, Lancaster,
  Penn., U.S.A. [N.F.P.] 1857. Swan. P.
„ James, Kinsale, merchant 1713. Swan. and W. Cork
„ Mrs. Margory 1806. Swan. Kilmore
„ Peter 1807. S.4. (H.I.)
„ Robert, Major in Waller's Regt.
  Dated 1658. Dub.
„ Robert, Killegone 1733. Swan.Kilmore
„ Thomas, Kinsale, merchant 1683. Swan. and W. Cork
„ Thomas, Stradone, Co. Cavan, gent. 1679. F.2.
„ Thomas, Cavan 1812. Swan. P.
„ Thomas, Rathdown, [Co. Wicklow,
  innkeeper] Dated 1692. Dub.
Burt, John, Castle Street, Dublin, tailor 1689. W.P.
Burton, Rev. Edmund, Dean of Killala,
  Tuam 1817. B.
„ Giles, Roper's Rest, Co. Dublin,
  skinner 1704. Dub.
„ John, victualler Dated 1678. Dub.
Bury, John, Shannon Grove, Co. Limerick 1722. B. and F.A.
„ John, Dublin, Spanish leather dresser 1664. Dub.
Bushop, Margery, Ludlow, Salop, widow 1682. Dub.
Bussell, Briscoe, Cork Dated 1669. F.
Busteed, Thomas, Jordanstown, Co. Cork 1677. F.
Butler, Amy, Dublin, widow [1565]. Dub.
„ Edmond, Kilkenny, Esq. 1785. F.D.
„ Edmund, Killinscar, Co. Kilkenny, gent.
  Dated 1635. Dub.

Butler, Gilbert, Tinehensy 1679. Dub.
„ Capt. James Bagshaw 1796. S.4. (H.BM.)
„ John, Dublin, shoemaker Dated 1678. Dub.
„ Hon. John, Clerk of the Pipe 1790. Ir.
„ Jonathan, Bandon Bridge, Co. Cork
  Dated 1657. Dub.
„ Mary [widow] Dated 1656. Dub.
„ Peter, Dublin, corn chandler Dated 1679. Dub.
„ Peter, Bunnahow, Co. Clare 1788. S.4. and M.
„ Richard, Dunleckny, Co. Carlow, clk. 1655. Dub.
„ Robert, Charlotteville, Carlow 1835. B.
„ Susanna, Cornmarket, widow Dated 1682. Dub.
„ Theobald Fitzwilliam, Raleyn, Co. Tipperary
  Dated 1649. Dub.
„ Thomas, Castlemartin 1616. Dub.
„ Whitwell 1798. S.4. (H.I.)
Butterworth, Isaac, Killester, Co. Dublin
  Dated 1671. Dub.
Buttolph, Anne, Stephen's Green, Dublin widow
  1685. Dub.
Butts, Abraham, [Patrick's Street] Dated 1649. Dub.
Bybbye [Bibby], Thomas, Bristol 1625. Dub.
Byckton, James, Dublin, yeoman Dated 1553. Dub.
„ James, Dublin, yeoman [1640]. Dub.
Byersall, Robt., Finglas, gent. Dated 1596. Dub.
Bygoe, Philip, Newtown, King's Co. 1664. F.P.
Byland, Thomas, Dublin, tailor Dated 1679. Dub.
Byrforde, Richard, Dublin, tallow chandler
  Dated 1599. Dub.
Byrforthe, Walter, Dublin Dated 1561. Dub.
Byrn, Gerald, Ballyronan, Co. Wicklow, gent.
  Dated 1617. Dub.
„ John, Dublin, weaver Dated 1699. Dub.
Byrne [Bryne], Callough, Courtpoll, Co. Wicklow, Esq.
  Dated 1623. Dub.
„ Charles, Dublin 1680. Dub.
„ Christopher, [Knockdreet, Co. Wicklow, farmer]
  Dated 1677. Dub.
„ Daniel, Ballydochan, Co. Wicklow, gent.
  Dated 1634. Dub.
„ Daniel, Wicklow, merchant 1708. Dub.
„ Darby, Dromin, Co. Wicklow Dated 1682. Dub.
„ Denis, Miltowne, [Co. Wicklow] 1688. Dub.
„ Donogh McDowling, Knockfadoe, Co. Wicklow, gent.
  Dated 1636. Dub.
„ Dontie [? Dudley] Dated 1632. Dub.

Byrne, Dowllyn McDonough, Knockefade, Co.
　　　　Wicklow, gent.　　　　　　Dated 1630. Dub.
　„　Dudley, Dublin　　　　　　　Dated 1632. Dub.
　„　Dudley, Banockemurrogh, [Co. Wick-
　　　　low]　　　　　　　　　　　[1633]. Dub.
　„　Gerald　　　　　　　　　　Dated 1618. Dub.
　„　Hugh, Ballimanus, Co. Wicklow　1707. Dub.
　„　James, Patrick Street, Dublin, tanner　1634. Dub.
　„　James, Ensign　　　　　　　1792. S.4. (H.BM.)
　„　John, Courtfoyle, Co. Wicklow, gent.
　　　　　　　　　　　　　　　　Dated 1629. Dub.
　„　John, Dublin, merchant　　Dated 1673. Dub.
　„　Laughlin als. Mellaghlin McEdmond,
　　　　Little Bray　　　　　　　　　1620. Dub.
　„　Lawrence, Saggard, Co. Dublin　1812. C.D.B.
　„　Maria als. Madden als. Carroll, Ballagh-
　　　　araline, Queen's Co.　　　Admon. 1697. F.A.
　„　Miles, Dublin, gent.　　　　　　1686. Dub.
　„　Patrick　　　　　　　　　　Dated 1583. Dub.
　„　Richard, New Street, shearman　Dated 1637. Dub.
　„　Richard, Dublin, cutler　　　Dated 1672. Dub.
　„　Teige　　　　　　　　　　　Dated 1653. Dub.
　„　Thady, Gallanstown, Co. Dublin, gent.
　　　　　　　　　　　　　　　　Dated 1652. Dub.
　„　Thomas Carey　　　　　　　1813. S.4. (H.O.,
　„　Tirloghe, Tomore, Co. Wicklow, gent.　[1639]. Dub.
　„　William, Ladicastell, Co. Kildare, yeo-
　　　　man　　　　　　　　　　Dated 1626. Dub.
Byron, Capt. John　　　　　　　Dated 1679. Dub.
Byrtch, John, Dublin, Doctor in Physic
　　　　　　　　　　　　　　　　Dated 1655. Dub.
　„　[Birch], Robert, [Colmine]　Dated 1619. Dub.
Bytagh, Edward, Kilgveran, Co. Galway　1802. C.D.B.

Caddell, John, Moreton, near Swords, gent.
　　　　　　　　　　　　　　　　Dated 1603. Dub.
　„　John, Graigesallaghe, Co. Kildare　[1611]. Dub.
　„　Patrick, Moole [The Moote], par. of
　　　　Kylleghe, Co. Dublin　　　1581. Dub.
　„　Patrick　　　　　　　　　　　1651. Dub.
　„　See Cadell.
Caddle, Michael, [Worganstown]　Dated 1635. Dub.
Cade, Peter, New Street, cutler　　1636. Dub.
Cadell [Caddell], Robert, [Dublin]　Dated 1614. Dub.
Cadwell, Bartholomew, Dublin, baker　1693. Dub.

Caffery, Edmund, Palmerston, Co. Dublin, farmer Dated 1650. Dub.
Cahill, Edmond, Fossey, Queen's Co., gent. 1753. F.2.
„ John, Youghal, Co. Cork Dated 1741. F.2.
„ John, Castle Blunden, Co. Kilkenny, farmer 1792. F.2.
„ John, South Gt. George's St., Dublin 1798. F.2.
„ Michael, Carlow [Not dated. 1805–1814] C.D.B.
„ Moses, Clare, Co. Kildare, gent. 1794. F.2.
„ Patrick, Cavan, merchant 1783. F.2.
„ Richard, Dublin, shoemaker 1637. Dub.
„ Richard, Dublin 1784. F.2.
„ William, Killylough, Co. Cork, gent. 1733. F.2.
Caillon, Mark Anthony, St. James', Westminster. 1703. Dub.
Caldwell, Christopher, Old Court, Co. Dublin, gent. 1727. Swan. Dublin
„ Sir Henry, Bt., Castle Caldwell, Co. Fermanagh 1726. B.
„ John, City of Dublin, Esq. Dated 1726. Swan.
Calf, Peter, clerk Dated 1596. Dub.
Calffe, Martin, Rathcow Dated 1536. Dub.
Callaghan, Dennis, Glin, Co. Cork 1768. S.2.P.
„ Dennis, Charles Street, Dublin 1778. S.2.P.
„ Henry, Enniskerry, miller 1699. Dub.
„ James, Clones, Co. Monaghan 1813. C.D.B.
„ John, King Street, Dublin 1762. S.2.P.
„ Mary, Clonmeen 1750. S.1.P.
„ Olivia, Limerick, widow 1804. Mol. P.
„ Robert, Clonmeen, Co. Cork 1727. S.1.P.
„ Thomas, Fleet Street, Dublin 1812. C.D.B.
„ Timothy, Mallow, Co. Cork 1776. S.2.P.
„ *See* O'Callaghan.
Calvert, Thomas, Wexford, merchant 1698. W. Ferns
Camac, Jacob, Greenmount, Co. Louth 1785. S.4. (H.I.)
Cambie, Solomon, Castletown, Co. Tipperary 1792. S.1.P.
„ Solomon, Ballycolleton, Co. Tipperary 1713. S.1. Killaloe
„ Thomas, Ballycolleton, Co. Tipperary 1743. S.1. Killaloe
Campbell, Archibald, [Dublin] 1689. Dub.
„ Charles, Anaghmallen, Co. Monaghan 1788. Swan. P.
„ Duncan, [Murogh, Co. Wicklow] 1663. Dub.
„ Eleanor. *See* Kerr.
„ George, Dublin 1812. C.D.B.
„ Rev. Wm., clk., Shurle, Co. Longford 1739. Swan. P.

Campion, Thomas, Leitrim, Co. Cork 1700. F. and W. Cork
" Thomas, Cork, gent. 1747. W. Cloyne
Cane, Thomas, master gunner 1637. Dub.
Canning, George, junr., Garrachy, Co. Londonderry 1710. F.P.
" George, Coleraine, Co. Derry, Esq. 1646. Dub.
" Robert 1644. F.2.
Canny, Mathew, Castlefergus, Co. Clare 1813. C.D.B.
Cantfield [Cantfild], John, New Row, skinner 1670. Dub.
Cantrill, Isaac. Wife Eliz. [N.F.P.] Dated 1707. S.4. Kildare
" Thomas, Shanbegg, Queen's Co. Dated 1705. S.4. Kildare
Cantwell, Geffrey, Dublin Dated 1595. Dub.
Capel, Joseph, Cloghroe, Co. Cork Dated 1798. F.P.
Capore [Capron], Francis, Dungannon 1640. Dub.
Caprett, Christopher, soldier, Clarke's Company 1659. Dub.
Capton or Capon, Robert, Ballincollinbeg, King's Co. Dated 1666. S.4. Kildare
Carden, John, Templemore, senr. 1728. S.1.P.
" John, Donore, Queen's Co. 1767. S.4.P.
Cardiff, Matthew, Dublin 1803. C.D.B.
Carew, John, Youghal, Co. Cork, gent. Dated 1630. F.2.
" Lynn, Castletown, Co. Waterford, gent. 1722. F.2.
" Mark, Deane Rock, South Libs. of Cork, gent. 1769. F.A.
" Robert, Ballinamona, Co. of city of Waterford, Esq. 1721. F. and W.P.
Carey, Frances, Monalty, Co. Monaghan, widow 1804. C.D.B.
" Mary, Coleraine, Co. Derry 1755. Ir.
" Capt. Peter, BallymacPatrick, Co. Cork, Esq. Admon. 1674. F.2.
" Peter, Careyville, Co. Cork, Esq. Admon. 1714. F.2.
" William. *See* Keary.
Carique, Henry, Esq. 1672. Ir.
" William, Tralee, Co. Kerry Dated 1729. Ir.
Caris, Thomas, Dublin, perfumer 1701. Dub.
Carleton, Christopher, Derry, gent. 1706. F.A.
" Ellen, Knockanenny [? Knockanderry], Co. Tipperary, widow 1695. F.P. and F.2.
" George, Dublin, clerk of Crown and Hanaper, Ireland Dated 1670. Dub.
Isabel, Ballylekin, Queen s Co., widow Dated 1697. S.4. Kildare

Carleton, Isabella, Welshstown, Co. Cork
    widow   1714. F.A. and W.P.
„   John, Darling Hill, Co. Tipperary
     Dated 1730. F.P.
„   Lancelot, Little Carleton, Co. Fermanagh   [1695]. F.2.
„   Rev. Robert, Dean of Cork   1735. F.P. and F.A.
Carlile, Andrew, Ashgrove, Newry   1845. Swan. P.
„   David, Newry   1787. Swan.
Carlingford, Theobald Earl of   1739. F.D.
Carloe, Darley, Opharrell, Dio. Dublin
     Dated 1683. Dub.
Carlton, Christopher, Dublin, Esq.   1703. F.A.
Carly, Stephen, Askingarrin, Co. Wexford   1813. C.D.B.
Carlyle, William, Bracklone, King's Co.
     Dated 1712/13. S.4. Kildare
Carmichael, Richard, M.D.   Dated 1849. F.
Carmicke [Cormick], George, Dublin, gent.
     Dated 1650. Dub.
Carney, Sir Richard, Dublin, Knt.   1692. Dub.
Caroe [Carow], St. (or Sir) Dennis, [clerk]
     Dated 1584. Dub.
Caroll [Carroll], Henry   1657. Dub.
Carpenter, George, Newmarket, Dublin   1699. Dub.
„   Joshua, Sigginstown, Co. Kildare   1657. Dub.
„   Martha, Co. Dublin, widow Dated 1701. Dub.
„   Richard, Dublin, gent.   1691. Dub.
„   William, Limerick, gent.   1684. F. Limerick
Carr, George   1662. F.2.
„   Henry, Powerscourt, Co. Wicklow, farmer   1676. Dub.
„   James, Bridge Street, Dublin   1803. C.D.B.
Carrger [Carryer], John, trooper, Morgan's Troop   [1658]. Dub.
Carrick, Ann, Youghal, widow   1666. F.2.
„   Simon, Dublin, merchant   1701. Dub.
Carricke, Dennis, Dublin   Dated 1651. Dub.
Carrill or Carroll [Carroll], Patrick, Cabragh, gent.   1685. Dub.
Carroll, Anthony, Lisheenboy   1724. Ir.
„   Cael, Kildare   Dated 1666. S.4. Kildare
„   Clara. *See* Bloomfield.
„   David, Rathwalken, Co. Kildare
     Dated 1694. S.4. Kildare
„   Daniel, soldier, Charlemont's Regt.
     Dated 1703. Ir.

Carroll, Daniel, Kilcregan, 1724. Ir.
„ Daniel, Nenagh 1749. Ir.
„ James, Tulla, Co. Tipperary 1728. S.1.P.
„ John, Dublin 1795. Ir.
„ Michael, Killoran, Co. Galway 1749. S.1. Clonfert.
„ als. Madden, Maria. *See* Byrne.
„ Richard, Emmill, King's Co., gent.
  Admon. 1781. Ir.
„ Thomas, Dublin, alderman 1616. Dub.
„ Willian, Ballycrenode, Co. Tipperary 1706. S.1. Killaloe and Ir.
„ *See* Caroll, Carrill.
Carryer. *See* Carrger.
Carson, James, Bishop's Court, Co. Down
  Dated 1694. F.P.
Carstens, William, Dublin, furrier 1705. Dub.
Carsusan, Jacob, Stephen's Green, gent. 1701. Dub.
Carter, Anne 1660. Dub.
„ Charles, Dublin, sadler 1694. Dub.
„ Honora, Ballycarroll, Queen's Co., widow 1703. S.4. Kildare
„ John, the elder, Dublin, webster 1672. Dub.
„ Simon, Straffan, Co. Kildare, gent. 1633. Dub.
„ Thomas, Mochollop, tanner Dated 1641. Dub.
„ Thomas, Dunard, Co. Wicklow 1670. Dub.
Cartland, George, Dublin 1792. S.1.P.
Carton, John, Glasnevin 1621. Dub.
Cartt, John, Philipstown, King's Co. Dated 1670. S.4. Kildare
Cary, Arthur, Coleraine, alderman 1723. Ir.
„ Arthur, Derryard, Co. Derry, gent.
  Admon. 1774. Ir.
„ [Mrs.] Avis, Redcastle, Co. Donegal 1670. Ir.
„ Chichester, Derry Dated 1670. Ir.
„ Edward, Dungiven, Co. Derry 1668. Ir.
„ Elizabeth, Brookend, Co. Tyrone 1718. Ir.
„ Elizabeth, widow of George C., of Redcastle, Co. Donegal 1759. Ir.
„ Elizabeth, wife of Tristram C., of Bushfield, Co. Donegal, Esq. 1780. Ir.
„ George, Redcastle, Co. Donegal 1669. Ir.
„ George, Finglas, gent. Dated 1559. Dub.
„ George, Whitecastle, Co. Donegal
  Dated 1718. Ir.
„ George, Fleet Street, Dublin 1749. Ir.
„ George, Drumhagart, Co. Donegal 1749. Ir.
„ George, Coleraine, Port surveyor 1758. Ir.

Cary, George, Redcastle, Co. Donegal   1772. Ir.
„ George, Londonderry   1773. Ir.
„ Henry, Dungiven, Esq.   1757. Ir. and S.3.P.
„ Henry, Archdeacon of Killala   1769. M. and Ir.
„ Jane, Parish of Killowen, Co. Derry, spinster   1762. Ir.
„ John, Dublin, merchant   1621. Dub.
„ Lucy, Whitecastle, Co. Donegal   1775. Ir.
„ Mary, Coleraine   1755. Ir.
„ Mordecai, Bishop of Killala   1751. M.
„ Oliver   1786. S.4. (H.I.)
„ Patrick, St. Andrew's, Holborn, Middlesex   1672. Ir.
„ Peter, Hazelbrook, Co. Antrim, clerk   1758. Ir.
„ Robert, Whitecastle, Co. Donegal, Esq.   1682. Ir.
„ Rose, Athlone, Co. Westmeath   1744. Ir.
„ Susanna, Coleraine, Co. Derry, spinster   1736. Ir.
„ Tristram, Coleraine   1676. Ir.
„ Tristram, Moy, Co. Limerick, Esq.   1723. Ir.
„ Tristram, Raphoe, Co. Donegal, gent.   Admon. 1726. Ir.
„ William, Birdstown, Co. Donegal   Dated 1707. Ir.
„ William, Birdstown, Fawn Parish, Co. Donegal   1707. Ir.
Caryke, Catherine, Dublin, widow   Dated 1617. Dub.
Case, Robert, Dewlyn, gent, yeoman of the Crown   Dated 1621. Dub.
Casey, Charles, Cork   1804. C.D.B.
„ John, Cork, starchman   1747. W.
„ Michael, Cork   1803. C.D.B.
Cashel, Archibald Hamilton, Archb. of   1641. B.
„ Malcolm Hamilton, Archb. of   1627. B.
Cashin, Thomas, Athy, tanner   1660. Dub.
„ Walter, Athy, tanner   1669. Dub.
Casie, Laurence, Lusk, gent.   1608. Dub.
„ Robert, Dublin, gent.   1651. Dub.
Casse, Laurence   Dated 1574. Dub.
Cassidy, Mary Anne, Newtown Avenue, Blackrock, Dublin   1813. C.D.B.
Casson, William, Donore, clothier   Dated 1650. Dub.
Castlefranc, Josias de, Ensign   Dated 1695. Dub.
Castle, Col. James, Dublin   1649. Dub.
„ Richard, Dublin, Esq.   1750. S.1.P.
Castleconnell, Edmond, Lord Baron of   [? Dated] 1638. F.E.

IN THE GENEALOGICAL OFFICE, DUBLIN 135

Casy, John, the Newton of Killmenane by
    Dublin [Kilmainham]   Dated 1599. Dub.
  "   William, Dublin, merchant   Dated 1603. Dub.
Cathcart, Allan, Enniskilling, Co. Fermanagh,
    Esq.   1720. W. Clogher
  "   Anna, Belcoo, Co. Fermanagh, widow 1735. W.P.
Catherye, Madame [de] la   1702. Dub.
Caulfeild, Sir Toby, 1st Lord Charlemount   1627. F.F.
  "   William   Dated 1670. F.
Caulfield, St. George, Donamon, [Co. Galway] 1778. F.A.
  "   St. George, Donamon, Co. Galway,
    Esq.   1810. F.A.
Caunt, William   1641. Dub.
Causabon, Thomas, Youghal   1673. F.2. and W.
     Cloyne
Cavan, Charles Lambert, Earl of   1660. B.
  "   Richard Lambert, Earl of   1742. B.
Cavanagh, Bryan, Newtown, Co. Carlow, gent. 1730. Cav. P.
  "   Derby, Ballenvallin, Dio. Leighlin
     D. 1678. Cav. P.
  "   Donnough McCahir, Moneyglass   1633. Cav. Ferns
  "   Harriet. *See* Kempstone.
  "   Kennedy, New Ross, Co. Wexford   1781. B. and Cav. P.
  "   Langrish, New Ross, merchant   1808. Cav. P.
  "   Laurence, Pimlico, brewer   1714. Cav. Dublin
  "   Morgan, Burrys   Dated 1670. Cav. Leighlin
  "   Murtagh, King St., Dublin   1707. Cav. P.
  "   *See* Kavanagh.
Cave, Andrew, Donnybrook, Co. Dublin   1718. B.
  "   Andrew, Brickfield, parish Donnybrook 1686. Dub.
  "   Elizabeth, [Dublin], widow   1690. Dub.
  "   Elizabeth, Dublin   1690. B.
  "   Thomas, Dublin   1637. B.
  "   Thomas, Dublin   1639. B.
Cave, Vincent, Archdeacon, Elphin   1669. B.
Cavenagh, Darby, Rathoe, Co. Carlow   1741. Cav. Leighlin
  "   Dennis, Dublin, hatter   1751. Cav. P.
  "   Edward, Dublin   1664. Cav. P.
  "   Griffin, Stillebegges, Co. Wexford 1679. Cav. Ferns
  "   James, Athy, Co. Kildare   1686. Cav. P., and
     Dub.
  "   James, Dublin, yeoman   1727. Cav. Dub.
  "   Matthew, Wexford   Dated 1819. Cav. P.
  "   Wentworth, New Ross, merchant 1795. Cav. P.
  "   *See* Kavanagh.
Cavinagh, James, Graige, Co. Kilkenny   1769. Cav. P.

Cawell, or Kavell, Cowell, Cormock, Dunshock,
   [Co. Dublin]   1638. B.
Chabert, Charles Andrew, St. Croix, West
   Indies   1801. C.D.B.
Chaddle, Robert, [Castle Street], surgeon 1666. Dub.
Chaigneau, Abraham, [? Dublin]   1780. Swan. P.
   „   D. [? David, Dublin]   1753. Swan.
   „   Jane. *See* Acheson.
   „   John, Dublin, gent.   1779. Swan. P.
   „   Lewis, Dublin   1724. Swan. P.
Chalk, Isaac, senr., Dublin, plasterer   1701. Dub.
Chalke, Jane, Dublin, widow   1702. Dub.
Challoner, Lucas (Luke), D.D. [Vice-Chancellor
   Dub. Univ.]   1613. Dub. and M.
Challonor, Thomas, Dublin, gent.   1676. Dub.
Chamberlain, Arthur. *See* Brownlow.
   „   John. *See* Brownlowe.
Chamberlaine, Elizabeth, Mountmellick,
   Queen's Co.   1802. C.D.B.
   „   John, Dublin, brewer   1701. Dub. and W.
                                                        Dublin
   „   Richard   Dated 1618. Dub.
   „   Robert, trooper at Naas   1658. Dub.
   „   Roger, Nizlyrath, Co. Louth,
          gent.   Dated 1625. Dub. and W.
                                                        Dublin
   „   als. Jans, Thomasine. *See* Crolly.
Chamberlin, John. *See* Chamberlaine.
Chamberline, Peter, Killenetower, Co. West-
   meath   1686. W.P.
Chamberlyn, John   Dated 1551. Dub.
   „   Michael, Dublin, alderman   1626. Dub.
Chambers, Susanna, wife of Thos. C., of Mangin,
   Co. Wexford   1768. W.
Chambre, Calcott, Carnew, Co. Wicklow   1635. B.
   „   Calcott, Carnew, Co. Wicklow   1638. B.
   „   John, Stormonstown, Co. Louth,
          Esq.   1670. W.P.
Chamney, Christopher, Keyle, Ferns   1729. B.
   „   Jane, Ballyshonock, Co. Wexford   1746. B.
   „   John, Ballard, Co. Wicklow   1733. B.
   „   Thomas, Ballyshonock, Co. Wex-
          ford   1727. B.
Champion, Jane, Cork   1687. W. Cork
   „   Thamzin, widow of Wm. C., of
          Cork   1689. W. Cork

Champion, William, senr., Cork, feltmaker   1668. W. Cork
Chandler, Thomas, Attlepeasse, Co. Dublin,
     farmer   Dated 1684. Dub.
Chaplaine, Elizabeth, Dublin, widow   1704. Dub.
Chaplin, Abraham, Ballindrin, Co. Wicklow,
     yeoman   1677. Dub.
   ,,   John, Dublin, feltmaker   1690. Dub.
Chapman, Arthur, Dublin, gardener   1660. Dub.
   ,,   Joseph, Rheban, Co. Kildare   1782. S.4. P.
   ,,   William, Killina, Westmeath, Esq. 1734. S.1. and W.P.
Chappel, Thomas, Rushtown, Co. Monaghan 1699. F.2.
Chappell, Robert, Athy, clothier   1637. Dub.
   ,,   Shelly   1654. Dub.
Charlemount, Sir Toby Caulfeild, Lord   1627. F.F.
Charles, James, Dublin, weaver   1706. Dub.
   ,,   Thomas, The Fort of Ballimore   1660. Dub.
Charlton, John, Aghabane, Co. Cavan   1678. B.
Charnocke, Geoffrey, [Kilmainham]   1621. Dub.
Chartres, John, Knockaloho, Co. Clare   1735. Mol. Killaloe
   ,,   John, Clondrala, Co. Clare   1767. Mol. Killaloe.
   ,,   John, Ennis, Co. Clare   1805. Mol. P.
   ,,   William, Cork, Esq.   1723. Mol. P.
   ,,   William, Cork   1740. Mol. P.
Chatterton, Sir James, City of Cork, Bart.   1806. S.1.P.
   ,,   Thomas, [Cork], mason   1733. Davis.
   ,,   Thomas, Cork   Dated 1733. pr. 1744. F.
Chearnley, Anne, Cappoquin, Co. Waterford,
     spinster   1813. C.D.B.
Cheatham, Eleanor, Dublin, widow   1696. F.2.
Cheevers, Christopher, Wexford   1602. Dub.
   ,,   Henry, Monkstown, [Co. Dublin],
     Esq.   1640. Dub.
   ,,   Thomas, Monkstown, [Co. Dublin]
     Dated 1651. Dub.
Chenerye, William, Wetherinsette, Co. Suffolk 1623. Dub.
Cherrye, Edward, Dublin, Esq.   Dated 1613. Dub.
Chester, Richard, Chesterfield, Cork   1778. Swan.
Chetham, Thomas, Hacketstown, Co. Dublin 1624. Dub. and B.
Chettle, Richard, [Dublin]   1637. Dub.
Chichester, Sir Arthur, Knt.   Dated 1621. Dub.
   ,,   John, Dungannon, Esq.   Dated 1657. Dub.
   ,,   Leonard, Dublin Castle, gent.
     Dated 1650. Dub.
   ,,   Mary. *See* Copley
Chillam, Patrick, Drogheda, alderman   1684. W.P.
   ,,   Robert, Drogheda, alderman   Dated 1632. W.P.

INDEX OF WILL ABSTRACTS

Chipeey [Chipsey], Edmond, Dublin, silk dyer
         Dated 1696. Dub.
Cholmondeley, Thomas, Hurleston, Co. Chester,
  [clerk]   1687. Dub.
Christian, Brabazon, Waterford, Esq. 1788. F.2.
  ,, Frances, Dublin, widow Dated 1686. Dub.
  ,, Rev. John, Kill, Co. Kildare, clk. 1773. F.2.
  ,, Michael, Dublin, merchant Dated 1692. F.2.
  ,, Rev. Patrick, Preb. of Killsossenty,
     Diocese of Lismore Dated 1687. F.2.
  ,, William, Old Grange, Co. Waterford,
     Esq.   1721. F.2.
Christmas, Elizabeth, widow   1770. F.A.
  ,, Richard, Waterford, Esq. 1723. F.A.
  ,, Thomas, Waterford, merchant 1704. F.A.
  ,, Thomas, Whitfield, Co. Waterford,
     Esq.   1747. F.A.
  ,, Thomas   Admon. 1749. F.A.
  ,, Thomas   1820. F.A.
  ,, William, clk., F., Trin. Coll. Dub. 1703. F.A.
  ,, William, Dublin, Esq.   1803. F.A.
Christofor [Christopher], Thomas, The Dow-
    lagh, Co. Dublin   1593. Dub.
Christopher, Patrick, Stubledekin Dated 1629. Dub.
Chudleigh, Thomas, Kinsale, shipwright 1707. F.
Chue, Edward, Dublin, weaver   1692. Dub.
Church, Hester   Dated 1657. Dub.
  ,, Jane, Dublin, formerly of Coleraine,
    spinster   1804. C.D.B.
Churchey, William, Dublin, yeoman 1621. Dub.
Chute, Francis, Tralee, Esq.   1753. Swan. P.
  ,, Rebecca, Montpelier Hill, Co. Dublin 1800. Swan. P.
  ,, Thos., Cork, merchant   1758. Swan. P.
Clanbrasill, Henry, Earl of   1675. Drogheda MSS.
Clancarty, Donough, Earl of Dated 1665. Gabbett MSS.
Clanchy, Roger   1655. Dub.
Clarcke [Clarke], Thomas, Corbally, Queen's
    Co.   1637. Dub.
Clare, Marmaduke, [Dublin, victualler] 1688. Dub.
  ,, Robert, Dublin, gent.   1612. Dub.
  ,, Thomas, [Cornmarket] Dublin, merchant 1650. Dub.
Clark, John   1699. Dub.
Clarke, Rev. Alexander, Lime Park, now of
    Ballycastle, Co. Antrim 1795. Swan.
  ,, Andrew   Dated 1702. Dub.
  ,, Andrew, Dublin   1690. B.

Clarke,	Ann, Dublin, widow	1752. W.P.
,,	Ann, Youghal, widow	1757. Swan.
,,	Daniel, Dublin, tailor	Dated 1641. Dub.
,,	Ellen, Drogheda, widow of Edward C., of Atherdee	1701. W. Armagh
,,	Gabriel, Lisnalea, Kilkenny	1729. F.
,,	George, Danesfort, [Kilkenny], servant	1658. Dub.
,,	Henry, Anaghsamry, Co. Armagh, Esq.	1727. Swan. and W.P.
,,	Hugh	Dated 1650. Dub.
,,	James, Proudstown, Co. Meath	1691. B.
,,	James, Dublin	1718. B.
,,	James, Dublin	1759. Swan.
,,	John	Dated 1650. Dub.
,,	John, [Patrick Street], Dublin, baker	1674. Dub.
,,	John, Portadown, Co. Armagh, gent.	1691. W.P.
,,	John, Carlow, publican	1812. C.D.B.
,,	als. Dupon, Mary, Woodpark, Co. Dublin, widow	1800. S.4. Dublin
,,	Mary, Dublin	Dated 1650. Dub.
,,	Michael, Dublin, Esq.	1774. Ir.
,,	Prudence, Portadown, Co. Armagh, widow	1727. W.P.
,,	Simon, Dublin	1729. W.P.
,,	Thomas, Drogheda	1630. B.
,,	Thomas, Dublin	1625. Dub.
,,	Thomas, Drumantine, Co. Down	1672. B.
,,	Thomas, Ardress, Co. Armagh	1708. W. Armagh
,,	See Clarcke, Clearke.	
Clarkson,	Thomas, Dublin, hosier	1701. Dub.
Clarksone,	John, Cullenadery, Co. Wicklow	Dated 1667. Dub.
Clarxton,	or Claxon, Thomas, Donard, [Co. Wicklow]	1683. Dub.
Clay,	Henry, Double Mills, par. of St. Nicholas, [Donore], miller	1717. Dub.
Claye,	Walter, Marshal to Archbishop of Dublin	1665. Dub.
Clayton,	Edward	1799. S.4. (H.I.)
,,	James, Dublin, musician	Dated 1666. Dub.
,,	John, Dean of Kildare	1726. B.
,,	Margaret	1696. B.
,,	Margaret, spinster	1696. F.P.
,,	Randall, Mallow, or Moyallow, Esq.	1684. F.P. and F.2.
,,	Robert, Dublin	1722. B.
Cleare	[Cleer], Mable, Dublin, widow	1691. Dub.
,,	Nicholas, Baldonan	Dated 1633. Dub.

Cleare, Robert, Dublin, gent. 1699. Dub.
Clearke, Lawrence, of the Baye 1576. Dub.
  ,, [Clarke], Susan, als. Usher Dated 1650. Dub.
Cleer, James, Dublin, weaver 1691. Dub.
  ,, *See* Cleare.
Cleere, James Dated 1569. Dub.
  ,, Patrick, Dublin, merchant Dated 1634. Dub.
  ,, Patrick, Dublin, merchant Dated 1701. Dub.
Cleghorne, William, [Lazy Hill, Werburgh's],
        Dublin, mariner Dated 1666. Dub.
Clement, Christopher, Lazy Hill, innkeeper 1680. Dub.
Clements, Christopher, Dublin, innkeeper
        Dated 1620. Dub.
  ,, Major Henry 1654 Dub. and Dated 1650. S.1.P.
  ,, Major Henry, Col. Johnson's Regt.
      of Foot 1745. Swan. P.
  ,, Richard, Cork, merchant 1692. F.2.
Clemett, John, senr., par. of Powerscourt, Co.
      Wicklow, parish clerk Dated 1698. Dub.
Clench, William, Finglas, gent. 1634. Dub.
Clere, Edmd., Newcastle, Co. Dublin, farmer [?]1691. Dub.
Clerke, John, Beye in par. of Mulhuddart
        Dated 1599. Dub.
  ,, Susanna, Dublin, widow 1657. Dub.
Cliffe, Anthony, Dungulph, Co. Wexford, gent. 1729. W. Ferns
  ,, Anthony, formerly of New Ross, late of
      par. of St. Michael, Worcester 1803. C.D.B.
  ,, Eleanor, Dungulph, Co. Wexford, widow 1700. W. Ferns
  ,, John, Dungulph, Co. Wexford, Esq. 1691. W.P.
  ,, John, New Ross, Esq. Dated 1727. W.P.
  ,, Loftus, Blarney, Co. Cork, Esq. 1729. W.P.
  ,, Robert, Sandbach, Chester, chirurgeon 1666. F.2. and W.P.
Clifford, Rt. Hon. Edward Baron de 1833. S.2. P.
  ,, Joseph 1693. W. Cork
  ,, Mary, Dublin, widow 1683. Dub.
  ,, Mathew, St. Audoen's, Dublin, tailor [1680]. Dub.
  ,, Miller, Castleannesey 1711. F.P.
  ,, William, Castle Annesly otherwise
      Maurice Castle, Co. Wexford, Esq. 1785. F.D.
Clince or Clune or Cline or Clinch [Clince],
      James Kilmartin, [Mallaghiddart],
      Dio. Dublin, farmer Dated 1676. Dub.
Clinch, Elizabeth, [St. Nicholas Without], Dub-
      lin 1640. Dub.

Clinch, James, Tubberrogan, Co. Dublin, farmer — Dated 1633. Dub.
  „ Laurence, Finglas — 1617. Dub.
Clinton, Arthur, Dublin, gent. — 1721. W. Dublin
  „ James, Clintonstowne, Co. Louth, Esq. — 1656. Dub. and W. Dublin
Close, Elizabeth, Lisburn, spinster — 1744. Swan. P.
Clotworthy, James, Monnimore, Londonderry — 1659. Dub.
Cloud, John, Knockmoura, Co. Cork, yeoman — 1678. W. Cork
Clowes, Thomas, Kilternan, Barony Rathdown — 1689. Dub.
Cloyne, Charles Crow, Bishop of — 1726. S.1.P.
  „ George Synge, Bishop of — 1663. F.2.
Clutterbuck, Richard, Derryluskin, Co. Tipperary — 1739. S.1.P.
Clune or Cline or Clinch, James. *See* Clince.
Clynton, Thomas — 1601. [? 1637]. Dub.
  „ Walter, Dublin — [1577]. Dub.
Coakley, Abraham, Curragh, Co. Cork — 1764. F.
  „ Darby, Clownings, par. Whitechurch — Dated 1663. Dub.
  „ Thomas, Gortahinny, Co. Kerry — Dated 1717. F.
Coan, John, baker — Dated 1586. Dub.
Coane, Anthony, Stradbally, Co. Tyrone, collector — 1757. Swan. P.
  „ Patience — 1790. Swan. P.
  „ Thady, Ballyshannon — 1723/4. Swan. P.
  „ William, Ballyshannon — 1789. Swan. P.
Coates, Catherine, Clinan, Co. Longford — 1802. S.4.
  „ Catherine, Clivein, Co. Longford, spinster — 1802. C.D.B.
  „ Ruth, spinster — 1821. S.4.
  „ Thomas, Newbridge, Co. Longford — 1809. S.4.
Coats, Robert, Dublin — 1700. Dub.
Cobb, Jane, Dublin, widow — Dated 1650. Dub.
  „ Thomas Alexander — 1836. S.4. (H.I.)
Cock. *See* Cook.
Cocke, John, Belturbet, Co. Cavan — 1658. Dub.
Cocks, Sarah, widow — 1679. W. Cork
Codd, Loftus, Castletown, Co. Wexford — 1696. W. Ferns
Coffey, Edward, [St. Bridget's] Dublin, baker — 1688. Dub.
Coghlan, Capt. John, Bandon, Co. Cork — 1709. F.
Cogly, Edmond, Dublin, cook — Dated 1634. Dub.
Coker, John, Dublin, gent. — Dated 1618. Dub.

Colclough, Adam, Tintern, Co. Wexford
                                   Dated 1651. Dub.
    ,,   Robert. *See* Leigh
    ,,   Sir Vesey, Tintern, Wexford, Bart.
                                   Dated 1794. M.
Colcoke [Colcock], Henry, Dublin   1650. Dub.
Cole, Capt. Abraham   1649. Dub.
    ,,   Andrew   Dated 1667. S.4. Kildare
    ,,   Francis, Ballileck, Co. Monaghan, Esq.
                                   Dated 1658. Dub.
    ,,   Robert, Dublin, merchant   Dated 1648. Dub.
    ,,   Thomas, Dublin, slater   1666. Dub.
Coleman, Anne, Drogheda, widow Dated 1803. C.D.B.
    ,,   Henry, Dublin, gent.   Dated 1661. Dub.
    ,,   James, Dublin, brewer   1695. Dub.
    ,,   Robert, Dublin, gent.   Dated 1680. Dub.
    ,,   Robert, Dublin, gilder   1689. Dub.
    ,,   *See* Collman.
Colemore, Abraham, Thomas Street, Co. Dublin,
          tanner   1706. Dub.
Coles, Samuel, Kildermod, Co. Wexford   1762. M.
Colgan, Richard, Dublin, baker   Dated 1624. Dub.
Colin, Patrick, Glassinmucky, Co. Dublin, far-
          mer   Dated 1698. Dub.
Colley, Dame Anne, Dublin, widow Dated 1650. Dub.
    ,,   Anne, Castlecarbury, Co. Kildare
                                   Dated 1686. S.4. Kildare
    ,,   Arthur, London, merchant   1772. S.1.
    ,,   Christopher, Dublin, gent.   1709. W.P.
    ,,   Frances, Dublin   1743. W.P.
    ,,   George, Rahin   1712. W.P.
    ,,   Henry, Castle Carbry, Co. Kildare, gent.
                                   Dated 1627. W.P.
    ,,   als. Cowley, Henry, Castlecarbry, Co.
          Kildare   1719. W.P.
    ,,   Sarah, Dublin   1746. W.P.
    ,,   Thomas, Killurin, King's Co.   1768. S.1.P.
    ,,   William, Edenderry, King's Co. 1646. W.P.
Collier, Nicholas, [? a soldier in Wade's Com-
          pany]   1656. Dub.
Collins, Barbara, Fleet Street, Dublin, widow 1813. C.D.B.
    ,,   James, Onagh, Co. Wicklow, farmer
                                   Dated 1699. Dub.
    ,,   James   1803. S.4. (H.I.)
    ,,   Patrick, trooper   Dated 1656. Dub.

Collion, Matthew, Killmurry, par. of Newcastle
                                             Dated 1625. Dub.
Collis, William, Dublin, merchant   1678. Dub.
Collman [Coleman], Ismay, Dublin   1625. Dub.
Colman [Coleman], Christopher, Dublin
                                             Dated 1635. Dub.
„   [Coleman], Thomas, Dublin, merchant 1625. Dub.
„   William, Castlecarbury, Co. Kildare
                                             Dated 1667. S.4. Kildare
Colson, John, Dublin, goldsmith   1629. Dub.
Colthurst, John, late of the Naas   1660. W.P.
„   John, Cooleneshanvally, Co. Cork 1681. F.2. and W.P.
„   Nicholas   Dated 1745. W. Ardfert
Colvill, Margaret, Wexford, widow   1686. F.2.
Comerford, Foulkes, Dublin, brewer   1700. Dub.
Comin, als. Power, Anstass, Blackcastle, Co.
       Kildare   Dated 1695. Dub.
Comyn, Edmund, Tullamayne, Co. Tipperary 1637. Dub.
„   Nicholas, Lisryan, Co. Longford, Esq.
               [Exor. renounces] 1744. Dub.
Conan, Cornelius, Kilbrack, Co. Kildare
                                           Dated 1719. S.4. Kildare.
„   William Nugent   1792. S.4. (H.BM.)
Conduitt, Deborah, Dame Street, widow 1675. Dub.
Coney, James, Baronstown, Co. Kildare
                                           Dated 1716. S.4. Kildare
Conian, Daniel, Rahine, Co. Dublin, farmer 1693. Dub.
Coniers [Conyers], Ralph   1665. Dub.
Conill [Connell], Richard, Tassagard   1622. Dub.
Coningham, Alexander, Dunduff, Co. Donegal 1747. B.
Connellan, Martin, Rahassane, Co. Galway 1801. C.D.B.
Connell, Abraham, Castlelyons   1785. Swan.
„   John, Irishtown, Co. Dublin   1680. F.P.
„   John, New Castle, near Lyons   1616. Dub.
„   Patrick, Ballygurtagh, Co. Meath 1802. C.D.B.
„   Richard, Dublin, tailor   Dated 1582. Dub.
„   *See* Conill.
Connelly, John, Morrell, Meath   1713. S.1.P.
„   Patrick, Ballybricken, Waterford 1812. C.D.B.
Connors, James, Killurin, King's Co. Dated 1719. S.4. Kildare
Connock, Richard, [trooper]   Dated 1658. Dub.
Connor, Ann. *See* Molony.
„   Bartholomew, Phecullen, Co. Kildare 1813. C.D.B.
„   Bryan, Dublin   1813. C.D.B.
„   Cornelius, Bandon   1719. F. Cork
„   Donnogh, Killen   Dated 1657. Dub.

INDEX OF WILL ABSTRACTS

Connor, Edward, Ballycarney, Co. Wexford   1813. C.D.B.
"   Honnor, Portarlington, Queen's Co.
                                            Dated 1719. S.4. Kildare
"   Hugh   Dated 1650. Dub.
"   als. Fitzharris, Mary, Dublin, widow   1672. Dub.
"   Mary, widow   1801. C.D.B.
"   Morragh, Ballinrahin, King's Co.
         [N.F.P.]   Dated 1668. S.4. Kildare
"   Walter, Dublin, gent.   1673. Dub.
"   William, Kildrought   Dated 1640. Dub.
Connye, Daniel   Dated 1620. Dub.
Connyngham, Robert, Minister of Taboyne
                                            Dated 1652. Dub.
Conolly, Mrs. Katherine, Castletown, Co. Kil-
         dare   1752. S.1.P.
"   Mathew, Kilgreag, Meath   1794. S.1.
"   Terence, Dundalk   1841. S.1.
"   Rt. Hon. Wm.   1729. W.P.
Conrahy, Carroll, Graigefolly, Queen's Co.
         Brother Jas. [N.F.P.]   1697. S.4. Kildare
"   Hugh, Derrymore, King's Co., Esq.   1835. S.4.P.
Conran, George Henry, Dublin   1812. C.D.B.
"   Walter, The Corough, Co. Dublin   1585. Dub.
"   Capt. William, Co. Antrim   1813. C.D.B.
Conron, George, Annagh, Co. Cork   1732. F. Cloyne
"   Robert, Walshstown, Co. Cork   1730. F.P.
Conroy, Thomas, Dublin, wine merchant   1813. C.D.B.
Consedene, Capt. Mathew   Dated 1661. Dub.
Constable, Captain William   Dated 1669. Dub.
Constantin, Anne, Dublin, spinster   1700. Dub.
Conway, Alice, Dublin, widow   Dated 1650. Dub.
"   Patrick, Galway, native of Cashel
                                            Dated 1660. Dub.
"   Thomas   Dated 1600. Dub.
Conyers, Charles, Rathkeale, Co. Limerick   1802. C.D.B.
"   Ralph   1665. Dub.
"   *See* Coniers.
Conyngham, Alexander, Co. Donegal   1754. B.
"   Lieut. Alexander, Dublin   1784. B.
"   Rev. Alexander, Millbrook, Co.
         Donegal   1789. B.
"   *See* Connyngham.
Cook or Cock [Cock], Thomas, Ballagh   1691. Dub.
Cooke, Anne, Dublin, [widow]   1660. Dub.
"   Dame Anne, Dungiven, Co. Derry   1680. Ir.
"   Daniel, Dublin, gent.   Not dated   S.I.P.

Cooke,	Daniel, Dublin	1719. S.4.P.
,,	Digby, Geashill, King's Co.	1784. S.1.P.
,,	Edward, Castletown, Co. Kilkenny	1751. S.1.P.
,,	Eliza, Maryborough, Queen's Co.	1813. C.D.B.
,,	Emilia, Wexford, widow	1813. C.D.B.
,,	Francis, Dublin, chirurgeon	1702. Dub.
,,	George, Dublin, brewer	1668. S.4.P.
,,	George, [St. Catherine's], Dublin, tanner	1678. Dub.
,,	Henry, Dublin	1650. Dub.
,,	James, Dublin	1653. Dub.
,,	Jane, Ballyavil, King's Co.	1793. S.1. Kildare
,,	John, soldier, Clarke's Regt.	1654. Dub.
,,	Margaret, Dublin, widow	1703. S.1.P.
,,	Mary, Dublin, spinster	1813. C.D.B.
,,	Phaniel, Clonomelehon, Co. Tipperary	1733. B.
,,	Randal, Burro, Co. Tipperary	1713. S.1.P.
,,	Richard, St. James Parish, [Dublin]	1640. Dub.
,,	Richard, soldier, Clarke's Regt.	1659. Dub.
,,	Thomas, Dublin	1726. S.1.P.
,,	Thomas, Alderman of Dublin Not dated	S.1.P.
,,	Samuel, Darondell, Co. Dublin Dated	1686. Dub.
,,	Susannah, Dublin	1719. S.1.P.
Cooley,	Charles, [St. Bridget's], Dublin, tailor	1687. Dub.
Cooper,	Edward, Stoneybatter, yeoman	1677. Dub.
,,	Edward, Markry, Co. Sligo, Esq.	1680. F.A.
,,	Edward, Sragh, Queen's Co. Dated	1739. F.A.
,,	Experience, Dublin, widow, late of Cooper's Hill, Queen's Co.	1773. F.A.
,,	George, Dublin, butcher	1657. Dub.
,,	Thomas, Vicar Choral, St. Patrick's, Dublin	1624. Dub.
,,	William, Major Davis's Company Dated	1656. Dub.
,,	Sir William, Dublin, Bart. Dated	1760. S.1.P.
,,	William, Sackville St., Dublin	1812. C.D.B.
Coote,	Chidly, Esq.	1697. W.P.
,,	Chidly, Kilmallock, Co. Limerick	1702. W.P.
,,	Chidley, Dublin, Esq.	1719. W.P.
Cope,	Anne, Drumully, Co. Armagh	1743. B.
,,	Erasmus, Dublin	1750. B.
,,	George, Knowle, Warwickshire	1652. B.
,,	George, Knowle, Warwick, gent. Dated	1652. Dub.
,,	Henry, M.D., Dublin	1742. B.

Cope, Henry, Dublin — 1775. B.
„ Richard, Sidon, Co. Meath, Capt. in Hamilton's Regt. — 1699. F.2.
„ Robert, Loughgall, Co. Armagh — 1753. Swan. P.
„ Thomas, Dublin — 1740. B.
„ Walter, Drumully, Co. Armagh, Esq. — 1658. Dub.
Copeland, William, Monaghan — 1714. Swan. Kilmore
„ William, Lr. Belnager, Co. Meath — 1734. Swan. P.
Coplen, John, Kilcosgrave, Co. Limerick — 1719. Ir. and S.1.
Copley, Anthony, Newcastle, Co. Limerick — 1744. Sullivan MSS. and W.P.
Coply, John, Cork, Esq. — 1758. W.P.
„ als. Chichester, Mary — 1673. W.P.
Coppinger, James, Cloghane, Co. Cork — 1666. F. Cork
„ Stephen, Bullock — Dated 1624. Dub.
Corballie, Simon, Jordanstown, Co. Dublin — 1638. Dub.
Corbally, John, Killcragh — 1626. Dub.
„ Robert, Reignoldston, Dio. Dublin, farmer — 1634. Dub.
„ Walter, Notstown, farmer — Dated 1629. Dub.
„ William, Nutstown, Co. Dublin, farmer — 1636. Dub.
Corcoran, Laurence, Borris, Co. Carlow — 1802. C.D.B.
Cork, Francis Moylan, Bishop of — 1815. S.1.
Cork, Cloyne and Ross, Edward Synge, Bishop of — 1678. F.2.
Cork and Ross, Peter Browne, Bishop of — 1735. F.A.
Corker, John, Dublin, merchant — Dated 1651. Dub.
Corkran, Brian, [Oxmantown], Dublin, stabler — Dated 1637. Dub.
Corles, Thomas, Chester, merchant. Codicil 1788. [No date of probate] — C.D.B.
Cormick, Nicholas, Dublin, gent. — Dated 1630. Dub.
Cormicke. See Carmicke.
Cornell, Daniel, Dublin, cooper — 1688. Dub.
Cornwall, Leonard, Rathmines, Co. Dublin — 1823. S.1.P.
Corry, Rt. Hon. Isaac — 1813. C.D.B.
„ James, Chantinee, Co. Monaghan — 1819. Swan. P.
„ Joseph, Dawson's Grove, Co. Armagh — 1769. Swan. P.
„ Mathew, Co. Monaghan — 1740. Swan. P.
„ Nicholas Henry Walter, Drumsna, Co. Leitrim — 1805. Swan. P.
„ Ralph, Kinsale — 1775. Swan. P.
„ Rebecca, Fairfield, Co. Monaghan, widow — 1805. Swan. P.
„ Walter, Glen, Co. Monaghan — 1699/1700. Swan. P.

Cosby, Ann, Stradbally, Queen's Co., widow 1749. Swan. P.
„ Arnold, Dublin, Esq. Dated 1652. Dub.
„ Arnold, Lismore, Co. Cavan 1722. Swan.
„ John, trooper, Ireton's troop
  Dated 1652. Dub.
Coscre, or Crosbe, John, curate of St. Audeon's [1575]. Dub.
Coscrowe, or Cosgrave, Thomas, Dublin, alder-
  man Dated 1585. Dub.
Cosens, John, Dublin, yeoman 1634. Dub.
Cosgrave, Christopher, Dublin, gent. Dated 1610. Dub.
„ John, Lucan, cottier Dated 1604. Dub.
Coskeleye [Coskely], Daniel or Donell, Dublin,
  citizen and blacksmith 1598. Dub.
Coskorowe, William Dated 1601. Dub.
Coskre, Edmond Dated 1575. Dub.
Cossart, Peter, Cork, merchant 1744. W.P.
Costello, Walter, South Earl St., Dublin 1812. C.D.B.
Cottell, Walter, New Ross, Co. Wexford, Esq.
  Dated 1631. W.P.
Cotter, Edmond, Ballinspaig 1661. F. Cork
Cottgrave, Margaret, Little Cabragh, widow 1677. Dub.
Cottle, Charles, Killininy, Co. Dublin, gent.
  Dated 1662. Dub.
Cotton, Felix, [Dublin, coachman] 1675. Dub.
Cottrell, als. Miles, Alson Dated 1638. Dub.
„ William, Naas, Co. Kildare Dated 1677. S.4. Kildare
Coulman, William, Dublin, butcher Dated 1626. Dub.
Coulter, Alexander, butler of the King's Hos-
  pital, Oxmantown 1701. Dub.
Coulthurst, John, Naas 1660. Dub.
Coulton, Marmaduke, Edenderry, King's Co. 1683. S.4. Kildare
Court, Richard, Belfast, glasier 1698. W. Connor
„ Lieut. Richard Dated 1701. W. Ardagh
„ William, Dublin, perukemaker 1728. W.P.
Courtenay, Francis, Newcastle, Esq. 1660. S.2.P.
„ George, Ballytrasney, Co. Cork 1710. S.2. and W.
    Cloyne
„ Sir William, Newcastle, Co.
    Limerick 1652. S.1.
Courteney, Maurice, Middleton 1782. S.2. Cloyne
Courthop, Sir Peter, Little Island, Co. Cork,
  Knt. 1680. F.2.
„ Peter, Grenane, Co. Tipperary 1685. F.2.
Courthopp. See Cowrtopp.
Couthorp, Peter, gent. 1685. F.P.
Covert, Richard, Cork, alderman 1684. F. Cork

INDEX OF WILL ABSTRACTS

Cowley, Henry.   *See* Colley.
Cowly [Cowley], als. Shee, Lettice, widow   1657. Dub.
Cowrtopp [Courthopp], Ellenor, Dublin, widow   1622. Dub.
Cox, Jasper, Youghal, alderman   1663. F.2. and W. Cork
„ Mary, Donore, widow   1706. Dub.
„ Olivia.   *See* Berry.
„ Capt. Richard   1650. W. Cork.
„ Richard, Dunmanway, Esq.   1731. W. Cork
„ Robert, Youghal, merchant   1650. W. Cork
„ Susanna, Arlandstowne   1730. W. Cork
„ Thomas, Coolkirky, gent.   1732. W. Cork
„ William, Dublin, brewer   1663. F.2.
„ William, Arlandstown, Co. Cork   Dated 1728. W. Cork
Coxe, Thomas, Athy   Dated 1624. Dub.
Coyle, Patrick   Dated 1575. Dub.
„ Richard, Dublin, tanner   1622. Dub.
„ Robert   1590. Dub.
„ Simon, Dublin, gent.   1639. Dub.
Coyne, als. Eccles, Anne, Ballyshannon, widow   1791. Swan.
„ James, Lackeen, Co. Westmeath   1752. Swan.
„ John, Dublin, alderman   1699. Swan. P.
„ Nicholas, Dublin   1764. Swan.
Crabb, Alexander, New Street   1642. Dub.
„ Nathaniel, Oldtown, par. of Coolock, farmer   1681. Dub.
Cradock, Michael   Dated 1678. S. 4. Kildare
Cradocke, Stephen, Dublin, barber   Dated 1577. Dub.
Craford, David, Belfast, gent.   1737. S.I.P.
„ [Crafford], Dorothy, [Dublin, widow]   1680. Dub.
Craforde, Alexander, Dublin, yeoman   Dated 1667. Dub.
Cragg, Winifred, Dublin, widow   1705. Dub.
Craggs, John, Dublin, brewer   Dated 1700. Dub.
Craig, Edward   D. 1822. S.4. (H.O.)
Cramer, Ambrose, Newry, Esq.   Dated 1768. F.A.
„ Balthasar, Dublin, Esq.   1741. F.A.
„ Jane, Dublin, spinster   1790. F.A.
„ Marmaduke, Rathmore, Co. Cork   1817. F.A.
„ Tobias, Co. Kilkenny   1684. F.P.
Crane, Simon, Great Forrest, Dublin, Esq.   1685. F.2.
„ *See* Creane.
Cranmer, George   Dated 1600. Dub.
Cranshawe, William, Dublin   1604. Dub.
Cransie, als. Owen, Ellinor   [1623]. Dub.
Cranwell, Elizabeth, Dublin, widow   Dated 1687. Dub.
„ John, Dublin, alderman   1674. Dub.

Crase, Edward, New Row, Dublin, gent.	1694.	Dub.
Craw, John, [Dublin], gent.	1658.	Dub.
Crawford, Eliz., Laurencetown, Co. Meath	1816.	Swan. P.
,, Gustavius, Lurganboy, Co. Leitrim Dated	1759.	Swan.
,, James, Crawford's Burn, Co. Down	1777.	S.I. Down
,, James	1830.	Swan. P.
,, Jason, Laurencetown, Co. Meath	1769.	Swan.
,, John, Wexford	1660.	Dub.
,, Robert, Ballysallagh, Co. Down, gent.	1658.	Dub.
,, Robert, Aughnacloy, Co. Fermanagh, gent.	1734.	Swan. P.
,, William, Dublin, tailor	1702.	Dub.
,, William, Lurganboy, gent.	1764.	Swan.
,, William, Enort Hill, Co. Fermanagh	1749.	Swan. P.
,, William, Lakelands, South Libs. of Cork	1835.	F.A.
Crawley, Patrick, Dublin, shoemaker	1623.	Dub.
,, Rev. Patrick	1803.	C.D.B.
Creane [Crane], Peter, Sligo, merchant	1659.	Dub.
Creave, John, Mountmellick, Queen's Co. Dated	1715.	S.4. Kildare
Creefe, Roger, Dublin, baker	1619.	Dub.
Crehalle, Nicholas, Rathsallagh, [Co. Wicklow] Dated	1617.	Dub.
Creighton, Abraham, Dublin	1800.	Swan. P.
,, John	1738.	Swan. P.
,, Mary, Dublin, spinster	1741.	Swan. P.
,, Rev. Wm.	1743.	Swan.
Crenan, Michael	1694.	Dub.
Cressey, Elizabeth, Dublin, widow Dated	1670.	Dub.
Cressy, George, Dublin, Esq.	1663.	Dub.
Crew [Crewe], Joshua, Dublin, gent.	1637.	Dub.
Crewe, James, Dublin, gent. Dated	1618.	Dub.
Crewes, John, [Patrick Street], Dublin, vintner	1672.	Dub.
Crewse [Cruise], Richard, Damalston	[1653].	Dub.
Crilly, Edward, Newtown, Co. Dublin.	1812.	C.D.B.
Croft, Philip, Dublin, gent.	1712.	Dub.
Crofton, Asheligh, Castlefish, Co. Kildare	1767.	B.
,, Edward, Athy, Co. Kildare	1741.	B.
,, or Croston, George, Dublin, girdler	1670.	Dub.
,, George, Galey, gent.	1764.	Ir.
,, John	1750.	Ir.
,, Michael, Parke, Co. Meath, gent.	1721.	Ir.
,, Sir Morgan, Dublin, Bart.	1802.	C.D.B.

Crofton, Philip, Dublin — 1783. B.
" Richard, Lissidorne, Co. Roscommon — 1668. Ir.
Crofts, Christopher, Cork — 1712. F.P.
" Daniel, Dublin — 1651. Dub.
" George, Velvextown, Co. Cork Dated 1718. F. and W. Cloyne
" George, Churchtown, Esq. Dated 1730. W.P.
" Mary, Churchtown — 1741. W.P.
" Philip, Cork — 1730. F. and W.P.
" Roger, Cnockbarry, Co. Cork Dated 1724. F. and W. Cloyne
" William, Downdamore, Co. Cork — 1648. F. Cork
Croker, Edward, Rawleighstown, Co. Limerick, Esq. — 1732/3. F.D.
" Edward, Dublin, apothecary — 1759. F.2.
" Elizabeth, Limerick, widow Not dated — S.1.P.
" Hugh, Ballyhamlis, Co. Waterford, gent. — 1668. F.2.
" John, Ariglin Bridge, Co. Cork — 1684. F.P. and F.2.
" Richard, Nadrid, Co. Cork — 1726. F.D.
" Richard, North suburbs of Cork — 1732. F.D.
" Strangman — 1784. S.4. (H.BM.)
" Thomas, Cahirereely, Co. Limerick — 1684. F.P. and F.2.
" Thomas, Ballyanker, Co. Waterford, gent. — 1704. F.D.
" Thomas, Youghal, alderman — 1718. F.D.
" Walter, Whitestown, Co. Dublin — 1714. F.D.
" William, Johnstown, Co. Cork — 1801. C.D.B.
Crolle, Edmond — Dated 1597. Dub.
Crollie, Thomas, Dublin, tanner — Dated 1641. Dub.
Crollis [Croly], Dominick, Dublin, gent. — 1668. Dub.
Crolly, als. Chamberlaine als. Jans, Thomasine, Dublin, widow — Dated 1670. Dub. and W. Dublin
Crommelin, Ann, Lisburn — 1756. Swan. P.
Crompton, Thomas, Poulemalow, Co. Wexford, gent. — 1696. F.2.
Cromwell, Thomas, Arklow, yeoman — 1675. Dub.
Crone, John, City of Limerick, Esq. — 1790. Swan. P.
Croocke [Crooks], James, Carrickfergus, burgess — Dated 1656. Dub.
Crooke, Sir Samuel, Bart. — Dated 1635. F.2.
" Thomas, Esq. — Dated 1682. F.2.
" Thomas, Nicherabilly — 1682. F. Cork
Crooks. *See* Croocke.
Crosbe or Coscre, John, curate of St. Audeons — [1575]. Dub.

Crosbie, Agnes 1803. C.D.B.
„ Anne, Limerick, widow 1813. C.D.B.
„ Col. David, Ardfert, Co. Kerry 1658. Dub. and S.2.P.
„ David, Ardfert, Co. Kerry 1717. B.
„ Lucy, Dublin, spinster 1801. C.D.B.
„ Thomas, Ballengee, Co. Wexford
 Dated 1729. S.2. Ferns
Croshan, Thomas, Miltowne, Co. Wicklow,
 yeoman 1632. Dub.
Cross, Epenetus, St. Dominick's nigh Cork,
 Esq. 1704/5. F.A.
„ Michael, St. Finn Barrs 1680. F. Cork
„ Philip Hawes, Cronody, Co. Cork 1734. F.P.
„ Sylvester, Cork, merchant 1643. F.2.
Crosse, Captain John 1656. Dub.
„ Philip Hawes, Cronody, Co. Cork,
 Esq. 1734. F.A.
„ Sylvester, Dublin, Esq. 1730. F.A.
„ William, Lazie Hill, merchant 1667. Dub.
Crosthwaite, Thomas, Dublin, clothier 1701. Dub.
Croston or Crofton, George, Dublin, girdler 1670. Dub.
Crostred, George, Kilboggot, Co. Dublin
 yeoman Dated 1680. Dub.
Crotty, Capt. Michael 1786. S.4. (H.BM.)
Crow, Anne, Dublin, widow 1782. S.1.P.
„ Baldwin, Bellmount, King's Co. 1772. S.1.P.
„ Charles, Bishop of Cloyne 1726. S.1.P.
„ Charles, Summerhill, Dublin 1836. S.1.P.
„ Edward, Spruce Hall, Co. Galway 1715. S.1.P.
„ Edward, Tullamore Dated 1814. S.1.P.
„ John, Dublin 1718. S.1.P.
„ Rev. John, Dublin 1740. S.1.P.
„ Margery, Tullamore, King's Co., widow 1777. S.1.P.
„ Richard 1713. M.
„ Thomas, Capt. in Molstyn's Dragoons 1767. S.1.P.
Crowe, Rev. Dawson, Kells, Co. Meath 1798. Swan.
„ Eliza, Dungarberry Lodge, Co. Leitrim 1890. Swan.
„ John, London, late of Monaghan 1829. Swan. Clogher
„ Richard, senr., Paston, Co. Norfolk,
 gent. Dated 1656. Dub.
„ Richard, Dowhill 1713. M.
„ Very Rev. William, Dean of Clonfert 1767. M.
Crozier, als. Rosborough, ——[Mrs.] 1845. Swan.
„ John, Magherydunbar 1717/1718. Swan.
 Clogher

Crozier, John, Magherydunbar, Co. Fermanagh 1750. Swan.
,, John, Moorfield, Co. Fermanagh 1764. Swan. Clogher
,, John, Drumlyon, Enniskillen 1791. Swan. Clogher
,, John, Dublin 1816. Swan.
,, Mary Anne, Killyleagh, Co. Down, widow 1834. Swan. P.
,, William, Magheradunbar, Co. Fermanagh 1737. Swan.
,, Wm. Pigott, at Killyleagh, Co. Down, gent. 1858. Swan.
Cruchley, William, Lazyhill, Dublin 1693. Dub.
Cruise, See Crewse.
Cruse, Donogh Dated 1583. Dub.
Cuffe, Joseph, Grove, Co. Tipperary 1761. S.1.P.
Cullen, Christopher, Dublin, gent. 1693. Dub.
,, Daniel, Ballybeg, Co. Kildare, physician 1674. Dub.
,, George, [Co. Wicklow] Dated 1627. Dub.
,, Jane. See Plunkett.
,, Judith 1796. S.1.P.
,, Matthew, Tagony, farmer Dated 1628. Dub.
,, Nicholas, Dublin, gent. 1633. Dub.
,, Nicholas, Kulnekilly 1703. Dub.
,, Patrick, Skreeny, Co. Leitrim 1775. S.1.P.
,, Patrick, Skreen, Co. Leitrim 1786. S.1.P.
Cullin, Nicholas, Tintern, Co. Wexford 1812. C.D.B.
Cullon, Doyne Corone, Dublin, surgeon Dated 1670. Dub.
,, Keane, Dublin, chirurgeon Dated 1641. Dub.
,, See O'Cullon.
Culme, Nicholas, Rector of Cloghran, Swords 1640. Dub.
,, Robert, London, citizen and merchant tailor Dated 1638. Dub.
Cumming, Andrew, Bull Alley, Dublin 1803. C.D.B.
Cundy, Joseph, Clonmore, King's Co. Dated 1705. S.4. Kildare
Cuningham, Major Thomas, chirurgeon 1700. Dub.
Cunningham, George, Killinlesseragh, Co. Longford, Esq. Dated 1684. Dub.
,, John, Dublin, tailor Dated 1640. Dub.
,, Nichola, Killinlesserah, Co. Longford, widow Dated 1685. Dub.
,, Thomas, Maynooth, chapman 1678. Dub.
Cuppadge, Thomas, Lambstown, Co. Wexford 1709. F.P.
Cuppage, Alexr., Lurgan 1831. Swan. P.
,, Ann, Lurgan, Co. Armagh, linen draper 1793. Swan. P.

IN THE GENEALOGICAL OFFICE, DUBLIN 153

Cuppage, Elizabeth, Glenbank, Co. Antrim   1839. Swan. P.
"   Faustin, Dublin, Esq.   1726. Swan. P.
"   George, City of Dublin, Esq.
            Not dated   Swan. P.
"   John, Garden Hill, Co. Antrim   1759. Swan. P.
"   John, Glenbank, Co. Antrim   1799. Swan. P.
"   John, Col. retd., Hon. East India Coy. 1809. Swan. P.
"   Robert, Lambstown   Not dated   Swan.
"   Robert, Lambstown, Co. Wexford   1683. F.2.
"   Stephen, alderman of Coleraine   1666. Swan. P. and F.2.
"   Stephen, Col. in H.M.S.   1855. Swan. P.
Cuppaidge, Ffaustin, Colemine, Co. Dublin, gent.   1680. Swan. P.
"   John, Magheralin, clk.   1725. Swan. P.
"   Mary, Athlone, spinster   1855. Swan. P.
"   Richard, Moat, Co. Westmeath   1764. Swan. P.
Curphey, Lt. Col. William   Died 1856. S.4. (H.O.)
Curran, Lieut. James   Died 1815. S.4. (H.O.)
Curry, John, Barrister-at-Law, Londonderry   1835. Swan.
Curteis, Jane. *See* Ball.
Curtis, Jane, Dublin, widow   1744. S.1.P.
"   William, Dublin   1739. S.1.P.
"   John, Mt. Hanover, Co. Meath   1775. Swan. P.
Curwain, John, Dublin, carpenter   1701. Dub.
Cusack, Begnet. *See* Bor.
"   Catherine, Ennis, Co. Clare, widow   1793. Mol. P.
"   Christopher, Kildare   Dated 1668. S.4. Kildare
"   John, Kilkishine, Co. Clare   1719. Mol. P.
"   Walter, Chapelizod   1593. Dub.
Cusacke, Mathew, Rush   1669. Dub.
"   Walter, Colemine, Co. Dublin   1678. Dub.
Cusake, Margery   Dated 1603. Dub.
Cushion, James   Dated 1698. Dub.
Cuthbert, Mabelle, Dublin, widow   1700. Dub.
"   William, the elder, Dublin   1675. F.2.
Cutherbert [Cuthbert], als. Rutherford, Margery, Lazy Hill, widow   1703. Dub.
Cutt, Robert, London, citizen and ironmonger   1610. Dub.

Daker, Anne Clancy. *See* Drought.
Dalacourt, James, Ballinknahane   Not dated   F. Cork
Dale, Capt. Donel, Moretown, Co. Wexford   1699. Dub.
"   John, Ardnamullan   Dated 1654. Dub.
"   Robert, Bishop of Kildare   Da ed 1582. Dub.

INDEX OF WILL ABSTRACTS

Dale, Thomas, butcher   Dated 1563. Dub.
,,   Thomas, Dublin, baker   Dated 1624. Dub.
Dallaghan, Hugh, Lisktoonie, [Lisktoony, King's Co.]   1641. Dub.
Dalliner, Richard, Dublin, coppersmith   1718. Dub.
Dalrymple, [Thomas], Dublin   1782. Swan.
Dalton, Amy, Dublin, widow   Dated 1629. Dub.
,,   Charles, Milton, Co. Westmeath, gent.   Dated 1652. Dub.
,,   Charles, Sergt. in Kerr's Regt.   1718. Dub.
Daly, Elizabeth, Queen Street, Dublin   1813. C.D.B.
,,   John, Skerries, Co. Dublin   Dated 1695. Dub.
,,   William, Dublin   Dated 1672. Dub.
Dambrick [Dambruck], John, trooper, Morgan's troop   1657. Dub.
Dames, Ann, Greenhills, King's Co.   1776. B.
Dancer, Joshua, Shinrone   1840. S.I. Killaloe
,,   Richard, Shinrone   1818. S.I. Killaloe
,,   Thomas, eldest s. of Richd. D. decd.   1773. S.I. Killaloe
,,   Sir Thomas, Modreeny   1777. S.I.P.
Dancey, Paul, Grenage, Co. Meath, gent.   1707. Swan.
Dancy, Pochrich, Navan, Esq.   1790. Swan. P.
Daniel, James, Kildare   Dated 1655. Dub.
,,   Peter, Languedoc, [France], refugee to Ireland   Dated 1716. Dub.
,,   Rice, trooper, Perry's Troop   1656. Dub.
,,   Sarah, St. Stephen's Green, Dublin, widow   1827. S.I.P.
Daniell, John   Dated 1647. Dub.
Darbishire, William, [Finglas]   Dated 1631. Dub.
Darby, Bryan, Trim, Co. Eastmeath, gent.   Dated 1658. Dub.
,,   Damer, Dublin, merchant   1792. S.I.P.
,,   Frances   1802. C.D.B.
,,   Jonathan, Leap   1685. F.2.
,,   Jonathan, Leap, King's Co.   1776. S.I.P.
D'Arcy, Margaret, Eccles Street, Dublin, spinster   1860. F.A.
,,   de Burgh, Dublin   1801. C.D.B.
Darcy [Darsy], Dominick, Rockvale, Co. Clare   1804. C.D.B.
,,   Patrick, Bishop St., Dublin   1803. C.D.B.
,,   *See* Darsy.
Dardes [Dardis], Patrick, Dublin, gent.   Dated 1602. Dub.

Dardis, Elinor, Jigginstown, Westmeath, spinster 1801. C.D.B.
Darlenton, Randle, Ballygleron, Co. Wicklow Dated 1712. Dub.
Darling, Richard, Dublin, gent. Dated 1705. S.4. P.
Darsy [Darcy], Edward 1615. Dub.
" *See* Darcy.
Dartas, James, Dublin 1576. Dub.
Daton, William Dated 1592. Dub.
Daunt, Achilles, Tracton Abbey, Cork Dated 1708. W. Cork
" Achilles, Tracton Abbey, Cork 1711. F. Cork and Davis
" Emanuel, Kinsale 1735. F., Ir. and W. Cork
" Francis, Ballingarry, Cork 1747. F.
" Francis, Willowhill, Co. Cork, gent. 1719. F. and W. Cork
" Francis, Knockatour, Co. Cork, gent. 1722. F. and W. Cork
" Francis, Ballingarry, Co. Cork, farmer 1747. W. Cork
" George, Novohal, Co. Cork, gent. 1733. F. and W. Cork
" George, Knockatour 1735. F. and W. Cork
" Henry, Fahalea, Co. Cork, gent. 1739. W.P.
" Henry, Dublin 1741. W.P.
" Jane, Tracton Abbey, Co. Cork, widow 1680. F. and W. Cork
" Martha, relict of Geo. D., of Gortigrenane, Co. Cork 1710. W.P.
" Mary, Britfieldstown 1631. F. and Davis
" Mary, Knockatour, widow of Francis D., senr. 1733. F. and W. Cork
" Mary, Cork, widow 1762. F.
" Swithin, Cork 1761. F.
" Thomas, Owlpen, Gloucestershire, endorsed Gortigrenan, Co. Cork 1670. Davis
" Thomas, Owlpen, Gloucestershire 1670. F. and W. Cork
" Thomas, Tracton Abbey, Cork 1736. F. and W. Cork
" Thomas, Owlpen, Gloucestershire 1745. F.
" Thomas, Cork 1754. F.
" Thomas, Gurtagrenan Not dated F.
" William, Grillagh 1682. F. and W. Cork
" William, Willowhill, Co. Cork, gent. 1735. F. and W. Cork

Davenport, Francis   Dated 1656. Dub.
„   Mabel, spinster   1811. Swan. Dublin
„   Simon, Dublin, Esq.   1809. Swan. P.
„   Thomas, Ballincurrig, Co. Cork,
         gent.   1695. F.2.
„   Thomas, Ballincurrig   1700. F. Cloyne
„   Thomas, Ennis, Co. Clare, apothe-
         cary   1732. W.P.
„   Thomas, Ennis, Co. Clare, apothe-
         cary   1748. W.P.
„   William, Dublin, gent.   1599. Dub.
„   William, Bregoge, Co. Cork   1669. F. Cloyne
Daves, George, [Kilmainham]   1617. Dub.
„   John, soldier, Clarke's Regt.   Dated 1654. Dub.
Davies, Jenkin, Oxmantown, yeoman Dated 1678. Dub.
„   Pierce, Dublin, feltmaker   1700. Dub.
„   Robert, Dublin   Dated 1621. Dub.
Davis, David, Limerick, burgess   1727. F.A.
„   Elizabeth, Limerick, widow   1792. F.A.
„   Elizabeth, widow   1796. F.A.
„   Elizabeth   1802. C.D.B.
„   George, Dublin, brewer   1679. Dub.
„   George, Limerick, victualler   1718. F.A.
„   George, Limerick, Esq.   1794. F.A.
„   Grizell, Dublin, widow   1714. Dub.
„   Henry, Youghal, chandler   1671. Swan. Cork
„   Henry, Carrickfergus, Co. Antrim   1710. Ir.
„   James, Martinstown, Co. Roscommon 1803. C.D.B.
„   James, Drogheda   1804. C.D.B.
„   Jane, Rathfarnham, widow   1653. Dub.
„   Jane, Limerick, spinster   1763. F.A.
„   John, Capt. in Huson's Regt.   1653. Dub.
„   John, Co. Antrim   1668. Ir.
„   John, Dublin   Dated 1676. Dub.
„   John, Killeagh, gent.   1774. Swan. Cloyne
„   Marcus, Dublin, merchant and maltster 1653. Dub.
„   Peter, Dublin, fringemaker   1719. Dub.
„   Richard, Murphystown, Co. Dublin,
         gent.   Dated 1707. Dub.
„   Robert, [Balmastowne, Co. Dublin], far-
         mer   1691. Dub.
„   Robert, Limerick, burgess   1780. F.A.
„   Rowland, Ardnemullen, Co. Meath 1659. Dub.
„   Samuel, Dublin, Esq.   Dated 1635. Dub.
„   Samuel, Limerick, apothecary   1778. F.A.
„   Sarah, Lazyhill, widow   Dated 1687. Dub.

Davis,	Thomas, Col. Warren's Coy.	1660. Dub.
,,	Thomas, Dublin, tallow chandler	1680. Dub.
,,	Thomas, Dublin, brewer	Dated 1692. Dub.
,,	Thomas, Kilmainham, tanner	1697. Dub.
,,	Thomas, Dublin, merchant	Dated 1711. Dub.
,,	William, Knockballymore, Co. Fermanagh	Admon. 1668. Ir.
,,	See Davys.	
Davison,	Richard, [Hangman Lane], Dublin, victualler	1703. Dub.
,,	William, Skeriffe, par. Tomgreny, Co. Clare	1634. Dub.
,,	See Davyson.	
Davock,	Michael	1812. C.D.B.
Davoren,	als. Dutton, Elizabeth	Dated 1666. Dub.
,,	Michael Constance	1800. S.4. (H.I.)
Davys,	Thomas, Lyons, husbandman	Dated 1584. Dub.
,,	Elizabeth, Dublin, widow	1736. Ir.
,,	John, Moulchanstowne, Co. Dublin	1683. Dub.
,,	John, Carrickfergus	1710. Ir.
,,	[Davis], Rosis [Rouse], Kilmainham, gent.	Dated 1669. Dub.
,,	Samuel, Carrickfergus	1718. S.I.P.
,,	William	Dated 1559. Dub.
,,	William, Knockballimore, Co. Fermanagh, Esq.	Dated 1661. Dub.
Davyson	[Davison], Alexander, Dublin, [pewterer]	Dated 1694. Dub.
Dawley,	Edward, Little Island	1691. W. Cork
,,	Henry, Ballydaheene, Co. Cork, Esq.	1694. W.P.
,,	Walter, Donnonstowne, gent.	Dated 1681. W. Cloyne
Dawly,	Dennis, Ballynookerry	Dated 1741. W. Cloyne
,,	Elizabeth, [Macromp, widow]	1653. W. Cork
,,	John, Cork, gardener	1735. W. Cork
Dawson,	Lieut. Edward	Dated 1653. Dub.
,,	Edward, Enagh, par. of Ematris	1737. Swan. Clogher
,,	Elizabeth, Dublin, widow	1812. C.D.B.
,,	Francis, Drumcall, Co. Monaghan	1813. C.D.B.
,,	Jeremy, Ballinderry, Co. Wicklow, clerk	1699. Dub.
,,	John, Swaffham, Co. Norfolk, now of Dublin	1667. F.2.
,,	John	1695. Dub.
,,	Richard, Drumenton, par. of Emetris	1717/18. Swan. Clogher

Dawson, Robert, drummer, Clarke's Regt.
Dated 1654. Dub.
„ Samuel, Londonderry, alderman 1658. Dub.
„ [? Danson], Rev. Thomas, Rector of Aughnamullen 1724/5. Swan. P.
„ [? Danson], Thomas, Gilford, Co. Down Esq. 1729. Swan. P.
„ Thomas, Castle Dawson, Co. Derry 1732. Ir.
„ Rev. William, Ematris, Co. Monaghan 1803. C.D.B.
Day, John, (Grecian), Dublin, jeweller 1691. Dub.
Dayly, Joyce, [Dublin] 1713. Dub.
Deane, Catherine, Dublin, widow 1713. Dub.
„ Edward, Kilkenny, gent. 1637. Dub.
„ Edward, Dublin, tanner Dated 1653. Dub.
„ Jane, widow of Titus D., Dublin 1662. Dub.
„ Joseph, Carmell, Co. Meath 1669. F.
„ Joseph, Dublin, shearman 1694. F.2.
„ Thomas, Dublin, skinner 1633. Dub.
„ Titus, Dublin, shoemaker Dated 1660. Dub.
„ William, senr., Dublin, dyer 1718. Dub.
Dearinge [Dering], John, Moate, Co. Kildare, gent. 1623. Dub.
Deaves, Henry, Crumlin, Co. Dublin 1804. C.D.B.
Deberney or Barney [Debernay], James [Jaque], pensioner Dated 1706. Dub.
De Clifford, Edward, Baron 1833. S.2.P.
De Courcey, John 1824. S.4. (H.I.)
Dee, Catherine, Dublin, widow 1690. Dub.
Deeke, John, St. Edmond's in Lombard Street, London 1661. Dub.
Deering, Isabell, Dublin, widow Dated 1699. Dub.
Deey, Abraham, Ballyteige, Co. Kildare 1683. Dub.
„ Alice, Dublin, widow 1689. Dub.
Deishagh, Walter, Ballymaddo, farmer
Not dated Dub.
Delacluse, John, Lazyhill, Dublin, winecooper 1663. Dub.
Delacour, Gabriel, Portarlington, Queen's Co. 1804. C.D.B.
Delacourt, James, Ballinahane, gent.
Not dated Davis
„ John, Cork 1741. F.
Delafield, Nicholas Dated 1582. Dub.
Delahoyde, Anthony, Loghshiny, Co. Dublin, gent. 1621. Dub.
„ Cassimere, Drogheda, merchant 1813. C.D.B.

Delahoyde, Christopher Fitzgeorge, Drogheda 1636. Dub.
" Peter, Dublin, Esq. Dated 1625. Dub.
" Rowland, Cork 1734. F.P.
Delan, Daniel, [Rathfarnham] [1631]. Dub.
" Daniel Dated 1632. Dub.
Delany, Robert, Ballinacarrig, King's Co., gent. 1827. S.4. P.
De la Sale, Paul, Dublin 1686. Dub.
Delaune, Anne, Dublin 1727. B.
" Henry, Gortinroe, Esq. 1660. B. and Dub.
" Henry, (ex. Lieut. Colonel) 1746. B.
Delelan, Barnabas, Byon in France, merchant 1597. Dub.
Dellanty, John, Thomas Court, glover and skinner 1706. Dub.
Den [Denn], Frances, [St. Katherine's], Dublin, widow 1621. Dub.
Denham, John 1719. Dub.
" *See* Dennham.
Denis, John, D.D., Diocese of Clogher 1745/6. Swan. P.
Denison, John, junr., Enniscorthy, Co. Wexford gent. 16th Oct. 1693. F.2. and W.P.
" John, Enniscorthy, gent. 18th Dec. 1693. F.2. and W.P.
Denn, John, Saggard, gent. 1706. Dub.
" Philip, [New St.], Dublin, tanner Dated 1635. Dub.
" William, Saggard, [Co. Dublin], gent. 1713. Dub.
" *See* Den.
Dennham [Denham], Mary, Athy Dated 1638. Dub.
Dennis, James, Cork, merchant 1757. F.A.
" John, Cork, joiner 1743. F.A.
" John, D.D., Diocese of Clogher 1745. W.P.
" Samuel, Waterford 1701. F.A.
" Samuel, Waterford, gent. 1739. F.A.
" *See* Tracton, Lord.
Denny, Sir Arthur, Tralee 1673. W.P.
" Edward, Castlelyons, Cork 1695. W.P.
" Edward, Tralee 1709. W.P.
De Renzi [De Renzy], Mathew, [Dublin], Esq. Dated 1653. Dub.
Dering. *See* Dearinge.
Dermot, Connor, Dublin, joiner 1632. Dub.
" Edward, Dublin, gent. Dated 1684. Dub.
" Richard, Dublin, plateworker Dated 1642. Dub.
" Thomas, Palmerston, Co. Dublin, husbandman 1639. Dub.
Dermott, John, Dublin, victualler Dated 1718. Dub.

Dermott, Thomas, Lazyhill, cooper   Dated 1666. Dub.
„   William   Dated 1685. Dub.
Derry, St. George Ashe, Bishop of   1718. W.P.
De St. Julien, Mary. *See* Adlecron.
Desly [Desley], Edward, Dublin, carpenter
                                         Dated 1655. Dub.
Desmond, Thomas, [Finglass], miller   1594. Dub.
Despard, Green, Queen's Co.   1786. S.1. Ossory
„   William, Killaghy, Co. Tipperary   1720. S.1.P.
Destare, John, Ballyloghlane, Diocese of Dublin,
            merchant   1713. Dub.
D'Esterre, Henry Martin   D. 1801. S.4. (H.I.)
Dethiche, Walter, Balynaid   Dated 1596. Dub.
Develin, Thomas, Dublin, tailor   1711. Dub.
Devenish, Ann, Dublin, widow   1801. Ir.
„   Alice, Dublin, widow   1712. Dub.
„   Christopher, Keelogues   1747. Ir.
„   William, Carnclogher, Co. Ros-
            common   1729. Ir.
Devenishe, Edmond, Dublin, alderman
                                         Dated 1582. Dub.
Devenysh, Edmond, [Thomas St.], Dublin   1578. Dub.
Devereux, Catherine, Enniscorthy, Co. Wexford,
            widow   1813. C.D.B.
„   George, Dublin, founder   Dated 1714. Dub.
„   James, Carrigmanon, Co. Wexford   1697. F.2.
„   John, Depis, Co. Wexford, gent.
                                         Dated 1615. Dub.
„   Mary, Dublin, widow   1709. Dub.
„   Michael, Two Pott House alias Foun-
            tainville, Co. Cork, formerly of
            Kilfinan   1763. Mol. P.
„   Paul, Bayliestown, Co. Wexford
                                         Dated 1659. Dub.
Devlene, Nicholas, Dublin, tailor   Dated 1594. Dub.
Devonsher, Elizabeth, Cork, spinster   1757. F.A.
„   Jonas, Cork, merchant   1756. F.A.
„   Sarah, Cork, widow   1757. F.A.
„   Thomas, Cork   1693. F.P.
Devy, James, Dublin, tailor   1718. Dub.
Dewdenny, Thomas, soldier   1655. Dub.
Dick, Elizabeth, Dublin   1862. Swan.
„   Samuel, Dublin   1802. C.D.B.
Dickenson, Elizabeth, [Ballinoge, Co. Wicklow]
                                         Dated 1640. Dub.

Dickering, Martin, trooper, Capt. Perry's Troop
                          Dated 1656. Dub.
Dickeson, Henry   Dated 1669. Dub.
Dickinson, Peter, tanner   Dated 1635. Dub.
Dickson, Ezekiel, Ballyheyd [Ballyhide], Co.
        Kildare, shepherd   1665. Dub.
    „   Francis, Dublin, gent.   Dated 1713. Dub.
    „   Hugh, Ballybrickan, Co. Cork, Esq. 1737. W.P.
Digby, Benjamin, Geashill, clk.   1764. S.1.P.
    „   John, Landenstown, Co. Kildare   1786. S.1.P.
    „   Simon, Bishop of Elphin   1720. S.1.P.
    „   Rev. William, Dean of Clonfert   1812. C.D.B.
Digles, Hugh, [New St.], Dublin, shoemaker
                          Dated 1650. Dub.
Dikes, Thomas   1656. Dub.
Dillon (or Dyllon), Anne, Dundrum, Co. Down 1634. Dub.
    „   als. Ball, Anne   Dated 1657. Dub.
    „   Arthur, Quartertown, Co. Cork   1693. F.2.
    „   Catherine, Carlow, widow   1804. C.D.B.
    „   Daniel, Rathcoole, Co. Dublin   1801. C.D.B.
    „   Edmond, Holywell, Co. Mayo   1801. C.D.B.
    „   Luke, Killine, Co. Galway   1803. C.D.B
    „   Nicholas, Dublin, merchant   1638. Dub.
    „   Thomas, Dublin, merchant   1713. Dub.
    „   William, Dublin, joiner   1653. Dub.
    „   *See* Dyllon.
Dingley, Mrs. Elizabeth. *See* Dobson.
    „   John, Dublin, Esq.   Dated 1678. Dub.
Disborow, Charity, Cullenwaine, King's Co.,
        widow   1696. S.1.P.
Disnee [Disney], Thomas, [Butcher-leas, near
        Dublin]   1658. Dub.
Disney, Susanna, Stebanon, Co. Louth, widow 1684. F.2.
Divin, als. Toole, Elizabeth, Dublin, widow
                          Dated 1686. Dub.
    „   William, [Skinner Roe], Dublin, baker
                          Dated 1679. Dub.
Dix, Martin, Dublin, Esq.   1659. Dub.
Dixon, Anthony, Munckstowne, Co. Dublin,
        farmer   1671. Dub.
    „   Elizabeth, Ballycaran, Co. Dublin,
        widow   Dated 1599. Dub.
    „   John, Wiestown, par. Ballmadon, Dio.
        Dublin   1625. Dub.
    „   John, Dublin   1642. Dub.
    „   John, Ballimore, Co. Cork, victualler 1729. W. Cork

Dixon, Maude. *See* Bee.
" Sir Robert, Knt., Dublin 1654. Dub.
" Robert, Calverstown, Co. Kildare 1725. S.1.
" Robert, Calverstown, Co. Kildare 1731. S.1.P.
" William, Knockline, Co. Dublin, gent. 1599. Dub.
" William, Swords, cooper Dated 1615. Dub.
" William, Dublin, gent. 1687. Dub.
Dixsone, John, [St. Andrew's, Dublin] 1642. Dub.
Dobar, Bethell, [St. Nicholas Without], Dublin,
    weaver 1681. Dub.
Dobbe, John, Dublin, gent. Dated 1620. Dub.
" Marmaduke Dated 1637. Dub.
Dobben, Michael, Waterford, gent. 1602. Dub.
Dobbin, Anthony, Gotladoe, Co. Donegal
    Dated 1696. W. Derry
" Anthony, Golodoe, par. of Moville, Co.
    Donegal, gent. Dated 1714. W. Derry
" Charles, Maghercreagh, Co. Antrim,
    gent. Dated 1739. W. Connor
" Dorothea, widow of Major John D.,
    Duneane, Co. Antrim 1743. W.P.
" Eliza, Goleduff, widow of Anthony D.
    Dated 1728. W. Derry
" Hugh, Ballymagarachan, Co. Down 1700. W. Dromore
" Isabella, Maghercreagh, Co. Antrim,
    gentlewoman 1731. W. Connor
" James, Duneane, Co. Antrim 1682. W. Connor
" James, Inishbrush, Co. Londonderry 1718. W.P.
" James, Carrickfergus, now of Belfast,
    M.D. 1757. F.A.
" Capt. John, Dublin 1740. W.P.
" Mary. *See* McManus
" Moses, Ballymenock 1713. W. Connor
" Peter, Ballydonalland, parish of Dun-
    eane, Co. Antrim 1733. W. Connor
" Stephen, Ballydonellan, Co. Antrim,
    gent. 1733. W. Connor
" Thomas, Drumsook, Co. Antrim, Esq. 1673. W. Connor
" Thomas, Carrickfergus 1678. W. Connor
" Thomas, Eskeleane, Co. Antrim, gent. 1718. W.P.
" William, Carrickfergus Dated 1683. W. Connor
" William, Carrickfergus, burgess 1703. W. Connor
" William, Cullnegeechan 1722. W. Connor
" William, Ediegrove, par. of Dromore,
    Co. Down 1728. W. Dromore
" William, Cork, gent. 1770. F.A.

Dobbins, Elizabeth, Carrickmacross, Co. Monaghan　　　　　　　　　　　　1796. S.4.
Dobbs, Anthony, Dublin, sergeant at mace　1662. Dub.
Dobbyn, James, Inishrush, Co. Derry, gent.　1718. F.A.
Dobin, John, Belfast, weaver　　　　1741. W. Connor
Dobson, Elizabeth, Dublin, widow　　1709. Dub.
　" 　　als. Dingley, Elizabeth, Mullingare, widow of Thos. D., clk.　1733. S.4. P.
　" 　　George, Dublin, merchant tailor
　　　　　　　　　　　　　Dated 1685. Dub.
　" 　　John, [St. Mary's Lane], gardener　1635. Dub.
　" 　　Thomas, Kevin Street, Co. Dublin, smith　　　　　　　　1701. Dub.
Dobyns, William, Dublin, merchant　1716. Dub.
Dodd, Margaret, Camden Street, Dublin, spinster　　　　　　　　　　1813. C.D.B.
　" 　　Nicholas, Brownstown, Co. Dublin　1800. C.D.B.
Dodridge, Andrew, Thomas Street, Co. Dublin, beer brewer　　　　　1706. Dub.
Dodson, als. Vepy, Jane, Dundalk　Dated 1658. Dub.
Dodsworth, Edward, Maryborough, Esq.　1730. Swan. P.
Dodwell, John, Dublin, gent.　　　1652. Dub.
Doe, Mathew, Dublin, baker　　　1676. Dub.
Doelittle, Thomas, Pimlico, Dublin, clothier　1666. Dub.
Doghtie [Doghter], Walter, Coulmyne
　　　　　　　　　　　　　Dated 1602. Dub.
Doherty, Rev. John, Cashel　　　1715. W. P.
Doine [Doyne], Walter, Moneycullie, par. Laraghbirne, farmer　Dated 1638. Dub.
Dollan, Charles　　　　　　　1700. Dub.
Domney, Murtagh, Miskeane, Co. Cork
　　　　　　　　　　　　　Dated 1692. Cav.
Domvill, John, Dublin, gent.　Dated 1634. Dub.
Donalley [Dunally], Henry Lord　1801. C.D.B.
Donaghe, Elizabeth　　　Dated 1566. Dub.
Done, John, [senr.,], Dublin, chapman　1653. Dub.
Donell, William, Greenock, Co. Dublin, freeholder　　　　　　Dated 1623. Dub.
Donellan, Francis, Portumna, Co. Galway, yeoman　　　　　　　　1656. Dub.
Doner, William, Dublin, gent.　　1699. Dub.
Dongan, Anne, widow　　Dated 1670. Dub.
　" 　　Edward, Dublin, yeoman　Dated 1597. Dub.
　" 　　Edward, Kiltaghan, Co. Kildare, Esq.　　　　　　Dated 1639. W.
　" 　　John, Thomastown　Dated 1601. Dub.

Dognan, John, Possickstowne, Co. Kildare,
    Esq.   Dated 1665. Dub. and W. Dublin
  „ Sir Walter, Castletown, Kildrought, Co. Kildare, Bart.   1626. W.P.
  „ William, Dublin, Recorder of Dublin Dated 1622. Dub.
Donil, or Donat, Morine, Rathno, widow   1593. Dub.
Donking, Roscarrick, Dublin, Esq.   1714. S.1.P.
Donnell, Francis   1719. Dub.
Donnellan, Catherine Nixon, Artane, Co. Dublin   1801. C.D.B.
  „ Mary, Dublin, widow   1812. C.D.B.
  „ Nehemiah, Artane   1772. S.1.P.
Donogh, Jane, Dublin, widow   Dated 1664. Dub.
Donovan, Anne, Ballymore, Co. Wexford   1713. F.
Donughe, Elizabeth   Dated 1566. Dub.
Dooke, William, Ballymacarrat, yeoman Dated 1657. Dub.
Doolan, John, Shinrone, King's Co.   1796. S.1.Killaloe
  „ Joseph, Shinrone   Dated 1767. S.1.Killaloe
  „ Thomas, Portumna   1776. S.1.P.
  „ William, Fairy Hill, Co. Galway   1813. S.1.P.
  „ William, Shinrone   1812. S.1.P.
Dopping, Anthony   1794. F.A.
  „ Margaret   1758. F.A.
  „ Samuel, Dublin, Esq.   1720. F.A.
Dore, Alice, Co. Waterford   1728. F.P.
  „ William, Bantyre, Co. Cork   1726. F.P.
Dorman, Daniel, Limerick, late of Dublin   1692. Dub.
  „ Richard, Monygormy, liberties of Cork   1749. W. Cork
Dormor, Edward, Dublin, gent.   Dated 1669. Dub.
Doude, Thomas, Kellystown, Maynooth, farmer 1635. Dub.
Doughertie, als. Gavan, Alson, Dublin, widow 1630. Dub.
Dougherty, Thomas, Belfast   1812. C.D.B.
Doughty, William, Dublin, gent.   Dated 1679. Dub.
Douglass, Robert, Gracehall, Co. Down   1803. C.D.B.
Dowane, Anne   Dated 1615. Dub.
Dowd. *See* Doude.
Dowdall, Edward, Monktown, Co. Meath, Esq.   1666. W.P.
  „ Edward, Dublin, maltster   Dated 1700. Dub.
  „ George, Drogheda, alderman   1580. Dub.
  „ Jane, widow of Laurence D.   1697. Dub. and W. Dublin

„ John Fitzwalter, Ardye, gent. 1603. Dub.
„ Mathew, Dublin, joiner 1714. Dub.
„ Nicholas, The Curragh, Co. Dublin,
farmer Dated 1638. Dub.
„ Robert Dated 1681. Dub.
„ Stephen, Drogheda, alderman
Dated 1649. Dub.
Dowde, Christopher, Dublin, cordwainer
Dated 1692. Dub.
Dowden, Christopher, Bandon, linen weaver 1729. W. Cork
Dowdinge, Henry, Ballymore Eustace, Co. Dublin 1685. Dub.
„ Nicholas, Swords Dated 1622. Dub.
Dowe, Ann, Coolerowe, Co. Cork, widow 1717. W. Cork
„ Isaac, Melane, Co. Cork, gent. 1723. W. Cork
„ Joshua, Cooleross, Co. Cork, gent. 1714. W. Cork
„ Joshua, Rusnascalp, Co. Cork 1804. C.D.B.
„ Richard, Carrigrohane 1617. W. Cork
Dowgan, Barnaby, Dublin, tailor Dated 1662. Dub.
„ William, Dublin, mason 1578. Dub.
Dowile, Margaret, Ballemolchan, Co. Dublin, widow Dated 1600. Dub.
Dowlen, William, Rathsillagh, Co. Kildare, farmer 1625. Dub.
Dowling, James, Ballymore, Co. Dublin 1640. Dub.
„ Thomas 1593. Dub.
Downell, Patrick, Greenock, Co. Dublin, farmer
Dated 1625. Dub.
Downes, Elizabeth, wife of Dive D., Bp. of
Cork and Ross 1707. F.2.
„ John, late of Sheffield, Co. York,
[cutler] 1665. Dub.
„ Michael, Knockrea, Co. Wexford 1813. C.D.B.
Downham, Very Rev. James, Dean of Armagh 1681. Ir.
Downton, Roger, Dublin 1621. Dub.
Downy, Joshua, Dublin, gent. 1617. Dub.
Downyll, Richard Dated 1560. Dub.
Doyle, Allen, Dublin, merchant 1812. C.D.B.
„ Daniel, Dublin, merchant Dated 1679. Dub.
„ Darby, Dalkey Dated 1616. Dub.
„ Edmund, [Dublin], Priest 1638. Dub.
„ James, Arklow Dated 1638. Dub.
„ John, The Big Eel Ford, or Athnahasgunny 1713. Dub.
„ Michael, Merrion St., Dublin 1813. C.D.B.

Doyle, Nicholas, Coollencullenduffe, Co. Wicklow, gent. 1675. Dub.
„ Oliver, Blancherstown, P.P. of Castleknock 1714. Dub.
„ Patrick, Harristown, Co. Kildare, yeoman 1653. Dub.
„ Patrick Dated 1659. Dub.
„ Philip, soldier, Clarke's Regt. Dated 1654. Dub.
„ Thomas, Dublin, carpenter 1705. Dub.
„ William, Dublin, merchant Dated 1621. Dub.
Doyn, Patrick [? 1538]. Dub.
Doyne, Henry, Dublin, merchant 1641. Dub.
„ James, Dublin, merchant Dated 1600. Dub.
„ Samuel, Dublin, pewterer 1689. Dub.
„ *See* Doine.
Doze, Isaac, [Dublin] 1709. Dub.
Draper, John, Ballymodane 1668. W. Cork
„ Peter, Rostrevor 1782. Swan. P.
„ Sarah Dated 1731. W. Dublin
„ William, Bandon 1642. W. Cork
Draycott, John, Maryverton, Co. Meath 1641. Dub.
Drayton, William, Dublin, baker 1670. Dub.
Dreaper, Rachel, Kinsale, spinster 1708. W. Cork
Drew, Thomasin, (? als. Gibbons), Dublin, widow Circa 1650. Dub.
Drewe, John, Dublin, yeoman Dated 1603. Dub.
„ Thomas, Dublin, gent. 1634. Dub.
Dring, Robert, Cork, Esq. 1759. F.A.
„ Simon, Cork, Esq. 1721. W.P.
Drinkell. *See* Drynckell.
Drinkwater. Mary, Dublin, widow 1686. Dub.
Driscoll (Driskoll), John, Cork 1671. W. Cork
„ Mary, ne Teige 1684. W. Cork
„ Thomas, Kilkenny, clk. 1750. W.P.
Drogheda, Henry Francis, Marquis of 1896. Drogheda MSS.
Dromore, Mathew Lennon Bishop of Dated 22 Jan. 1801. [N.F.P.] C.D.B.
Drope, James, Ballihaise 1758. Swan. P.
„ John, Cootehill, Co. Cavan 1774. Swan. P.
„ John, Ballihaise, Co. Cavan 1800. Swan.
„ William, Ballihaise, Co. Cavan 1754. Swan. P.
Drought, Alice, Cappagolan, King's Co. 1778. Dr. P.
„ Rev. Adolphus Theodore Admon. 1875. Dr.
„ Albert E., **Knockfin,** Queen's Co., farmer Admon.1897. Dr.

Drought, Andrew Smerger, Woodend, Victoria,
        police sergeant   Probate 1897. Dr.
„   Ann, Kilnagarvoge, Co. Carlow   1715. Dr. Leighlin
„   Anna, Harristown, Queen's Co.   1856. D. P.
„   Anne Charlotte, Parsonstown
        Dated 1841. Dr. P.
„   als. Daker, Anne Clancy Probate 1868. Dr.
„   Arthur, The Heath, King's Co., gent 1730. Dr. P.
„   Arthur, Cappagollan, King's Co.
        Admon. 1744. Dr.
„   Bartholomew E., Banagher, King's
        Co.   1841. Dr. P.
„   Bridget, Mountrath, Co. Westmeath,
        widow   Admon. 1900. Dr.
„   Caroline Susannah, Birr, King's Co.,
        widow   Probate 1891. Dr.
„   Caroline, 8 Clifton Terrace, Monkstown, Co. Dublin, widow Probate 1899. Dr.
„   Rev. Charles Bristow, Wheatley,
        near Ilkley, Co. York
        Admon. Intest. 1869. Dr.
„   Dorothea Alicia, 30 Fitzroy St., Co.
        Middlesex, widow Probate 1889. Dr.
„   Edward, Frankford, King's Co. 1838. Dr. P.
„   Edward, Oaklawn, Kinnitty, King's
        Co.   Admon. 1872. Dr.
„   Elinor, 10 Aughrim St., Dublin 1838. Dr. P.
„   Eliza, 18 Duke St., Dublin, spinster
        Admon. 1874. Dr.
„   Eliza Harriet, Glencarrig, Glenealy,
        Co. Wicklow, spinster Admon. 1893. Dr.
„   Elizabeth, Birr, King's Co., spinster 1771. Dr. P.
„   Elizabeth, Ricketstown, Co. Carlow 1811. Dr. P.
„   Elizabeth, 15 Middle Mountjoy Street
        Admon. 1895. Dr.
„   Eusebius, Bannagher, King's Co.,
        gent.   1801. Dr. P.
„   Eusebius [original grant, 1801]
        Admon. 1817. Dr.
„   Eusebius. Will unadministered 1817. Dr. P.
„   Fanny, Ballybrack, Co. Wicklow,
        formerly of Elm Park, Co. Armagh,
        spinster   Probate 1894. Dr.
„   Frances Diana, Aughrim St., Dublin 1839. Dr. P.
„   Francis E., Croghan House, Co. Tipperary   1845. Dr. P.

Drought, [Mrs.] Frederick Drought alias Scott
Admon. 1798. Dr.
,, Frederick, Birr, King's Co. 1805. Dr. P.
,, Frederick, Richmond, Co. Dublin
Two admons. 1868. Dr.
,, George, Castletown, King's Co. 1806. Dr. P.
,, George, 11 Old Mount Pleasant, Ranelagh, Co. Dublin, printer Probate 1885. Dr.
,, George, Glebe View, Ballybritt, King's Co., farmer Probate 1889. Dr.
,, George, Ballyhenry, Roscrea, Co. Tipperary, farmer Probate 1897. Dr.
,, George M. J., Glencarrig, Co. Wicklow 1844. Dr. P.
,, George Perceval, Montpelier Parade, Monkstown, Co. Dublin Admon. 1869. Dr.
,, George Warburton, Cargins, Co. Roscommon Admon. 1881. Dr.
,, Hanna, Parsonstown, King's Co. 1841. Dr. P.
,, Henry, Oak Lawn, King's Co., and Toronto, Canada 1852. Dr. P.
,, Henry, Bow Lane, Dublin Admon. 1867. Dr.
,, Henry, Ballybritt, Roscrea, King's Co., farmer Probate 1894. Dr.
,, Henry Pigott, London, Canada
Probate 1885. Dr.
,, James, Ballyboy, King's Co., gent. 1781. Dr.
,, Rev. James, city of Bath 1828. Dr. P.
,, James, Kilbreedy, Queen's Co.
Probate 1875. Dr.
,, James, Monevane, Portarlington, King's Co., farmer Admon. 1901. Dr.
,, James Morris, Thomas St., Dublin 1849. Dr. P.
,, Jane, Kilrown, King's Co. 1828. Dr. Killaloe.
,, John, Cappagolan, King's Co., gent. 1724. Dr. P.
,, John, Ballyboe, King's Co., gent. 1747. Dr. P.
,, John, Ballyboy, King's Co., gent.
Probate 1748. Dr.
,, John, Heath, King's Co., gent. 1758. Dr. P.
,, John, Whigsborough, King's Co.
Probate 1780. Dr.
,, John, Whigsborough, King's Co. 1780. Dr. P.
,, John, Ricketstown, Co. Carlow, Esq. 1794. Dr. P.
,, John, Ricketstown, Co. Carlow, Esq.
Admon. 1806. Dr.

Drought, John, Ricketstown, Co. Carlow
 Will unadministered 1813. Dr. P.
 " John, Ricketstown, Co. Carlow, Esq.
 [original grant, 1794] Admon. 1813. Dr.
 " John, Whigsborough, King's Co. 1815. Dr. P.
 " John, Lavally, Queen's Co. 1822. Dr. P.
 " John, formerly of Droughtville, late
 of Wellfield, King's Co. 1826. Dr. P.
 " John, Tullamore, King's Co. 1839. Dr.
 " John, Kerawn, Roscrea, farmer
 Admon. 1896. Dr.
 " John Armstrong, Lettybrooke, near
 Kinnetty, King's Co. 1838. Dr.
 " John Head, Lettybrook, King's Co. 1876. Dr.
 " John Wm., Whigsborough, King's Co.
 Probate 1888. Dr.
 " Rev. John Wm., Glencarrig, Glenealy, Co. Wicklow Admon. 1891. Dr.
 " Mary, Cappogolan, King's Co.,
 widow 1745. Dr. P.
 " Mary, Powersgrove, Co. Kildare,
 spinster 1792. Dr. P.
 " Maria, Power's Grove, Co. Kildare,
 spinster Admons. 1805 and 1808. Dr.
 " Mary, Camden St., Dublin, spinster
 Dated 1817. Dr. P.
 " Mary Anne, Ballyboy, King's Co. 1834. Dr. P.
 " Morris, 31 Denzille St., Dublin 1838. Dr. P.
 " Phillippa, Lazer's Hill, Dublin,
 widow 1779. Dr. P.
 " Peter, Mountrath, Co. Westmeath,
 farmer Admon. 1900. Dr.
 " Ralph, High St., Dublin, ironmonger 1787. Dr. P.
 " Richard, Ballybritt, King's Co., farmer 1802. Dr. P.
 " Robert, Park, King's Co. gent. 1726. Dr. P.
 " Robert, Grantstown, Queen's Co. 1746. Dr.
 " Robert, Ballyoran, King's Co. 1784. Dr. P. and
 S.I.P.
 " Robert, Oldglass, Queen's Co. 1801. Dr. P. and
 C.D.B.
 " Robert, Plunketstown, Co. Kildare,
 clerk 1809. Dr. P. and S.I.
 " Robert, Frankford, King's Co. 1827. Dr. P.
 " Robert, Cullen's Wood, Co. Dublin 1831. Dr. P. and
 S.I.P.

Drought, Robert, Durrow, Co. Kilkenny,
M.D. 1834. Dr. P.
„ Robert, Nelson St., Dublin 1848. Dr. P.
„ Robert, Ballygeehan House, Ballacolla, Queen's Co., M.D. Admon. 1862. Dr.
„ Robert Seymour, Pembroke, Passage West, Co. Cork Probate 1900. Dr.
„ Sarah, Parsonstown 1852. Dr. P.
„ Steuart, Dublin 1835. Dr. P.
„ Stewart, Ballybrie, King's Co., Esq.
Admons. 1796 and 1807. Dr.
„ Stewart, Dromoyle, King's Co., Esq. [original grant, 1796] Admon. 1807. Dr.
„ Susan, Banagher, King's Co., widow
Admon. 1876. Dr.
„ Thomas, Plunketstown, Co. Kildare 1753. Dr. P.
„ Thomas, Cappagolan, King's Co., Esq., Admon. 1768. Dr.
„ Thomas, Cappagolan, King's Co. 1769. Dr. P.
„ Thomas, Droughtville, King's Co. 1782. Dr. P.
„ Thomas, Ricketstown, Co. Carlow
Admons. 1799. and 1813. Dr.
„ Thomas, Cappagolan, King's Co. 1808. Dr. P.
„ Thomas, Oldglass, Queen's Co. 1813. Dr.
„ Thomas, Moate, Co. Westmeath 1830. Dr. P.
„ Thomas, Droughtville Forrest, King's Co. 1833. Dr. P.
„ Rev. Thomas Acton, Clonoulty Glebe, Co. Tipperary Admon. 1893. Dr.
„ Thomas Wilder, Carraghmore, King's Co. 1790. Dr. Meath
„ Thomas, Ballywilliam, King's Co., farmer Probate 1902. Dr.
„ William, Kilmagarvogue, Co. Carlow, gent. 1698. Dr. P. and F.2.
„ William, Commonstown, Co. Kildare, farmer 1751. Dr.
„ William, Boherard, Queen's Co. 1780. Dr. P.
„ William, Ricketstown, Co. Carlow 1793. Dr. P.
„ William, city of Westminster 1797. Dr. P.
„ William, Dublin 1816. Dr. Dublin
„ William, Lieut. in H.M.'s Dragoon Guards 1817. Dr. P.
„ William, Balliboy, King's Co.
Dated 1840. Dr. P.

Drought, Rev. William, 15 Montpelier Parade, Monkstown, Co. Dublin, clerk
                                Probate 1884. Dr.
„   William, Ballybritt, King's Co., farmer   Probate 1898. Dr.
„   William, Parsonstown, King's Co., gent.   Probate 1902. Dr.
„   William Beasley, Birr, King's Co.   1816. Dr. P.
„   William Beasley, Birr, King's Co., Esq.   Admon. 1816. Dr.
Drumond [Drummond], Sir John, The Rathe, Co. Tyrone, Knt.   Dated 1625. Dub.
Drury, Edward, Kingsland, Esq.   Admon. 1723. Ir.
„   John, Dublin, gent.   1698. Dub.
Drynckell [Drinkell], Edward, [Dublin]
                                Dated 1595. Dub.
Dublin, Robert Fowler, Archbishop of   1797. C.D.B.
„   Adam Loftus, Archbishop of Dated 1604. M.
„   Francis Marsh, Archbishop of   1693. F.2.
Duckart, Davis (Daviso de Arcort), engineer   1786. S.1.P.
Duckenfeild, Francis, Quartermaster, King's Troop   1658. Dub.
Dudghen, Barbara. *See* Beatty.
Dudley, Elizabeth, Dublin, widow   Dated 1660. Dub.
„   John, Castledermot, gent.   Dated 1660. Dub.
„   Mary, Athy, widow   Dated 1640. Dub.
Duff [Duffe], Lawrence, [Dublin, butcher] 1644. Dub.
„   Sheemus, the Forthuddunte, husbandman   Dated 1577. Dub.
„   Thomas   Dated 1600. Dub.
Duffe, Edmund, Kilmainham   Dated 1569. Dub.
„   als. Taaffe, Elizabeth   Dated 1658. Dub.
„   Loughlin, husbandman of the 3 Castles   Dated 1593. Dub.
„   Morrough, Tyncilly, husbandman
                                Dated 1621. Dub.
„   Nicholas, Howth, fisherman   Dated 1502. Dub.
„   Nicholas, Dublin, alderman   Dated 1582. Dub.
„   Richard, Dublin, baker   Dated 1540. Dub.
„   Thady, Dublin, alderman   Dated 1580. Dub.
„   Tirlagh McHugh O'Doyle, Ballecuke, Arklow   1629. Dub.
„   William, Dublin, butcher   Dated 1641. Dub.
Duffey, Brian, Dublin, worsted comber   1701. Dub.
Duffill, John, Crannagh, Co. Wicklow   1701. Dub.
Duffin, Lt. Col. Adam   1839. S.4. (H.I.)

Dufour, Peter, [Pierre, Dublin] 1717. Dub.
Duine, Edmund, Priest, of St. Catherine's,
   Dublin   Dated 1689. Dub.
Dullen, Donnogh, Castledermot, Co. Kildare 1638. Dub.
Dunalley, Henry, 1st Lord, Kilboy, Co. Tip-
   perary   1801. C.D.B.
 „ Catherine, Lady, Kilboy   1821. S.1.P.
 „ *See* Donally.
Dun, Dermot   1640. Dub.
 „ James, Kilmacredock, Co. Kildare
    ? Dated 1596. [1600]. Dub.
 „ Patrick, Ballybeg, Co. Wexford, farmer 1813. C.D.B.
Duncan, William, Derriaghy, Co. Antrim 1812. C.D.B.
Dungan, als. Holiwood, Margaret. *See*
   Andrewes.
 „ William, now in garrison of Killen-
   hargie   1656. Dub.
Dunkin, Anne Elizabeth, Co. Fermanagh 1755. S.4.
 „ Elizabeth   1766. S.4.
 „ Jane   1785. S.4.
 „ Patrick   1723. S.4.
 „ als. Babington, als. Wray, Rebecca,
   Dublin   1752. S.4.
 „ Rev. William,   Admon. 1766. S.4.
Dunlop, John   1841. S.4. (H.I.)
Dunn, Barnaby, Rathleen, King's Co. 1723. S.1.P.
 „ Charles, Master in Chancery Dated 1617. F.2.
 „ Charles, Brittas, Queen's Co. 1681. F.2.
 „ Margaret, Ballynakill, Queen's Co. 1722. S.1.P.
 „ Frances, Loughrea, Co. Galway, widow 1804. C.D.B.
 „ Grace, Dublin, widow   1801. C.D.B.
 „ James, St. Patrick Street   1672. Dub.
 „ James, Ballinakill, Queen's Co. 1801. C.D.B.
 „ Thomas, Frankford, King's Co. 1770. S.1.P.
 „ Thady, Dublin   Dated 1625. F.2.
 „ Thady, Dublin, shoemaker Dated 1626. Dub.
Dunne, Mary, Logamarla, King's Co.,
   widow   1735. S.1.P.
 „ Rev. Patrick, P.P. of Naas 1812. C.D.B.
Dunscombe, Noblett, Mount Desart, Co. of city
   of Cork, Esq.   Dated 1740. W.P.
Dupleacks, George, Edenderry, King's Co.,
   senr.   1744. W.P.
 „ Thomas, Edenderry, King's Co.,
   gent.   1747. W.P.

Dupon, Mary. *See* Clarke.
„ Stephen 1796. S.4. Dub.
Durand, Peter, [St. Anne's], Westminster, Co.
　Middlesex, Esq. Dated 1716. Dub.
Durning, John Dated 1604. Dub.
Durninge, John, Dublin Dated 1591. Dub.
„ Richard, Garristown 1552. Dub.
Dutens, Alexander, Capt. in Peirce's Dragoons 1712. Dub.
Dutton, Elizabeth. *See* Davoren.
„ Joan, [Dublin], widow Dated 1635. Dub.
„ Richard, Dublin, gent. 1631. Dub.
Duxbury, George, Dublin, clothier 1706. Dub.
Duxon, Nicholas, Ballygibbon 1740. F.
Dwyer, Joseph 1801. C.D.B.
Dyamond [Dymond], Peter, Dublin, merchant 1649. Dub.
Dye, Richard 1715. Dub.
Dyer, John, Knockroe, gent. 1639. W. Cork
„ Thomas, Baltimore 1722. W. Cork
„ Thomas, s. suburbs of Cork city, clothier 1735. W. Cork
Dygname, Robert Dated 1543. Dub.
Dykes, Arthur, Dublin, gent. 1685. Dub.
Dyllon [Dillon], Anne, Dundrum, Co. Down, widow 1634. Dub.
Dymond, Elizabeth, Cork, widow 1690. W. Cork
„ Philip, Cork, merchant 1679. F.2.
„ *See* Dyamond.
Dyne, John, Dublin, cordwainer Dated 1681. Dub.
Dynham, Anne, widow of Edward D., late of Dublin. Renounces Admon. of his Will in 1668. Dub.

Earbery, Mathias, Ballincollig, Co. Cork, Esq. 1730. W.P.
„ Nicholas, Ballincollig, gent. 1729. W.P.
Eastwood, Francis, Falmore, Co. Louth, Esq. 1834. Swan. P.
Eccles, Anne. *See* Coyne.
„ Elizabeth, Dublin, widow 1697. W.P.
„ Lady Elizabeth, wife of Sir John E., Kt. 1728. W. Dublin
„ Francis, Dublin 1652. W. Dublin
„ Gilbert, Shannock, Co. Fermanagh, Esq. 1719. Swan and W. Clogher
,, Hugh, Belfast, merchant 1680. W.P.

Eccles, Hugh, Tamnadowy, par. of Desertlin,
    Co. Londonderry, yeoman   1709. W. Armagh
    ,,   Hugh, Eccles Grove, Co. Wicklow,
    Esq.   1716. W. Dublin
    ,,   Jane, Belfast, widow   1747. W. Connor
    ,,   John, Malone   1704. W. Connor
    ,,   John, Belfast   1726. W.P.
    ,,   John, Belfast   1739. W.P.
    ,,   Joseph, Rathmoran, Co. Fermanagh   1723. W.P.
    ,,   Joyce, wife of Alderman John E.,
    Dublin   1709. W.P.
    ,,   Mary, als. Yarner, wife of Hugh E.,
    Dublin   Dated 1706. W.P.
    ,,   Mary, Waterford, widow   1710. W.P.
    ,,   Samuel, Roan, Co. Armagh   1713. W. Armagh
    ,,   William, Dundesarl, Co. Antrim   1688. W. Connor
    ,,   William, Tamnadny, par. of Desertlyn,
    Co. Londonderry   1715. W. Armagh
    ,,   William, Shanock, Co. Fermanagh,
    gent.   1742. Swan. and W.P.
Eddis, James, senr., Dublin, tanner   1647. Dub.
Edmonds, Anthony, Lynch's Cross, Co. Louth   1747. B.
    ,,   Robert, Dunmore, Co. Kilkenny   1735. B.
Edwards, Anthony, Dublin, brewer   1765. S.1.P.
Elane, Donell   1578. Dub.
Elles, Francis, Royal Crescent, Bath   1842. Swan. P.
Ellicott, als. Keaghry, Honor, Galway, widow   1798. S.2.P.
Elliott, Bartholomew B., Birr, King's Co.   1813. C.D.B.
    ,,   James, Drumrollagh, Co. Fermanagh,
    gent.   1773. Swan. P.
    ,,   William, Rathmoran, Co. Fermanagh,
    Esq.   1696/7. Swan. P.
Ellis, Dorothy. *See* Reynolds.
    ,,   James, Booterstown, Co. Dublin   1825. B.
    ,,   Jane, Dunbar, Co. Fermanagh   1782. Swan. P.
    ,,   Thomas, Monaghan   1714. Swan. Clogher
Ellot, Leonard, Dublin   1676. S.1. Dublin
Ellwell, Elizabeth. *See* Sutton.
Elphin, Simon Digby, Bishop of   1720. S.1.P.
Ely, Thomas, Eminisky, Co. Tipperary   1799. S.1.Killaloe.
Emmet, Christopher, Tipperary, Co. Tipperary   1743. F.
End, William, Cork, merchant   1704. W. Cork
Enery, Dorothy, widow   1776. Swan
    ,,   John, Bawnboy   1756. Swan.
    ,,   Patrick, Garden Hill, Co. Fermanagh   1741. Swan. P.
England, Walter, Dublin, merchant   Dated 1568. Dub.

Enos, Anthony Dated 1581. Dub.
Enraght, Thomas, Rathkeale, Co. Limerick 1813. C.D.B.
Entwistle. See Aentwyssyll.
Erbery, Elizabeth, Cork, widow 1687. W. Cork
Erskine, John, Muff, Templemore parish 1694. Swan. Derry
„ als. Patton, Margaret 1803. Swan. Derry
„ William, Ballishannon, Co. Donegal 1837. Swan. Raphoe
„ See Arisken.
Espie, als. Adaire, Jane. See Getty.
Eustace, Ann 1802. C.D.B.
„ Edward, Elwardstown, Co. Dublin gent. 1597. Dub.
„ John, Castlemartin, [Co. Kildare] 1580. Dub.
„ John, Confy, Co. Kildare Dated 1597. Dub.
„ John, New Ross, Co. Wexford 1802. C.D.B.
„ Margaret, Walterstown, Dio. Kildare, widow Dated 1588. Dub.
„ Oliver, Killemanoge, Co. Dublin 1595. Dub.
„ Robert, [Blackhall, Co. Kildare] Dated 1577. Dub.
Evans, als. Brewster, Anne, Ballywilliam Roe, Co. Carlow 1787. F.A.
„ Eugene, Cork, gent. Admon. 1673. Ir.
„ Francis, Philipstown, King's Co. 1659. Ir.
„ George, Ballygrenane, Co. Limerick 1710. Ir.
„ George, Ballygrenon 1707. F.
Evanson, Maria Townsend Baldwin, Bandon, spinster 1855. Swan. P.
Evory, George, Londonderry 1774. B.
„ James, Dublin 1789. B.
„ Margaret, Dublin 1789. B.
Ewing, John, Carimoney [? Carnmoney], Co. Antrim 1812. C.D.B.
Exham, John, Dublin, Esq. Dated 1668. F.A.
„ John, Greek St., Dublin, Esq. 1777. F.A.
„ Thomas, Frankford, King's Co., gent. 1771. F.A.
„ Thomas, Cork 1824. Swan.
Exshaw, John, Dublin, merchant Dated 1747. Eu.
„ John, Grafton St., Dublin 1776. Eu.
„ Thomasina, widow of John E., of Dublin 1767. Eu.
Eyre, Jane, Eyrecourt 1743. S.1.P.
„ John, Eyrecourt, Co. Galway, Esq. 1685. S.4.P.
„ Robert, Galway 1792. S.1.P.
„ Lieut. Samuel Blake 1795. S.4. (H.BM.)

Eyre, Thomas, Dromoyle, King's Co.   1775. S.1.
  „   Thomas, Eyreville, Co. Galway   1799. S.1.P.

Faggetter, Mary, Cork, spinster   1749. W. Cork
Fahy, Francis, Balleighter and Calfhill, Co.
       Galway   1810. S.2.P.
  „   Malachy, Walgin, Co. Mayo   1804. S.2.P.
  „   Murtagh, Oranmore, Co. Galway   1705. S.2. Tuam
  „   Owen, Darr, Co. Kildare   1616. S.2.P.
  „   William, Ballydulgare, Co. Westmeath   1680. S.2.P.
Falkiner, Caleb, Cork, merchant   1745. W.P.
  „   Richard, Dublin, clothier   1698. F.2.
  „   Richard, Mt. Falcon   Dated 1785. S.1.P.
Falkner, William, Lissbryne, Co. Tipperary   1724. S.1. Killaloe
Fallis, Francis, Emla, Co. Kerry, gent.   1746. F.2.
Fallon, Catherine, Boyle, widow   Dated 1801. C.D.B.
Falls, Alexander, Ballygawley, Co. Tyrone,
       distiller   1788. S.2. P.
  „   Eliz., Aughnacloy, widow   Dated 1803. S.2. Armagh
  „   Henry, Aughnacloy   1810. S.2. Armagh
  „   James, Killygiven, Co. Tyrone   1784. S.2. P.
  „   James, Aughnacloy, Co. Tyrone   1831. S.2. P.
  „   James, Aughnacloy   1851. S.2. P.
  „   James O'Neill, Cloughcastle, Co.
       Antrim   1852. S.2.P.
  „   John, Cock Hill, als. Cavan Kilgreen,
       Co. Armagh   1816. S.2. Armagh
  „   John, Fallbrook, Co. Tyrone   1838. S.2. Armagh
  „   John, Dungannon   1844. S.2. P.
  „   Mary, Fallbrook, Co. Tyrone   1839. S.2. P.
  „   Thomas, Fallbrook   1796. S.2. Armagh
  „   Thomas, Fallbrook   Dated 1837. S.2. Armagh
  „   Thomas, Cavan Kilgreen, Co. Tyrone   1841 S.2. Armagh
Falvey, Daniel, Moynoe   1793. Mol. P.
Fanning, Rev. Edward, Grafton St., Dublin   1791. Swan.
Faris, David, Clodrum, Co. Cavan   1729. Swan. Kilmore
  „   John, Carrigallen   1707. Swan. Kilmore
Farmer, James, Kilrush, Co. Clare   1739. W. Killaloe
  „   Major Jasper   1686. W.
  „   Jasper, Ardevolane, Co. Tipperary,
       Esq.   1715. W.P.
  „   John, Kilshinane   1697. W. Cashel
  „   John, Youghal, mariner   1735. W. Cloyne
  „   Mary, Youghal, Co. Cork, widow   1724. W. Cloyne
  „   Richard, Ardra, Co. Cork   1691. W.P.
  „   Robert, Cork   1749. W.P.

IN THE GENEALOGICAL OFFICE, DUBLIN 177

Farrell, Daniel, Moods, Co. Kildare   1804. C.D.B.
  ,,   Fergus, Dublin, gent.   1720. Cr. and W.P.
  ,,   Fergus, London, merchant   1732. Cr. and W.P.
  ,,   James, Clonaquin, Co. Roscommon, Esq.   Dated 1682. F.2.
  ,,   James, Cloonyquin   1682. Ir.
  ,,   James   1738. Ir.
  ,,   Margaret, Longford, spinster   1831. M.
Farren, Thomas, Cork, alderman   1761. F.A.
Faussett, John, Coolarkin, Co. Fermanagh, gent. 1785. Swan. P.
Fegan, Byron   1813. C.D.B.
Fendall, als. Brocklesby, Elizabeth, widow of James F.   1694. W. Cork
Fennell, Algernon, Manning, gent.   1709. W. Cloyne
  ,,   Blessing, Youghal, widow   1735. W. Cloyne
  ,,   Gerald, M.D.   1665. W.P.
  ,,   Hester   1736. W.P.
  ,,   John, Mahon   1674. W. Cork
  ,,   John, Cork, merchant   1682. W.P.
  ,,   John, Curraghivore, Co. Cork   1710. W. Cloyne
  ,,   John, Ballymorelly, Co. Limerick, gent.   1733. W.P.
  ,,   John, Youghal   Dated 1741. W. Cloyne
  ,,   John, Cloanfady, Co. Waterford, gent. Dated 1744. W. Waterford
  ,,   John   1751. W. Waterford
  ,,   Jowan Fitz James, widow of John Butler   Dated 1666. W.P.
  ,,   Richard, Coleigh, Co. Tipperary   Dated 1606. W.P.
  ,,   Robert, Ballyquain, Co. Cork, gent. 1728. W. Cloyne
Fenner, Alexander   1801. C.D.B.
Fenton, Sir Maurice, Mitchelstown, Co. Cork, Bart.   1664. W.P.
  ,,   Sir William, Mitchelstown, Co. Cork, Kt.   1667. W. Cork
  ,,   Sir William, Mitchelstown, Co. Cork, Bart.   1671. W.P.
  ,,   Sir William, Mitchelstown, Co. Cork, Kt.   1671. W.P.
Fenwick, Ann, Bandonbridge, Co. Cork, spinster   1681. W. Cork
  ,,   Joshua, Clonmore, Co. Carlow, Esq. 1665. F.2.
  ,,   Ralph, Mahoony, Co. Cork, Esq. 1675. F.2.
Ferguson, Agnes. *See* Fife.
Fernley, Mary. *See* Poë.

Ferns, Thomas Ram, Bishop of   Dated 1633. F.2.
Ferrall, Andrew, Athlone, Co. Roscommon   1802. C.D.B.
   „   Richard, Barn, Co. Longford, Esq.   1669. F.2.
Fetherston, Eliz., Whiterock, Co. Longford,
                widow   1766. Ir.
   „   Francis, Whiterock, Co. Longford 1748. Ir.
   „   Francis   1757. Ir.
   „   Gertrude, widow   1788. Ir.
   „   Robert, Dublin   1779. Ir.
   „   Thomas, Castlekearan, Co. Meath 1729. S.4. P.
Fiddes, Alexr., Co. Fermanagh   1742. B.
   „   Edward   1776. B.
   „   Rev. James, Killydonnellan, Co. Mon-
           aghan   1820. B.
   „   James, Tullycreevy, Co. Fermanagh   1779. B.
   „   Margaret, Enniskillen, spinster   1841. Swan. P.
   „   Richard, Enniskillen   1813. B.
   „   Richard, Enniskillen, late of Tully-
           creevy   1813. Swan.
   „   Sarah, Enniskillen   1821. B.
Fiddis, Alexr., Tullycreevy, Co. Fermanagh   1742. Ir.
Fife, als. Ferguson, Agnes, Newtownards, Co.
       Down   1812. C.D.B.
Finey, Eliz. *See* Blumfield.
Finin, John, Peter's Well   1750. Cr. Tuam
Finn, William, Carlow   1813. C.D.B.
Finucane, Morgan, The Cottage, Ennistimon,
         Co. Clare   1836. Mol. P.
Fisher, George, Carneville, Co. Meath, Esq.   1790. Swan. P.
   „   Reuben, Youghal   Dated 1714. F.
   „   William, Dublin, merchant   1739. W.P.
Fitzgerald, als. Langford, Catherine   1800. S.1.
   „   Capt. Hugh Massey   1805. S.4. (H.BM.)
   „   James, [? Clucary], Co. Clare   1664. F.
   „   James, Lackagh, Co. Kildare   1670. Cav.
   „   John, Buttikeale, Co. Limerick   1801. Mol. P.
   „   John, Newtown Pery, City of
             Limerick   1806. Mol. P.
Fitzgerald, Louisa Petitot   1827. F.E.
   „   als. Power, Mary, Ballykenelly, Co.
             Cork, widow   1752. S.1.
   „   Michael Gould, Cork   1705. Cav. Cork
   „   Nicholas, John Street, Limerick   1797. Mol. P.
   „   William, Ballynard, Co. Limerck,
             gent.   Dated 1716. W. Cashel
   „   William, Lacharne, Co. Kerry   1731. W. Cashel

Fitzharris, Mary. *See* Connor.
Fitzhenry, William, Ballymakesey, Co. Wexford 1812. C.D.B.
Fitz Maurice, Raymond, Dublin   1714. W.P.
  „   Gertrude Margaret, Dublin   1812. C.D.B.
  „   William, Gullane, Co. Kerry   1711. W.P.
FitzPatrick, Florence, Galway, merchant   1709. S.4.
  „   Thomas, Coole, Co. Galway, farmer   1747. Cr. Clonfert
FitzSimons, Rev. Wm., Sydenham Hall, Co. Meath 1801. C.D.B.
Flanagan, Mary, Clencaron, Co. Fermanagh   1774. Swan. Dublin.
Fleetwood, Charles, Athy, Co. Kildare   1739. B.
  „   Charles, Jane Villa, Co. Kildare   1774. B.
  „   Charles, Dublin   1830. B.
  „   Dora, Dublin   1862. B.
  „   Francis, Ballingarry, Co. Meath   1770. B.
  „   George, Dublin   1862. B.
  „   Mary, Dublin, widow   1763. B.
  „   Robert, Shanco, Co. Meath   1776. B.
  „   Sarah, Willow Lodge, Co. Tipperary   1835. B.
  „   Sibella, Downpatrick and Dublin   1868. B.
  „   Thomas, Ballydearaven, Co. Cork   1632. B.
  „   Thomas, Banagher, King's Co.   1843. B.
Fleming, Arthur, Belville   1766. Swan. P.
  „   Arthur, Belville, Co. Cavan   1821. Swan. P.
  „   James, city of Londonderry   1824. Swan. P.
  „   Randal. *See* Slane, Lord.
  „   Lieut. Robert   D. 1805. S.4. (H.O.)
  „   Thomas, Lisnelong, Co. Cavan   1708. Swan. Kilmore
  „   Thomas, Cavan   1793. Swan. Kilmore
  „   Thomas, Castlecosby, Co. Cavan   1824. Swan. P.
  „   William, Belturbet   1834. Swan. P.
Fletcher, Elizabeth, Belfast, widow   1722. Swan. P.
  „   Honora   1782. Swan. P.
  „   Jane, Lisburn, Co. Antrim, widow   1804. C.D.B.
  „   William, Bolakeale, Co. Tipperary   1787. B.
Flood, Peter, President of the College of Maynooth 1803. C.D.B.
Flower, Sir William, Finglas, Co. Dublin   1681. F.2.
Fogarty, Cornelius, Garrane, Co. Tipperary, gent. Dated 1730. S.4.
Fogerty, Philip, Ballintonty, Co. Tipperary 27 Jan., 1813 [N.F.P.]   C.D.B.
Folliott, Capt. Anthony, Londonderry   1670. B.
  „   Frances, Boyle, Co. Roscommon   1672. F.2.

Folliott, Henry, Termalin, Londonderry — 1719. B.
Folque, Henry, Killavy, Co. Fermanagh — 1725. M. and Swan.
Foord, John, Limerick, alderman — 1712. W.P.
Foott, George, [Moyallow] — 1677. W. Cloyne
Forbes, Ann, Dublin, widow — 1801. C.D.B.
„ Michael (? Mabel), Chester, spinster — 1804. C.D.B.
„ Thomas — 1802. C.D.B.
Ford, Alice, Kevin Street, Dublin, widow — Not dated [? 1813.] C.D.B.
„ Dame Jane Allen, widow — 1802. C.D.B.
„ John, Cork — 1698. F. and Davis
„ Nicholas, Cork, brewer — 1713. F. and Davis
Forde, Elizabeth, Seaford, Co. Down, widow — 1812. C.D.B.
„ Matthew, Seaforde, Co. Down — 1812. C.D.B.
Forstall, James, Forstallstown, Co. Kilkenny, gent. — Admon. 1661. F.A.
„ Peter, Carrigloning, Co. Kilkenny, gent. — 1683. F.A.
Forster, Anne, widow — 1737. Swan. P.
„ Francis, Dublin, brewer — 1773. Swan. P.
„ John, Dublin — 1613. B.
„ John, Clanvally — 1719. Swan. Clogher
„ John, Tullaghan, Co. Monaghan — 1738/9. Swan. P.
„ John, Cavan, Co. Cavan, merchant — 1753. Swan. P.
„ Margaret. *See* Johnston.
„ Margaret, Lisnagole, Co. Fermanagh — 1801. Swan.
„ Margaret, Cavan, spinster — 1859. Swan.
„ Mark, Lisnaskea, Co. Fermanagh — 1805. Swan. Clogher
„ Mary, widow — 1736. Swan. P.
„ Rev. Nicholas, Stradbally, Queen's Co. — 1813. C.D.B.
„ Rev. Richard, Co. Dublin — 1657. B.
„ Richard, Clonsasaley, Co. Dublin — 1711. F.
„ Samuel, Kilmurry, Co. Meath — 1807. Swan. P.
„ Thos., Roristown, Co. Meath, gent. — 1775. Swan. P.
„ William, Cork, mariner — 1745. W. Cork
„ William, Kilmurry, now of Trim — 1763. Swan. P.
Forth, James, Dublin — 1731. S.I.P.
Fosbery, Francis, Kilcoroly, Co. Limerick — Dated 1700. F.
„ Francis — Dated 1717. F.
„ George, [? Kildemo], Co. Limerick — 1774. F.P.
Foster, Abraham, Ballymallo, Co. Cork — 1802. C.D.B.
„ Arthur, Dungoone — 1688. Swan. P.
„ Charles Thomas — D. 1822. S.4. (H.O.)
„ William, Dowdstown, Co. Meath — 1803. Swan. P.

Foukes, Ellen, Monasterevan, Co. Kildare,
　　　　widow　　　　　　　　　　　　1726. F.E.
　　„　　als. White, Frances, Kilkenny　　1685. F.E.
Foulke, Anne, Youghal, Co. Cork, widow　1763. F. and F.E.
　　„　　Deborah, Rathoath, Co. Meath, widow 1728. F. and F.E.
　　„　　Digby, Tallow, Co. Waterford, Esq.　1783. F. and F.E.
　　„　　Digby, Young Grove, Co. Cork　　1810. F. and F.E.
　　„　　Elizabeth, Strawhall, Co. Cork, widow 1732. F.E. and W.P.
　　„　　Francis, Shanegarry, Co. Cork, Esq. 1702. F.E.
　　„　　Francis, Ratoath, Co. Meath, clk.　1713. F.E.
　　„　　Robt., Youghal, Esq.　　　　　　1741. F.E.
Foulks, George, N. Suburbs of Cork, innkeeper 1731. W. Cork
Fowke, Matthew, Cork, apothecary　　　1709. W. Cork
Fowler, Most Rev. Robert, Archbishop of Dublin
　　　　　　　　　　　　　　Dated 1797. C.D.B.
Fox, Joseph, Graige, Lr. Ormond, Co. Tipperary　　　　　　　　　　　　1689. S.4.
　　„　Hon. Luke [Hon. Mr. Justice Fox]　1819. Swan. P.
Franck, Thomas, Franckfort, King's Co.　1731. S.1.P.
Frankland, Agnes, widow of Richard F., of Cork,
　　　　M.D.　　　　　　　　　　　　1787. F.A.
　　„　　Barry, Cork, gent.　　　　　　1734. F.A.
　　„　　Richard, Cork, M.D.　　　　　1763. F.A.
　　„　　[Franckland], Thomas　　　　1686. F.2.
Freeman, Daniel, Rapla, Co. Tipperary　1744. S.1.P.
　　„　　Jane, Cavan, widow　　　　　1824. Swan. P.
　　„　　John, Ringrone, Co. Cork, gent.　1667. F.
　　„　　John, Cork　　　　　　　　　1667. F.
　　„　　John, Cork　　　　　　　　　1710. F.
　　„　　Mary, Finoe, Co. Tipperary　Dated 1752. S.1.Killaloe
　　„　　Mary, city of Dublin, widow　1789. S.1.
　　„　　Richard, Cork　　　　　　　　1688. F.
　　„　　Richard, Ballinguile, Co. Cork, gent. 1718. W.P.
　　„　　Thomas, Dublin, merchant　　1668. Swan.
　　„　　Thomas, Esker, Queen's Co.　1733. S.1.P.
　　„　　William, Kilmusky, Co. Cork　1672. F.
　　„　　William, Castlecor　　　　　　1732. W.P.
French, Agnes, Galway, widow　　　　　1802. C.D.B.
　　„　　Alexander, Galway, mercht.　Dated 1593. Ir.
　　„　　Arthur, Clooneyquin, Co. Roscommon,
　　　　Esq.　　　　　　　　　　　　1729. Ir.
　　„　　Arthur, Tyrone, now of Tuam　1779. Ir.
　　„　　Catherine, widow of Aldn. Richd. F. 1800. Swan.
　　„　　Christopher, Tyrone, Co. Galway　1720. Ir.
　　„　　Lt. Col. Christopher, 52nd Regt. of
　　　　Foot　　　　　　　　　　　　**1797. Ir.**

French, Christopher, Curraghboy, Co. Mayo
	Not dated	Ir.
„	Daniel, Belturbet, Co. Cavan
	Admons. 1702. Swan. P.
„	Daniel, Dublin, gent.	1736. Swan. Dublin
„	Dominick, Dungar, Co. Roscommon	1670. Ir.
„	Elizabeth, St. Finbarr's, Cork, widow	1668. F.2.
„	Geoffrey, Galway	1528. Ir.
„	Henry Walter, Clooneyquin	1817. Ir.
„	Henry Walter	1820. Ir.
„	Rev. Humphrey, D.D., Dunshaughlin, Co. Meath	1788. Swan. P.
„	Isabella, wife of Daniel F.	1718. Swan. P.
„	James, Cork, alderman	1710. F. and W.P.
„	Jeffrey, Leicester Fields, Middlesex, and Middle Temple	1754. Ir.
„	John (FitzStephen)	1669. Ir.
„	John, Cork, gent.	Admon. 1730. F. and Davis
„	John (FitzValentine), Galway	1635. Ir.
„	Katherine	Dated 1544. Ir.
„	Marcus, Rahassane, Co. Galway, Esq.	1723. Ir.
„	Margaret, Kinsale, widow	1639. F.
„	Dame Marie, widow of Sir Peter F.	1685. Ir.
„	Martin, Frenchgrove, Co. Mayo	1801. C.D.B.
„	Mathew, Belturbet, Esq.	1691. Swan. P.
„	Mathew, Ballyhublock, Co. Wicklow	1731. Swan.
„	Matthew, Dublin, merchant	1755. Swan.
„	Rev. Mathew, Preb. of Kilroot	1722. Swan.
„	Patrick, Monivea, Galway	Dated 1618. Ir.
„	Patrick, Dungar, Co. Roscommon	1671. Ir.
„	Patrick, Duras, Co. Galway, Registered 27th Jan. [Registry of Deeds]	1709. Cr.
„	Patrick, Duras, Registered 4th Feb., [Registry of Deeds]	1709. Cr.
„	Sir Peter, Galway	1636. Ir.
„	Pitter FitzJohn, Galway, alderman
	Dated 1584. Ir.
„	Richard, Belturbet	1638. Swan. P.
„	Richard, St. Finn Barrys	1651. F.
„	Richard, Dublin	1686/7. Swan. P.
„	Richard, Johnstown, Co. Dublin	1779. Swan.
„	Richard, Baltinglass, Co. Wicklow	1782. Swan. P.
„	Robert, Rahasane, Co. Galway	1789. M.
„	Roboche (FitzJohn)	1602. Ir.
„	Sarah, widow	1803. C.D.B.

French, Thomas FitzMarcus, sometime of Galway, now in Bilboa, Spain   Dated 1716. Cr. Tuam
„   Thomas, Moycullen, Co. Galway   1785. S.4.
„   Walter, Galway   1638. Ir.
„   Walter, Kinsale, merchant   1658. F.2.
Frend, John, Carrickareely, Co. Limerick   1675. S.1.P. and F.2.
Friend, Jonathan, Kilmurney, Co. Kilkenny, gent.   1671. F.2.
„   [Frend], Samuel, Carrickereely, Co. Limerick   1683. F.2.
Frizell, Chas., Holles Street, Dublin   Dated 1810. S.4.
„   Charles, senr., Holles St., Dublin   1812. C.D.B.
Fuller, Anne, Bandonbridge, widow   1630. F. and W.P.
„   George, Cork, Esq.   1739. F.
„   George, Cork, Esq.   1745. W. Cork
„   Mary, Bandonbridge   1686. F.
„   Ralph, Oldcastle   1766. F.
„   Richard, Finn Barrys, Cork   1641. F. and W. Cork
„   Robert, Kinsale   1666. F. and W. Cork
„   Thomas, Bandonbridge, yeoman   1643. F. and W. Cork
„   Thomas, Iniskeene   1672. F. and W. Cork
„   Thomas, Iniskeene   1687. F. and W. Cork
Fuller, William, Ballymodan, Co. Cork   1677. F. and W. Cork
„   William, Church Lane, Cork   1775. F.A.
Fullerton, Mary. *See* Gregory.
Furlong, Bridget, Wexford, Co. Wexford   1683. W. Ferns
„   Mary, Ballyhack, Co. Wexford, widow   1813. C.D.B.
„   Humphrey, Munnega   1714. S.2. Cloyne

Gabbott, William   1736. F.
Gahan, George, Coolquil, Co. Tipperary   1731. S.1.P.
„   Robert   1818. S.4. (H.I.)
Gaich, John, Gaichborough, King's Co.   Dated 1705. S.1.P.
„   Ruth, Griffinrath, Co. Kildare, widow   1712. B.
Galbalie, Maude. *See* Archbold.
Galbraith, James, Ramorane, Co. Fermanagh   1673. F.2.
„   James, Roscavey, Co. Tyrone   1787. S.2.P.
„   Jane, Donish, Co. Donegal, widow   1675. F.2.
„   Jane, Ramorane, Co. Fermanagh   1676. S.2. P.
„   Josias, Crachadooey, Co. Donegal   1676. S.2.P.
„   Thomas, Up. Cooladerry, Co. Donegal   1720. S.3. Raphoe
Gallwey, Francis, Glanmire Road, Cork   1804. C.D.B.

Galt, Charles, Coleraine — 1801. C.D.B.
Galwey, John, Malaga, Spain — 1812. C.D.B.
Gambell, Elizabeth, Waterford — 1731. W. Waterford
Gamble, Arthur, Waterford — 1741. W. Waterford
„ Elizabeth, Cork — 1749. W.P.
„ John, Oldcourt, Cork, gent. — 1724. W.P.
Gard, Richard, Garrymore, Co. Cork — 1801. C.D.B.
Gardiner, Katherine, Bandon, Co. Cork, now of Wexford — Dated 1813. M.
Garner, James — D. 1825. S.4. (H.O.)
„ Joseph — D. 1851. S.4. (H.O.)
„ Thomas — D. 1848. S.4. (H.O.)
Garvey, als. Burke als. Lynch, Annabel. *See* Keaghry.
Gash, John, Castle Lyons, Co. Corke, gent. — 1681. W.P.
„ John, junr., now prisoner in Co. Cork gaol — 1741. W. Cork
„ Margaret — 1712. W. Cloyne
Gason, John, Richmond, Co. Tipperary — 1759. S.1.P.
„ Joseph, Ballycumine, Co. Tipperary — Dated 1712. S.1.Killaloe
„ Joseph, Nenagh — 1777. S.1.Killaloe
„ Richard, Killashalloe (Richmond) — 1772. S.1.P.
„ Samuel, Nenagh — 1772. S.1.P.
Gaussen, Charles, Gardiner's Place, Dublin — 1887. Swan.
Gavan, Alson. *See* Doughertie.
Gay, Anne, Dublin, widow — Dated 1693. F.
„ John, Dublin — 1692. F.
Geale, Benjamin, Lismore, Co. Tipperary, gent. — 1732. W. Cashel
Geasley, Roger, Curraglasse, Co. Cork — 1666. Swan. Cork
Geaseley, Roger, Tullogh, Co. Waterford — 1739. Swan. P.
Geasly, Elizabeth, Youghal, widow — 1679. Swan. Cork
„ Roger, Tullough, Co. Waterford — 1744. Swan. P.
Gentleman, Mary, Kanturk, spinster Admon. — 1801. F.A.
„ Capt. Patrick, Paystown, Co. Dublin — Admon. 1749. F.A.
„ Robert, Kanturk, Co. Cork — 1802. C.D.B and F.A.
Gerald, Henry, Monard, Co. Cork — 1700. F.2.
Gething, Richard, Ballefenatyr, Co. Cork — 1679. F.2.
Getty, Jane, als. Espie, als. Adaire, Maghera, Co. Londonderry, widow — Admon. 1694. F.A.
Gibbings, Arthur, Lieut.-Col. Madras Army — 1842. Swan.
„ John, Garrane, Co. Cork — 1732. F. and W. Cloyne
„ John, Lieut. Hon. East India Company — 1831. Swan P.

Gibbings, Rev. Richard, Gibbings Grove, Co.
        Cork   1813. C.D.B.
„   Thomas, Cork   1813. C.D.B.
Gibbon, Robert, Kilworth, Diocese of Cloyne,
        clk.   1721. W.P.
Gibbons, John, Kindlestown, parish of Delgany,
        Co. Wicklow   1749. F.D.
„   Simon, Youghal, merchant   Admon. 1639. F.A.
„   Thomasin. *See* Drew.
Gifford, Henry, New Ross, Co. Wexford   1760. W. Ferns
„   John, Castlejordan   1676. F.2.
„   John, Ahern, Co. Cork   1741. Swan.
„   Ravenscroft, New Ross, Co. Wexford,
        Esq.   1736. W. Ferns
Gilbert, Jane. *See* Blood.
Gill, Katherine, relict of John G., Lurgan Clan-
        brazil, Co. Armagh   1721/22. W.P.
Gillespie, Hugh, Cherry Valley, par. of Cumber,
        Co. Down   1755. W. Down
„   James, Gortclowry, Co. Tyrone   1741. W.P.
„   Robert, Parsonstown, King's Co.   1735. W.P.
Gillis, Grove   1783. S.4. (H.BM.)
Gillman, Henry, Killneglary, Co. Cork, gent. 1724. W. Cork
„   Herbert, Shanacloyne, Co. Cork, gent. 1765. F.E.
„   Heyward, St. Finbarrys, Cork   1733. W.P.
„   John, senr., Curryheene, Co. Cork,
        gent.   Dated 1724. W. Cork
„   John, Curriheen, South Libs. of Cork,
        gent.   1746. W.P.
„   Philip   Dated 1724. W. Cork
„   Silvester   Not dated   W. Cork
„   Stephen, Curryheene, Co. Cork, gent. 1679. W. Cork
„   Stephen, Clasmartel, Co. Cork   1710. W. Cork
„   Stephen, now of Curraheen, Cork,
        Esq.   1748. W.P.
„   Stephen, Cove of Kinsale, Esq.   1829. F.A.
Gillmor, Hugh, Monaghan, merchant   1715. Swan. Clogher
Gilman, Bridget, Ballymodan, widow   1689. W. Cork
„   John, Currine, Co. Cork, gent.   1644. W. Cork
Glanally, Dame Susanna, Baroness of   1690. W.P.
Glenny, Isaac, Saullmore, Co. Down   1770. Swan.
Glover, Margaret, Mallow, widow   1654. F.
Goddard, Sarah, Kilkenny   1802. C.D.B.
Godfrey, William, Knockgraffan, Co. Tipperary 1696. S.1.P. and F.2.
„   William, Bushfield, Co. Kerry   1747. Cav.

Godsell, Amos, Moorestown, Co. Limerick
                                Dated 1714. F., F.E. and Mol.P.
Godwin, Robert, Drogheda   1642. B.
Goff, Rev. Thos., Eccles St., Dublin, clk.   1844. F.A.
Goldsmith, Edward, Dean of Elphin Admon. 1723. Ir.
    ,,   Edward, Limerick   1762. S.4. P.
    ,,   Robert, Ballyoughter, Co. Roscommon, gent.   1711. Ir.
Good, William, St. George's Troop   1663. F.2.
Goodman, James, Mabeg, par. of Marragh, Co. Cork, maltsman   1669. W. Cork
Goodriche, Thos., Cahir [? Cahirucha], Co. Limerick   1742. F.
Goodwin, Simon, Talbotstown, Co. Wicklow, Esq.   Dated 1723. S.4.
Gookin, Robert, Courtmasherry, Co. Cork   1666. F. and F.2.
    ,,   Robert, Currageen, Co. Cork, Esq. 1752. F. and F.E.
Goold, Francis, Cork, merchant   1770. F.2.
    ,,   Helen, Cork, widow   1746. F.2.
    ,,   Michael, Jamesbrook, Co. Cork   1722. Cav. P. and F.2.
Gordon, Ainegier, Robertstown   1723. Swan. Ardagh
    ,,   Alex., Capt. in Herbert's Regt.   1691. Swan. P.
    ,,   Alex., Ardandreagh, Co. Longford 1691. S.2.P. and M.
    ,,   Alex., Lesise, par. of Dromballyroney, Co. Down   Dated 1708/9. S.4.
    ,,   Anne, Racavan, Co. Antrim   1813. C.D.B.
    ,,   Thos. Knox, Loyalty Lodge, Co. Down   1796. S.1.P.
    ,,   Charles, Park Place, Co. Dublin   1792. Swan. P.
    ,,   Hannah, Mackenagh, Co. Tyrone   1755. Swan. P.
Gore, Clements   D. 1795. S.4. (H.I.)
    ,,   Thomas   1813. C.D.B.
    ,,   Sir William, Bart.   1705. Ir.
Gorman, Capt. Robert Johnston   1802. S.4. (H.BM.)
Gough, Francis, Cork, gent.   1695. F.2.
    ,,   Jane, Cork, widow   1710. F.
    ,,   Mercy, widow of Capt. Wm. G., Doonassy, Co. Clare   Dated 1671. F.2.
    ,,   William, Doonasa, Co. Clare, gent.
                                     Dated 1664. F.2.
    ,,   William, Cork, merchant   1671. F.
Gould, Garrett, Knockrahee (or Knockrahan), Co. Cork   1697. F. and F.2.
    ,,   Garrett, Knockraheen, Co. Cork   1766. F. and F.2.
    ,,   Patrick, Cork, merchant   1681. F.2.

Grady, Henry, parish of St. James, Westmin-
ster, late of Paris 1783. S.2.P.
„ Thomas, Harley Street, London 1788. S.2.
„ Rev. Thomas, Barne 1804. C.D.B.
Graham, Anthony Dated 1682. F.
„ James, Ballymore Allen, Co. Cork 1718. Swan. Cork
„ John 1657. F.
„ John, Ballygrane, Queen's Co. 1667. F.
„ John, Drogheda, alderman 1714. S.4.
„ John 1724. W.P.
„ John, St. George's St., Dublin 1777. S.1.P.
„ John, city of Cork, shopkeeper
Dated 1738. Swan. and
W. Cork
„ Peter, Castlelyons 1749. F.
„ Pierce, Orell, Co. Limerick Dated 1682. F.
„ Robert, Balliheridon, Co. Armagh,
gent. 1680. F.2.
„ Major Thomas Dated 1652. Swan.
„ Major Thomas 1666. F.
„ Brig. Gen. William 1747. S.4.
„ Rt. Hon. William, Platten, Meath 1748. S.1.P.
„ William, Drumgoon, Co. Cavan 1797. Swan.
„ William D. 1829. S.4. (H.O.)
Grant, Jasper 1698. F. and F.2.
Gratan, Patrick, Belcamp, Co. Dublin, D.D. 1707. F.2.
Grattan, Rt. Hon. James 1854. F.E.
„ John, Clonmeen, Co. Kildare 1750. S.3.
„ Rev. Patrick, Belcamp, Dublin
[Notes, no Will] D. 1703. Swan.
„ Rev. Ralph, D.D., Brookfield, Co.
Tipperary 1772. S.1.P.
„ Rose Anna, widow 1802. C.D.B.
„ Rev. William, Tullycleagh, Co. Fer-
managh, clk. Admon. 1719. Ir.
„ Rev. William, Swanlinbar 1844. Swan.
Gratton, Daniel, Rabbitfield 1772. S.1.P.
Grave, Abigail, Ballycommon, widow 1780. S.1. Kildare
„ Anne, Killeigh, widow of Rev. Joseph
G. 1803. S.1. Kildare
„ Elizabeth, widow Dated 1814. S.1.
„ John, Dublin, merchant, now in Mary-
land 1742. S.1. Dublin
„ Rev. Joseph, Ballycommon Dated 1743. S.1.P.
„ Joseph, Killeigh, King's Co., clk. 1802. S.1. Kildare
„ Mary, Dublin, widow 1747. S.1.

Grave, Mary, Dublin, spinster	1754. S.1.	
" Rev. William, Kenagh, Co. Longford	1839. S.1.P.	
Graves, Anthony, a trooper at Dungarvan	1658. B.	
" Grace, Drogheda, widow	Dated 1672. S.1. Meath	
Gray, Anne, Donard, Co. Wicklow, widow	1791. C.D.B.	
" Charles, Drury Lane, Dublin	1804. C.D.B.	
" Martha, Portobello, widow	1802. C.D.B.	
" Terence, Ballymodan	1698/9. W. Cork	
" William, Dublin	1705. B.	
" William, north suburbs of Cork, chandler	1748. W. Cork	
Grayson, Abraham, Hugh St., Dublin	1756. Swan.	
" Anthony, Londonderry, formerly of Dublin	1809. Swan. P.	
Greatrakes, Alice	1685. F.	
" Edmund, New Affane, Esq.	Admon. 1692. F.A.	
" Valentine	1684. F.	
" Valentine, New Affane	Admon. 1691. F.A.	
" William, [? New Affane], Co. Waterford	1685. F.	
Greatreaks, William, Affane, Co. Waterford	1686. F.2.	
Greatricks, Edward, Cornrosse, Co. Wexford, Esq.	Admon. 1676. F.A.	
" Elizabeth, Aughamayne, Co. Waterford, widow	Admon. 1630. F.A.	
" William, Aughmayne, Co. Waterford, Esq.	Admon. 1628. F.A.	
Greatrix, William, Aghane, Co. Waterford, Esq.	Admon. 1663. F.A.	
Green, Edward, Youghall, innkeeper Cloyne	Admon. 1671. Swan.	
" Godfrey, Kilmanahan, Co. Waterford	1683. F.	
" Henry, Dublin	1738. F.	
" Nicholas, Dublin, gent.	1656. F.	
" Simon, junr., Youghal	1731/2. Swan.	
" William, Ballinaboy	1623. Swan. Cork	
" William, Rushane, Co. Clare	1768. Mol. P.	
Greene, Eliah, College Green, Dublin, Esq.	1677. F.2.	
" Henry, Dresternan, Co. Fermanagh	1691. W.	
" Nicholas, Dublin, cornet	1656. W. Dublin	
" Nicholas	Dated 1725. F.	
" Richard, Pimlicoe	1665. W. Dublin	
" William Sheppey	D. 1811. S.4. (H.I.)	
Greer, als. Poge, Mary, Stranlorlar, Co. Donegal	1724. B.	
Gregory, Benjamin, Manooth, Co. Kildare	1742. S.4. P.	
" Catherine, Athlone, Co. Westmeath, widow	Dated 1668. S.2. Meath	

Gregory, als. Broome, Eliz., city of Derry 1707. S.2. Derry
„ George, Castlebar, Co. Mayo Dated 1757. S.2. Tuam
„ Rev. George, curate of parish of
    Down   Dated 1732. S.1.
„ Giles 1664. F.
„ Joshua, H.M.S. Severn 1742. S.2. Dublin
„ als. Fullerton, Mary, widow 1731. S.2. P.
„ Robert, Mt. Etna, Co. Kerry, Esq. 1775. S.2. Ardfert
„ Robert, Galway 1741. S.2. Tuam
„ Robert Burke 1824. S.4. (H.I.)
„ Samuel, Dublin 1776. S.2. Dublin
Gregg, Jean, als. Jinn, Knockcarn, Co. Antrim 1780. F.E.
„ Thomas, Knockcano 1780. F.E.
„ William, Parkmount, Co. Antrim, merchant, formerly of Belfast 1782. F.E.
Grey, Lt. Col. John, lying wounded in Clonmel 1650. W. Cork
„ William, Clonoghill, King's Co. Dated 1742. Sadleir Deeds
Grice, Richard 1667. F.2.
Grier, Thomas, Rhonehill 1803. C.D.B.
Griffin, Ann, Dublin, widow 1745. W. Dublin
„ Lt. Col. Daniel Fitzgerald 1804. S.4. (H.BM.)
„ Henry, Clonbrien, Co. Kerry Dated 1741. Davis
„ Mortogh, Killarney, Co. Kerry, Esq.
     Dated 1712. Davis
Griffith, Richard, Dean of Ross 1717. W.P.
Grigg, John, Ardmore, Co. Cork 1670. S.2. Cloyne
„ John, Ardprior 1724. S.2. Cloyne
„ Richard, Ardprior, Co. Cork 1741. S.2. Cloyne
Grogan, Edward, Dublin 1813. C.D.B.
Grueber, Nicholas. Dated 19 June 1783.
     Proved 17 Feb. 1784 [N.F.P.] 1784. S.4. (H. BM.)
„ Richard 1805. S.4. (H.I.)
Guilliam, Henrici, Drumcassidy, Co. Cavan
     Admon. 1720. Ir.
Gumbleton, Richard, the elder, Tallow, Co.
     Waterford 1757. F.A.
„ Richard, Castle Richard, Co.
     Waterford, Esq. 1776. F.A.
„ Richard, Castle Richard, Co.
     Waterford, Esq. 1793. F.A.
Gumley, Rev. James, Belturbet 1838. S.1.P.
Gun, William, Limerick 1615. W.P.
Guning, Bryan, Castlecoote, Co. Roscommon 1717. Ky.
Gunn, George, Carrickfoyle, Co. Kerry 1744. W.P.
„ William, Ratow, Co. Kerry, Esq. 1691. W.P.
„ William, Ratow, Co. Kerry, gent. 1723. W.P.

Gwyllym, Lt. Col. Meredith, Gyllymsbrook, Co.
　　　　　　Cavan　　　　　　　　　　1719. Ir. and Swan.P.
　　„　　Thomas, Ballyconnell, Co. Cavan,
　　　　　　Esq.　　　　　　　　　　　1681. Ir.
Gyles, John, Dundalk, Co. Louth, gent.　1745. Ir.

Haddock, Joseph, Cork　　　　Dated 1701. W. Cork
　　„　　Thomas, Ballygroman　　　　1718. W. Cork.
Hall, Rev. John, Ardstraw, Co. Donegal　1735. F. and W.P.
　　„　　William, Leamcon, Co. Cork　1726. F.
Hallam, John, Hallam Hill, King's Co.　1673. S.I.P.
　　„　　John, Waterford　　　　　　1699. S.I.P.
Hallaran, William, Castlemartyr, Esq.
　　　　　　　　　　　　　　　Dated 1794. F.
Hallisy, Elizabeth. *See* Ashe.
Haly, Ellen, Cork, spinster　　　　　1801. C.D.B.
Haman, John, Marsham St., Westminster
　　　　　　　　　　　　　　　Dated 1755. M.
Hamil, Francis, Dublin, merchant　　1803. C.D.B.
Hamilton, Adam, Crossdoney, Co. Cavan　1714/15. W. Kilmore
　　„　　Alexander, Lisnalinney　　　1726/7. W. Derry
　　„　　Rev. Alexander, Moneyrea　　1740. W.P.
　　„　　als. Ramage, Ally, widow, Dublin　1803. Swan. P.
　　„　　Andrew, Co. Donegal　　　　1655. F.
　　„　　Andrew, Ballymacdonnell, Co. Donegal　　　　　　　　　　　　1768. Swan. P.
　　„　　Andrew, Francis St., Dublin　1674. F.
　　„　　Anna　　　　　　　Admon. 1715. Ir.
　　„　　Archibald, Archbishop of Cashel　1641. B.
　　„　　Archibald, Crehanan, Co. Donegal 1694. W. Derry
　　„　　Archibald, Lieut.-Col. Mountjoy's
　　　　　　Regt.　　　　　　　　　　1712. F.A.
　　„　　Archibald, Cornet, Strabane, Co.
　　　　　　Tyrone　　　　　　　　　1753. F.A.
　　„　　Archibald, Dublin, Doctor of
　　　　　　Physick　　　　　　　　　1777. F.A.
　　„　　Catherine　　　　　Admon. 1715. Ir.
　　„　　als. Bredin, Clements. *See* Hassard.
　　„　　Digby, Maj.-Gen.　　　　　　1820. S.4.
　　„　　Sir Francis, Castle Hamilton, Co.
　　　　　　Cavan　　　　　　　　　　1674. B.
　　„　　Galbraith, Dublin, merchant　1791. F.A.
　　„　　George, Co. Tyrone　　　　　1699. W.P.
　　„　　George, clk., rector of Devenish and
　　　　　　Bohoe　　　　　　　　　　1702. W. Clogher
　　„　　George, Kattigolan, Co. Monaghan 1718. W. Clogher

Hamilton,	George	1724. W. Clogher
"	Col. George, Milburn	1728. Ir.
"	Gustavus, Dublin	1754. B.
"	Rev. Gustavus	1795. B.
"	Hugh, Donagheady Dated	1689. W. Derry
"	James, Strabane, Co. Tyrone, merchant	1703. F.A.
"	James, Ardnacinny, Co. Tyrone	1714. W. Clogher
"	James, Carrowitragh, Co. Monaghan	1717. W. Clogher
"	Capt. James, Ballyfatton, par. of Urney, Co. Tyrone	1731. F.A. and F.E.
"	James, Roscrea, Co. Tipperary	1658. F.
"	James, par. of Clownish, Co. Fermanagh	1736. W. Clogher
"	James, Donemanagh	1742. Swan. P.
"	James, Derrycullin, par. of Aughalurcher, Co. Fermanagh	1746. W. Clogher
"	James, Mt. Charles, Co. Donegal	1763. Swan. P.
"	Jane, Down, widow	1658. F.
"	Jane, Currinshegoe	1726. W. Clogher
"	Jane, Belturbet, Co. Cavan, widow	1727. W. Kilmore
"	John, Cornemucklack	1703. W. Clogher
"	John, Edergoll, Co. Tyrone	1707. W. Clogher
"	John, Carbeg, Co. Tyrone	1708. W.P.
"	John, Drummurcher	1726. W. Clogher
"	Letitia, widow of Cornet Archibald H.	1761. F.A.
"	Lettice, widow of Col. Geo. H.	1741. Ir.,S.2. and W.P
"	Malcolm, Archbishop of Cashel	1627. B.
"	Patrick, Strabane, Co. Tyrone, merchant	1662. W.P.
"	Patrick, Garrison, Co. Fermanagh	1776. Swan. P.
"	Robert, Clady Dated	1678. W. Derry
"	Robert, Killiclunie, Co. Tyrone, gent.	1689. W.P.
"	Robert, par. of Clonfeckle	1712. W. Armagh
"	Robert, Drumsonas	1736. W. Clogher
"	Thomas, Currenshegoe, Co. Monaghan	1709. W.P.
"	William, Downpatrick Dated	1656. F.
"	William, Hamilton's Bawn, Co. Cavan	1670. B.
"	William, Lisclooney, King's Co.	1679. B.
"	William, Cornemucklagh, Co. Tyrone Dated	1694. W. Clogher

Hamilton, William, junr., Killycoran, par. of
        Clogher, Co. Tyrone   1744. W. Clogher
„   William, Donemana, Co. Tyrone
                Dated 1747. Swan. P.
„   William, Beltrim, Co. Tyrone, Esq. 1747. W.P.
„   William, Londonderry, merchant   1758. F.A.
„   William, Dunnamana, par. of Don-
        oughhedy, Co. Tyrone, Esq.   1793. F.A.
Hamersley, George, Clunkeen, Co. Monaghan 1754. S.1.P.
„   Richard, Holy Cross, Co. Tipperary 1747. S.1. Cashel
Hamerton, Denis, Orchardstown, Co. Tipperary
                Dated 1766. S.1. Cashel
Hamon, Hector, Portarlington   1769. S.1.P.
„   John, Cork, senr.   1692. F.2.
Handcock, Robert, Dublin, apothecary
                Dated 1704. M.
Handcock(e), William, Recorder of Dublin city 1701. W.P.
Hansard, Frances, Rathgorey   1759. W.
„   Mary, Dublin, widow   1709. W.P.
„   Nicholas, Dublin, gent.   1749. W.P.
„   Rev. Ralph, Baltinglass, Co. Wick-
       low   1749. W.P.
„   Sir Richard, Lifford, Co. Donegal,
       Knt.   1628. W.P.
„   Richard, Atherdee   1748. W. Drogheda
Harden, George, Donnybrook, Co. Tipperary 1798. B. and S.1.
                                        Killaloe
Hardiman, Robert, Loughrea   1801. C.D.B.
Harding, Ambrose, Dublin, Esq.   1772. S.1.P.
 ,   (or Hardy), Arthur, Rathcurah, [Co.
        Carlow], yeoman   1666. W. Leighlin
Hardman, Robert, Drogheda   Dated 1681. M.
Hardy, Arthur, Tinry Lane, Co. Catherlogh 1716. W. Leighlin
„   Edward, Ballybarr, Co. Catherlogh 1720. W. Leighlin
„   Thomas, Tinry Lane, Co. Catherlogh,
      Esq.   1716. W. Leighlin
„   *See* Harding.
Hare, Andrew, Cork, merchant   1728. F.
„   John, Cork, merchant   1745. F.
Harloe, Caleb, Castlebar, als. Eglish, Co. Mayo
                   Admon. 1712. Ir.
„   John, Rathmullen, Co. Sligo   1757. Ir.
„   William, Rathmullen, Co. Sligo   1705. Ir.
Harman, Christopher, Congarvie   1783. Swan. Kilmore
„   Thomas   Dated 1667. F.2.
„   William, Congarvie, Co. Cavan   1783. Swan. Kilmore

Harman, William, Cargrove, Ballyhaise
Admon. 1861. Swan.
Harmer, William, Inner Temple, Esq. 1697. W. Cloyne
Harnett, James Fuller, Aghamore, Co. Kerry,
Esq. 1794. F.A.
Harris, Alexander, Q.M. in Roche's Regt.
Dated 1730. Ir.
" Sir Edward Dated 1632. F.A.
" Dame Jane, Dublin, widow 1638. F.A.
" Joseph, Cork 1723. W.P.
" Laungharne, Mountmellick 1727. Ir.
" Richard, Bannistowne Riesk, Co. Meath 1687. Ir.
" Richard, Bandonbridge, tanner 1714. W. Cork
" Robert, Dublin 1701. Ky.
" Robert, Cork 1731. W.Cork
" Robert, Dublin 1740. Ky.
" Stephen, Cork 1670. W. Cork
" Thomas, Kinsale, cordwainer 1670. W. Cork
" Thomas, Bantry 1718. W. Cork
" Thomas, Dublin 1762. Ir.
" Walter, Dublin 1695. Ir.
" Walter, Dublin, Esq. 1723. Ir. and Ky.
" Walter, Dublin 1790. Ir.
" William, Ballyvoloone, gent. Dated 1721. W. [? Cloyne]
" William, Kinsale, Co. Cork, cooper 1728. W. Cork
Harrison, Anne, Ballyhobartye, par. of Ballyglissane, Co. Cork, widow 1629. Swan.
" Henry, Ballyglissane, Cork, now in Bristol 1648. Swan.
" John, Dublin, merchant 1670. Ir.
" John, Castlequin [? Castlelyons], Esq. 1746. Swan. P.
" Michael, Dublin, Esq. 1709. Ir.
Hart, Anne, Dublin, widow 1760. S.2.
" Christopher, Dublin, baker 1724. S.2.
" Christopher, Dublin, gent. 1679. S.2.
" David, Dublin, hosier 1747. S.2.
" Edward, Sword Bearer of Cork 1721. F.
" Eliz., Dublin, widow 1762. S.2.
" Henry, Coolrue 1742. F.
" Henry, Dublin, alderman 1763. S. 2. P.
" John, Ensign in Dunbar's Foot 1755. S.2. P.
" als. Russell, Mary, Dublin 1750. S.2.
" Paul, Ballykyly, Co. Dublin 1751. S.2.
" Percival, Dublin, Esq. 1664. S.2.

Hart, Richard, Cloghannagh, Co. Limerick,
    Esq.   1662. F.2.
  "   Richard, Galistowne, Co. Meath, gent. 1705. S.2.
  "   Simon, Dublin, Esq.   1780. S.2.
Hartigan, Edward, Dublin, apothecary   1767. F.E.
Hartwell, Frances, widow   1681. W. Cloyne
  "   Joseph, Limerick, burgess   1727. W. Limerick
Harvey, Henry, Ballyhackett, Co. Carlow, farmer   1718. F.2.
  "   Thomas, Dublin   1711. F.
Hasart, James, Mullimorkan, Co. Fermanagh 1692. Swan.
Hassard, als. Bredin, als. Hamilton, Clements 1795. Swan.
  "   Jason, Dublin, merchant   1745. Swan.
  "   Jason, Legregeymore   1746. Swan. Clogher
  "   Jason, Skea, Co. Fermanagh
    [Full copy]   Dated 1761. Swan.
  "   Jason, Garden Hill   1809. Swan
  "   Jason, Levaghey, Co. Fermanagh   1841. Swan. Clogher
  "   John, Youghal, merchant   [?] 1661. Swan. P.
  "   John, Cara, Co. Fermanagh Dated 1804. Swan. P.
  "   John, Carna Green, Co. Fermanagh 1817. Swan. P.
  "   Richard, Carna Green   1813. Swan. P.
  "   Robert, Legnageamore, Co. Fermanagh   1713. Swan. Clogher
  "   William, Carn Green   1841. Swan. P.
Hasshie, Michael, Maunsmore, Co. Clare   1803. C.D.B.
Hatchell, John Hore   D. 1844. S.4. (H.O.)
Hattin, Jonathan, Dublin, slater   1727. W.P.
Haugh, John, Kilskoran, Co. Wexford, clk.   1738. W. Ferns
Haughton, Arthur   Dated 1689. W. Connor
  "   Eleanor, relict of Geo H., Esq.   1685. F.2., F.E., and W.P.
  "   James, Wexford   1664. W. Ferns
  "   John, Dublin, gent.   1651. F.2.
  "   Robert, vicar of Strabannon, Co. Louth   1699. F.E.
  "   Stephen   1653. W. Dublin
  "   Thomas, Dublin, merchant   1668. F.E.
  "   Thomas, St. Martin's, Co. of Middlesex   1738. W.P.
  "   Thomas, Roskath, Co. Wicklow, farmer   1743. W.
Hawkins, Anne, Cork, widow   1736. F.A.
  "   Anne, Cork, widow   Admon. 1745. F.A.
  "   Edward, Cork, skinner   1693. F.

Hawkins, Henry, weaver [Undated. Stated to
　　　　be early]　　　　　　　　　　　　F.
　„　　Jane. *See* Allin.
　„　　John, the elder, Cork, alderman　1685. F.
　„　　John, Cork, merchant　　　　　　1707. F.A.
　„　　John, Cork, gent.　　　　　　　　1734. F.A.
　„　　John, Cork, gent.　　Admon. 1745. F.A.
　„　　Joseph, Cork　　　　　　　　　　1689. F.
　„　　Richard, Cork, gent.　　　　　　1629. F.
Hawkshaw, Richard, Millbrook, Co. Tipperary 1803. C.D.B.
　„　　　Thomas, Dublin, gent.　　　　1683. F.2.
Hawksworth, Amory, Leeson Street, Dublin
　　　　　　Admon. Intestate 1812. S.4.
　„　　　Amory, Leeson Street, Dublin
　　　　　　　　　Admon. 1819. S.4.
　„　　　Elizabeth, Ennis, Co. Clare　1819. S.4. P.
　„　　　William, Rathmines, formerly of
　　　　　　London　　　　　　　　　1817. S.4. P.
Hawthorne, Sophia, Downpatrick, Co. Down,
　　　　spinster　　　　　　　　　　　1801. C.D.B.
　„　　　Steele　　　　　　　　　D. 1853. S.4. (H.O.)
Hayes, Ottiwell, Knocknagore, gent.　1705. F. and Davis
　„　　William Henry　　　　　　D. 1825. S.4. (H.O.)
Hayman, Jane, Dublin, widow　　　　1724. F.A.
　„　　John, Polmore, Co. Cork, Esq.　1736. F.A.
　„　　Samuel, Youghal, merchant　　1672. F.2.
　„　　Samuel, Youghal, alderman　　1724. F.A.
Haynes, John　　　　　　　　　　D. 1822. S.4. (H.I.)
Hazard, Elizabeth, Dublin, widow　　1732. Swan.
Head, Michael, Waterford, alderman　1711. F.D.
　„　　Michael, London, grocer　　　　1713. F.D.
　„　　Michael, Derry, Co. Tipperary, Esq. 1749. F.D.
　„　　Thomas, Headsgrove, Co. Kilkenny,
　　　　Esq.　　　　　　　　　　　　　1723. F.D.
Heard, Anne, Kinsale, Co. Cork, widow　1768. F.A.
　„　　Anne, Cork, spinster　　　　　　1780. F.A.
　„　　Bickford, Cork, gent.　　　　　　1780. F.A.
　„　　Edward, Kinsale, merchant　　　1775. F.A.
　„　　George　　　　　　　　　　　　1792. S.4. (H.I.)
　„　　James John Bickford　　　　　　1814. S.4. (H.BM.)
　„　　John, Kinsale, Esq.　　　　　　1789. F.A.
　„　　John, Dublin, Esq.　　　　　　　1799. F.A.
　„　　William, Cork, gent.　　　　　　1782. F.A.
Heckelfield, Anne. *See* Stanford.
Hemmings, William　　　　　　　　1810. S.4. (H .:
Hemsworth, Mary, relict of John H.　1747. S.1.P

Henderson, Daniel, Ruskey, Raphoe, Co. Donegal 1752. S.4. Raphoe
„ Elizabeth, Castlepin, Co. Donegal 1778. S.4. Raphoe
„ George, Ballyshannon, Co. Donegal 1776. S.4. P.
„ Hugh, Ganvachan, Co. Tyrone 1746. S.4. Derry
„ Isabella, Dublin 1773. S.4. P.
„ James, [? Brockles] 1736. S.4. Derry
„ James, Raphoe 1776. S.4. Raphoe
„ James, Dungiven, Co. Londonderry 1783. S.4. Derry
„ James, Drumcounis 1798. S.4. Clogher
„ Jane 1784. S.4. Clogher
„ Capt. John, Donoughmore, Co. Donegal 1735. S.4. P.
„ John, Putterley, Co. Donegal 1740. S.4. Derry
„ John, senr., Lisnuentegly, Co. Donegal 1745. S.4. Raphoe
„ John, Powderly, Co. Donegal 1778. S.4. Derry
„ John, Waterside, Liberties of Londonderry 1801. S.4. P.
„ Joseph, Toyfin, Co. Donegal 1799. S.4. Derry
„ Patrick, par. of Kilowen, Co. Derry 1740. S.4. Derry
„ Samuel, Magheracrigan, Co. Tyrone 1798. S.4. Derry
„ William, Drumbulcon, Co. Fermanagh 1781. S.4. Clogher
Henn, Rt. Hon. William Dated 1784. F.
Hennessey, Mathias 1821. S.4. (H.BM.)
Henry, Helena, Henry St., Dublin 1801. C.D.B.
Henzey (Henzell), Bigoe, Barnegrotty, King's Co. 1732. S.1.P.
Hepburne, William, Londonderry, gent. 1666. F.2.
Hepenstall, Anne Isabella, spinster 1801. F.A.
„ Benjamin, Harold's Cross, Dublin, gent. 1806. F.A.
„ George, Sandymount, Dublin 1806. F.A.
„ John, Cornagower, Co. Wicklow, farmer, late of Newcastle 1792. F.A.
„ John, Athleague, Co. Roscommon 1802. F.A.
„ Mary, Rockmount, Co. Down, spinster 1805. F.A.
Hereing, Thos., Tom's Coffee House, Dublin 1712. S.2.
Herrin, Nicholas, Butlerstown, Co. Wexford 1743. S.2.
Herring, Anne, Graigue, Queen's Co., widow 1805. S.2.
„ Darby, Carlow, Co. Carlow, Esq. 1807. S.2.
Heslip, James, Killinchy, Co. Down 1812. C.D.B.

Heverin,	Francis, the elder, Ballinasloe, Co. Galway	1802. C.D.B.
Hewetson,	Christopher, Dublin	1633. B. and F.2.
,,	Christopher, clerk	1658. F.2.
,,	Christopher, Clonuff, Co. Kildare	1699. B.
,,	John, Kildare	1658. B. and F.2.
,,	Michael, Coolbeg, Co. Donegal	1753. B.
,,	Moses, Clane, Co. Kildare	1721. B.
,,	Thomas, Kildare	1688. B.
Hewett,	Easter, [Cork, widow]	1774. F.D.
,,	(or Hewitt), Francis	D. 1846. S.4. (H.O.)
,,	Isaac, Dublin, gent.	1699. F.D.
Hewitt,	Henry, Dublin, Esq.	1782. F.D.
,,	John	1783. F.D.
,,	Thomas, Cork, Esq.	1811. F.D.
Hewson,	George, Ballyengland, Co. Limerick	1737. S.1. Limerick
Hiatt,	William	1825. S.4. (H.I.)
Hickes,	George, Bushy Park, Co. Roscommon, clk.	1780. Ir.
,,	Richard, Creaghta, Co. Roscommon, gent.	Admon. 1743. Ir.
,,	Richard, Creta, Co. Roscommon	1766. Ir.
Hickey,	John, Cullane, Co. Clare	1730. S.4. Killaloe
Hickman,	Andrew	1685. F.2.
,,	Hannah, Limerick	1804. C.D.B.
,,	Thomas, Ballyhyman, Co. Clare, gent.	1678. F.2.
Hicks,	George, Creta, Co. Roscommon	1776. Ir.
Hicky,	Andrew, Drumgillinagan, Co. Clare	1730. S.4. Killaloe
Hiffernan,	Pierce	1792. S.4. (H.BM.)
Higginbotham,	Andrew, Nutfield, Co. Cavan	1765. Swan. P.
,,	Lt. Col. Charles, Dublin	D. 1882. Swan.
,,	Henry, Linenhall Street, Dublin	1789. Swan. P.
,,	John, Bolton, Co. Kildare	1781. Swan. P.
,,	Rev. Robert, Dublin Admon.	1818. Swan.
,,	Thomas, Drumcondra, Dublin	Not dated Swan. P.
,,	Rev. Thomas	1762. Swan. P.
,,	Thomas, Mountjoy Sq., Dublin	1826. Swan.
Higgins,	Edward, Lieut. and Surgeon	1737. B.
,,	Francis, St. Stephen's Green, Dublin	1802. C.D.B.
,,	Luke, Dublin	1790. B.
,,	Mathew, Mayfield, Co. Meath	1814. B.
,,	Mathew, London. [Pr. in Dublin]	1815. B.
,,	Paul, Dublin	1746. B.
,,	Ralph, Bellewstown, Co. Meath	1745. B.

Higgins, William, Arbour Hill, Dublin   1759. B.
Higinbotham, Mrs. Anne Elizabeth, Summer-
    hill, Dublin   1800. Swan.
  "   Frances (Fanny), Dublin, spin-
    ster   D. 1882. Swan.
  "   George, Largy, Co. Cavan   1768. Swan. P.
  "   Ralph, Banbridge   D. 1884. Swan.
  "   Rev. Ralph, Enniskillen   1752. Swan. Clogher
  "   Rev. Robert, Laurel Hill, Co.
    Derry   1758. Swan. P.
Hill, Adam, Claggan   1698. W. Armagh
  "   Adam, Derrykeighan, Co. Antrim   1749. W. Connor
  "   Anne. *See* Barton.
  "   Edward, Rathbane, Co. Mayo   1675. B.
  "   Elizabeth, Ballynabowly   1740. W. Cork
  "   John, Cork, clothier   1735. W. Cork
  "   John, Cork, clothier   Dated   1737. W. Cork
  "   Robert, Carrickmacross, Co. Monaghan,
    gent.   1688. W.P.
  "   Sarah, Cork, widow   1718. W. Cork
  "   Thomas, trooper in Prittie's Regt.   1655. W.P.
  "   Thomas, Dublin, gent.   1672. W.P.
  "   Thomas, D.D., Kilkenny   1673. W.P.
  "   Thomas, Cork, merchant   1691. W. Cork
  "   Thomas, clothier   1702. W. Cork
  "   Capt. Thomas, Stewart's Regt. of Foot 1710. W. Dublin
  "   William, Bristol, merchant   1615. W. Cork
  "   William, Kilbrogan, Co. Cork, yeoman 1640. W. Cork
  "   William   1800. S.4. (H.I.)
Hind, Thomas, D.D., Dean of Limerick   1689. Ir.
  "   Thomas, Killoy   1690. Ir.
Hinde, Anne, Dublin, widow   1674. Ir.
  "   Dorothy, Dublin   1728. Ir.
  "   Edmond, Lower Ballinegar, Co. Meath
                                 Dated 1687. Ir.
  "   George, Castlemihan, Co. Roscommon
                                Admon. 1751. Ir.
  "   Jervis, Anadown, Co. Galway, Esq.   1779. Ir.
  "   John, London   Dated   1668. Ir.
  "   John, Dublin, merchant   1737. Ir.
  "   Richard, city of Waterford, gent.   1767. Ir.
  "   Richard, the elder, Waterford Admon. 1767. Ir.
  "   Richard, Dublin, gent.   1769. Ir.
  "   Richard, late of Waterford, now of
    Dublin, Esq.   1770. Ir.
  "   Richard, Shannon Lawn, Co. Limerick   1869. Ir.

Hinde, Samuel, Dublin — 1719. Ir.
„ Thomas, Kilboy — 1690. Ir.
Hoare, Abraham, Dublin, gent. — 1670. W.P.
„ Edward, Dunkittle, Esq. — 1709. S.4. P. and M.
„ Joseph, Cork, merchant — 1730. M. and W.P.
„ Joseph, Cork, merchant — 1741. W.P.
„ Richard, Dublin, Esq. — 1724. W.P.
Hobson, Mary, Dublin, widow — Dated 1715. W. Dublin
Hodder, Francis, Cork, Esq. — 1774. F.D.
„ Jane, Bridgetown, widow — 1673. F. and Davis
„ John, Cork, merchant — 1730. F.
„ John, Bridgetown, Co. Cork — Dated 1671. F.
„ William, Coolmore, Co. Cork — Dated 1665. F.
„ William, Hoddersfield, Co. Cork gent. — 1726. F.D.
Hodges, William, Shanagolden, Co. Limerick — 1750. W.P.
Hodson, Elizabeth, Coolkenno, Co. Wicklow, widow — 1760. S.4.
„ Lorenzo, Coolkenno, Co. Wicklow, Esq. — 1774. F.D.
Holiwood, als. Dungan, Margaret. *See* Andrewes.
Holland, George, Borris-in-Ossory — 1744. S.1. Ossory
Holmes, Alice, London — 1775. B.
„ Allicia, Drogheda, widow — 1828. B.
„ Elizabeth, Ballyart, King's Co. — 1785. B.
„ Garner Joseph, Lisduff, Co. Tipperary — 1845. B.
„ George, Lisclooney, King's Co. — 1737. B.
„ George, Drogheda — 1824. B.
„ George, Drogheda — 1843. B.
„ George Arbuthnot, Moorock, King's Co. — 1847. B.
„ Gilbert, Dean of Ardfert, King's Co. — 1847. B.
„ Henry Joy, Holywell, Co. Antrim — 1835. B.
„ Isabella, widow of Geo. H. — 1759. S.1.P.
„ James, Antrim — 1752. B.
„ John, Belfast — 1626. B.
„ Joseph, (Diocese of Clogher) — 1785. B.
„ Peter, St. Mary's Parish, Oxmantown — 1675. F.2.
„ Peter, Peterfield, Co. Tipperary — 1803. B.
„ Robert, Clongorey, Co. Kildare — 1683. B.
„ Sir Robt. — Dated 1692. S.4.
„ Samuel, Kells, Co. Meath — 1789. B.
„ Thomas, Drumnafinchin, Co. Cork, clk. — 1718. W. Cork
„ Rev. Wm. Anthony, D.D., Templemore, Co. Tipperary — 1844. B.

Holmes, William, Cork Hill, Dublin, saddler 1812. C.D.B.
Homan, John, Mote Grange, Co. Westmeath 1683. F.2.
Honnor, John, Madam, Co. Cork 1670. F.2.
Hooker, Charles, Dublin 1667. B. and Cav. P.
Hopkins, Benjamin, Tomacork, Co. Wicklow, farmer 1812. C.D.B.
,, Francis, Tullow, Co. Carlow, clk. 1776. F.A.
,, Francis, Dariestown, Co. Meath, gent. 1778. Swan. P.
,, Francis, Dublin, Esq. 1789. F.A.
,, Francis, Bagot St., M.D. 1819. Swan. P.
,, John, Mullingar, Co. Westmeath 1763. F.A.
,, John, Munsborough, Co. Roscommon, gent. 1768. F.A.
,, Joseph, Waterford, Esq. 1724. F.A.
,, Rev. Richard, Co. Dublin, clk. 1788. F.A.
,, Samuel, Ramelton, Co. Donegal 1700. F.A.
,, William, Gillstown, Co. Meath 1819. Swan. P.
Hopper, William 1844. S.4. (H.I.)
Horan, Thomas, junr., Manor Hamilton, Co. Leitrim 1848. S.2. Kilmore
Hore, Edmd., Cork, merchant 1662. W. Cloyne
,, James. [Mentions debts only. ? Dated 1682]. F.2.
,, William, Harperstown, Co. Wexford, Esq. 1700. W. Ferns
Horncastle, Christopher, Dublin, gent. 1711. Swan. P.
Houghton, Ann, Dublin, widow 1747. W.
,, Edward, Ash Street, Co. Dublin 1746. W.P.
,, Elizabeth, Dublin, widow 1740. W. Dublin
,, Henry, Dublin, carver 1729. W. Dublin
,, Mathew, Dublin, merchant 1743. W.P.
,, Rev. Robert, Vicar of Strabannon, Co. Louth 1699. W.P.
,, Roger, Ballendesig, Co. Cork 1702. W. Cork
,, Thomas, Dublin, merchant 1668. W.P.
,, Thomas, Kilmanock, Co. Wexford 1744. F.E. and W.P.
Hovell, William, Cork, alderman [1698]. F.2.
Howard, Alfred, Dublin, gent. 1776. Swan. P.
,, Joan. *See* Jones.
,, John, Waterford, now of Milford, S. Wales 1807. Cav. P.
,, Thomas, Dublin 1664. F.2.
,, William, Waterford city, yeoman 1750. Cav. Waterford and Lismore
Howes, Robert, Dublin, stationer Dated 1671. W. Dublin
Howse, Edwd., Bandon bridge, Co. Cork 1704. W.P.

Howth, Rt. Hon. Thomas, Earl of	1802.	C.D.B.
Hoystead, Thomas, Mount Ophaly, Esq.	1744.	S.4.
Huband, Edmund, Dublin, merchant	1758.	Ir.
Hubbart, Nicholas, Cork, merchant	1713.	W. Cork
Hubbert, Francis, Killeightroy, Co. Cork	1670.	W. Cork
Hudson, Rev. Alex., Templeton, Co. Longford	1856.	Swan.
„ Charles, Rear Admiral, R.N. Dated	1802.	Swan.
„ Rev. Edward	1757.	Swan.
„ Eliza, Lr. Mount St., Dublin	1837.	Swan.
„ Jane, Enniskillen, widow	1816.	Swan. Clogher
„ Letturnal, Enniskillen	1781.	Swan.
„ Margaret, Ballymoney, widow	1764.	Swan. P.
„ Sir Walter, Enniskillen, Knt.	1803.	Swan.
Hughes, Abraham, Ballytrent	1739.	W. Ferns
„ Elinor, Enniscorthy, widow	1752.	W. Ferns
Hull, Elizabeth	1705.	F.
„ Esther, Clonakilty, widow	1639.	F.
„ George, Ballyculter, Co. Down	1640.	F.
„ John, Innisbegcleary, Co. Cork, late of Lorr, near Baltimore	1692.	F.
„ Randal, Cork	1685.	F.
„ Sir Richard, Leamcon	1691.	F.
„ William, Cork, merchant Dated	1658.	F.
„ William, Leamcon	1665.	F.
„ William, Cork, merchant	1691.	F.
Hume, Sir John, Bt.	1695.	Ir.
Humphrey, John, Dublin	1775.	S.4.
Hungerford, Walter, D.D., Bunward's [? estate] in Berks Dated	1681.	F.
Hunt, Dorcas, spinster	1839.	Swan.
„ Elizabeth, Dublin Not dated		Swan.
„ Henry, Limerick	1747.	S.1. Limerick.
„ Henry, Fruistown [? Friarstown, lib. of Limerick]	1752.	Swan.
„ John, Dublin	1800.	Swan.
„ John, Dublin	1844.	Swan. P.
„ Rev. John William, Portarlington	1876.	Swan.
„ Samuel Dated	1797.	S.4. (H.I.)
Hunter, George D.	1819.	S.4. (H.O.)
Huson, Benjamin, Drumiskin, Co. Louth, clk.	1720.	W.P.
„ Rev. Charles, Wexford	1777.	Swan. Ferns
„ Elizabeth, Tomnaboley	1736.	W. Ferns
Hutchinson, Anne, wid. of Bp. of Down	1749.	Swan. P.
„ Edward, Knocklofty	1699.	F.2.
„ Sir James, Bart.	1813.	C.D.B.
Hutton, Mary, Dublin, widow	1736.	Ir.
„ Maxwell, Dublin	1797.	S.2. P.

Hutton, William, Donaghclooney, Co. Down 1720. S.2. Dromore
Hyde, John Fleming, Capt. 30th Native Infantry till 1826. [Notes. No Will] S.4. (H.O.)
Hynde, Geo., Castlemeaghan, Co. Roscommon, gent. 1711. Ir.
   ,, John, Roscommon 1702. Ir.

Inchiquin, Morogh, Earl of 1674. W.P.
Innos, John, Saintfield, Co. Down 1812. C.D.B.
Irvine, Dame Elizabeth. *See* Bunbury.
   ,, Henry, Dawson Street, Dublin, Esq. 1812. F.A.
Irving, James, Ballybridge, Co. Roscommon Admon. 1684. Ir.
Irwin, James, Alexander 1814. S.4. (H.I.)
   ,, John, the elder, Carnabrook, Co. Monaghan, gent. 1770. Swan.
   ,, John, Woodhill, Co. Donegal, late of Drumsilla, Co. Leitrim 1773. M.
   ,, Thomas, Sligo, gent. Admon. 1719. Ir.
Irwine, Thomas, Dublin, apothecary 1710. Ir.
Isaac, Peter, Dublin, gent. 1694. F.A.
   ,, Simon, Ballywalter, Co. Down Dated 1727. S.1.P.
Iveagh, Sir Arthur Magenis, Lord Viscount 1629. W.P.

Jackson, Benj. Murdock, Youghal 1818. Swan. P.
   ,, Beresford, Maghryenan, gent. 1730. W.P.
   ,, Isaac, Dublin 1772. B.
   ,, Isabella, Londonderry, widow 1741. W.P.
   ,, Michael, Lisburn, Co. Antrim 1710. B.
   ,, Nathaniel, Mountmellick 1803. C.D.B.
   ,, Nichola Ann, Forkhill, Co. Armagh 1804. C.D.B.
   ,, Thomas, Ballyduff, Co. Waterford 1672. F.2.
   ,, Thomas, Creekstowne, Co. Meath Dated 1750. S.2.P.
   ,, Thomas, Lisnabow, Meath, gent. 1796. S.1.P.
   ,, William, Youghal, alderman 1781. Swan. P.
Jacob, Abigail, Clonmel, spinster 1765. S.1.Cashel
   ,, Ann, Dublin, widow 1802. C.D.B.
   ,, Mary, Clonmel, widow 1762. S.1.Cashel
   ,, William, Sigginstown 1668. W. Ferns
Jacobs, Mary. *See* Poë.
James, Ann, par. of Drumsnatt, Co. Monaghan, widow 1788. Swan. Clogher
   ,, Lydia, Smithborough, Co. Monaghan 1810. Swan. Clogher
   ,, Michael, Newbliss 1800. Swan. Clogher
   ,, Richard, Carnew 1730. W. Ferns

James, Robert, par. of Drumsnatt, Co. Mon-
aghan, gent. 1744. Swan. Clogher
Jameson, Hugh, Cork, merchant 1773. F.A.
„ John, Gortnessy 1792. S.2. Derry
„ Jonathan, Tamlacht, farmer 1755. S.2. Derry
„ Robert, Strabane 1741. S.2. Derry
„ Robert, senr., Strabane 1786. S.2. Derry
Jans, als. Chamberlaine, Thomasine. *See* Crolly.
Janns, Richard, Black Castle, Co. Meath, Esq. 1688. B. and F.2.
Jarvis, Charles, Cleveland Court, Westminster 1739. S.2.
„ Penelope, Somerset House, Strand,
widow 1746. S.2.
Jefferyes, [Jeffrys], Sir James, Blarney 1722. Swan. P.
„ James, Blarney, Co. Cork 1749. S.4. P.
„ James 1740. Swan.
„ James St. John, Blarney Castle 1780. Swan. P.
Jellett, Rev. Matthew, Lisburn 1821. S.1.P.
Jennett, Mary, Dublin 1812. C.D.B.
Jennings, George, Castletown, Co. Mayo 1761. S.1.P.
Jephson, Henry, Knockangriffin, Co. Cork 1733. W. Cloyne
„ Sir John, Froille, Knt. 1638. W.
„ John, now in Dublin 1693. F.2. and W.P.
„ John, Limerick 1724. W. Limerick
„ Dame Mary 1655. W.P.
„ Michael, Dean of St. Patrick's 1693. F. and W.P.
„ William, Froyle, Co. Southampton,
Esq. 1658. F.2. and W.P.
„ William, Dean of Lismore 1720. F. and W.P.
Jervis, Basil, Dublin 1750. B.
„ John, Birr, King's Co. 1762. B.
Jervois, Joseph Admon. 1798. F.A.
„ Sampson, Cork, Esq. 1750. F.A.
„ Sampson, Bandon, Co. Cork, Esq. 1806. F.A.
„ Samuel, Droome, Barony of East Car-
bury, Co. Cork, Esq. 1725. F.D.
„ Samuel, Brade, Co. Cork, Esq. 1795. F.A.
Jessop, Anthony, Doory, Co. Longford
[Commission to widow] 1767. Ir.
„ Francis, Dundrum, Co. Dublin, formerly
of Ballintampin, Co. Longford
Admon. 1749. Ir.
„ Capt. John, Dublin Admon. 1667. Ir.
„ Hannah, Birr, King's Co. 1836. S.2. P.
„ Robert, Doory, Co. Longford, Esq. 1730. Ir.
„ Robert, Ballintampin 1746. Ir.

Jessop, Robert, Dury, Co. Longford, Esq.
　　　　　　　　　　　　　　　　Admon. 1745. Ir.
　,, 　　Robert, Dury, Co. Longford, Esq.
　　　　　　　　　　　　　　　　Admon. 1748. Ir.
　,, 　　Robert, the younger, Doory Admon. 1768. Ir.
　,, 　　Robert, Mount Jessop, Co. Longford,
　　　　　Esq. [From Prerog. Cause Papers].
　　　　　　　　　　　　　　　　Dated 1782. Ir.
　,, 　　Sarah, Ferbane, King's Co.　　　1849. S.2. P.
　,, 　　Thomas, Mount Jessop, Co. Longford,
　　　　　Esq.　　　　　　　　　　　　1773. M.
　,, 　　Thomas, Mt. Jessop, Co. Roscommon,
　　　　　Esq.　　　　　　　　　　　　1776. Ir.
　,, 　　William, Ferbane, King's Co.　　1849. S.2. P.
Jewel, Ann, Ballinelard, Co. Tipperary, widow 1706. W. Cashel
Jewell, William, Ballynelard, Co. Tipperary 1705. W. Cashel
Johnson, Anthony, Quarrymount, Queen's Co. 1821. S.1.P.
　,, 　　Christopher, Dublin, Esq.　　　1682. F.2.
　,, 　　George, Cork, chandler　　　　 1724. F.2.
　,, 　　Mary, Clough, Co. Down　　　　1784. Swan. P.
　,, 　　Robert, 2nd Justice of Court of Com-
　　　　　mon Pleas　　　　　　　　　 1687. F.2.
　,, 　　Lieut. Robert O'Hara　　　　　 1792. S.4. (H.BM.)
　,, 　　née Judge, Ruth, Dublin and St.
　　　　　Omer　　　　　　　　　　　　1774. B.
　,, 　　Walter, Mewlick, Co. Fermanagh 1693. F.2.
　,, 　　William, Cork, weaver　　　　　1743. F.2.
　,, 　　William, Cork, merchant　　　　1764. F.2.
Johnston, Alice　　　　　　　　　　　1777. Swan. Clogher
　,, 　　Andrew　　　　　　　　　　　　1709. Swan. Clogher
　,, 　　Andrew, Adragold, Co. Leitrim　1808. S.2. P. and
　　　　　　　　　　　　　　　　　　　　　　　　Swan. P.
　,, 　　Anne, Derrycholanght, Co. Fer-
　　　　　managh, widow　　　　　　　 1768. Swan. P.
　,, 　　Arthur, Ederney, Co. Fermanagh 1751. Swan.
　,, 　　Arthur, Dublin, late Capt., 8th Dra-
　　　　　goons　　　　　　　　　　　　1785. Swan.
　,, 　　Arthur, Enniskillen　　　　　　1797. Swan.
　,, 　　Arthur, Littlemount　　　　　　1807. Swan.
　,, 　　Baptist, Tully, Co. Monaghan　 1755. S.2. P.
　,, 　　Catherine, The Ring, Co. Fermanagh,
　　　　　widow　　　　　　　　　　　　1812. Swan. Clogher
　,, 　　Charles, Drum, Co. Monaghan　 1812. Swan. P.
　,, 　　Edward, Anaghore, Tyholland　 1754. Swan. P.
　,, 　　Francis, Kilmore, Co. Fermanagh 1743. Swan. P.
　,, 　　George, Aghacashill, Co. Leitrim 1781. S.2. P.

IN THE GENEALOGICAL OFFICE, DUBLIN 205

Johnston, [Johnson], Henry, Aghlecky, Co.
  Limerick, gent.   Dated 1671. F.2.
" Hugh, Redemon, Co. Down 1742. S.1.Down
" Irvine, Co. Fermanagh 1834. Swan. P.
" James, Aghnacldony, Co. Fermanagh, gent. 1676. F.
" James, Enniskillen 1699. Swan. P.
" James, Aghanure, Co. Fermanagh 1693/4. Swan. P.
" James, Magheramena, Co. Fermanagh 1731. Swan. P.
" James, Rutland Sq., Dublin 1834. Swan. P.
" Jane. *See* Wilson.
" John, Dublin 1731. Swan.
" John, Roxborrow, Co. Armagh 1759. Swan.
" John, Killaneal, par. of Tyholland, gent. 1774. Swan.
" Katherine 1802. Swan. P.
" Lancelot, Johnstown, Co. Fermanagh Dated 1754. Swan. Clogher
" Margaret, als. Forster, Maguiresbridge 1837. Swan. P.
" Mary, widow 1782. Swan. P.
" Richard, Cornewall, parish of Aughaboy, Co. Monaghan 1727. F.D.
" Richard, Tully, Co. Monaghan 1739. S.2. P.
" Robert, Hollymount, Co. Fermanagh 1792. Swan.
" Sophia 1834. Swan.
" Thomas, Belturbet, Co. Cavan 1748. S.2. P.
" Walter, Mewlick, Co. Fermanagh 1693. S.2. P.
Jones, Ambrose, Cashel, Esq. 1697. F.A. and W.P
" Ambrose, Drewstown, Co. Meath 1734. W. Meath
" Arthur, Dublin, Esq. 1716. W.P.
" Christopher, Lisgrehan 1639. Ir.
" David, Clonmoyle, Co. Westmeath 1817. S.2. P.
" David, Beauparc, Co. Meath 1786. Swan.
" Edward, Dublin, cork cutter 1727. W. Dublin
" Elizabeth. *See* Stanford.
" Frances, Dublin, spinster 1673. W.P.
" Frances, Lynn, Co. Westmeath, widow 1833. S.2. Meath
" Hugh, Ticknicke, par. of Tullogh, Co. Dublin 1728. W. Dublin
" Humphrey, Belturbet 1771. Swan.
" Jane, Kilkenny, widow 1693. F.A.
" als. Howard, Joan, Dublin, widow 1695. Ir. and W.
" John, Moyallow 1688. W. [Cloyne]
" John, Belturbet, Co. Cavan 1733. Swan.

Jones, John, Belturbet — 1757. Swan.
" John, Newtown — 1803. C.D.B.
" Rev. John — 1849. Swan. P.
" Martha, Droghenure, King's Co. — 1709. S.1.Kildare
" Morris, Dublin — 1664. W. Dublin
" Nicholas, Dublin — Dated 1695. Ir. and W. Dublin
" Col. Oliver — 1664. Ir.
" Oliver, 2nd Justice, King's Bench — 1695. Ir. and W.P.
" Owen, Dublin, gent. — Dated 1688. W. Dublin
" Rev. Richard, Dean of Elphin — 1643. Ir.
" Richard, Dublin, gent. — Dated 1695. W. Dublin
" Robert, Dublin, baker — 1719. W. Dublin
" Roger, Dollardstown, Co. Meath, Esq. — 1748. W.P.
" Roth, [Dublin, Esq.] — 1725. W.P.
" Thomas, Dublin, brewer — 1667. W. Dublin
" Thomas, Dublin, brewer — 1719. W. Dublin
" Thomas, Oldcastle, Co. Meath — 1738. W. Meath
" Valentine, Kilmacmarcarty, Co. Armagh, gent. — 1693. W.P.
" William, Castleconrath, Co. Westmeath — 1687. W. Meath
" William, Dublin, gent. — 1696. W. Dublin
" William Morris, Moneyglass, Co. Antrim — 1735. W.P.
" William, Athlone — Dated 1746. Ir.

Judge, Arthur, senr., Mosstown, Co. Westmeath — 1721. B.
" Arthur, Mosstown, Co. Westmeath — 1729. B.
" Jane, née Magan, St. Omer, France — 1774. B.
" John, Gagebrook, King's Co. — 1731. B.
" Judith, Carpenterstown, Co. Westmeath — 1783. B.
" Juliana, Dublin — 1774. B.
" Mary, Ballinacard, King's Co. — 1764. B.
" Peter, Ballyshiel, King's Co. — 1746. B.
" Ruth. *See* Johnson.

Judkin, Elizabeth, Greenhill, Co. Tipperary, widow — 1731. S.I.P.

Kane, Richard, Carrickfergus — Dated 1735. W.
" Redmond — Not dated — Swan.
" Thomas, Dublin, vintner — 1747. W.P.

Kavanagh, or Cavenagh, Arthur, Ballycronnigen, Co. Carlow — 1730. Cav. Leighlin
" Arthur, Dublin, merchant — 1717. Cav. Dublin
" Brian, Borris, Co. Carlow — 1663. Cav. P.

Kavanagh, Bryan, Capel St., Dublin   Dated 1768. Cav. P.
,,   Charles, Rocksavage, Co. Carlow   1768. Cav. P.
,,   Darby, Graiguesmotten, Queen's
             Co.   Dated 1700. Cav. Leighlin
,,   Dennis   1770. Cav. Ferns
,,   Donnell [Daniel], als. Spaniagh,
             Clonmullen, Co. Carlow   1632. Cav. P.
,,   Edmund McBrene, Templeudigan
                                 D. 1634. Cav. Ferns.
,,   Elinor, Marley, Co. Carlow, widow   1749. Cav. P.
,,   Felix, Ballybeggs, Co. Carlow, gent.   1791. Cav. P.
,,   Gerald, Ballynattin, Co. Carlow
                                 Dated 1753. Cav. Leighlin
,,   Gerald, Dublin   1768. Cav. Dublin.
,,   Gerald, Marly, Co. Carlow   1791. Cav. P.
,,   Griffin, Shelbagga, Co. Wexford
                              Dated 1675. Cav. P. and F.2
,,   Griffin, Boderene, Co. Wexford   1679. Cav. P.
,,   Hugh, Ballyhacken, Co. Wexford   1769. Cav. Ferns
,,   John   1662. Cav. Ferns
,,   Mary, Leperstown, Co. Wicklow,
             widow   Dated 1671. Cav. P.
,,   Morgan McBrian, Borris, Co. Car-
             low   1631. Cav. P.
,,   Morgan   Dated 1664. Cav. Leighlin
,,   Michael, New Ross, Co. Wexford   1718. Cav. P.
,,   als. Cavanagh, Morrogh Backagh,
             als. Morgan, Carrigleod, Co. Carlow
                               Dated 1622. Cav. P.
,,   Murtagh, Knockduffe, Co. Carlow
                               Dated 1747. Cav. P.

Kavell. *See* Cawell.
Kavenagh, Dennis, Castleroot, Co. Kildare, inn-
             keeper   1741. Cav. P.
Keaghry, Anthony, Tynagh, Co. Galway   1763. S.2. Clonfert
,,   als. Garvey, als. Burke, als. Lynch,
             Annabel   1750. S.2. Tuam
,,   Cecily, Galway, spinster   1800. S.2.
,,   Flan, Tuam, Co. Galway, farmer   1772. S.2.
,,   Honor. *See* Ellicott
,,   John, Creavaghbann, Co. Galway   1746. S.2. Tuam
,,   Loughlen, Dr. of Physick   1736. S.2. Tuam
,,   Michael, town of Galway   1797. S.2. Tuam
Kearin, Alice, Donoony, Co. Wexford, widow   1802. C.D.B.
Kearney, Edmond, Kilmallock, Co. Limerick,
             merchant   1680. F.2.

Keary, Rev. John, Tuam, Co. Galway — 1816. S.2. P.
„ John — 1820. S.2. Elphin
„ James, Tuam, gent. — 1812. S.2. P.
„ Malachy, Careen, Co. Galway — 1818. S.2. Clonfert
„ Mary, Tuam, late of Ballinrobe — 1829. S.2.
„ [Carey], William, Clonsingle, Co. Tipperary — 1780. S.2.
„ William, Rathfryland, Co. Down — '38. S.2.
Keating, Alice, Dublin, widow — 1774. F.A.
„ Edmond, Possickstown, Co. Meath, Esq. — 1639. F.A.
„ Edmond, Dublin, Esq. — 1671. F.A.
„ Gerald, Castlewaring, Co. Kildare, gent. — Dated 1637. F.A.
„ John, Gurteen, Co. Waterford, gent. — Admon. 1679. F.A.
„ John, Garranlea, Co. Tipperary, Esq. — 1787. F.A.
„ Katherine, Dublin — 1773. F.A.
„ Leonard, Knockagh, Co. Tipperary, gent. — Dated 1770. F.A.
„ Margaret, Dublin, spinster — 1774. F.A.
„ Maurice, Dublin, gent. — 1696. F.A.
„ Maurice, Arborhill, Co. Tipperary, gent. — 1772. F.A.
„ Michael, Shanballyduff, Co. Tipperary, gent. — 1753. F.A.
„ Michael, Rossertown, Co. Tipperary — 1775. F.A.
„ Michael — D. 1829. S.4. (H.O.)
„ Nicholas, Dublin, merchant — 1767. F.A.
„ Oliver, Ballyninmory, Co. Carlow, Esq. — 1680. F.A.
„ Oliver, Kiculling, Co. Kildare — 1715. F.A.
„ Thomas, Kells, Co. Meath — 1813. M.
„ William, Dublin, merchant — 1715. F.A.
„ William, Dublin, gent. — 1719. F.A.
Keeffe, Rose, Milltown, Queen's Co., widow — 1813. C.D.B.
Keene, Ann, Rathfarnham — 1749/50. F.A.
Keighry, Thomas, Priest — 1718. S.2. Tuam
Keine, Mary, Dublin — 1802. C.D.B.
Keith, John, born Nisbettstown, Co. Westmeath [N.F.P.] — 1805. S.4. (H.O.)
Kellett, Charles, Cornesesk, Co. Cavan — 1746. Swan. Kilmore
„ John, Rathburee, Co. Meath — 1752. Swan. P.
Kelly, Alice, Greenmount — 1791. Ky.
„ Anthony, Drimgriffin, Co. Galway — 1771. Ky.
„ Anthony, Clooneasse, Co. Roscommon — 1772. Ky.

Kelly,	Bridget, Loughrea, Co. Galway	1810. Ky.
,,	Bryan, Balaforen, Co. Roscommon	1706. Ky.
,,	Bryan, Dublin	1742. Ky.
,,	Bryan, Mullaghmore, Co. Galway	1800. Ky.
,,	Colla, Dublin	1663. Ky.
,,	Colla, Corante, Mount Lynch	1731. Ky.
,,	Daniel, Dublin	1733. Ky.
,,	Daniel, P.P., Killasolanin, Co. Galway	1768. Ky.
,,	Daniel, Cargin, Co. Roscommon	1789. Ky.
,,	Denis, Aughran, Co. Galway	1740. Ky.
,,	Denis, Kellybrook, Co. Roscommon	1756. Ky. and F.E.
,,	Denis, Castlekelly, Co. Galway D.	1788. Ky.
,,	Denis, Loughrea, Co. Galway	1789. Ky.
,,	Edmond, Scregg, Co. Roscommon	1733. Ky.
,,	Elinor, Loughrea, Co. Galway, spinster	1803. C.D.B.
,,	Elizabeth, Dublin, widow	1789. Ky.
,,	Elizabeth, Dublin	1793. Ky.
,,	Elizabeth, Churchborough, Co. Roscommon, widow	1810. Ky.
,,	Festus, Dublin	1808. Ky.
,,	Frances, Knockmore, Co. Roscommon, widow	1791. Ky.
,,	Francis, Earl of Meath's Liberty	1795. Ky.
,,	Hannah, Dublin, widow	1793. Ky.
,,	Henry, Dublin	1741. Ky.
,,	Isabele, Lysmoyle, Co. Roscommon	1808. Ky.
,,	James, Lakanin, Co. Roscommon	1768. Ky.
,,	James, Dublin	1793. Ky.
,,	James, Mus. Doc. [? Dublin]	1800. Ky.
,,	John, Dublin	1652. Ky.
,,	John, Clonlyon, Co. Galway	1694. Ky.
,,	John, Tulsk, Co. Roscommon	1713. Ky.
,,	John, Clonlyon, Co. Galway	1714. Ky.
,,	John, Keneagh, Co. Roscommon	1732. Ky.
,,	John, Dublin	1755. Ky.
,,	John, Ballybane, Co. Galway	1787. Ky.
,,	John, Drogheda	1808. Ky.
,,	John, Lyscoffy, Co. Roscommon	1810. Ky.
,,	Joseph, Dublin	1791. Ky.
,,	Joseph, Co. Galway Not dated	Ky.
,,	Luke, Dublin	1791. Ky.
,,	Mary, Portarlington, Queen's Co.	1802. C.D.B.
,,	Mary, Dublin	1803. C.D.B.
,,	Patrick, Scregg, Co. Roscommon	1741. Ky.
,,	Patrick, Grangegorman Lane	1808. Ky.
,,	Patrick, Knockeen, Co. Carlow	1812. C.D.B.

Kelly,	Richard, Athlone	1684. Ky.
„	Lt. Col. Robert	1791. S.4. (H.BM.)
„	Rose, Dublin, widow	1793. Ky.
„	Thomas, junr. [Not dated. Lands in Co. Kildare]	Ky.
„	Tobias, Clondoyle, Co. Galway	1796. Ky.
„	William, Dublin	1597. Ky.
„	William, Turrock, Co. Roscommon	1719. Ky.
„	William, Cork	1732. Ky.
„	William, Buckfield	1762. Ky.
Kemeys,	Lewis, Kilmogue, Island of Allen, Co. Kildare	1731. F.E.
Kemmis,	Charles, Queen's Co., Esq. Admon.	1838. F.D.
„	Thomas, Killeenlinah, Queen's Co.	1774. F.E.
„	Thomas, S[t]raboe, clk.	1839. F.D.
Kempson,	Nicholas, Drummurry, Co. Cavan	1676. Swan.
Kempstone,	als. Cavanagh, Harriet, widow of H. H. Kempstone	D. 1874. Cav.
Kemys,	Nicholas, Dublin	1712. F.
Kenah,	James, Youghal	1690. Swan.
„	Mary, Garryentragh, widow	1788. Swan.
„	Richard	1769. Swan.
„	Robert, Garryentragh	1766. Swan.
„	William, Garryentragh, Co. Cork	1772. Swan.
„	William, Castlemartyr	1789. Swan. P.
Kenedy,	als. Brymingham, Jane, widow Dated	1615. Dub.
Kennedy,	Anne, Lady, Mountkennedy, Co. Wicklow	1703. S.I.P.
„	als. Killikelly, Ann, Bullanagh	1742. Cr. Clonfert
„	David, Ballycultra, Co. Down	1699. S.1. and W.P.
„	Hugh, Ballycultra, Co. Down, Doctor of Physick	1685. W.P.
„	Hugh, Derfraghrog, Co. Tyrone	1695. W. Armagh
„	James, Donegal, clk.	1662. W.P.
„	James, Mullinahack, city of Dublin	1803. C.D.B.
„	John, Ballimcgown, Co. Tyrone	1681. W. Clogher
„	Sir Richard, 2nd Baron of the Exchequer	1701. S.I.P. and F.2
„	William, Mullo, Co. Longford, Esq.	1744. W.P.
Kenny,	Richard, Wexford, Esq.	1682. F.2.
Kent,	Francis, Ennis, Co. Clare	1770. Mol. P.
„	Thomas, Dawestown	1664. F.
Keogh,	Edmund, Sralea, Co. Roscommon	1791. Ky.
„	Laurence, Keoghville, Co. Roscommon	1804. Ky.
Kerdiff,	als. Boran, Allson, widow Dated	1643. Dub.

Kerin, Patrick, Corofin, gent. 1785. Mol. P.
Kerr, née Campbell, Eleanor 1839. Swan.
Kieran, Francis, Dublin, Esq. 1809. F.A.
Kilbee, William 1797. Swan. P.
Kilcawly, Michael, Carrowinree, Co. Sligo,
    farmer 1789. Cr. Killala and Achonry
„   Patrick, parish of Emlyfadd 1811. Cr. Killala and Achonry
Kildare, Elizabeth, Countess of, widow 1666. Cav.
„   Robert Dale, Bishop of Dated 1582. Dub.
Kilkelly, Ann 1847. Cr. Clonfert
„   Daniel, Beaghmore, par. of Donoghpatrick, Co. Galway, yeoman
    Admons. 1707, 1712. Cr. Tuam
„   James, late of Tuam, now of Dublin, Esq. 1815. Cr. Tuam
„   James, Athlone, shopkeeper 1874. Cr.
„   Joseph, 23 Innisfallen Parade, Dublin, R.I.C. Pensioner 1888. Cr.
„   Judy. *See* Boughan.
Killala, Mordecai Cary, Bishop of 1751. M.
Killaloe, Edward Worth, Bishop of 1670. F.2.
„   Henry Ryder, Bishop of 1696. F.2.
Killikelly, Ann. *See* Kennedy
„   Bryan, Muniscribegh, Co. Galway, gent. 1755. Cr. P.
„   Daniel Moore, Summerville, Co. Galway, Esq. 1854. Cr. P.
„   Edmond, Coolragh, Co. Galway 1770. Cr. Clonfert
„   Edmd., Camla, Co. Roscommon 1835. Cr. P.
„   Fargus, Caronamadra, Co. Galway 1767. Cr. Clonfert
„   Fergus, late of Carrownamadra, now at the Windmill, Co. Galway 1768. Cr. P.
„   James, formerly of Wellpark, late of Duras, both in Co. Galway, Esq. 1850. Cr. P.
„   Luke 1735. Cr. P.
„   Martin, Dublin, merchant 1746. Cr. P.
Killkelly, Mortagh, Beaghmore, yeoman 1713. Cr. Tuam
„   Murtogh, Shancluan, Co. Galway 1771. Cr. Tuam
Kilmore, Joseph Story, Bishop of 1757. Ir.
King, David, Dublin, goldsmith 1738. Swan. P.
„   Nicholas, Cork, vintner 1664. F.
„   Richard, parish of Keneigh, Co. Cork 1636. W. Cork
„   Simon, Dublin 1801. C.D.B.
„   Sir William, Kilpeacon, Co. Limerick, Knt. 1706. F.2.

Kinkead, Moses, Hillsborough 1762. Swan. P.
Kirby, Samuel, Dromkeen 1813. C.D.B.
„ William Bagwell, Cornet 7th Lt. Cav. till
    1827. [Notes. No Will] S.4. (H.O.
Kirk, Patrick, late of Castle St., now of Weston
    Park, Co. Dublin 1836. S.1.
Kirkpatrick, Archibald, Donegor, Co. Antrim 1813. C.D.B.
Kirwan, Margaret. *See* Madden
Kisling, Elinor, Dublin, widow 1812. C.D.B.
Kitson, George, Dublin, gent. 1781. F.A.
„ William, Ballyng, Co. Kilkenny, gent. 1777. F.A.
Kittson, Richard, surgeon mate, 28 Regt. of
    Foot 1794. F.A.
Knight, Christopher, Ballymore, Co. Cork 1728. F.
„ James, Dublin, gent. Dated 1725. Sullivan MSS.
Knipe, Arthur, Ballymatrim, Co. Armagh 1754. S.2.P.
„ Charlotte, Mid. Gardiner St., Dublin,
    widow 1829. S.2.P.
„ Dorothea, Dublin 1823. S.2.P.
„ Elizabeth, the elder, 14 Summer Hill,
    Dublin 1832. S.2.P.
„ Elizabeth, 2 Mountjoy Place, Dublin 1854. S.2.P.
„ Rev. George, Castlerickard, Co. Meath
    Admon. 1797. S.2.
„ John Augustus, 30 Chester Terrace,
    Regent's Park 1850. S.2.P.
„ John, Belturbet, Co. Cavan 1788. S.2.P. and
    Swan. P.
„ John, Strandville, Co. Dublin 1813. S.2.P.
„ Samuel, Ballyinastrum 1758. S.2. P. and
    Swan. P.
„ Samuel, Belturbet, Co. Cavan 1804. S.2.P. and
    Swan. P.
„ Thomas, Kealogh, Co. Waterford 1660. S.2.P.
„ Rev. Thos. Frederick 1835. S.2.P.
„ William, Strandville, Clontarf, late of
    Dublin 1825. S.2.P.
Knott, John, Dublin, clothier 1667. Ir.
„ John, Sligo 1708. Ir.
„ Mary. *See* Thomas.
„ William, Knockadoe, par. of Boyle, Co.
    Roscommon Dated 1729. Ir.
Knox, Alexander, Balibofey, par. of Stranorlar,
    Co. Donegal 1756. Swan.
„ George, Munimore, [Co. Donegal], Esq. 1681. F.2.
„ Major George 1805. S.4. (H.BM.)

Knox,	Randfurlie	1764. S.4. (H.I.)
„	Robert Trotter D. 20 Nov.	1841. S.4. (H.O.)
„	William	1782. S.4. (H.I.)
Kyan,	Francis	1815. S.4. (H.I.)
Kyfte,	Nicholas, an Irishman, then in Portugal	1588. W.P.

Laban,	Samuel, Harristown, King's Co.	1718. Cav. Kildare
Ladaveze,	John, Dublin	1804. C.D.B.
Lamb,	Edward, formerly of Thomas Street, late of Naas	1803. C.D.B.
„	Hall, Dublin	1801. C.D.B.
Lambert,	Charles, Earl of Cavan	1660. B.
„	George, Downpatrick, Co. Down	1723/4. Swan. P.
„	James, Carnagh, Co. Wexford	1700. Mol. P.
„	John, Kilcrony, Co. Wicklow, gent.	1749. F.A.
„	Montague, Dublin, Esq.	1740. Swan. P.
„	Major Oliver Richard	1796. F.A.
„	Patrick, Carnagh, Co. Wexford	1730. Mol. P.
„	Ralph, Knockenarny, Co. Down	1762. Swan. P.
„	Richard, Earl of Cavan	1742. B.
„	Robert	1782. Swan. P.
„	Thomas, Dromiskin, Co. Louth, clerk	1661. F.2.
Lanauze,	Geo., Kill, Co. Cavan	1800. Swan. P.
Lancruze	(? Lanauze), Joseph	1786. S.4. (H.BM.)
Lane,	Abraham, Cork, brewer	1758. F. Cork
„	Ambrose, Killeen, als. Lane's Park, Co. Tipperary	1725. Cav. P. and F.D
„	Anne, Cork, widow	1756. F. Cork and Cav.
„	Elizabeth, Cork, widow	1734. F. Cork
„	Francis, Cork, innkeeper	1704. F. Cork
„	Gawen, Cork, merchant	Dated 1728. W. Cloyne
„	Henry, junr., Cork, merchant	1730. F. Cork
„	John, Laragh	1667. F. Cork
„	John, Cork, clothier	1695. F.2.
„	Mathew, Rosbercon, Co. Kilkenny	1774. Cav. P.
„	Richard, par. of Christ Church, Cork	Dated 1662. F. and W. Cork
„	Richard, Galway, chandler	1693. S.1. Tuam
„	Samuel, Cork, common brewer	1782. F. Cork
„	Sarah, Cork, widow	1791. F. Cork
„	Thomas, Dromagh, Co. Cork	1700. F.2. and W.P.
„	Walter, Cork, gent.	1720. F. and W. Cork
„	William, Cattiganstown, Co. Tipperary	Dated 1672. Cav. P. and F.D.

Lane, William, Killeens, Co. Tipperary
                                           Dated 1698. Cav. Ossory
Langford, Anne, Tullah, Co. Limerick   1798. F.A.
- Catherine. *See* Fitzgerald.
- Elizabeth, Kells, Co. Limerick, widow   1768. F.A.
- George, Glakestown, Co. Westmeath 1728. S.1. Meath
- George Coplen, Reen, Co. Kerry   1814. S.1.
- Gertrude, Doneraile, Co., Cork, widow   1734. F.A. and W.P.
- Hercules, Viscount   1798. S.1.P.
- Sir Hercules, Carrickfergus, Knt. 1639. S.1.P.
- James, Banemore, Co. Limerick   1732. Ir.
- James, Banemore, Co. Limerick   1733. Ir. and S.1. Limerick
- James, Charleville, Co. Cork   1806. S.1. Limerick
- John Coplin, Kilcosgrave, Co. Limerick   1719. Ir.
- John, Tullagha, Co. Limerick   1729. Ir. and S.1. Limerick
- John, Kells, Co. Limerick   Dated 1745. S.1.
- John, Kells, Co. Limerick, gent.   1755. Ir., F.A., and W.P.
- John, Castleconway, Co. Kerry   1782. S.1.P. and F.A.
- John Coplen, Kilcosgriff, Co. Limerick   1799. S.1. Limerick
- Jonas, Castletown, Co. Limerick   1764. S.1. Limerick
- Richard, Dublin, gent.   1606. S.1. Dublin
- Richard Coplin, Kilcosgrave, Co. Limerick   1736. Ir.
- Richard Coplin, Kilcosgrave [? 1736] 1756. S.1.
- Robert, Banemore, Co. Limerick, gent.   1738. F.A. and W.P.
- Susanna, par. of St. Paul's, Covent Garden, spinster   1726. W.P.
- Theophilus, Kinsale, Esq.   1713. W.P.
- William   1650. W. Cork
- William, Gardenfield, Co. Limerick, Esq.   1718. Ir. and 1719. F.A. and W.P.

Langley, Henry, Killmaninge, Co. Waterford 1672. F.2. P.
- Henry   1763. F.
- John, Blackkettle   Dated 1674. F.
- Roger, Fort Lewis, Co. Cork   1803. C.D.B.

Langor, John [? of Youghal]   Dated 1671. F. and Davis
Lapp, John, Waterford   1714. F.D.
- Mary, Cork, widow   1721. W. Cork

Lapp, Richard, Archdeacon of Cork   1691. W. Cork
- "   Thomas, Cork, tanner   1706. W. Cork
- "   William, Bandon, gent.   1721. W. Cork

Latham, John, Meldrum, Co. Tipperary   1762. S.1. Cashel
- "   John, Brookville, Co. Cork, and Meldrum, Co. Tipperary   1806. S.1.P.

Lauder, John, Youghal   1783. Swan.
- "   Robert, Moyclare, King's Co.   1740. S.1.P.

Law, John, Ballydown, Co. Down. [Recited in deed betw. Sarah L., widow, and James Law, registered 1758]   S.4.

Lawder, David, Ballysheen, Co. Kerry, Esq.   1767. F.A.
- "   Robert, Moyclare, King's Co., gent.   1740. F.A.

Lawless, Anne, Dublin   1723. B.
- "   Christopher, Dublin   1722. B.
- "   James, Shankill, Co. Dublin   1738. B.
- "   John, Crumlin, Co. Dublin   1679. B.
- "   John, Dublin   1795. B.
- "   Luke, Dublin   1778. B.
- "   Luke, Dublin   1783. B.
- "   Mary, Kilkenny, widow   1726. B.
- "   Mary, Shankill, Co. Dublin, widow   1729. B.
- "   Mary, Shankill, Co. Dublin, widow   1744. B.
- "   Mary, Dublin, widow   1776. B.
- "   Michael, Dublin   1776. B.
- "   Peter, Shankill, Co. Dublin   1727. B.
- "   Richard, Clonshagh, Co. Dublin   1609. B.
- "   Richard, Talbot's Inch, Kilkenny   1663. B. and F.2.
- "   Richard, Dublin   1778. B.
- "   Richard, Dublin   1799. B.
- "   Robert, Dublin   1779. B.
- "   Thomas, Dublin   1767. B.
- "   Thomas, Cabinteely, Co. Dublin   1775. B.
- "   Walter, Newhall, Co. Dublin   1623. B.
- "   Walter, Kilkenny   1627. B.

Lawndy, Agnes, Youghal, Co. Cork, widow   1697. F.2.
- "   Edward, Youghal, merchant   Admon. 1686. F.A.
- "   Edward, Muckridge, Esq.   1730/1. F.A.
- "   Passivere, Youghal, merchant   Admons. 1686, 1697. F.A.

Lawton, Abraham, Mallow, gent.   1703. W. Cloyne
- "   Hugh, Ballybeg, Co. Cork, farmer   1726. W.P.
- "   John, Cork, merchant   1773. F.A.

Lawton, Richard, Cork, merchant   1804. C.D.B. and F.A.
- "   Trayer, Cork, merchant   1758. F.A.

Layng, James, Gurtinardross, gent. 1756. Swan.
Lea, als. Roe, Mary. *See* Thomas.
„ Henry 1785. S.4. (H.BM.)
Leader, Henry, Tully, Co. Cork 1738. F.
„ John, Mountleader, Co. Cork 1731. F.P.
Leake, Ezekiel, Holycross 1727. S.1.P.
„ als. Newhouse, Elizabeth, Cloughjordan 1752. S.1.P.
Leary, Lewis, Kinsale, Co. Cork 1790. S.2.P.
Leathes, Margaret, Hillsborough, Co. Down, widow 1738. W.P.
Leavens, Robert, Churchtown, Co. Louth 1804. C.D.B.
Leckey, Robert Dated 1707. F.P.
Ledbeater, Robert, Dublin, gent. 1656. F.2.
Ledger, Elizabeth. *See* Lhoyd.
„ Edward, Sedgemoor, Co. Tipperary 1817. S.1. Killaloe
„ John, Burrisakane, Co. Tipperary 1778. S.1.
„ Richard, Whitehaven, Cumberland and Dublin 1768. S.1.P.
„ William, Derrynaslin, Co. Tipperary Dated 1752. S.1. Killaloe
„ William, Dublin, coal merchant 1768. S.1.P.
Ledwich, Peter Wilkinson, Weston Lodge, Co. Kildare 1839. S.1.P.
„ Susanna, Dublin, widow 1797. S.1.P.
Lee, Benjamin, Merrion, Co. Dublin, gent. 1745. F.D.
„ Edward, Barnarusacully, Co. Tipperary, gent. 1726. F.D.
„ James, Sunday's Well, Cork 1776. S.1. Cork
„ John, Kinsale, baker 1797. S.1. Cork
„ Richard, Clonderslaw, Co. Clare 1708. F.2. and F.D.
„ Samuel, Dublin, printer 1694. F.D.
„ Thomas, Dublin, cook Admon. 1673. F.D.
„ Rev. Ussher, Dean of Waterford 1859. S.1.P.
„ William, Cork 1728. S.1.
Leeson, Joseph, the elder, Dublin, Esq. 1741. F.D.
„ Rev. Hugh, Dublin, clk. 1719. F.D.
Legard, Edward, Bandon 1678. S.1. Cork
Legge (Legg), Francis, Cappagh, Co. Tipperary 1691. S.1.P. and F.2
Le Hunt, Mary, Cashel, widow 1688. F.2.
„ Richard, Cashel, Esq. 1668. F.2.
Le Hunte, George, St. Martins in the town and county of Haverfordwest, Esq. 1697. F.2.
„ Richard, Artramount, Co. Wexford 1783. Swan.
Leicester, John, Kilkarnuck, King's Co. 1684. F. and F.2.
Leigh, Andrew, Frierstown, Co. Kildare 1706. F.2.

Leigh, Francis, Cullinmore, Co. Meath	1692.	F.2.
„ Francis, Robert, Dublin, Esq.	1727.	F.D.
„ Judith, Dublin, spinster Dated	1700.	F.2.
„ als. Colclogh, Robert	1694.	F.2.
„ Robert, Rosgarland, Co. Wexford, Esq.	1803.	F.E.
Leitrim, Robert, Earl of	1804.	C.D.B.
Lennon, Matthew, R. C. Bp. of Dromore Dated 22 Jan., 1801. [N.F.P.]		C.D.B.
„ Thos. Bunbury, Carlow	1798.	B.
Leslie, Charles, Cork, Esq.	1793.	F.A.
„ Rev. Dr. George, Ballyconnell, Co. Cavan	1754.	F.A.
„ James, Tarbert, Co. Kerry	1724.	S.4.
L'Estrange, Henry, Moystown, King's Co.	1666.	B.
„ William, Castlecuffe, Queen's Co.	1677.	F. and F.2.
Lewis, Richard, Lismore, Co. Cavan	1691.	Swan.
Leycester, Robt., Kilcarmicke, King's Co.	1643.	S.1. Dublin
Lhoyd, als. Ledger, Elizabeth	1759.	S.1.P.
Limerick, John Molony, Bishop of [in French] Dated	1701.	Mol.
Lindrum, Capt. John	1784.	S.4. (H.BM.)
Lindsay, Andrew, Ballinderlan, Co. Donegal, gent. Dated	1698.	S.2.P.
„ Helen, Ballinderlan, widow	1699.	S.2.P.
Lindsey, John, Lindville, Esq. Not dated.	[? after 1770].	Swan.
Linn, Anne, Caledon, Co. Tyrone, widow	1804.	C.D.B.
Little, George, Lemangh, Co. Longford	1768.	Swan. P.
„ John, Largy, Co. Fermanagh	1722.	Swan. Clogher
„ John, Carterstown, Co. Louth	1768.	Swan. P.
Lloyd, John, Athlone, Co. Westmeath	1802.	C.D.B.
Loane, John, Charleville, Co. Cork	1784.	F.E.
Lochard, Peter, Pimlico, Liberty of Thomas Court, Dublin Dated	1672.	W.P.
Lockett, Abraham D.	1834.	S.4. (H.O.)
Lockhard, Arthur, Christianstown, Co. Kildare	1734.	W.P.
Lodge, Katherine. *See* Arsticken.		
Loftus, Adam, Lord Chancellor of Ireland and Lord Archbishop of Dublin Dated	1604.	M.
„ Dudley, Isle of Wight	1772.	S.1.P.
„ Nicholas, Fethard, Co. Wexford, Esq. Dated	1666.	F.2.
„ Sarah	1772.	S.1.P.
Lombard, Edmond, Cork	1643.	W. Cork
„ Rev. Edmund, Lombardstown, Co. Cork, clk.	1799.	Swan. P. and F.E.

Lombard, George, the younger, Cork, merchant   1749. F.E. and W.P.
"   George, Cork, merchant   1769. F.E.
"   James, Cork, merchant   1639. W. Cork
"   James, Cork, alderman   1652. W. Cork
"   James, Gortvolire, Co. Cork, gent.   1685. F.E.
"   James, formerly of Lombardstown, Co. Cork   1769. Swan. and F.E
"   James, Cork, merchant   1783. F.E.
"   John, Gortmalyre, Co. Cork, gent.   1764. F.E.
"   Nicholas, Cork, gent.   1626. W. Cork
"   Rev. Peter, Dublin, clk.   1773. F.E.
"   William, Cork, Esq.   1718. F.E. and W.P.
"   William, Cork, merchant   1754. Swan. P. and F.E.
"   William, Danesfort, Co. Cork   1831. Swan.
Lonergan, Francis   1802. C.D.B.
Long, Lt. Col. Henry   1803. S.4. (H.BM.)
"   John, Derrynasera, Queen's Co., farmer   1763. F.E.
"   Thomas   1819. S.4. (H.I.)
Longfield, Hawnby, [Ballynascarty, Co. Cork]   1740. W.P.
"   John, Castlemary, als. Carrigacotta, Co. Cork Esq.   1730. W.P.
"   Robt., Kilbride   1711. F.
Longworth, Francis, Cragan, Co. Westmeath   1803. C.D.B.
Looby, Baptist, Cork, cordwainer   1686. W. Cork
"   George, Cork, brewer   1714. W. Cork
"   Margaret. *See* Williams.
Lopdell, Christopher, Derryowne, Co. Clare   1801. C.D.B.
Lovett, Verney, East Sheen, Surrey, Esq.   1771. Sadleir Deeds
Lowe, Elizabeth, Hamilton Row, Dublin, spinster   1813. C.D.B.
Lowry, Robert Rogers, Killinchy, Co. Down   1812. C.D.B
Lowther, Sir Gerard, Knt.   1624. B.
"   Sir Gerrard, Knt.   1660. B.
Lucas, Gilbert, Drogheda, tanner   1689. F.2.
"   Jasker [? Jasper], Youghal   1710. Swan. P.
"   Richard   1804. S.4. (H.I.)
Ludlow, Stephen, Dublin, Esq.   1724. W.P.
Luffkin, Grizzel, Farrenebane, Co. Cork   1686. W. Cork
"   John, Raheen   1710. W. Cork
"   Roger, Knocknaheilan, Co. Cork, gent.   1724. W. Cork
Lumm, Elnathan, Dublin, banker   1708. W.P.
Luther, Elizabeth, Youghal, widow   1702. W. Cloyne
"   John, Youghal, merchant   1697. F.2.

IN THE GENEALOGICAL OFFICE, DUBLIN 219

Luxbury, Samuel. *See* Suxbury.
Lynar, Alexander, Capel St., Dublin — 1802. C.D.B.
Lynch, als. Garvey, als. Burke, Annabel. *See* Keaghry.
" Edward, Rathorpe — 1731. W.P.
" James, formerly of Drogheda, late of Dublin — 1812. C.D.B.
" Patrick, Jamaica — D. 1773. Ky.
Lyndon, Edward, Esq., Master in Chancery — 1727. W.P.
" Jane, Carrickfergus — Dated 1698. W. Connor
" Sir John, Dublin, Kt. — 1699. W.P.
Lyon, Edward — D. 1825. S.4. (H.O.)
" John, Cork — 1751. W. Cork
Lyons, Charles, Mucklagh, King's Co. — 1709. S.1. Kildare
" Daniel — D. 1819. S.4. (H.I.)
" Geoffrey, Killeen, King's Co. — 1709. S.1. and S.4. Kildare
" Hannah, Dublin, widow — 1804. C.D.B.
Lysaght, Major Arthur — 1784. S.4. (H.BM.)
" Nicholas — 1726. F.

McAboy, David, Knockasmullane — 1739. W. Cloyne
McBride, David, Dublin, M.D. — 1779. B.
" Dorcas, Dublin, widow — 1790. B.
" John, Magherlin, Co. Down — 1694. B.
" Rev. John, Belfast — 1718. B.
" John, Seapatrick, Co. Down — 1728. B.
Macan, Richard — 1812. S.4. (H.I.)
McCann, Luke, Armagh, M.D. — 1813. C.D.B.
McCarthy, Callaghan, [? Cahircreveen] — 1715. W. Cloyne
" Charles, Ballyshoneen, Co. Cork — 1727. W. Cloyne
" Cormac McDonough, Duhallow. Dated 1656. W. Cloyne
" (Donogh McCarthy Reagh) Dated 1663. F.2.
" Donough, Derry, Co. Cork — 1732. W. Cloyne
MacCarthy, Patrick, Lieut. 1st Native Infantry till 1814. [Notes. No Will] S.4. (H.O.)
Macartney, John — 1813. S.4. (H.I.)
McCausland, Oliver, Strabane, Co. Tyrone, Esq. — 1722. W.P.
" Oliver, Strabane, Co. Tyrone, Esq. — 1741. W.P.
McDermott, Bridget, Dundalk, Co. Louth, widow — 1802. C.D.B

McDermott, Hugh — 1787. S.4. (H.I.)
McDonagh, James — 1818. S.4. (H.I.) and S.4. (H.O.)
McDonnell, Catherine, New Sackville St. — 1803. C.D.B.
   ,,   Christopher, Killeen, Co. Dublin, Esq. — 1852. F.A.
McEvers, James, Abbey St., Dublin — 1804. C.D.B.
McEvoy, Francis, Abbey St., Dublin, surgeon — 1808. F.A.
MacGeogh (Mageogh or M'Geaugh), Samuel — 1791. S.4. (H.I.) and S.4. (H.O.)
M'Ginis, Con, Drumbenagh, Co. Monaghan, farmer — 1736. W. Clogher
McGrath, Daniel, Charleville, Co. Cork, publican — 1813. C.D.B.
   ,,   Deborah, Dublin, late of Cork — 1791. Swan. P.
   ,,   James, Derryvackney, Co. Cavan, gent. — Dated 1727. Swan. Kilmore
   ,,   John — 1804. S.4. (H.I.)
McGregor, Patrick, Drumale — 1725/6. Swan. Clogher
McGuire, Richard, Dublin, banker — 1727. W.P.
McGusty, Rev. Barry, Vicar of Galtrim, [Co. Meath] — 1814. Swan.
M'Gwyre, Bryan, Carrick McGriffin, Co. Tipperary, gent. — 1700. W.P.
Machell, Jane, Dublin — 1738. S.2. P.
   ,,   Hugh, Strangford, Co. Down — 1732. S.2. P.
McIllree, Robert — Admon. 1785. Swan. Kilmore
McIlravey, David, Glenavey, Co. Antrim — 1812. C.D.B.
M'Kay, William, Merrion Sq., Dublin [N.F.P.] — 1812. C.D.B.
McKenny, Francis — 1792. S.4. (H.BM.)
Mackey, John, Coleraine, Co. Derry — 1765. B.
McLaughlin, Capt. Richard, Ballydowney, Co. Kerry — Dated 1670. F.2.
McLorinan, Hugh, Anaghmore, Co. Antrim, gent. — 1727. W. Connor
   ,,   als. Morris, Margaret, Aghadrimdirige, Co. Tyrone, widow — 1697. W.P.
   ,,   Mathew, Killcross, par. of Killead, Co. Antrim — 1744. W. Conn
McMahon, Alexander — D. 1887. S.4. (H.C.)
McManus, als. Dobbin, Mary, Carradaughy, Co. Antrim, widow — 1722. W.P.
McMath, Andrew, Aughadreena — 1809. Swan. Clogher
McMullin, Robt. — D. 1865. S.4. (H.O.)
McMurrogh, Tirlagh Boy, Kilbride — Dated 1624. Dub.
McNamara, Lott, Coley, Co. Clare, gent. — 1750. F.A.

McNamara, als. O'Callaghan, Mary, Ard-
cloneyn, Co. Clare, widow
                        Admon. 1772. F.E.
Macnamara, William, Rathany, Co. Limerick,
    gent.   1775. Mol.P.
McNeil, John, Dublin   1802. C.D.B.
McNemara, Donough, Gortiderry, Co. Clare 1770. Mol. Killaloe
,,   Elizabeth, Limerick, widow   1779. Mol. Limerick
,,   Honora   1733. Mol. Killaloe
,,   Hugh, Clonnole, Co. Limerick   1729. Mol. Limerick
,,   John, Limerick, merchant   1708. Mol. P.
,,   John, Rathkeale   Dated 1738. Mol. Limerick
,,   John, Limerick, gent.   1739. Mol. Limerick
,,   John FitzJohn, Limerick   1742. Mol. P.
,,   Mathew, Limerick, clothier   1712. Mol. Limerick
,,   Norcott, Limerick, gent.   1747. Mol. P.
,,   Thady FitzFlorence, Gurrane, near
       Parteen, Co. Clare   1724. Mol. Limerick
,,   Thomas, Clounfaddy, Co. Clare 1740. Mol. P.
,,   William, Rathany, Co. Limerick,
       gent.   1775. Mol. P.
McSweeny, John, Cork, shoemaker   1738. W. Cork
Madden, Ambrose, Lacken, Co. Kerry, gent. 1707. F.A.
,,   Anniagh, Ballyheene, Co. Kerry,
       gent.   Admon. 1674. F.A.
,,   Anthony, Wexford   Admon. 1658. F.A.
,,   Barnaby, Athlone, Co. Westmeath,
       gent.   1672. F.A.
,,   Edward, Lacken, Esq.   Admon. 1705. F.A.
,,   Elizabeth, Dublin, widow Admon. 1674. F.A.
,,   Eugene, Ballyheene, Co. Kerry, gent.
                        Admon. 1674. F.A.
,,   Fergus, Lismore, Co. Galway, Esq.,
                        Admon. 1687. F.A.
,,   Capt. Hugh, Clonedagare, Co. Galway
                        Admon. 1658. F.A.
,,   Hugh, Gortnekelly, Co. Galway,
       gent.   1668. F.A.
,,   John, Enfield, Co. Middlesex, gent.
                        Admon. 1661. F.A.
,,   John, Enfield, Co. Middlesex, gent.
                        Admon. 1681. F.A.
,,   Rev. John, Kilmoone, Co. Meath 1745. Ir.
,,   John, Maddenstown   1791. Swan.
,,   als. Kirwan, Margaret, Galway.
                        Admon. 1690. F.A.

Madden, als. Carroll, Maria. *See* Byrne.
" Robert, Donore, Co. Dublin Admon. 1637. F.A.
Maddin, Patrick, Aghnure, Co. Fermanagh,
gent. Admon. 1675. F.A.
Magan, Jane. *See* Judge.
Magenis, Arthur, Rathfriland, Co. Down, Knt.,
Lord Viscount of Iveagh 1629. W.P.
" Arthur, Cabragh, Co. Down, gent. 1735. W.P.
" Con, Newry, late of Corbolly 1755. W. Dromore
" Constantine, King's Inns, Dublin 1684. W.P.
" Daniel, Castlewellan 1726. W.P.
" Mary, [? Drumaul] 1747. W. Connor
" Phelemy, Castlewellan, Co. Down,
Esq. 1706. W.P.
Maghan, Thos., Derrincourt, Co. Galway, gent.
Dated 1747. S.2. Clonfert
" Thos., Bellville, Co. Galway 1819. S.2. P.
Magin, John, surgeon, of Dromore Diocese 1812. C.D.B.
Maginnis, Andrew Ferguson D. 1830. S.4. (H.O.)
" Edmund, Londonderry 1748. W. Derry
Maginniss, John, Dublin 1803. C.D.B.
Magnise, Hugh FitzJohn, Newry, Co. Down 1640. W.
Mahaffy, Ninian, Earl St., Dublin 1827. S.1.
" Rev. Robert, Carrygart, Co. Donegal 1835. S.1.
" Samuel, Meenhoney, Co. Donegal 1792. S.1.Derry
Mahon, Elizabeth, Dublin, spinster 1803. C.D.B.
" Michael, Bride St., Dublin, shoemaker 1803. C.D.B.
" Nicholas, Ballinernly, Co. Roscommon,
Esq. 1681/2. F.A.
" Capt. Robert 1801. S.4. (H.BM.)
" Ross, Castlegar 1767. S.2.
Mahoney, Lt.-Col. Dennis 1816. S.4. (H.BM.)
Mahony, Denis, Dromore Dated 1788. F.
" John, Dunloe, Co. Kerry Dated 1706/7.F.
Major, Anne, Wentworth Place, Dublin, widow 1814. Swan. P.
" Henry, Ballyshannon, Co. Donegal 1798. Swan. P.
" Rev. John, Camlin, Co. Donegal, clk. 1775. Swan.
Manders, Isaac, junr., Rathmines, Co. Dublin 1813. S.4.
" Jane, Lr. Mount St., Dublin, widow 1825. S.4.
" John, Blackpool, Cork, clothier 1796. S.4.
" John, Athy, Co. Kildare, carpenter 1833. S.4.
" Jonathan, Cork, merchant 1786. S.4.
" Joshua, Dublin 1813. S.4.
" Margaret, 12 Herbert Place, Dublin 1847. S.4.
" Richard, Brackenstown, Co. Dublin,
alderman 1824. S.4.

Manders, Robert, Merrion Square 1853. S.4.
Mangin, Alexander, Dublin 1802. C.D.B.
Manly, George, Keelogue, Co. Wicklow 1853. S.2. P.
„ Isaac, Dublin 1765. S.2. P.
„ Isaac, Ballygammon, Co. Wicklow 1830. S.2. Dublin
„ John, Ledcrop, Kent. 1743. S.2. P.
„ James, Castle Fleming, Queen's Co., gent. 1662. S.2. Ossory
„ Thomas, Ballyrone 1677. S.2.
Mansergh, Bryan, Ballyburr, Co. Kilkenny 1688. F.2.
„ Daniel, Macrony, Co. Cork, Esq. 1725. F.D.
„ Elizabeth, Cashel, widow 1786. S.4. and F.D.
„ James, Macrony, Co. Cork, Esq. 1704. F.D.
„ James, Parliament Street, Westminster, late of Macrony, Co. Cork, Esq. 1774. F.D.
„ James, Limerick 1813. S.4. P.
„ Nicholas, Grenane, Co. Tipperary, Esq. 1768. F.D.
„ als. Wemys, Sarah, widow 1754. F.D.
„ William, par. of St. Clements Danes, Co. Middlesex 1707. F.D.
Manwaring, William, Maynooth, Co. Kildare D. 1727. Cav.
Manypenny, Thomas, Pimlico, Dublin 1802. C.D.B.
Maquay, Susanna, Gloucester Street, Dublin, widow 1809. Swan. P.
Mara, Richard, Roscrea, Co. Tipperary 1803. C.D.B.
Markham, George, New Abbey, Co. Tipperary, gent. 1750. S.2.P.
„ James, Kinsale, Co. Cork Dated 1704. S.2. Cork
„ Moses, Dublin, weaver 1693. F.2.
„ Stephen, Tuitstown, Co. Westmeath, gent. 1694. Swan. and F.2.
„ William, Tuitstown, Co. Westmeath 1671. S.2. P.
Marlay, Thomas, Lord Chief Justice 1756. B.
„ Thomas, Celbridge, Co. Kildare 1784. M.
Marsh, Francis, Archbishop of Dublin 1693. F.2.
„ Mary, Dublin, widow of Francis, Archbishop of Dublin 1695. Ir. and F.2.
„ Peter, Moyally, King's Co. 1737. B.
„ Peter, Moyally, King's Co. 1740. S.1.P. and B.
Marshal, Gregory, Gowran, late of Cloghala 1749. S.1.
Marshall, Walter 1800. S.4. (H. BM.)
Marston, Teresa, Dublin 1813. C.D.B.
Martell, Patrick, Cork, merchant 1699. W. Cork

Martell, Philip, Cork, burgess — 1653. W. Cork
Marten, Thomas, Kilkenny, clk. — 1730. F.D.
Martin, Alexander, [Cork], cordwainer — 1758. W.P.
" Dominick, Galway, merchant Dated 1656. F.2.
" Ellinor, Lurgan, Co. Armagh, widow — 1692, F.A.
" Francis, Galway, alderman — 1603. F.2.
" John, Bandonbridge, yeoman — 1624. W. Cork
" John, [Kinsale] — 1646. W. Cork
" Peter, Pollagh — 1745. Cr. Tuam
" Robert, Galway, merchant Dated 1594. F.2.
" Robert, Galway, alderman Dated 1621. F.2.
" Robert, Co. Tyrone — 1724. F.
Martley, James Frederick, M.D. — 1813. Swan.
" John, Ballyfallen, Co. Meath — 1729. Swan. and W. Meath
" John, Dublin, merchant — [? 1796]. F.A.
" John, Athboy — 1797. Swan.
" John, 9 Rutland Sq., Dublin, b.-at-law — 1839. Swan.
" William, Newtown, Ballyfallen, Co. Meath, Esq. — 1807. F.A.
Martyn, William, Galway, alderman — 1593. F.2.
Mason, Sarah, Waterford — [Dated 1714]. F.
Massey, Humphrey, Killnihill — 1712. F.
Massy, Charles, Dean of Limerick — 1766. F.A.
" Elizabeth, Ballyvier, Co. Tipperary, widow — 1764. F.A.
" Godfrey, Tinnerana, Co. Clare, clk. — 1770. F.A.
" Hugh, Duntrileage, Co. Limerick, Esq. — 1701. F.A.
Masters, Elizabeth, Ampthill, Co. Bedford, widow — Dated 1801 C.D.B.
Masterson, Roger, Prospect, Co. Wexford — 1680. F.2.
" Rowland, Barre'hanon, Co. Wexford — 1630. Cav. Ferns
" Thos., Moneyseede, Co. Wexford — 1718. F.
Mathers, John, Belfast, Co. Antrim — 1803. C.D.B.
Mathews, Catherine, Usher's Quay, Dublin — 1803. C.D.B.
" Rev. John, Newcastle, Co. Down — 1733. Swan. P.
" Matthew, Kilmurry, Co. Wicklow — 1801. C.D.B.
Matthews, Constantine, Dublin, malster — 1735. Swan. P.
Maughon, Hannah. *See* Burke.
Maunder, William, Galway, butcher — 1658. S.4.
Maunsell, John, Ballyvornane — 1685. F. and F.D.
" Thomas, Thorpmolson, Northants. — 1744. F.
Max, John, Killough, Co. Tipperary — 1769. S.4. P.
" Simon, Gaile, Co. Tipperary — 1733. S.4.

Max, Thomas, Killough, Co. Tipperary	1776.	S.4. P.
Maxenal, John, Ballyriskbegg, Co. Londonderry	1715.	S.1. Derry
Maxwell, Agnes, Drombegg, widow	1684.	W. Down
,, Ann, Fellows Hall, par. of Tynan, Co. Armagh	1740.	Swan. P.
,, Alex., Cork, merchant	1720.	S.2.
,, Arthur, Drumbeg, Co. Down	1722.	W.P.
,, Grace, Dublin, spinster	1803.	C.D.B.
,, Henry, College Hall, Co. Armagh, clerk	1709.	F.E.
,, James, Drumbeg, Co. Down, gent.	1682.	W.P.
,, James, the elder, Omagh, Co. Tyrone	1772.	S.2. P.
,, John, Ballyriskbegg, Co. Londonderry	Dated 1715.	W. Derry
,, Mary, Strabane, Co. Tyrone	Dated 1709.	W. Derry
,, Thomas, Strabane, merchant	Dated 1702.	W. Derry
,, William, Strabane, Co. Tyrone, merchant	1709.	W.P.
Maynard, [Sir] Boyle, Curryglass, Co. Cork, Knt.	1690.	F.2.
,, [Sir] William, Curriglass, Knt.	1658.	F.2.
Mayne, Charles, Dynan, Co. Monaghan	1780.	B.
Meade, Robert, Dublin, brewer	1677.	Swan. P.
Meagher, William	1804.	C.D.B.
Meares, Charles, Dalestown, Co. Meath	1775.	Swan. P.
,, Rev. Charles, Prospect, Co. Dublin	1795.	Swan. P.
,, Mary, Mearescourt, Westmeath, widow	1813.	C.D.B.
Meath, Grace, Viscountess	1812.	C.D.B.
,, Richard Tennison, Bishop of	1705.	B.
Medlicott, James D., Youngstown, Co. Kildare	1812.	C.D.B.
Medlycott, Thomas, Dublin	1738.	S.1.P.
Mee, Alice, Leixlip	1795.	Swan. P.
,, Grace. *See* Alsop.		
,, William, Kilrush, Co. Westmeath	1656.	W.P.
Mercer, John, Dublin, gent.	1702.	S.1.P.
,, Mary, Dublin, widow	1702.	S.1.P.
Meredith, Philip, Lachenmore, Queen's Co.	1809.	S.4. Kildare
,, Rice, Clonegark, Queen's Co.	1801.	B.
,, Sir Robert	1668.	F.2.
,, Thomas, Rerymore, Queen's Co.	1761.	S.4. Kildare
,, Rev. Thos., Ardtrea, Co. Tyrone	1819.	B.
,, William, Dublin	1822.	B.
Meredyth, Frances, Sackville St., Dublin, widow	1798.	S.1.P.
,, Henry, Dublin	1789.	S.1.P.
Metge, Peter, senr., Navan, Esq.	1735/6.	Swan. P.

INDEX OF WILL ABSTRACTS

Metge, Peter — 1777. Swan. P.
Meulh, Thomas — 1797. S.4. (H. BM.)
„ William — 1788. S.4. (H.BM.)
Meyler, Nicholas, Shelebeggan, Co. Wexford — 1658. F.2.
Midleton, Alan, Lord Viscount — 1728. W.P.
„ Lady Ann. Viscountess Dowager — 1747. W.P.
„ Lord — 1747. W.
Miles, Alson. *See* Cottrell.
Miller, Hugh, Coleraine, Co. Derry — 1671. B.
„ James, Lismoghry, Co. Donegal — 1740. B.
„ James, Rossyvolan, Co. Donegal — 1841. B.
„ John, Dublin, merchant — Dated 1646. W.P.
„ Jonathan, Greenhill, Co. Donegal — 1790. B.
„ Joseph, Rossgarland, Co. Wexford [gent.] — 1658. W.P.
„ Joseph, Blackmore, Co. Wexford, clk. — 1729. W. Ferns
„ Lewis, Drinagh, Co. Wexford, gent. — Dated 1704. W. Ferns
„ Ralph — 1650. W.P.
„ Robert — D. 1804. S.4. (H.BM.
„ Thomas, Limerick, alderman — 1687. W.P.
„ Capt. William, Inglesby's Regt. — 1653. W.P.
„ William, Morris Castle, Co. Wexford, gent. — 1696. W. Ferns
Millerd, Thomas, Cork, maltster — 1691. W. Cork
Millett, Thomas, Kyle, Co. Tipperary — 1756. S.[1]. Cashel
Milling, Nathaniel, Ardee, Co. Louth — 1799. Swan. P.
„ Oliver, Ardee, Doctor in Physick — 1790. Swan. P.
Mills, Francis — 1843. Swan.
„ Henry, Dromore — 1659. F.
„ Michael, Collinstown — 1835. Swan.
„ Thomas, Ballybeg, [Co. Cork] — 1699. F. and W.P.
„ Thomas, Ballymodan, Co. Cork, clk. — 1720. W. Cork
„ Thomas, Cork, gent. — 1737. W. Cork
„ Thomas, Collinstown, M.D. — 1831. Swan. P.
Milward, Clement, Dublin, merchant — Dated 1697. F.2.
„ Clement, Enniscorthy, Co. Wexford, gent. — 1696. F.2.
Minchin, Charles, Moneygall, King's Co., gent. — 1681. F.2.
„ Humphrey, Inchemore, Co. Kilkenny — 1748. Cav. P.
„ John, Inchemore, Co. Kilkenny — 1734. Cav. P.
„ Paul, Bough, Co. Carlow — 1764. F.
„ William, Dublin — 1759. S.1.P.
Minnitt, John, Chapman Park, Co. Tipperary — 1732. S.1. Killaloe
„ Joshua, Annaghbegg, Co. Tipperary — 1788. S.1.P.
Mitchell, George, Clonmylan, Queen's Co. — 1761. S.4. Kildare

Mitchell, John, Frolick, Co. Roscommon 1801. C.D.B.
" Mary, Dublin, widow 1802. C.D.B.
" Thomas, Cork, merchant 1691. F.2.
" Thomas, Cork, merchant 1711. W. Cork
" Thomas, Aghadda, Co. Cork, gent. 1721. W.P.
Moderwell, Adam, the elder, parish Donagh-
    more, Co. Donegal Dated 1632. W. Derry
" John, Strabane, merchant 1679. W.P.
Moign, Abigail. *See* Moore
Moland, Edward 1778. Swan.
Molesworth, William, Holles St., Dublin 1803. C.D.B.
Molloy, Arthur, Killyon, King's Co. 1794. B.
" Daniel, Kilcreagh, Co. Westmeath 1760. B.
" Dorothy, Mt. Bolus, King's Co. 1790. S.1.
" Francis, Frankford, King's Co.
    [No date, ? 1804. N.F.P.] C.D.B.
" James 1788. S.4. (H.BM.)
" John, Clonbeale, King's Co. 1803. B.
" Joseph, Rathrobin, King's Co. 1805. S.1.P.
" William, Doughill, King's Co. 1770. B.
" William, Streamstown, King's Co. 1777. B.
Molony, als. Connor, Ann 1776. Mol. P.
" Bartholomew, Limerick, merchant 1736. Mol. Limerick
" Bartholomew, Limerick, merchant 1746. Mol. P.
" David, Ballyclohessy, Co. Clare 1772. Mol. Killaloe
" Denis, Gray's Inn, late of Lincoln's Inn,
    Esq. 1726/7. Mol.
" Denis, par. of St. Michael, Limerick 1729. Mol. Limerick
" Denis, Lacharroo, Co. Clare Admon. 1779. Mol. Killaloe
" Denis, Lackarugh, farmer 1785. Mol. P.
" Eleanor, William's Lane, near New
    Street, Co. Dublin, widow 1809. Mol. P.
" Garrett, Limerick, gent. 1820. Mol. Killaloe
" Henry, Cregg, Co. Clare Dated 1819. Mol.
" James, Ballynahiny, Co. Clare 1733. Mol.
" James, the Abbey of Athy, Co. Kildare,
    Esq. 1794. Mol. P.
" James, Limerick, grocer 1808. Mol. P.
" James FitzDavid, Crossderry
    Admon. 1765. Mol. Killaloe
" Jeremiah, Cullinagh, Co. Clare 1819. Mol. Killaloe
" John, Bishop of Limerick, then of Issy,
    France. [In French] Dated 1701. Mol.
" John Dated 1759. Mol.
" John, Dooras, Co. Clare, gent. Admon. 1771. Mol. Killaloe

Molony, John, Carrubane, Co. Clare, farmer
　　　　　　　　　　　　　　　Admon. 1781. Mol. Killaloe
,,　　John, Ballycarado, par. of Castle-
　　　town, Co. Tipperary　　　1795. Mol. Killaloe
,,　　John, Cragg, Co. Clare　　Dated 1804. Mol.
,,　　John　　　　　　　　　　1804. Mol. Killaloe
,,　　John, Phenagh, Co. Clare, gent.　1809. Mol. P.
,,　　Mathew, Dourish, clerk　　1729. Mol. Killaloe
,,　　Mathew, Sixmilebridge, Co. Clare
　　　　　　　　　　　　　　　Admon. 1756. Mol. Killaloe
,,　　Rev. Mathew, Donaha, Co. Clare
　　　　　　　　　　　　　　　Admon. 1808. Mol. Killaloe
,,　　Michael　　　　　　　　Admon. 1768. Mol. Killaloe
,,　　Michael, Acres, par. of Feakill, Co.
　　　Clare, gent.　　　　　　　1769. Mol. P.
,,　　Michael, Ballyhurly　　Admon. 1772. Mol. Killaloe
,,　　Michael, Rossfadda, Co. Clare
　　　　　　　　　　　　　　　Admon. 1793. Mol. Killaloe
,,　　Miles, Fickle, Co. Clare, farmer　1767. Mol. Killaloe
,,　　Miles, Fickle　　　　　Admon. 1767. Mol. Killaloe
,,　　Patrick, Drimininagan, Co. Clare　1814. Mol. Killaloe
,,　　Stephen, Knockadoon, Co. Clare, far-
　　　mer　　　　　　　　　　Admon. 1781. Mol. Killaloe
,,　　Teige　　　　　　　　　Dated 1700. Mol. Killaloe
,,　　Thady, Curruemore, Co. Clare, gent.
　　　　　　　　　　　　　　　Admon. 1762. Mol. Killaloe
,,　　Timothy, Derasalagh　　　1828. Mol. Killaloe
,,　　William, par. of St. Munchin,
　　　Limerick　　　　　　　　1792. Mol. Limerick
Monckton, George, Liskennett, Co. Limerick,
　　　Esq.　　　　　　　　　　1730. Ir.
,,　　Nicholas, Liskennett, Co. Limerick,
　　　Esq.　　　　　　　　　　1725. Ir.
,,　　Thomas, Ballyfranky, Co. Limerick,
　　　gent.　　　　　　　Dated 1687. Ir.
Monear, William, Belfast　　　　1812. C.D.B.
Montgomery, Alexander, Bessmount　1808. Swan. P.
,,　　　George, Drumrollagh, Co. Fer-
　　　　managh　　　　　　　　1761. Swan. P.
Moore, als. Moign, Abigail, Moign Hall, Co.
　　　Cavan, widow　　　　　　1732. Swan. P.
,,　　Alice, Boley, Co. Wexford, widow　1740. F.D.
,,　　Allan, Caldroome, Co. Tyrone　1633. B.
,,　　Ann, Belfast, Co. Antrim　Dated 1797. C.D.B.
,,　　Boyle, Dublin　　　　　　1742. B.
,,　　Christian, Eccles St., Dublin, widow　1789. F.D.

Moore, Christopher, Carlingford — 1747. Swan. P.
" Frances. *See* Burridge.
" Francis, Raheenduff, Queen's Co. — 1730. B. and Cav. P.
" Garret, Feernane, Co. Kerry — 1773. S.3. Ardfert
" Henry, Ballyaglish, Co. Limerick — 1787. M.
" Henry William, Drumbanagher, Co. Armagh — 1762. M.
" Hugh, Ballyhalaghan, Co. Tyrone — 1751. B.
" Ignatius, Ballintry, Co. Meath — 1728. F.D.
" James, Ballintry, Co. Meath — 1658. B.
" Rev. James, Athy — 1703. Cav. P.
" James, Ardstraw — 1712. Swan. Armagh
" James, Dorset Street, Dublin — 1803. C.D.B.
" John, Glenhoyes, Co. Tyrone — 1701. B.
" John, Ballyneclogh, Co. Limerick — 1742. S.4.
" Lewis, Creemorgan, Queen's Co., Esq. — 1746. B. and F.D.
" Lewis, Cremorgan, Queen's Co., Esq. — 1776. F.D.
" Lewis, Dublin, gent. — 1777. F.D.
" Lorenzo — 1804. F.D.
" Nicholas, Ardaghstown, Co. Louth, Esq. — 1673. Swan. P. and F.2.
" Nicholas, Mooremount, Co. Louth — 1756. Swan. P.
, Pierce, Loran, Queen's Co., gent. — 1746. B. and F.D.
" Randal, Mount Terrible, Co. Monaghan 1746. M.
" Robert, Ardmayle, Co. Tipperary — 1775. M.
" Thomas, Grange, Queen's Co. — 1660. F.D.
" Thomas, Aghearren, Co. Cork — ? 1761. Swan. Cork
" William, lately of Youghal, Dio Cloyne, gent. — 1705. Swan.
" William, Atherdee, Co. Cork — 1735. M.
" William, Drumon, Co. Tyrone — 1749. B.
" William, city of Cork, mariner — 1753. Eu.
" William, Tinrahan, Co. Wexford — 1756. F.D.
" William, Drumon, Co. Tyrone — 1789. B.
" William, Tullyvin, Co. Cavan — 1803. C.D.B. and Swan. P.

More [Moore], Barry, Shenton, Co. Leicester, gent. — 1706. F.D.

Moriarty, als. Rice, Alice, Dingle — 1767. Cav. Ardfert
" Rev. Dennys, D.D., Dingle Dated 1735. Cav. Ardfert
" Mathew, Dingle Dated 1743. Cav. Ardfert
" Maurice, Miltown, Co. Kerry Dated 1781. Cav. Ardfert
" Dr. Melchior — 1747. Cav. Ardfert
" Michael, Ballymacalla, Co. Clare Dated 1729. Cav. Ardfert

Moriarty, Murtagh, Knockana Coolteen, Co.
Kerry   Dated 1730/31. Cav. Ardfert
„   Thomas, Tuoreen, Co. Clare   Dated 1719. Cav. Ardfert
„   Thos., Dingle   Dated 1785. Cav. P.
„   Thomas James, Dingle   1806. Cav. Ardfert
Morland, Joseph, Esq.   Dated 1716. Cav. P.
Mornington, Earl of (Garret Wesley)   1781. S.2.
Morris, Abraham, Cork, merchant   Dated 1721. F.
„   Andrew, Galway, gent.   1780. S.4.P.
„   Edward, Oldcourt, Co. Dublin, gent.   1717. W.P.
„   Edward, senr., Mullagha, Co. Meath   1718. W.P.
„   Jane, Dublin, widow of John M.,
        gent.   1730. W.P.
„   Jasper, Ballinarig, Co. Kerry, Esq.   1729. Ir.
„   John, par. of Desertcreagh, Co. Tyrone,
        clk.   1708. W.P.
„   John   D. 1814. S.4. (H.O.)
„   Jonas, Cork   1736. F.A.
„   Margaret. See McLorinan.
„   Patrick, Silverwood, Co. Armagh   1735. W.P.
„   Samuel, Ballybegan, Co. Kerry, Esq.   1694. Ir., F.2. and
                                              W.P.
„   Samuel, Littleton, alias Ballybegan,
        Co. Kerry, Esq.   1722. Ir.
„   Rev. Samuel, Glebe Lodge, Co. Tyrone 1804. C.D.B.
„   Rev. Samuel, Glebe Lodge, Co. Tyrone,
        clk.   1806. Swan.
„   William, Dublin, barrister-at-law   1724. W.P.
Morrison, Samuel, Dublin, gent.   Dated 1690. Swan.
Mortimer, Rev. Robert, clk.   1797. Swan.
Mothee, Joseph, Ringsend, Dublin   1801. C.D.B.
Mounckton, Nicholas, Knockany, Co. Limerick 1675. Ir.
Moylan, Francis, R.C. Bishop of Cork   1815. S.1.
Mulcaile, James Philip, George's Hill, Dublin   1802. C.D.B.
Mulhollan, John, Conaghie, Co. Monaghan,
        gent.   1671. Swan. P.
Mullally, William, Shankill, Co. Monaghan   1811. C.D.B.
Mullane, James, Cork, merchant   1728. W. Cork
Mulligan, Edward, Abbey Street, Dublin, mer-
        chant   1812. C.D.B.
Mullony, Darby, Derrynafeigh, Co. Clare, gent.
                                       Admon. 1743. Mol. Killaloe
„   John   Admon. 1709. Mol. Killaloe
„   Mary, Ballyclinshane, Co. Clare,
        widow   1790. Mol. Limerick
„   Simon, Barrane   Admon. 1796. Mol. Killaloe

Mulock, Henry Vans, Lusna, King's Co. 1836. B.
„ Rev. John, Bellair, King's Co. 1800. B.
„ Joshua, Clara, King's Co. 1835. B.
„ Luke, Limerick 1834. B.
„ Maria Sophia, Bath, widow 1841. B.
„ Rachel, Dublin 1870. B.
„ Robert, Banagher, King's Co. 1791. B.
„ Robert, Dublin, M.D. 1868. B.
„ Sarah 1806. B.
„ Thomas, Limerick 1774. B.
„ Thomas 1818. B.
Mulony, John, Clenagh, Co. Clare Admon. 1738. Mol. Killaloe
Murdock, Rev. Benezer, Killshannick 1747. F.
„ Joseph, Youghal, merchant 1670. F.P.
Murphy, Daniel, Terenure, Dublin, farmer 1803. C.D.B.
„ Elinor, Whitefriar Street, Dublin, widow 1803. C.D.B.
„ James, Clonmel, Co. Tipperary 1812. C.D.B.
„ Jane. *See* Adair.
„ Capt. Lawrence 1783. S.4. (H.BM.)
Murphy, Phelim, Myaugh, Co. Wexford, farmer 1813. C.D.B.
„ Thos. Turner D. 1808. S.4. (H.O.)
„ Thomas, Inistioge, Co. Kilkenny 1803. C.D.B.
Murray, Emmanuel, Kilkenny, merchant 1803. C.D.B.
„ James D. 1850. S.4. (H.O.)
„ Rev. John Walton, Dean of Connor
Dated 1883. Swan.

Nagle, Edmond, Clogher, Co. Cork, Esq. 1796. F.A.
„ Garrett, Ballynamona, Co. Cork, Esq. 1805. F.A.
„ James, Garnavelly, Co. Tipperary, gent. 1710. F.A.
„ Joseph, Calverleigh, Devon 1813. C.D.B.
„ Richard, Fethard, Co. Tipperary, Esq. 1719. F.A.
Naper, Dorothy, Loughcrew, Co. Meath 1692. F.2.
„ James, Loghrow [? Loughcrew], Co. Meath, Esq. 1676. F.2.
„ James, Tobercurry, Co. Sligo 1786. S.4.
„ William, Billsborough, Co. Meath, Esq. 1741. W.P.
Nash, Richard, Ive Gallahoe, Co. Limerick, gent. 1714. Ir.
„ Richard, Ardtaget, Co. Clare, gent. 1725. Ir.
Nason, Elizabeth, Youghal, late of Newtown, Co. Cork 1804. C.D.B.
„ William, Rahenity, Co. Cork, gent. 1736. W. Cork
„ William, Cork, merchant 1740. W.P.

Naylor, Rev. Charles, Carlow 23 Jan. 1804.
[N.F.P.] C.D.B.
Neal, Mathias 1769. S.4. (H.1.)
Neale, Barbara, Kinsale, Co. Cork, widow 1624. W. Cork
  ,,   Constantine, Wexford town, Esq. 1692. F.2.
Nelson, John 1793. S.4. (H.BM.)
Nesbit, Thomas, Kilmacredon, Co. Donegal 1802. C.D.B.
Nesbitt, Cosby, Lismore 1791. Swan. Lismore
  ,,   James, Green Hills, Co. Donegal 1791. Swan. P.
  ,,   Gifford, Tubberdally, King's Co. 1773. S.1.P.
  ,,   Louisa, Lismore 1803. Swan. P.
  ,,   Nathaniel Sneyd D. 1876. S.4. (H.O.)
  ,,   Thomas, Lismore, Co. Cavan, gent. 1752. Swan. P.
  ,,   William, Drumalee, Co. Cavan 1744. Swan. P.
Netterville, Margaret, Brunswick St. Convent,
    widow 1802. C.D.B.
  ,,   William, Dublin 1801. C.D.B.
Nettles, Robert, [? Maghubaragh], Co. Cork,
    Esq. 1712. F.
Nevill, Gen. Clement, Dollardstown, Co. Kildare 1744. S.1.P.
  ,,   Garrett, Dublin, merchant 1737. F.E.
Neville, Richard, Phornaghs, Co. Kildare, Esq. 1682. F.2. and F.E.
  ,,   Robert, Great Fornaghts, gent. 1688. F.2. and F.E.
Newburgh, Anne, Killiter, Co. Tyrone, widow 1712. Ir.
  ,,   Arthur 1675. Ir.
  ,,   Brockhill, Ballyhays, Co. Cavan,
    Esq. 1741. Ir.
  ,,   Brockhill, Ballyhaise 1798. Ir.
  ,,   Broghill, Ballyhaise 1798. Ir.
  ,,   Lt.-Col. Thomas 1660. Ir.
  ,,   Thomas, Ballyhaise. [Exemplification] 1696. Ir.
  ,,   Thomas, Ballyhaise, Co. Cavan 1702. Ir.
  ,,   Thomas, Ballyhaise 1776. Swan. P.
  ,,   William, Drumcarn 1777. Ir.
  ,,   William Perrott, Ballyhaise 1790. Ir.
Newcomb, John, Aughenville, King's Co. 1712. S.1.P.
Newcomen, Arabella, Dublin 1802. C.D.B.
  ,,   Robert D. 1819. S.4. (H.O.)
Newell, Alexr., par. of Mitchellstown
    Admon. 1694. W. Cloyne
Newenham, George, Cork, merchant 1793. F.A.
  ,,   John, Cork, Esq. 1706. F.A. and W.P.
  ,,   John, Cork, clothier 1735. F.A. and W.P.

Newenham, John, Maryboro', South Liberties of
  Cork, Esq.   1787. F.A.
 ,, Richard, Cork, merchant 1759. F.A.
 ,, Thomas, Cork, Esq.   1725. F.A. and W.P.
 ,, William, Cork, Esq.   1736. F.A.
Newhouse, Elizabeth. *See* Leake.
Newman, Charles, Kilshanig, Co. Cork, gent. 1731. W.P.
 ,, Dillon, Dromore, Co. Cork, Esq. 1733. F.
 ,, Edward   1662. W. Cork
 ,, Elizabeth, Cork, widow   1717. F.A. and W.P.
 ,, Rev. Henry, Newberry, Co. Cork 1801. C.D.B.
 ,, John, Kinsale, apothecary
          Dated 1728. W. Cork
 ,, Philip, Kinsale Dated 1737. W. Cork
 ,, Richard, Cork   1693. F. and W.P.
Newstead, William, Derryneslyn, Co. Tipperary 1749. S.1. Killaloe
Newton, Major-Genl. John Dated 1714. F.
 ,, Thomas, Drogheda, Alderman 1696. F.2.
Nicholls, Simon, Shancer, Co. Cavan, gent. 1784. Swan. P.
Nicholson, George, Drogheda 1802. C.D.B.
 ,, Thomas, Tallagh, Co. Dublin
        Admon. 1610. Drogheda MSS.
Nickson, Abraham, Collattin, Co. Wicklow,
  Esq.   1720. S.4., F.D. and
            Eu.
 ,, Abrahan, Munny, Wicklow, Esq. 1759. S.4. and F.D.
 ,, Abraham Augustus, Munny, Wicklow 1798. S.4.
 ,, Isabella, Killinure, Co. Wicklow,
   widow   1751. F.D.
 ,, John, Cornarry, Co. Cavan 1750. Swan.
 ,, John, Gibralter   1765. S.4. and Eu.
 ,, Lorenzo, Chapel Izod   1806. S.4.
 ,, Lydia, Munny, Co. Wicklow, widow 1748. S.4. P. and
            F.D.
 ,, Richard, Killanure   1797. S.4. Leighlin
 ,, Timothy, Ballymurphy   1783. S.4.
 ,, *See* Nixon.
Nicolls, George, Lossett, Co. Cavan 1736. Swan. P.
Nihell, James (James Nihell David), Limerick 1733. Mol. P.
 ,, Patrick, Glasclowen, Co. Clare 1703. Mol. P.
Nisbitt, Thomas, Strabane, Co. Tyrone, mer-
  chant   1757. Swan. P.
Nixon, Adam, Cranly Begg   1721. Swan. Ardagh
 ,, Rev. Adam, vicar of Clontibret, Co.
  Monaghan   1767. Swan. and F.D
 ,, Adam, Lurgan Lodge   1843. Swan.

Nixon, Adam, Belturbet, Co. Cavan Admon. 1808. Swan.
,, Adam, Graan 1845. Swan.
,, Alexander, Nixon Hall, Co. Fermanagh 1791. Swan.
,, Andrew, Tullyharney 1753. Swan.
,, Andrew, Feaghmore, Co. Tyrone 1765. Swan. Derry
,, Rev. Andrew, Belturbet 1774. Swan.
,, Andrew, Derryinch, Cleenish, Co. Fermanagh 1825. Swan. Clogher
,, Archibald, par. of Rosory, Co. Fermanagh Admon. 1673. Swan.
,, Rev. Brinsley Not dated Swan. P.
,, Dorothea Rose 1867. Swan.
,, Edward, Aughrim, Cleenish, Co. Fermanagh 1742. Swan. Clogher
,, Elizabeth, Enniskillen, spinster 1845. Swan. P.
,, George, Drumwhillin, Co. Cavan 1696. Swan. Kilmore
,, George, Coragh Admon. 1737. Swan. Clogher
,, George, Mullinhasher or Mullinashe 1757. Swan. Clogher
,, George, Lisnarrow, Clones, Co. Monaghan 1783. Swan. Clogher
,, George, Lieut. 12th Regt. Admon. 1800. Swan.
,, George, Dunbar, Co. Fermanagh 1822. Swan.
,, George, Milford, near Athy, Queen's Co. 1840. Swan. P.
,, Humphrey, Balfaghan, Co. Meath 1825. Swan.
,, James [? of Granshagh] 1702. Swan. Clogher
,, James, Aughafadda, par. of Ematris, Co. Monaghan 1737. Swan. P.
,, James, Dublin, gent. Dated 1752. Swan.
,, James, Rockcorry, Co. Monaghan 1779. Swan. P.
,, James, Toppedmountain, Enniskillen, Co. Fermanagh 1799. Swan. Clogher
,, Jane 1840. Swan. P.
,, John, Newtownbutler 1708. Swan. Clogher
,, John, Corinary, Co. Cavan 1750. Swan. Meath
,, John, Lisneynagrovah, Co. Leitrim 1769. Swan. Kilmore and Ardagh
,, John, Redmills, Co. Dublin, gent. 1773. F.E.
,, Katherine, Albemarle Row, Clifton, Gloucester, widow 1812. Swan. P.
,, Leonard, Inisburgh, par. of Burrishoole, Co. Mayo 1764. Swan. P.
,, Mary, Antrim, Co. Antrim, widow Admon. 1789. Swan.
,, Mathew, Ballyhaise, late of Belturbet 1800. Swan. P.

Nixon, Richard, Sheestown, Co. Wexford 1713. F. and F.D.
„ Richard Phepoe, Lieut. 19th Foot 1815. Swan. P.
„ Robert, Temple Court, Castle Street, Dublin 1750. Swan.
„ Robert, Cranullagh, par. of Mostrim Not dated Swan. Ardagh
„ Robert, city of Dublin, gent. 1786. Swan. P.
„ Rev. Robert, Killala, Co. Mayo 1812. Swan. P.
„ Robert, Laughan, Co. Cavan, gent. 1850. Swan. P.
„ Thomas, Kingstown, Co. Fermanagh 1739. Swan. Clogher
„ Thomas, Capt. 56th Regt. 1797. Swan. P.
„ Thomas, Dunbar 1815. Swan.
„ William, Drummish 1699. Swan. Clogher
„ Rev. William, Galway D. 1761. Swan.
„ William, Mullaghacluff, Co. Fermanagh 1806. Swan. P.
„ William, Thornhill, par. of Killenagh, Co. Cavan 1837. Swan. P.
„ See Nickson.
Noble, Adam, Longfield, Co. Monaghan 1793. Swan. P.
„ Archibald, Lisdow, par. of Aghalurcher 1727. Swan. Clogher
„ Archibald, Lisnaskea, Co. Fermanagh 1766. Swan. Clogher
„ Arthur, Derrwin, Co. Fermanagh 1732. Swan. Clogher
„ Arthur, Churchill, Co. Monaghan 1817. Swan. P.
„ Brabazon, Donamoine, Co. Monaghan 1776. Swan. P.
„ Elizabeth, Dublin, widow 1801. Swan. P.
„ Francis, Peterborrow, par. of Donamoine, Co. Monaghan 1740. Swan. Clogher
„ Francis, Raheens, Co. Monaghan, Esq. 1790. Swan. P.
„ James, Clones 1709/10. Swan. Clogher
„ James 1720. Swan.
„ James, Lisnaskea, Co. Fermanagh 1777. Swan. Clogher
„ James, Donagh House, Co. Fermanagh Dated 1829. Swan. P.
„ Jane, Enniskillen, widow 1817. Swan. P.
„ Jerome, Summer Hill, Co. Down 1874. Swan. P.
„ Joseph Story, clk. 1855. Swan. P.
„ Samuel, late Major Hon. East India Coy., Moyne Hall, Co. Cavan 1843. Swan. P.
„ Thomas, Dublin, gent. 1750. Swan. P.
Nolan, Joseph Edward, Clonalis, Co. Roscommon 1802. C.D.B.
Norcott, Edward, Ballyellis, Co. Cork 1735. F.
„ Rev. John, Kilshanig Not dated F.
„ William, Springfield 1742. F.
Norman, Samuel, Londonderry, Alderman 1692. F.2.
North, Eleanor, Dublin, widow 1776. Swan. P.

INDEX OF WILL ABSTRACTS

North, Philip, Tubberbonny, Co. Dublin   1772. Swan. P.
Noy, Edward, Newbrook, Co. Dublin Dated 1777. S.4.
Nugent, Hon. Alice, Dublin, widow   1736. S.1.
„   als. Barnewall, Alicia, Ballinacor, Co. Westmeath   1803. C.D.B.
„   Jane, Derrymore, Co. Westmeath   1737. S.4.P.
„   Lt.-Col. John   1792. S.4. (H.BM.)
„   Mary, dau. of Thos. N., of Clonlost   1757. Swan.
„   Thomas, Smithfield, Dublin, saddler   Dated 1791. C.D.B.
Nunan, James, Cork   1813. C.D.B.
Nunn, Ebenezer   1782. S.4. (H.I.)
„   Rev. Joshua   1802. C.D.B.
„   Richard, Hill Castle, Co. Wexford   1692. S.1.
„   Richard, Hill Castle, Co. Wexford   1714. S.1.
Nuttall, Charles, Bolybeggs, Co. Kildare   1727. S.1.P.
„   Richard, Dublin, gent.   1713. S.1.P.
Nuttle, James, Clonmel, innkeeper   1715. S.1. Waterford

O'Barne, Hugh Bane, the Mill, [Rathnew], Co. Wicklow, farmer   Dated 1618. Dub.
O'Beirne, Thomas Ormsby   1839. S.4. (H.I.)
Obre, Edward, Lisburn, Co. Antrim   1791. Swan. P.
„   Francis, Cantilew, Co. Armagh   1758. Swan. P.
„   Mary, Lisburn, Co. Antrim   1827. Swan. P.
O'Brien, Catherine, Portobello, Co. Dublin   1803. C.D.B.
„   Cnogher, Coylnocorry   1661. F.2.
„   Ellinor, Clonfadda, Co. Clare, widow   1764. Mol. P.
„   Henry, Mallow   Dated 1742. W. Cloyne
„   James, Kilrush   Dated 1845. Mol.
„   John Perkins, Garryhill, Co. Carlow   1811. S.1. Leighlin
„   Lucius Robert   1825. S.4. (H.I.)
„   Richard, Ballinacloonagh, gent.   1767. S.1.P.
„   Terlagh, Knockdroma, Co. Clare   1743. Mol. P.
„   William, Killinacahill, Co. Cork, gent.   1707. F.2. and W.P.
O'Bryen, Terlagh, Glagesiagh, Co. Galway   1732. Mol. Clonfert
„   William, Coolnacurra, Co. Cork   1640. W.P.
„   William, Cork, clothier   1708. W. Cork
„   William, Bealavaddy   1730. W. Cloyne
O'Callaghan, Cahir, Curra, Co. Cork, gent.   Dated 1678. F. and W.P.
„   Catherine, Loughmoe, Co. Tipperary, widow   1731. F.P.
„   Catherine, Loughmore, Co. Tipperary   1732. S.1.P.

O'Callaghan,	Conogher, Co. Kerry	1637. F.
"	Cornelius, Bantyre	1737. F. and S.2.P.
"	Cornelius, Co. Cork	1739. S.2. P. and F.E.
"	Cornelius, senr., gent.	1739. F.
"	Cornelius	Dated 1740. F. and S.1.P.
"	Cornelius, Droumskeaghy, Co. Cork	1749. F. and S.1.P.
"	Cornelius, Bantire, Co. Cork	1772. S.2.P.
"	Cornelius, Shanbally, Co. Tipperary	1782. S.1.P.
"	Daniel, Kilgorey, Co. Clare	1772. F.
"	Donogh, Clonlunan, Co. Louth, farmer	1672. F.2.
"	Donough, Kilgorey, Co. Clare	Dated 1698. F.
"	Hannah, Dublin, widow	Admon. 1771. F.E.
"	Mary. See McNamara.	
"	Robert, Clonmeen, Co. Cork	1727. F.
"	Robert, Shanbally, Co. Tipperary	1761. S.1.P.
"	Robert, Cork, late of Clonmeen	1778. S.1.P.
"	Roger	1747. F.
"	Roger, Dirgallon, Co. Cork	1747. S.1.P.
"	Thady, Mount Allen, Co. Cork, Esq.	Admon. 1772. F.E.
"	Timothy, Bregoge, Co. Cork	1758. F.
"	Timothy, Bregoge, Co. Cork	1759. S.2.P.
"	See Callaghan.	
O'Collyn,	Colan	Dated 1595. Dub.
O'Connell,	Daniel, Portmagee, Co. Kerry. Dated 21 Feb., 1812. [N.F.P.]	C.D.B.
O'Connor,	Monica, Dominick St., Dublin	1812. C.D.B.
O'Connovan,	Daniel, Athy, husbandman	Dated 1625. Dub.
O'Connowe,	Donnogh, Narraghmore	1636. Dub.
O'Cullon,	Gillananowe, Crookstown	1620. Dub.
O'Dale.	See Adale.	
Odell,	Lieut. Christopher	1656. Ir. and W.P.
"	Eleanor, widow	Not dated Swan. P.
"	John, Ballingarry, Co. Limerick, Esq.	1699. Ir. and Swan. P.
"	John, Ballingarry	1725. Ir. and Swan. P.
"	John, Bealduregy	1761. Swan. P.
"	Richard, of the College of Dublin, gent.	Dated 1701. W. Waterford

Odell, Thomas, Shannongrove, Co. Limerick 1763. Swan. P.
Odlum, Henry 1781. S.1.P.
O'Donnell, James Moore 1801. C.D.B.
„ James, city of Waterford 1812. C.D.B.
O'Donoghue, Daniel [? of Killarney] 1804. F.
„ Jeffrey, Co. Kerry 1678. F.
„ Jeffrey, Cork 1790. F.P.
Ogden, John, Dublin 1653. B.
O'Halloran, Thady, Ballycuneen, Co. Clare 1797. M.
O'Hara, Charles King, Nymphs Field, Co. Sligo 1860. F.A.
„ Geffry (or Jeffrie), West Lodge, Galway, Esq. 1796. Ir.
„ James Admon. 1785. S.4. (H.BM.)
O'Hea, James, Killkierane, Co. Cork, gent. 1720. W.P.
O'Hehir, Ensign Charles 1791. S.4. (H.BM.)
O'Heyne, Francis, Laurence, Dublin, gent. [From Prerogative Cause Papers.] 1741. Cr.
Oldfield, Margaret, St. Andrews, Dublin, spinster 1680. Drogheda MSS.
Oliver, Christopher, Cork, alderman 1691. F.
„ Robert, Cloughnodfry or Clonadfoy, Co. Limerick 1679. S.1.P. and F.2.
„ Robert, Clonodfoy, Co. Limerick 1737. F.
O'Loghlen, Dr. Colman, Ennis, Co. Clare, late of Ballilee, Co. Galway 1784. F.A.
O'Moore, Garrett, Cloghan Castle 1833. S.1.P.
O'Neil, Barbara, York Street, Dublin, widow 1804. C.D.B.
O'Neill, Sir Bryan, Backistown, Co. Dublin, Bart. 1670. W.P.
„ Henry, Dublin, merchant 1738. W.P.
„ John, Edenduffcarrick, Co. Antrim, Esq. 1739. W.P.
„ Neal, Tauriaghmore East, C.o Antrim, gent. 1728. W.P.
O'Reilly, Edward Sterling 1837. Swan. P.
„ James, Tullicoe, Co. Cavan 1800. Swan. Kilmore
Ormsby, Anthony, Lissegallane, Co. Roscommon 1631. Ky.
„ Arthur, Co. Limerick 1692. F.
„ Arthur, Rookwood, Co. Galway 1735. Ky.
„ Arthur, Bath, late of Dublin 1809. S.1.P.
„ Joseph 1705. F.
„ Margaret, Balanamore, Co. Mayo, widow 1714. Ky.
„ Robert, Cloghans, Co. Mayo 1714. S.1.P.

Orrery, Margaret, Countess of — Dated 1682. W.P.
" Margaret Dowager Countess of, widow
    of Roger Earl of O. — 1696. W.P.
" Roger, Earl of — 1682. W.P.
Orson, Mary, Dublin, widow — 1743. Swan. P.
Osborn, Capt. Edward — 1691. Ky.
Osborne, William, Youghal, merchant — Dated 1681. Swan. P.
O'Shaghnussie, Sir Dermott, Gortinsigorye, Co.
    Galway, Knt. — Dated 1671. Cr. P.
Ossory, Thomas Otway, Bishop of — 1693. B.
O'Sullivan, John, Coleck, Co. Cork, gent. — 1790. Davis
" Owen, Kilcumen parish — 1743. Davis
" Timothy, Dublin, formerly a vintner — 1744. Davis
" Murlogh, Conlagh — 1708. F.
Otway, Anthony. [Proved in London] — 1650. B.
" Henry, Castle Otway, Co. Tipperary — 1737. B.
" Loftus, Nenagh, Co. Tipperary — 1789. S.1.P.
" Sir John, Knt., Ingmer Hall, Yorkshire — 1693. B.
" Thomas, Bishop of Ossory — 1693. B.
" Thomas, Lissenhall, Co. Tipperary — 1724. B.
Ously, Jasper, Ballycogly, Co. Wexford — 1710. B.
Ovens, Elizabeth, Highwood Parsonage, near Chelmsford — 1850. Swan. P.
" Jane, Enniskillen, widow — 1847. Swan. P.
" John, Rahalton, Co. Fermanagh — 1802. Swan. P.
" John, Careclone, Co. Fermanagh — 1849. Swan. P.
" See Owens.
Owen, Edward, Kilmore, Co. Monaghan, gent. — 1733. W. Clogher
" Ellinor. See Cransie.
" Henry, Ballenadrumney, Co. Meath, Esq. — 1739. W.P.
" John, Dublin, gent. — 1696. W.P.
Owens, Hugh (*recte* Ovens), Saint Catherine's, par. of Innismcsaint, Co. Fermanagh — 1794. Swan. Clogher
O'Witheroe, Mary — 1718. F.
Owlton, Luke, Dublin — 1668. B.

Pagett, James, Milltown, Co. Dublin, gent. — 1787. Swan. P.
Paine, Judith [? of Carrickfergus] — 1761. Ir.
Pakenham, Anne, Bracklin, Co. Westmeath, widow — 1708. F.2.
Palliser, Philip, Castletown — 1784. Cav. P.
" Thomas, Portobello — 1756. Cav. P.
" Thomas, The Great Island — 1758. Cav. P.

Palmer, Amos, Derry, King's Co. 1806. S.1.P.
,, Cassandra, Dublin, widow 1690. B. and F.2
,, Elizabeth, Dublin, spinster 1836. S.1. Dublin
,, Francis, Dublin 1801. C.D.B.
,, Henry, senr., Birr 1739. S.1.P.
,, James, Cloghan, King's Co. 1773. S.1.P.
,, John, Dublin 1715. Swan. Kilmore
,, John, Annaghnerrig, Co. Tipperary 1731. S.1. Killaloe
,, Joseph, Derrensallagh, Co. Tipperary 1765. S.1. Killaloe
,, Joseph, Nenagh 1761. S.1.P.
,, Joseph, Glannacurragh, King's Co. 1730. S.1. Killaloe
,, Mary, Shinrone, King's Co. 1808. S.1.P.
,, Richard, Snugboro, King's Co. 1809. S.1. Killaloe
,, Stephen, Dublin, vintner 1667. B. and F.2.
,, Thomas, Kilballyshea, King's Co. 1715. S.1. Killaloe
,, Thomas, Birr 1742. S.1. Killaloe
,, William, Dublin 1727. B. S.1. and W.P.
Paradise, Richard, Youghal, merchant 1688. F.2.
Parke, Gilbert, Castlecarr, Co. Leitrim, Esq.
 Admon. 1715. Ir.
Parker, Anthony, Castlelough, Co. Tipperary 1785. S.1.P.
,, John, Dunkip, Co. Limerick 1700. S.1.P.
,, John Neville 1781. S.4. (H.I.)
,, Robert, Gortroe, Co. Cork, gent. 1715. F.
,, Thomas, Coume, Co. Tipperary 1766. S.1. Killaloe
Parks, John, Cork, clothier 1750. F.E.
Parr, Edward, s. suburbs of Cork city, innholder 1738. W. Cork
,, Martha, Dingle, Co. Kerry, widow
 Dated 1744. W. Ardfert
,, William, Dingle Dated 1742. W. Ardfert
Parsons, Anne, Birr, King's Co. 1676. W.P.
,, Francis, Garridyce, Co. Leitrim 1668. Ir.
,, Michael, Tomduff, Co. Wexford, Esq. 1699. W.P.
,, Peter, Larkhill, Co. Fermanagh 1812. S.1. Clogher
,, Samuel, Powertstown, Co. Tipperary 1761. S.2. Waterford
,, Sa ah, Kinsale 1651. W. Cork
,, William, Tomduff, Co. Wexford 1705. W. Ferns
,, William, St. John's, Co. Wexford, gent. 1737. W. Ferns
,, William, Mt. Sidney, Co. Dublin 1852. S.1.P.
Patten, Robert, Dublin, merchant 1773. S.1.P.
Patterson, William, Knocknagappull, Co. Cork 1817. S.1. Cloyne
Pattin, Ellinor, Dublin, widow 1813. C.D.B.
Patton, Margaret. *See* Erskine.
Paul, Jeffrey, Balleraglin 1690. F.

IN THE GENEALOGICAL OFFICE, DUBLIN 241

Paul, John, Dublin — 1801. C.D.B.
  „ Urith, John's Hill, Co. Waterford — 1812. C.D.B.
Peacock, Richard, Rothwell, York, late of Grange, Co. Limerick — 1693. F.2.
Pearce, John, Kilbree, Co. Cork, gent. — 1721. W. Cloyne
  „ Nicholas, Ballyhaunder, Co. Cork — 1677. W. Cork
Peard, Richard, Castlelyons, Co. Cork — Dated 1716. F.
Pearde, Henry, Coole, gent. — 1738. Mol. and W. Cloyne
  „ Richard, Coole — 1689. Mol.
Pearson, Samuel, Clonin, King's Co. — 1767. B.
  „ Thomas, Beamore, Co. Meath — 1736. B.
  „ William, Clonmel, Co. Tipperary — 1812. C.D.B
Peirce, Robert, Ballygormans, Barony Barretts, Co. Cork — 1721. W.
Peirson, Eleazer, Dublin — 1739. B.
  „ Samuel, Killinsonkin, Co. Westmeath — 1701. B.
  „ Thomas, Stoneyford, Co. Westmeath — 1753. B.
Peisley, Sir Fras, Roscrea Co. Tipperary — 1666. F.
Pembroke, William, Cork, cardmaker — 1711. W. Cork
Pentland, Barbara, Dublin, widow — 1835. S.1.P.
  „ Charles, Dublin — 1848. S.1.
  „ Edward, Thornhill, Co. Tyrone — 1826. S.1.P.
  „ (Rev.) Francis, Rathmacnee — 1840. S.1.
  „ George, Cootehill, apothecary — 1733. S.1. Kilmore
  „ George, Drumkirk, Co. Down — 1783. S.1. Down
  „ George, Athboy — 1826. S.1.P.
  „ George, Blackhall — 1834. S.1.P.
  „ Jane, Cootehill, widow — 1742. S.1.P.
  „ John, Dublin, gent. — 1808. S.1.P. and M
  „ John, Strandvilla, Co. Wicklow — 1809. S.1.P.
  „ John, Dublin, M.D. Dated 1825. S.1.P.
  „ Mary, Seaview, Co. Wicklow — 1841. S.1.
  „ Robert, Drogheda, merchant — 1808. S.1.P.
  „ Robert, Blessington Street, Dublin Dated 1832. S.1.P.
  „ Rev. William — 1779. S.1.P.
  „ William, Letterkenny — 1810. S.1.P.
Pepper, Martin, Drogheda, merchant — 1684. F.2.
  „ Simon, Ballygarth, gent. — 1701. F.2.
  „ William, Rathgorey, Co. Louth — 1871. S.2.
Percival, Major Charles Dated 1710. W.P.
  „ Charles, Callan, Co. Kilkenny, Esq. Dated 1713. W.P.
  „ Edmond, Ballydinane — 1714. W. Cork

Percival, Edward, Dublin, pewterer   Dated 1685. W. Dublin
"   George   D. 1805. S.4. (H.O.)
"   John, Wexford   1737. W.P.
"   King   D. 1815. S.4. (H.O.)
"   William, Dean of Emly   1734. W.P.
Percivall, Dame Cath., widow of Sir Philip P., Knt.   1681. W.P.
"   Lady Catherine, Kinsale   1686. W.P.
"   David, Dublin, merchant   1719. W. Dublin
"   Edward, Clonkeen, Co. Louth, clk.   1737. W.P.
"   Elizabeth   1656. W. Dublin
"   George, Dublin, Esq.   Dated 1674. W.P.
"   Hugh, Kinsale, merchant   1652. W. Cork
"   Hugh, Gortadroma, Co. Clare, gent.   1683. W.P.
"   John, Dublin, tailor   1693. W. Dublin
"   John, Knightsbrook, Co. Meath, Esq.   1718. W.P.
"   Martha, widow   1745. W.P.
"   Sir Philip, Knt.   1653. W. Cork
"   Thomas, Drogheda, alderman   1703. W.P.
"   Rev. William, Aghanlow, Co. Derry, clk.   1747. W.P.
Percivell, Mary, Bandonbridge, Co. Cork, widow   1682. W. Cork
Percy, Sir Anthony, Kt., Dublin   1704. B. and Ir.
"   Francis, Ballintemple, King's Co.   1744. B. and S.1.P. and Ir.
"   George, Limerick   1769. B.
"   Henry, Seskin, Co. Wicklow   1725. B. and Ir.
"   Jane, Cloneraken, Co. Wicklow, widow   1768. B. and S.1.P.
"   Sarah, Ballintemple, King's Co.   1745. B. and Ir.
"   William, Aghatavny, Co. Leitrim   1738. B. and Ir.
"   Rev. William, Esker, Co. Dublin   1795. B. and Ir.
Percyvall, Christopher, Dublin, merchant   1607. W. Dublin
Perkins, John, Ballinharne, Co. Carlow, Esq.   1781. F.A.
Perrie, Ann, Cork, widow of Jonathan P.   1752. W. Cork
"   Jonathan   1712. F.
Perrier, John, Dublin, wine merchant   1737. F.A.
Perrott, Abraham   Dated 1665. Ir.
"   Conyers, Drumhome, Co. Cavan   1715. Ir.
"   Elizabeth, Ballyhays, Co. Cavan   1696. Ir.
"   Humphrey, Drumhome, Co. Cavan   1688. Ir.
"   Humphrey   1695. Swan.
Perry, John, Woodroffe, Co. Tipperary   Dated 1709. F.
"   Philip, Kilbrogan   1619. W. Cork
Persevall, Matthias, Bandon, gent.   1673. W. Cork

IN THE GENEALOGICAL OFFICE, DUBLIN 243

Persse, Parsons, Castleboy, Co. Galway   1812. C.D.B.
Phair, Edward, Waterford   1786. F. Waterford.
Phaire, Aldworth, St. John's, Co. Wexford   1762. F.
„   Onesiphorus, Grange, Co. Cork, Esq.
     Admon. 1702. F.2.
„   Onesiphorus, Temple Shannon, Co. Wexford, Esq.   1767. F.2.
„   Robert, Grange, Co. Cork   1682. F.
„   Robert, Grange, [Co. Cork]   1712. F.2. and W.
„   Robert, Grange, Co. Cork, gent.   Admon. 1742. F.2.
„   Thomas   1716. F.
„   Thomas, Enniscorthy   1749. W. Ferns
Phelan, Thomas, Ballyragget, Co. Kilkenny   1812. C.D.B.
Phepoe, John, Fairview Avenue, Clontarf   1812. Swan. P.
„   Richard, Dublin   1777. Swan.
„   Richard, Richmond, near Ballybough Bridge   1838. Swan. P.
„   Samuel, Nealstown, Co. Meath   1752. Swan. Meath
„   Thomas, Kells, Co. Meath   1733. Swan. P.
„   Thomas, Hardwicke St., Dublin   1840. Swan. P.
„   Thomas, Clanbrassell St., Dublin   1853. Swan. Dublin
Phillips, Edward, Kilkenny   1684. B.
„   Thomas, Kilkenny   1718. B. and S.1.P.
Philpot, Edward, Belturbet   1669. Swan.
„   Lieut. John   Dated 1706. F.
Phipps, Lieut. Richard, Kilmainham   Dated 1629. Ir.
Pickhaver, Sarah, Dublin   1813. C.D.B.
Pidgeon, Peter, Castlegrange, Co. Wicklow   1804. C.D.B.
Pierce, Edwd., Cork, merchant   1742. W.P.
„   James, Dublin   1748. W. Dublin
„   Joan, Kinsale, widow   Dated 1724. W. Cork
„   Richard, Ballynagara, Co. Kerry, gent.   1732. W.P.
„   Robert, Ballygroman, gent.   Admon. 1723. W.
Piers, Henry, Tristernagh, Co. Westmeath   1623. B.
„   Sir Henry, Tristernagh, Co. Westmeath, Bart.   1691. B. and Gabbett MSS.
Pierse, Thomas, Ballynagaragh, Co. Kerry, gent.   1734. W.P.
Piersy, George, Cork   1711. W. Cork
„   James, par. of St. Mary's Shandon   1685. W. Cork
„   Richard, Shandon   1626. W. Cork
Pigott, Alexander, Inishonan, Co. Cork   1681. W.P.
„   Emanuel   1760. F.
„   John, Mallow Lane, Cork City   1812. C.D.B.
„   Mary, widow   1797. Swan. P.

Pike (Pyke), Joseph, Cork   1728. F.D.
„   Wright, Dublin, merchant   1801. C.D.B.
Pilkington, Alice, late of Grange, Co. Meath,
         widow   1749. Ir.
„   Daniel, Waterford   1720. Ir.
„   Elizabeth, Newton, Co. Westmeath,
         widow   1714. Ir.
„   Richard, Grange, Co. Meath
         Dated 1705. Ir.
„   Richard, Rathgaret, Co.. West-
         meath   1711. Ir. and F.
„   Richard, Grange, Dirkpatrick, Co.
         Meath   1753. Ir.
Pilot, Joshua, Portarlington, M.D.   1772. S.1.P.
Pilsworth, Godwin, Dame Street, Dublin   1804. C.D.B.
Pim, Elizabeth, Anner Mills, Clonmel   1802. C.D.B.
„   Moses, Lackey, Queen's Co.   1801. C.D.B.
Pitt, Simon, Londonderry, alderman   1662. W. Derry
„   Thomas, Stoakestown, merchant   Dated 1666. W.P.
Pitts, Richard, Drogheda, alderman   Dated 1704. W. Armagh
Plunket, Alexander, Gormanstown, Co. Meath   1804. C.D.B.
Plunkett, als. Cullen, Jane, Ballydonnogh   1637. Dub.
„   John, Inn's Quay, Dublin   1801. C.D.B.
Poack, Robert, Belfast   1671. B.
„   William, Aghadoey, Co. Derry   1754. B.
Poak, David, Barony of Dunluce, Co. Antrim   1713. B.
Pochrich, Richard, Alinamalah, Co. Monaghan   1722. Swan. Clogher
Poë, Capt. Anthony, Skreen, Co. Meath   1654. B.
„   Bridget, Leighlin Bridge, Co. Carlow   1830. B.
„   David, Dring, Co. Cavan   1742. B.
„   Edward, Moyroe, Co. Tipperary   1785. B.
„   Elizabeth, Atherdee, Co. Louth, spinster   1778. B.
„   Emmanuel, Glanekilty, Co. Tipperary   1679. B.
„   Emmanuel, Clonmark, Co. Tipperary   1727. B.
„   Emmanuel, Moyroe, Co. Tipperary   1801. B. and S.1.P.
„   James, Rosneharley   1739. B. and S.4.
„   James, Rosneharley, Co. Tipperary   1756. B.
„   James, Drumgooldstown, Co. Louth   1768. B.
„   John, Salborough, Co. Tipperary   1771. B.
„   John Gabbett, Donnybrook, Co. Tipperary
         and Isle of Man   1848. B.
„   Jonas, Kilcomin, King's Co   1779. B.
„   Martha, Donnybrook   1831. B.
„   née Fernley, Mary, Dublin   1745. B.
„   née Jacobs, Mary   1795. B.
„   Mary, Atherdee, Co. Louth   1798. B.

Poe, Purefoy, Rosenharley, Co. Tipperary	1751. B.	
,, Sarah, Nenagh, widow	1769. B.	
,, Thomas, Cloghan, King's Co.	1683. B.	
,, Thomas, Clonmaghane, King's Co.	1700. B. and S.1.P.	
,, William, Manor Poe, Co. Fermanagh	1682. B.	
,, William, Bessborough, Co. Tipperary	1763. B.	
,, William, Donnybrook, Co. Tipperary	1830. B.	
Poel, Richard, Ballymackleduff, Co. Tyrone	1834. B.	
Poge, Mary. *See* Greer.		
Pogue, David, Ballyneary, Co. Cavan	1810. B.	
,, Wm., Ballyneary, Co. Cavan	1787. B.	
Pomeroy, Samuel, Palles, Co. Cork, gent.	1703. F. and F.A.	
,, Thomas Holmes, Palace, Co. Cork	1752. W.	
Ponsonby, George Connolly	D. 1866. S. 4. (H.O.)	
Pooel, John, Drumon, Co. Tyrone	1783. B.	
Porter, Thomas, Bandon	1630. F.	
Potter, John, Downpatrick	1802. C.D.B.	
,, Samuel, Camden St., Co. Dublin	1802. C.D.B.	
,, Thomas, Fartha, Barony of Kinalea	Dated 1762. W. Cork	
,, William, Killinchy, Co. Down	1812. C.D.B.	
Potts, John, Cammcourt, Co. Kildare, gent.	1626. Drogheda MSS.	
Poug, John, Stranorlar, Co. Donegal	1737. B.	
Powe, Anthony, Dublin	1680. B.	
Powel, Elinor, Drumbee, Co. Armagh	1700. B.	
Powell, Lady Ann	1801. C.D.B.	
,, George, Drumburee, Co. Fermanagh	1702. B.	
,, Giles, Poell, Co. Limerick	1692. F.	
,, Giles, Glintary, Co. Limerick	1730. F.	
,, John, Charlemont St., Dublin	1804. C.D.B.	
,, Jonathan, Ballybrolly, Co. Armagh	1713. B.	
,, Jonathan, Corr, Co. Cavan	1757. B.	
,, Robert, Monemore, Co. Tipperary	1674. S.4.	
,, Robert [? Cullen]	1785. F.	
,, Sarah, Drumbee, Co. Armagh	1730. B.	
,, Stratford	1783. S.4. (H.BM.)	
,, Thomas, Cabragh, Co. Armagh	1718. B.	
,, Thomas, Ballyreagh, Co. Armagh	1846. B.	
,, William, Dublin	1677. B.	
,, William, Drumon, Co. Armagh	1765. B.	
,, William, Ballyfin, Queen's Co., Esq.	Dated 1774. Drogheda MSS.	
Power, Ambrose, Barrettstown, Co. Tipperary	1776. B.	
,, Anstass. *See* Comin.		
,, Catherine. *See* Fitzgerald.		
,, Cisly. *See* **Burke.**		

Power, Cisly, Rathruddy 1724. S.2.
„ Edward, Knockaderry, Co. Waterford 1802. S.1.P.
„ Hugh, Clashmagarriffe 1750. S.2. Cloyne
„ James, Carrick-on-Suir, clothier 1812. C.D.B.
„ John, Barrettstown, Co. Tipperary 1743. B.
„ John, Stradbally, Co. Waterford 1813. C.D.B.
„ Mary. See Fitzgerald.
„ Mary, Waterford 1813. C.D.B.
„ Mathew, Rathruddy, Co. Galway 1716. S.2.
„ Milo, Kilkenny, Esq. 1679. F.2. and W.P.
„ Nicholas, Rockshare, Waterford 1813. C.D.B.
„ Patrick, Loughrea 1748. S.2.
„ Pierce, Knocklahar, Co. Waterford, gent. 1695. F.2.
„ Pierce, Clonmult, Co. Cork 1743. S.1.
„ Pierce, Clonmult, Co. Cork 1753. S.1.
„ Pierce, Clonmult, Co. Cork 1771. S.1.
„ Pierce, Clonmult, Co. Cork 1827. S.1.P.
„ Richard, Carrigaline, Co. Cork 1684. F.2. and W.P.
„ Richard, Castletown, Co. Waterford 1730. S.1.
„ Hon. Richard, 2nd Baron of the Exchequer 1794. B.
„ Robert, Waterford 1803. C.D.B.
„ Thomas, Rathruddy 1722. S.2.
„ William, Clonemult 1667. S.1.
Pratt, Barbara, Clonpriest, spinster 1670. Swan. Clogher
„ Benjamin, Dean of Down 1721. S.2.
„ James, Castle Martyr, Co. Cork 1804. Swan. and C.D.B.
„ John (? of Stoneville) Not dated Swan.
„ Robert, Carrignashinny, Co. Cork 1724. Swan.
„ Sarah, Hermitage, Co. Cork, widow 1803. Swan. P.
„ Thomas, Castlelyons 1718. Swan. Clogher
„ William, Kinsale 1853. Swan.
Prendergast, Richard, Tuam, Co. Galway 1788. Cr. Tuam
Price, Capt. Dunbar Hamilton, 5th Dragoon Guards 1802. S.4.
„ Francis Nicholas D. 1821. S.4. (H.O.)
Price, John, Bandon, weaver 1688. W. Cork
„ Richard, Ballyhooly, Co. Cork, Esq. 1712. W.P.
„ Thomas, Cork, maltster 1668. W. Cork
„ William, Cork, gent. 1699. W. Cork
Pringle, Hamilton, Caledon 1771. Swan. P.
„ Major Geo. Henry 1800. Swan.
„ John, Caledon 1742. Swan. P.
„ William, Caledon, Co. Tyrone 1799. Swan. P.

IN THE GENEALOGICAL OFFICE, DUBLIN 247

Prior, Thos.   1690. F.
"   Thomas, Rathdowney, Queen's Co., Esq. 1691. F.2.
Pritchard, Ann, Dublin, widow   1779. Mol. Dublin
"   Samuel, Dundrum, Co. Dublin   1776. Mol. Dublin
"   Thomas, Corygedol, par. of Llanddwyere, Co. Merioneth   1739. Mol. P.
"   William, Blackpool, city of Cork   1795. Mol. Cork
Pritchet, Mary, Dublin, widow   1715. Mol. Dublin
Pritchett, Francis, Dublin, mariner   1692. Mol. Dublin
Prittie (Prittee), Elizabeth, Kilboy, Nenagh   1701. S.1.P. and M.
"   Elizabeth, Killboy, widow   1702. F.2.
Pritty, Henry, Kilboy, Co. Tipperary   1738. M.
Prossor, Philip, Dublin   1766. B.
Proud, Alice, Ashfield, Co. Meath, widow   1686. F.2.
"   Nicholas, Dublin, D.D.   1669. F.2.
Puckle, John, New Ross, Co. Wexford, Esq. 1673. F.2.
Purcell, John, Dublin, merchant   1704. F.2.
"   John, Gortinard   1744. W.
"   John   1770. F.
"   Mary, Templemary, Co. Cork   1801. C.D.B.
"   Peter   1846. F.
"   Richard, senr., Canturk   1733. W.
"   Robert, Croah, Co. Limerick, Esq.   1692. F.
Purdon, Bartholomew, Garren James, Co. Cork, gent.   Dated 1776. F.2.
"   Helena, widow   Dated 1745. W.P.
"   Henry, Rockspring, Co. Cork   1689. F.
"   Henry   1738. F.
"   John, Dyshert, Co. Cork, gent.   1741. W. Ardfert
"   Mary, Gt. George St., Dublin   1803. C.D.B.
"   Nicholas, Dysert, Co. Cork, gent.   1702. F.2.
Purefoy, Alice, Dublin   1700. S.1. Dublin and S.4. Dublin
"   Arthur, Skreen, Co. Meath   1673/4. S.1.P.
"   Bartholomew, Ballyclogh, Co. Cork   1689. F.
"   Bazil, Dublin, gent.   1699. S.1.P. and S.4.P.
"   Gamaliel, Purefoy's Place, King's Co. 1707. S.1.P. and S.4.P.
"   James, Gortnakelly, Co. Galway   Not dated   S.1.P.
"   James, Gortnakelly, Co. Galway   1725. S.4.
"   John, Dublin, merchant   Dated 1701. S.1.P. and S.4.P.
"   Thomasan, Dublin, spinster   1790. S.1.P.
"   Thomas, Dublin   1818. S.1.P.
"   William, Purefoy's Place (Clonbulloge), King's Co.   1699. S.1.P. and P.S.4.

INDEX OF WILL ABSTRACTS

Purefoy, William, Dawson St., Dublin   1737. S.1.P. and S.4.P.
  „   William, Cork, Esq.   1797. F.2.
Purefield, Richard, Fleet St., Dublin, merchant 1812. C.D.B.
Pyke, John, Woodenstown, Co. Tipperary
                                               Dated 1682. F.2.
  „   See Pike.
Pyne, Henry, Ballyneglass, Co. Cork, gent.   1674. F.2. and W.P
  „   Henry, Waterpark, Co. Cork   1713. W.P.
  „   John, Youghal, Co. Cork   1690. W.
  „   Katherine, Dublin, widow of Thos. P.   1747. W. Dublin
  „   Nicholas   Dated 1604. W.P.
  „   Sir Richard   1711. F. and W.P.

Quane, David, Carigbon, gent.   Dated 1811. Eu.
Quayle, William, Dublin, alderman   1735. F.2.
Queade, Hon. Grace, Dublin   1803. C.D.B.
Quelsh, Capt. John, Dublin, gent.   1693. F.A.
  „   Mary, Dublin, widow   1694. F.A.
Quick, Catherine, Townsend St., Dublin, widow 1812. C.D.B.
Quin, Aeneas O.   Admon. 1791. S.4. (H.BM.)
  „   Chas. Wm., Ballyorman, Co. Wicklow   1819. S.1.P.
  „   Capt. Henry   1783. S.4. (H.BM.)
Quinn, Edward, Molesworth Lane, Dublin   1803. C.D.B.

Radford, William, Gurteens, Co. Wexford, gent. 1702. F.2.
Rainey, James   1817. S.4. (H.I.)
  „   William Henry   1832. S.4. (H.I.)
Ralph, John, Stephen St., Dublin   1801. C.D.B.
Ram, Sir Abel, Dublin, Knt.   1691. F.2.
  „   Abel, Ramsford, Co. Wexford   1740. F.
  „   Abel, Ramsfort, Co. Wexford, Esq.   1778. F.A.
  „   Andrew, Dublin   1699. F.
  „   Andrew, Clonattin, Co. Wexford, Esq. 1793. F.A.
  „   Mary, Dublin, widow   1800. F.A.
  „   Rebecca, Palace Row, Dublin, widow 1799. F.A
  „   Thomas, Bishop of Ferns   Dated 1633. F.2.
Ramage, Ally. See Hamilton
Randal, Francis, Deepes, Co. Wexford   1693. F.2.
  „   Henry, College Green, Dublin   1692. F.2.
Ranken, John Grant   D. 1812. S.4. (H.O
Rawleigh, Walter, Mitchelstown, Co. Cork, Esq. 1725. F.2.
Ray, Charles, Youghal, Co. Cork, gent.   1716. F.2.
Raymond, James, Ballyegan, Co. Kerry   1732. Ir.
  „   Philip, Cork   1697. F.2.
  „   Robert, Ballydulogher, Co. Cork,
         gent.   1692. F.2.

IN THE GENEALOGICAL OFFICE, DUBLIN 249

Rea, Thomas, Monaghan	1771. Swan. P.
Read, Elizabeth	1803. C.D.B.
,, Thomas, Parliament St., Dublin	1803. C.D.B.
Reading, Robert, Tullamore	1736. S.1.
,, Robert, Dublin	1764. S.1.P.
Reeves, Barbara, Youghal, widow	1771. Swan. P.
,, Boles	1794. Swan. P.
Reid, John, Portaferry, Co. Down	1804. C.D.B.
,, William, Limerick	1802. C.D.B.
Reilly, Bartholomew, Mountwatergrass	1782. S.4. Meath
,, Charles, Brananstown, Co. Meath, P.P.	1713. S.4. Meath
,, Christopher, Dean Hill, Co. Meath	1763. S.4. Meath
,, Edward, Cullentragh, Co. Cavan	1770. Swan. P.
,, Francis, Cornahuane, Co. Meath	1769. S.4. Meath
,, Hugh, Curaghtown, Co. Meath	1730. S.4. Meath
,, John, Foordstown, clk.	1722. S.4. Meath
,, John, Stephen's Green, Dublin	1791. Swan. P.
,, Luke, Baltrasny, Co. Meath	1729. S.4. Meath
,, Miles, Dublin	1732. S.4.P.
,, Miles, Dogstown, Co. Meath	1772. S.4. Meath
,, Myles, Stonefield, Co. Meath Dated	1768. S.4.P.
,, Philip, Cluntorcan, Co. Cavan	1730. S.4.
,, Terence, Rahiner, Co. Cavan	1702. S.4. Meath
,, Thomas, Robbinstown, Co. Meath Dated	1716. S.4. Meath
,, Thomas, Urney, Co. Cavan, gent.	1777. Swan. P.
,, Thomas, Roebuck, par. of Kilbride, Co. Cavan	1785. Swan. P
Render, William	? 1708. Ir.
,, William, Doudstown	1708. F.2.
Rennick, Alexander, Derryargue, Co. Fermanagh	1826. Swan. P
Renwick, Eliza, Derryargav, Co. Fermanagh, spinster	1853. Swan. P.
Reymes, William, Parkneshoge, Co. Wexford, gent.	1685. F.2.
Reynolds, née Ellis, Dorothy, Wardhouse, Co. Leitrim	1775. B.
,, John, Drummore, Co. Donegal	1757. B.
,, John, Coolbeg, Co. Donegal	1789. B.
,, Letitia, Magherychar, Co. Donegal	1761. B.
Reynolds, Michael, Surgeon of the Donegal Militia	1811. B.
,, Thomas	D. 1673. S.4. (H.O.)
,, William, Drummore, Co. Donegal	1753. B.
Ribton, David, Dublin, Esq.	1773. F.2.

Ribton, William, West Forrest, Co. Dublin,
    Esq.   1774. F.2.
Rice, Alice. *See* Moriarty.
  „ Dominick, Co. Kerry, gent.   1757. S.4.
  „ Edward, Dingle, gent.   1835. S.4.
  „ John, Dingle, gent.   1756. S.4.
  „ John, Ballymaquin, Co. Donegal   1788. S.4.
  „ John, Rathkanny   Dated 1786. S.4.
  „ als. Ronayne, Margaret, relict of James
    Ronayne, wife of Bartholomew Rice 1662. F.2.
Rich, Stephen, Wexford, gent.   1672. F.2. and W.P.
Richards, Catherine, Co. Wexford, widow   1758. F.2.
  „   Edward, Enniscorthy   1765. F.2.
  „   Goddard   1834. S.4. (H.I.)
  „   John, Co. Wexford   D. 1749. F.2.
  „   John   1770. F.2.
  „   Richard, Cork   Admon. 1752. F.2.
  „   Solomon, [Solsborough, Co. Wexford]   [1784.] F.2.
  „   Thomas, Rathaspeck   1788. F.2.
  „   William, Dublin   1766. F.2.
Richardson, Archibald, Augher, Co. Tyrone   1762. Swan. Clogher
  „   John, Summerhill, Co. Fermanagh 1820. Swan. P.
  „   Joseph, Shamore, Co. Down   1803. C.D.B.
  „   St. George, Dublin   1777. Swan. P.
  „   William, Tatukyl, Kildress, Co. Fermanagh   1690. Swan. Armagh
  „   William, Summerseat, Co. Londonderry   1755. Swan. P.
  „   William, Limerick, apothecary   1758. F.2.
  „   Rev. William, Clonfeacle House, Co. Tyrone, D.D.   1820. Swan. P.
Richman, Richard, New Ross, cooper   Dated 1663. W. Ferns
Richmond, Anne. *See* Shipward (Shepard).
  „   Elizabeth, Cork, spinster   1709. W. Cork
  „   George, parish of Ballymodan
        Admon. 1638. W. Cork
  „   als. Shepheard, George, Eastgully,
    Diocese of Cork, gent. Admon. 1683. W. Cork
  „   John. *See* Shipward.
  „   Prudence. *See* Shipward.
Rickotts, John, Cork, blacksmith   1713. W. Cork
    John, Cork, goldsmith   1738. W. Cork
  „ William, Cork, merchant   1745. W.P.
Rider, Thomas, Wyanstowne, Co. Dublin   1713. Ir.
  „ *See* Ryder.

Ridges, William, London, Esq., skinner
                                Dated 1670. F.2.
Ridgway, Henry, the elder, Ballycarroll,
       Queen's Co., yeoman   1691. W.P.
   ,,   Samuel, Dublin, shagweaver   1745. W.P.
Riggs, George, Milltown, Co. Limerick, Esq. 1721. F.2.
   ,,   George, Middle Temple, London, Esq. 1739. F.2.
Riky, John, Brown St., Dublin   1803. C.D.B.
Roberts, Avis, Cork, widow   1717. F.
   ,,   Benjamin   1739. F.
   ,,   Benjamin, Cork   1739. F.
   ,,   Browne   D. 1854. S.4. (H.I.)
   ,,   Francis, gent.   1707. F.
   ,,   Randall, Bridgetown, Co. Cork   1719. F.
   ,,   Thomas, Cork   1724. F.
   ,,   William, Cork, merchant   1727. F.D.
   ,,   William, Cork, alderman   1732. F.
   ,,   William, Cork, alderman   1736. F.
Robbins, George, New Ross, Co. Wexford,
       " Proved about 1692 "   [1693.] F.2.
Robinson, George, Ballinagarley, Co. West-
       meath, farmer   Dated 1801. C.D.B.
   ,,   John, Dublin, notary public   1803. C.D.B.
Roche, Elizabeth, Kilkenny, widow Dated 1803. C.D.B.
   ,,   George, Limerick, alderman   1706. W. Limerick
   ,,   Maurice fitz Richard, Dowenderow,
       Esq.   Dated 1665. F.
   ,,   Richard, Dublin   1730. Swan. P.
   ,,   Stephen (John)   1804. C.D.B.
Rodgers, Michael, senr., Moninteen   1729. Swan. Cloyne
   ,,   Samuel, Carrenca, Co. Monaghan 1732. Swan. Clogher
   ,,   Thomas, Anacray, Co. Monaghan 1735. Swan. P.
Roe, John, Two Pott House   1728. Mol. Cloyne
   ,,   als. Lea, Mary. *See* Thomas.
   ,,   Thomas, Roesboro, Co. Tipperary   1770. S.1.
Rogers, Benjamin, Tramore, Co. Waterford,
       gent.   1764. Ir.
   ,,   Bignell, Dublin, gent.   1750. Swan. P.
   ,,   Charles   D. 1841. S.4. (H.O.)
   ,,   Daniel, Ballynavin, Co. Tipperary 1741. S.1. Killaloe
   ,,   Daniel, Ballynavin, Co. Tipperary 1797. S.1.P.
   ,,   Elizabeth, Dublin, widow   1768. S.1.P.
   ,,   George, Ashgrove, Co. Cork   1709. F.
   ,,   George, Lota   1721. F. and W.P.
   ,,   George, Clough, Co. Antrim   1769. Swan. Connor
   ,,   Jane, Dublin, late of Monaghan 1814. Swan.

INDEX OF WILL ABSTRACTS

Rogers, John, Monaghan, atty. at law   1776. Swan. P.
"   Joseph, Co. Monaghan   1827. Swan. P.
"   Joseph, Esq.   1834. Sullivan MSS.
"   Robert, Lota, Co. Cork   1718. F.
"   Ruth, Parsonstown, King's Co., widow   1801. S.1. Dublin
"   Simon, Magheraclooney   1787. Swan. P.
"   Thomas, Killure, Co. Waterford, gent.   1784. Ir.
"   Thomas, Monaghan, gent.   1787. Swan. P.
Rogerson, Sir John, Dublin, Knight   1724. F.E.
"   John, Chief Justice of King's Bench   1741. F.E.
Ronayne, Edmond, Rochestown   1762. F.
"   James, Limerick city, merchant   1662. F.2.
"   Margaret. *See* Rice.
"   Nicholas, Limerick, merchant   1662. F.2.
"   Uniacke, College Green, Co. Waterford   1804. C.D.B.
Roper, Robert, Roscommon, apothecary   1802. C.D.B.
Rorke, John, Morristown Latten, Co. Kildare   1803. C.D.B.
Rosborough, Mrs. *See* Crozier.
"   Frances, widow   1816. Swan.
"   George   1739. S.4. Derry
"   John, Newtownbutler, Co. Fermanagh   1804. Swan. P.
"   Thomas, Newtownbutler, Co. Fermanagh   1810. Swan. Clogher
Rose, Alice, widow   1828. Swan. Limerick
"   Rev. George, Rathkeale   1802. Swan. Limerick
"   Gertrude, Limerick   1758. Swan. Limerick
"   Hickman, Cuffe St., Dublin   1823. Swan. P.
"   Jonas   1821. Swan. P.
Ross, George, Liskilloge, Co. Clare   1700. F.
"   James, Portavo, Co. Down   1696. S.1.P.
"   Robt., Rostrevor, Co. Down   1755. S.1.P.
"   Thomas, Limerick   1754. B.
Rothwell, John, Co. Meath   1750. Swan. P.
"   John, Cannonstown, Co. Meath   Dated 1801. S.3.
"   Mary, Berfordstown, Co. Meath   1735. S.3. P. and Swan. P.
"   Mary, Berfordstown, Co. Meath   1779. S.3. P. and Swan. P.
Rotton, John, Dublin, gent.   1713. F.A.
"   John, Dublin, Esq.   1724. F.A.
"   John, Templeoge, Co. Dublin, Esq.   1793. F.A.
Rowan, Andrew, Ballymaclereny, Co. Down   1736. Swan. Dromore

Rowan,	Rev. John, Ballynagappog	1728. Swan. P. and F.A.
,,	Rev. John, Ballynagappog	1749. Swan. Dromore
,,	Stewart, Ballynagappog, gent.	1741/2. Swan. Dromore
Rowe,	Nicholas, Ballyharty, barony Bargie, Co. Wexford	1696. W. Ferns
,,	Richard, Ballyharty, Co. Wexford, Esq.	1687. W. Ferns
Rowles,	William, Dunganstown, Co. Wexford, gent.	1683. F.2.
Rowley,	Geo., Maberath, Meath	1711. S.1.P.
,,	Henry, Maberath, Meath	1742. S.2.P.
,,	Hercules, Summerhill, Co. Meath	1744. S.1.P.
,,	Hugh, Culmore, Co. Londonderry	1701. S.1.P.
,,	James, Barrack St., Dublin	1780. S.2.P.
,,	Sir William	1768. S.1.P. and Ir.
,,	William, Carrick-on-Suir	1790. S.2. Waterford
Roycraft,	James, Bandon, gent.	1724. W. Cork
,,	William, Bandon, merchant	1742. W. Cork
Ruby,	Edward, Carrigrohan, Co. Cork, yeoman	1666. W. Cork
Ruddock,	John, parish of Wallstown, gent. Admon.	1701. W. Cloyne
Rudkin,	Ann, Wells, Co. Cavan	1762. B.
,,	Bernard, Tinnegarney, Co. Carlow	1760. B.
,,	Bernard, Carlow	1812. B.
,,	Eliza, Corres, Co. Carlow	1792. B.
,,	Gilbert Pickering, Carlow	1831. B.
,,	Henry, Kilkenny	1738. B.
,,	Henry, Wells, Co. Carlow	1815. B.
,,	Jemma, Ballymahon, Co. Longford	1821. B.
,,	Mark, Corres, Co. Carlow	1722. B.
,,	Mark, Tullow, Co. Carlow	1824. B.
,,	Mark, Corres, Co. Carlow	1870. B.
,,	Mary, Carlow	1794. B.
,,	William, Carlow	1819. B.
Rule,	Jane, widow	1744. Swan
Russell,	John, Rutland, Co. Carlow, gent.	1729. F.A.
,,	Mary. *See* Hart.	
,,	Philippa Maria, wife of Rev. Thos. R., Archdeacon of Cork Admon.	1745. F.A.
,,	Samuel Stone D.	1814. S.4. (H.O.)
,,	Thomas, Archdeacon of Cork	1745. F.A.
Rutherford,	Margery. *See* Cutherbert [Cuthbert].	
Ryan,	Bernard	1811. S.4. (H.I.)
,,	James, Kilkenny, merchant	1605. W. Dublin
Ryder,	Giles, Wyanstown, Co. Dublin, gent.	1744. Ir.
,,	Henry, Bishop of Killaloe	1694. Ir.

Ryder, Henry, Bishop of Killaloe   1696. F.2. and Ir.
„   (Rider), Thomas, Wyanstone, Co. Dublin   1713. Ir.
„   (Rider), Thomas, Wyanstown   1713. B.
„   Rev. Thomas, Mitchelstown, Co. Cork   1747. B.
Rynd, Christopher, Fenagh, Co. Leitrim, Esq.   Admon. 1734. F.A.
„   David, Derrivolan, Esq.   1758. F.A.
„   James, Derryvolan, Co. Fermanagh, clk.   1746. F.A.
„   John, Strabane, Co. Tyrone, Esq.   1784. F.A.
„   Thomas, Dublin, merchant   1709. F.A.
„   Thomas, Dublin   1783. F.A.
Rynde, David, Derrivallan, Co. Fermanagh, Esq.   1723. F.A.
Ryves, Charles, Dublin   1675. B.
„   Sir William, Kt., Dublin   1648. B.

Sadleir, Ambrose, Cork   1805. S.1. Cork
„   Clement, Ballintemple, Co. Tipperary, gent.   Dated 1715. S.1. Cashel
„   James, about to proceed to N.S.W.   1844. S.1. Cork
„   John, Cashel   1835. S.1.
„   Margaret, widow   1788. S.1.P.
„   Nicholas, Golden Garden, Co. Tipperary   1765. S.1. Cashel
„   Richard, Scalliheen, Co. Tipperary   1748. S.1. Cashel
„   Richard, Chapel St., Tipperary   1817. S.2.P.
„   Richard, Nelson St., Tipperary   1834. S.1.
„   Richard, Scallaheen, Co. Tipperary, Esq.   1846. Eu. P.
„   Samuel, Shanballymore, Co. Tipperary   1717. S.1. Cashel
„   Thomas Lefroy, Henry St., Tipperary   1861. Eu.
Sadler, John, Ballintemple, Co. Tipperary   Dated 1680. S.1. Cashel
St. Leger, Andrew, Ballyvoholane, Co. Cork, gent.   Dated 1729. W.P.
„   Barbara   1685. F.
„   Hayward, Cork, Esq.   1688. W.P.
„   Heyward, [Heywardshill House, Co. Cork]   1684. F., F.2. and W.P.
„   John, Doneraile, Esq.   1696. W. Cork
„   John, Cork   Dated 1727. W.P.
„   John, Kilkenny, gent.   1738. W.P.

St. Leger, Sir John [Knt.], second baron of
Exchequer   Dated 1741. W.P.
" Mary, Cork, spinster   Admon. 1735. W. Cork
" Robert, Newtown, Co. Kilkenny,
gent.   1738. W.P.
" Thomas, Dublin, grocer   1736. W.P.
" (Sentleger), Sir Warham, Knt.   1599. W.P.
" Sir William, Knt.   Admon. 1651. W. Cork
Salmon, Christopher, Clonmel   1736. S.I.P.
Salter, Gregory, Youghal, alderman   1755. Swan. P.
Sanderson, Alexander, Drumkeevill, Co. Cavan 1706. Swan. P.
Sandes, Elizabeth, Kilcavan, Queen's Co.,
widow   1757. Ir.
" Lancelot, Carrigfoyle, Co. Kerry, Esq.
Dated 1668. F.2.
Sandford, Henry, Collector of Coleraine, Esq. 1741. Ir.
" Theophilus, Major, Moyle's Regt. of
Foot   1741. Ir.
Sandys, Ann, Dublin, widow   1748. Ir.
" Charity, Lady   1722. Ir.
" Elizabeth, widow of Col. Robert S.   1748. Ir.
" Hester, widow of Rev. Abraham S.   1767. Ir.
" Col. Robert, Roscommon   1684. B. and F.2.
" William, Dublin, Esq.   1757. Ir.
" William, Crevaghmore, Co. Longford,
Esq.   1774. Ir.
Santry, Lord. *See* Barry. (1736, 1751).
Saunders, Elizabeth. *See* Boyle.
" Joseph, Dublin, Esq.   1682. F.2.
" Robert, Deepes, Co. Wexford, Esq.   1672. F.2.
" Thos., Breahigg, Co. Kerry   1780. Swan.
Savadge, Henry, Dublin   1653. W. Dublin
" Valentine, Dublin, gent.   Dated 1670. F.E.
Savage, Hugh, Downpatrick, Co. Down, gent. 1732. W.P.
" Margaret, Dublin, widow   1729. W. Dublin
" Mary, Dublin, widow   1718. W. Dublin
" Patrick, Dublin   1784. Swan. P.
" Rt. Hon. Philip, Chancellor of the
Exchequer in Ireland   1717. F.E. and W.P.
" Philip, Dungulph, Co. Wexford, Esq.   1751. F.E.
" Rowland, Dublin   Dated 1744. W. Dublin
" Thomas, Kilgarvan   1672. W. Meath
" William, Kirkistown, Co. Down, Esq.
Dated 1733. W.P.
Savary, John, the elder, parish of East Green-
wich, Kent, Esq.   1741. W.P.

Savery, Daniel, Mallow, merchant   1704. W. Cloyne
Sayers, Rev. Edward   1730. W. Cloyne
Scallan, Margaret, Wexford   1813. C.D.B.
Schuldham, Edmond, Dublin, gent.   1723. F.A.
   „   Elizabeth, Dublin, widow   1760. F.A.
   „   Rev. Lemuel, Dublin, clk.
                                                  Admon. 1719. F.A.
Scoals, als. Wileman, Margaret, Dromgriston,
      Co. Monaghan   1739/40. Swan. Clogher
Scott, Angel, Cahercon, Co. Clare   1756. S.I.P.
   „   Rev. Barlow, Dublin   1780. Swan. P.
   „   Forster, Co. Monaghan   Dated 1768. Swan. Clogher
   „   Mrs Frederick. *See* Drought.
   „   George, Boagh, Co. Monaghan   1697. Swan. P.
   „   Robert   1738. B.
   „   Robert, Dublin, knight   1800. Swan. P.
   „   Thomas, Patrick St., Dublin, gent.   1658. F.2.
   „   Thomas, Newbay, Co. Wexford, Esq.   1688. F.2.
   „   William, Baldongan, Co. Dublin, Dr. of
       Physic   1800. Swan. P.
   „   William, Scotsborough   1843. Swan.
   „   Rev. William, Hacketstown Not dated   Swan.
Scudamore, Richard, Gil[l] Abbey, in city of
      Cork   1679. F.2.
Scull, Josiah, Ballymacree, Co. Tipperary
                                    Dated 1716. W. Cashel
Sealy, John, Maglass, Co. Kerry, Esq.
                                    Dated 1756. Davis
Seaver, Nicholas, Bellaghy, Co. Armagh   1694/5. Swan. Armagh
Sedgrave, Mary. *See* Browne.
Sentleger, *See* St. Leger.
Servant, Thomas, Dublin   1711. B.
Servatt, Stephen, Kinsale, vintner   1721. W. Cork
Seward, John, Kilkannoway   1708. W. Cloyne
   „   Richard, Clashnegannuffe, Co. Cork,
       gent.   1680. W. Cloyne
   „   Robert, Corbeah   1702. W. Cloyne
   „   Simon, Bristol, late of parish of Knock-
       morne, Co. Cork, gent.   1643. W. Cloyne
Shapland, Ellen, widow of John S.   1727. W.P.
   „   John, Wexford, Esq.   1704. W.P.
Sharman, John, Grange, Co. Antrim   1746. W.P.
   „   Letitia, Dunleer, Co. Louth   1778. S.1. Drogheda
   „   William, Dublin   1775. S.1.P.
Shaw, Samuel, Melough, Co. Down   1771. S.4.
   „   Thos., Glastry, Co. Down   1794. S.4.

Shawe, Edward, Coolcor, Co. Kildare 1811. S.1.P.
" Samuel, Rahinbeg, King's Co. 1786. S.1.P.
" Sarah, Fairfield, Co. Galway, widow 1720. F.A.
Shea, Henry, Carrick, Co. Tipperary 1761. S.2. Waterford
" Richard, Ballylarken, Co. Kilkenny 1753. S.2. Ossory
Shearman, Thomas, Burntchurch, Co. Kilkenny 1702. B.
" Thomas 1720. B.
Shears, Humphrey, Cork, apothecary 1703. W. Cork
" Thomas, Cork, gent. 1712. F.
Shee, Lettice. *See* Cowly.
Sheehy, James, Tralee, Co. Kerry 1803. C.D.B.
Shegog, George, Castleblaney, Co. Monaghan 1789. Swan. Clogher
" James, Loughbrickland 1808. Swan. P.
" Jane, Bovenett, Co. Down 1820. Swan. P.
" John, Loughbrickland, Co. Down 1805. Swan. P.
" John, Mount Carmel, Co. Monaghan [Notes]. D. 1823. Swan.
" Samuel, Dermaclog, Clontibret, Co. Monaghan 1781. Swan.
Sheldon, Anne, widow 1711. F. and W.P.
Shelton, John, Dublin, alderman Dated 1563. M.
Shepard. *See* Shipward.
Shepheard, George. *See* Richmond.
Sheppard, George John, Grange, Co. Waterford 1803. C.D.B.
Shewcraft, Henry Cork, cooper 1744. W. Cork
" John, Ballynamona, yeoman 1702. W. Cork
Shinton, Alex., Proudfootstown, Co. Louth Admons. 1672. and 1673. Ir.
" Lancelot, Pranstown, Co. Meath, gent. 1772. Ir.
" Richard, Garrettstowne, Co. Meath, Esq. 1721. Ir.
" Richard, St. George's Dragoons 1745. Ir.
Shipward (Shepard) Anne, als. Richmond, Ballymodan, Co. Cork, widow 1643. W. Cork
" John, the elder, Castle Mauhonne, Co. Cork, gent. 1611. W.P.
" als. Richmond, John, Carrilucas 1637. W. Cork
" als. Richmond, Prudence, Ringrour, widow 1637. W. Cork
Shortt, Henry, Palmer D. 1817. S.4. (H.O.)
Shuler, Anne, Kinsale, widow 1705. F.
" Francis, Kinsale, merchant 1681. F.
" Jane, widow, Kinsale ? 1691. F.
" Michael, Kinsale, merchant 1717. F.
Silver, Owen, Youghal, Esq. 1688. F.2.

Simmons, Abigail, Dublin, widow	1802.	C.D.B.
Simpson, Daniel, Tullynanily, Co. Armagh	1788.	Swan.
Sinclair, Anne, Strabane, Co. Tyrone, widow	1728.	F.2.
„ George, Hollyhill, Co. Tyrone Dated	1774.	C.D.B.
Singleton, Sydenham, Gt. Quebec St., Middlesex	1801.	C.D.B.
Siree, Charles Moore, Summerhill, Co. Dublin	1809.	Swan. P.
„ Henry, Dublin	1842.	Swan. P.
Skelton, Katherine, Dublin, widow	1758.	Swan. P.
Skerrett, Edmond, Ballinduffe, par. of Killcoona, Co. Galway	1706.	Cr. Tuam.
„ Mary, Middle St., Galway, widow	1804.	C.D.B.
Slane, Randal Fleming, Lord	1676.	Drogheda MSS.
Sleigh, Francis	1734.	S.4. and W. Cork
Slingsby, Sir Henry, Newtown, Co. Cork, Knt.	1697.	F.2.
Sloane, Davis	1813.	S.4. (H.I.)
„ William D.	1795.	S.4. (H.O.)
Sloper, Constantine, Castlebar, Co. Mayo	1803.	C.D.B.
Smith, Anne, Rathcoursey, Co. Cork	1688.	B.
„ Aquilla, Shinrone, King's Co.	1815.	S.1.P.
„ Barecah, Corbally, Co. Tipperary	1768.	S.1.P.
„ Benjamin, Dunlaven, Co. Wicklow, merchant	1707.	F.A.
„ Catherine, Roscrea, widow	1808.	S.1.P.
„ Chas. Poles, Co. Cavan, gent.	1783.	Swan. P.
„ Major Cuthbert	1742.	S.2.P.
„ Cuthbert, Sligo	1770.	S.2.P.
„ Deborah, Dublin	1669.	W. Dublin
„ Edward, New Ross, Co. Wexford	1696.	F.2.
„ Edward, Clonlough, Co. Monaghan, gent.	1717.	W.P.
„ Henry, Dublin, merchant	1731.	W. Dublin
„ Henry D.	1805.	S.4. (H.O.)
„ James, Londonderry, merchant	1699.	W.P.
„ Isabella, Dublin, spinster	1802.	C.D.B.
„ Isaac, Anneville, Co. Westmeath	1763.	S.1.P.
„ John, Mahoran	1665.	W. Cork
„ John, Clonemare	1671.	W. Cork
„ John, Dublin, alderman	1703.	W.P.
„ John, Cork, chandler	1715.	W. Cork
„ John, Dunmanway	1734.	W. Cork
„ John, Corbally, Co. Tipperary	1737.	S.1.P.
„ John, Gathmore, Co. Meath	1737.	F.
„ Rev. John, Lismacrory, Co. Tipperary	1813.	C.D.B.
„ Joshua, Shinrone	1767.	S.1. Killaloe

Smith,	Mathias, Cork, gent.	1719. F.
,,	Capt. Peter, Sligo	1757. S.2. Elphin
,,	Philip, Monalty, Co. Meath	1784. Swan. P.
,,	Ralph, Ballymacash, Co. Antrim	1690. Swan. P.
,,	Robert, Vicar of Ballyloghloe, Co. Westmeath	1706. F.2.
,,	Samuel, Shinrone, King's Co.	1738. S.1.
,,	Samuel, Ballydona or Newgarden, King's Co.	1776. S.1.P.
,,	Rev. Stuart, Drumloon, Ballintemple, Co. Cavan	1849. Swan. P.
,,	Thomas, Bandonbridge, clothier	1629. W. Cork
,,	Thomas, Gillabbey, in parish of Finbarre, gent. Dated	1641. W. Cork
,,	Thomas, Ballymodane	1663. W. Cork
,,	Thomas, Ballingarry, Co. Tipperary	1754. S.1.P.
,,	Walter	1598. W.P.
,,	William, Archdeacon of Armagh	1673. W.P.
,,	Rev. William, Rector of Loghgilly, Co. Armagh, clk.	1716. W.P.
,,	William, Newgrove, Co. Tipperary	1765. S.1. Killaloe
,,	William, Ballingarry, Co. Tipperary	1771. S.1.P.
,,	William, Lisduffe, Co. Tipperary	1801. S.1.P. and C.D.B.
,,	William, Golden Bridge, Co. Dublin, Esq.	1810. F.A.
Smyth,	Anne, Loughane, King's Co.	1763. S.1.P.
,,	Boyle, Ballynatray, Co. Waterford Dated	1661. F.
,,	Rev. Charles, Castleconnell, clk.	1803. S.1. Limerick
,,	John, Ballynatray, Co. Waterford Dated	1688. F.
,,	Sir Percy, Ballynatray, Co. Waterford Dated	1657. F. and W.P.
,,	Percy, Ballynatray, Co. Waterford	1714. F.
Sneyd,	Edward, Cairncross	1826. S.4. (H.I.)
,,	Rev. Wetenhall, Archdeacon of Kilmore	1747. Ir.
,,	Rev. William, Fort Frederick, Co. Cavan	1813. C.D.B.
Southcote,	Nicholas, Greenane, Co. Tipperary Dated	1722. S.4. Cashel
Southwell,	Edward. *See* De Clifford.	
,,	Margaret, Countess Dowager	1802. C.D.B.
,,	Rev. Richard, Castlemartyr	1784. Swan. P.
Span,	Benjamin, Castleforbes	1746. W.P.
,,	William, Dublin	1791. Swan. P.

Spear, Robert, Stratharry, Co. Fermanagh 1778. Swan. Clogher
Spelissy, George D. 1828. S.4. (H.O.)
Spencer, Brent, formerly of Ballycastle, Co.
　　Down, now of Dublin 1772. Swan. P.
„　Charles Admon. 1636. W.
„　Henry, Fromragh, Co. Antrim 1686. Swan. and W.P.
„　Henry 1711. W.P.
„　Isaac, Kilbrogan Admon. 1624. W.
„　John, Kilkenny 1675. W. Ossory
„　John, Youghal, merchant 1688. F.2.
„　Joshua 1829. F.E.
„　Laurence, Bandonbridge 1654. W. Cloyne
„　Nathaniel 1734. W.P.
„　Pullein, Fort St. George
　　Not dated [? 1792.] Swan. P.
„　Richard, Youghal, hosier 1668. W. Cork
„　William, Fishamble Street, Dublin,
　　shoemaker 1669. W. Dublin
Spenser, John 1569. W. Dublin
Spiers, Mary 1757. S.4.
Spiller, Ferdinando, Ross 1711. W. Cork
„　Henry, Capt. in Sir John Hammer's
　　Regt. 1700. W.P.
„　Margaret, Bandon, widow 1737. W. Cork
„　Thomas, Cloghnakilty, gent. 1737. W. Cork
Sprigge, William, Cloonivoe, King's Co. 1735. S.1.P.
Spunner, Charles, Miltown, King's Co. 1759. S.1.P.
„　Charles Rolleston, Glasshouse, Shin-
　　rone, King's Co. 1888. Eu.
„　Robert, junr., Kellogues, King's Co.
　　Dated 1724. S.1. Kildare
„　Thomas, Glasshouse, King's Co. 1829. S.1.
Squier, Lewis 1634. W. Cork.
Stafford, Hugh 1819. S.4. (H.I.)
„　Capt. John, Ballywoodick, Co. Wex-
　　ford 1652. B.
„　Martin, Ballycleary, Co. Wexford 1812. C.D.B.
Stamer, George, Carnally, Co. Clare, Esq. 1707. F.2.
Stamers, George 1684. W. Cork
„　George, senr., par. of Ballinadee 1721. W. Cork
„　John, senr., Bandonbridge 1651. W. Cork
„　John, Radrough 1719. W. Cork
Standish, Hannah, par. of St. Andrew, Holburn,
　　London, widow 1697. Ir.
„　James, Hatton Garden, Holborn 1695. Ir.
„　James, Dublin, gent. Admon. 1732. Ir.

Standish, Sir Thomas, Bruff, Co. Limerick,
Knt. Dated 1635. Ir.
Stanford, als. Heckelfield, **Anne,** Belturbet,
Co. Cavan, widow 1755. Swan. P.
„ Bedell, Belturbet, Co. Cavan 1776. Swan. P.
„ Daniel, Dublin 1788. Swan. P.
„ Elizabeth, Belturbet, widow 1798. Swan. P.
„ John, Belturbet 1745. Swan.
„ Luke, Little Green, Dublin 1749. Swan. P.
„ William, Bilbury Hill, Co. Cavan 1775. Swan. P.
Stanley, John, Drogheda, apothecary 1813. C.D.B.
Stannard, Capt. Robert, Kilmallock 1655. F.2.
„ Robert, Chancellor of Ferns Dated 1686. W. Ferns
Stapleton, Michael, Mountjoy Place, Dublin
Dated 1801. C.D.B.
Starrett, Samuel Dated 1767. S.4. Raphoe
Staunton, Anthony, Galway 1812. C.D.B.
Stawell, Anthony 1685. F.
„ Anthony, Cork 1685. F. Cork
„ Jane, Kinsale, widow 1691. F.
„ Rev. Jonas, Kinsale, Archdeacon of
Ross 1671. F.
„ Jonas, Coolmain 1708. F.
„ Jonas, Madame, Co. Cork 1716. F.
Stear, John, Gennets, Co. Meath 1788. S.1.P.
Stearne, John, Dublin, gent. 1652. F.2.
„ Robert, Tullinally, Co. Westmeath,
Esq. about 1660. F.2.
Steele, Norman, Moynalty, Co. Dublin 1802. C.D.B
Stephens, Arabella, Dublin, spinster 1694. F.2.
„ Daniel, 5th Dragoon Guards 1832. S.2.P. and
Swan. P.
„ Edward, Ballincargy, Co. Cavan 1740. Swan. Kilmore
„ Sir John, Finglas, Knt. 1673. F.2.
„ Richard 1696. F.2.
Sterling, Edward, Dublin, Esq. 1777. Swan. P.
„ James, Dowras, als. Whiggsborrow,
King's Co. 1734. S.1.P. and
Swan. P.
„ John, Kilikean, par. of Kilmoe, Co.
Cavan 1746. Swan. P.
„ Luke, Dublin, Esq. 1783. Swan. P.
„ Marlborough, Dublin, gent. 1764. Swan. P.
„ William Parsons, Dublin 1796. Swan. P.
Stern, Enoch, Kilkenny Not dated Swan.
Steuart, Col. John, Dublin 1763. S.4. P.

Stevens, John, Athlone, Co. Westmeath, clerk 1682. F.2.
   „   Walter, Appleton, Co. Berks   1696. F.2.
Stevenson, Capt. St. George, Dromoyle, King's
     Co.   1769. S.1.P.
Stewart, Sir Annesley, Fort Stewart, Co.
     Donegal, Bart.   1801. F.A.
   „   Charles, Dublin, Esq.   1740. Swan. and S.4.P.
   „   Charles, Lisglin, Co. Armagh, gent. 1750. Swan. P.
   „   Ezekiel, Fort Stewart, Co. Donegal,
     Esq.   1734. F.A
   „   George, Omagh, Co. Tyrone   1729. S.4.
   „   John, Mondowey   Dated 1772. S.4. Raphoe
   „   John, Togher, Co. Donegal   1773. S.4. Raphoe
   „   John, Ballyscanlon   1777. S.4. Raphoe
   „   Katherine, Skeas, Co. Cavan   1720. Swan. P.
   „   Peter, Ballyscanlon   1766. S.4. Raphoe
   „   Robert, Prebendary of Freshford 1773. F.A.
   „   Robert, Ardmonan, Co. Donegal 1769. S.4. Raphoe
   „   Seth, Bouchen, Co. Donegal   1767. S.4. Raphoe
   „   Walter, par. of Iniskeel, Co. Donegal,
     clk.   1764. S.4. Raphoe
   „   William, Fort Stewart, Co. Donegal,
     Esq.   1713. F.A.
   „   William, Bailieborough Castle, Co.
     Cavan   1778 Swan. P.
Stiffe, Samuel, Moyallow, Co. Cork, mariner 1714. W. Cloyne
Stopford, Joseph, Dublin   Dated 1705. F.P.
   „   Rev. Joseph, Charleville, Co. Cork 1801. C.D.B.
Story, Frances Arabella, widow of Rev. Joseph
     S.   1806. Ir.
   „   Frances Arabella, Bingfield, Co. Cavan,
     widow   Admon. 1806. Ir.
   „   Joseph, Bishop of Kilmore   1757. Ir.
   „   Joseph, Archdeacon of Kilmore   1768. Ir.
Stott, Anne, Hillsboro', Co. Down   1680. S.2. Down
   „   James, Lisbane, Ballynahill, Co. Down 1839. S.2. Down
   „   Jonas, Hillsborough, Co. Down   1758. S.2. Down
   „   Mary Anne, Dromore, Co. Down 1835. S.2. Dromore
   „   Samuel, Fairview Ave., Co. Dublin 1845. S.2. Dublin
   „   Thomas, Dromore, Co. Down   1829. S.2. P.
   „   William, Hillsboro', Co. Down   1821. S.2. Down
   „   William, Ashfield, Belfast   1826. S.2. P.
Stowell, William, Dublin, alderman Dated 1700. F.2.
Stoyte, Sir Francis, Dublin   1707. F.
Stratford, Benjamin, Corbally, King's Co. 1771. S.1.P.
   „   Lady Hannah, Dublin   1801. C.D.B.

IN THE GENEALOGICAL OFFICE, DUBLIN

Stratford, Henry, Dublin — 1749. S.1.
Strelly, John, (Strelly, Nottingham), Reynold's Regt. — 1650. W. Dublin
Strettell, Abel, Dublin, merchant — 1732. F.A.
„ Abel, Dublin, merchant — circa 1742. F.
„ Abel, Ballytore, Co. Kildare, gent. Admon. 1748. F.A.
„ Amos, Dublin, Esq. — 1795. F.A.
„ Edward, Dublin, merchant — 1780. F.A.
„ Elizabeth, Dublin, widow — 1769. F.A.
„ Jonathan, Dublin, gent. — 1757. F.A.
„ Thomas, Dublin, merchant — 1750. F.A.
Strettle, Abigail, Lurgan, Co. Armagh — 1748. F.A.
„ Elizabeth, Dublin, widow — 1743. F.A.
Stuart, John, Drumgarth, Co. Down — 1774. Swan.
„ Mathew, Corky, Co. Donegal — 1764. S.4. Raphoe
Studdert, Elizabeth Mary, Clonderlaw — 1839. Swan. P.
„ Maurice, Nenagh — 1803. Swan. P.
Sullevan, James, Dublin — 1739. Davis
Sullivan, Benjamin, King Street, London, late of City of Cork, Esq. — 1767. Davis.
„ Cnoger — 1687. Davis Cork
„ Cornelius, Cork, merchant — 1740. Davis
„ Cornelius — 1767. Davis
„ Cornelius, Cork — 1768. Davis
„ Daniel — 1725. Davis Cork
„ Daniel, Shandon — 1728. Davis.
„ Daniel, Kilkenny, gent — 1737. Davis
„ Daniel — 1751. Davis. Cork
„ Darby — 1708. F.
„ Darby, Collatrim — 1753. Davis
„ Dennis, Cork, Capt. Bragg's Regt. — 1747. Davis
„ Florence, Gortnacullee, Diocese of Ross — 1723. Davis
„ Florence, Lahenebeg — 1762. Davis
„ Florence, Foramore, Co. Kerry, gent. — 1767. Davis
„ Jeremy, Kill, Co. Kildare, gent. — 1769. Davis
„ John, Mitchelstown, Co. Cork, gent. — 1701. Davis
„ John, Ballintubber, Co. Limerick, gent. — 1744. Davis
„ Juliana, Cork, widow — 1756. Davis
„ Michael, Headfort, Co. Galway — 1790. Davis
„ Owen, Fackanatoshane, farmer — 1727. Davis
„ Philip — 1746. Davis. Cork
„ Thomas, Mitchellstown, Co. Cork — 1761. Davis
„ Timothy — 1723. Davis. Cork

Sullivan, Timothy, Michael's Lane, Dublin,
    merchant   1756. Davis
  ,,   William, Cork, gent.   1744. Davis
Sullivane, John, Cork, mariner   1732. Davis
Sumpner, Thomas, Dublin   1650. B.
Sutton, als. Ellwell, Eliz., New Ross, Co. Wex-
    ford   Dated 1731. S.1.
Suxbury, Samuel, Cork, gent.   1711. F.
Swan, Barbara, Dublin, widow   1789. Ir.
  ,,   Rev. Bellingham, Desert, Co. Cork   1798. Ir.
  ,,   Edward, Dublin   1719. Ir.
  ,,   John, Rath, Co. Wicklow, Esq.
                               Admon. 1730. Ir.
  ,,   John, Dublin, Esq.   1783. Ir.
  ,,   John, Dublin, brewer   1798. Ir.
  ,,   Joseph, Tombrean, Co. Wicklow, Esq. 1796. Ir.
  ,,-   Robert, Caledon, Parish Aghalow, Co.
    Tyrone   1797. Ir.
  ,,   William, Farlagh, Co. Tyrone, gent. 1697. F.A.
  ,,   William, Rathfryland, Co. Down   1798. Ir.
Swanne, Richard, Templeport, Co. Cavan   1794. Ir.
Swansey, Hugh, parish of St. Dunstan's in the
    West, London   1680. Swan.
Swanzy, Anne, Harrymount, Co. Monaghan,
    widow   1822. Swan.
  ,,   James, Aveleagh   1784. Swan.
Swayne, Daniel, Ballincurrig, Co. Cork, gent. 1757. F.A.
  ,,   Hugh, Cork, Esq.   1760. F.A.
Sweeny, Elizabeth, Dublin, widow   1724. W. Dublin
  ,,   James, Thomas St., Dublin   1798. F.2.
  ,,   Myles, Enniskillen, Co. Fermanagh,
    butcher   1789. F.2.
Sweet, John, Mononagh   1684. F.
Sweete, John, Mohonagh   Dated 1676. Davis
  ,,   John, Mononagh   1681. F.
  ,,   William, Ballinody   Dated 1677. F. and Davis
Sweetenham, Killiner   1829. S.4. (H.I.)
Sweny, Owen, Newmarket, Co. Dublin   1741. W. Dublin
Swiney, Francis, Two Pott, Co. Cork, gen . 1730. F.2. and W.P.
  ,,   William, Ballyteige, Co. Wexford, Esq. 1729. F.2.
Swiny, Daniel, Wexford   1745. W. Ferns
  ,,   Myles, Wexford, clk.   1690. W.P.
  ,,   William, Ballyteige, Co. Wexford, Esq. 1729. W.P.
Swyney, Edmond, Capel St., [Dublin]   1779. F.2.
Swyny, Dermod, Currybehagh   Dated 1730. W. Cork
  ,,   John, Kilmurry   1702. W. Cork

IN THE GENEALOGICAL OFFICE, DUBLIN 265

Swyny, Francis. *See* Swiney.
" (or Swynye), Tirlogh (or Terence), Cork 1650. W. Cork
Symes, Andrew, Ballymoney, Co. Cork, clk. 1718. W. Cork
" George, Ballymodane 1698. W. Cork
" Mabella, Cork, spinster 1731. W. Cork
Symons, William, Cork, tanner 1630. W. Cork
Synge, Barbara, widow of Edward S., Bishop
    of Cork, Cloyne and Ross 1712. F.2.
" Edward, Bishop of Cork, Cloyne and
    Ross 1678. F.2.
" Edward, Archbishop of Tuam 1741. W.P.
" George, Bishop of Cloyne 1663. F.2.
" Margaret, widow of Rev. Samuel S.,
    Dean of Kildare 1710. F.2. and W.P.

Taaffe, Elizabeth. *See* Duffe.
Talbot, Joane, Dublin, widow   Dated 1671. F.2.
Tandy, Anne, Portobello, Co. Dublin, widow 1833. Swan. P.
" Burton, Drogheda, alderman 1814. Swan. P.
" Chas. Samuel, Sion Lodge, Co. Waterford 1850. Swan. P.
" Edward, Charlemont St., Dublin 1812. Swan. P.
" Elizabeth, South Quay, Drogheda,
    widow 1826. Swan. P.
" George, Drindally, Co. Meath, gent. 1746. W.P.
" George, Dublin, Esq. 1805. Swan. P.
" John, Drewstown, Co. Meath, Esq. 1741. Swan. and W.P.
" John O'Brien 1827. S.4. (H.I.)
" Marcus (? Maurice) 1800. Swan. P.
" Thomas, Drewstown, Co. Meath 1684. Swan. and W.P.
Tankerville, Elias, Galway   Admon. 1806. Ir.
Tanner, Charles, Cork, chandler 1739. W. Cork
" James, Donguihie, Co. Limerick, gent. 1626. W.P.
" Jonathan, senr., Bandon, merchant 1740. F.2. and W.P
" Jonathan, Bandon, Esq. 1776. F.2.
" Katherine, Ballynamuck, widow 1711. W. Cork
" Mary, Bandon, widow 1789. F.2.
Tarleton, Edward, Killeigh, King's Co., gent. 1695. S.1.P.
" Edward, Killeigh, King's Co. 1740. S.1.P.
" Gilbert, Killeigh, King's Co. 1740. S.1.P.
" John, Killeigh, King's Co. 1700. S.1.P.
" John Weldon, Fenter   Not dated   S.1.
Taverner, Jacob, Limerick 1715. W. Limerick
" Samuel, Lissanode, Co. Westmeath,
    formerly of Limerick   Dated 1744. W. Limerick
" William 1742. W. Cork

Tawton, Pasco, Nicholas St., Dublin — 1752. S.1.P.
Taylor, Berkeley, Ballynort, Co. Limerick, Esq. — 1736. W.P.
,, Christopher, Dublin, gent. — 1717. Mol. P.
,, Elizabeth, Dublin, widow — 1784. F.A.
,, James, Dublin — 1804. C.D.B.
,, John, Bandonbridge, gent. Dated 1690. W. Cork
,, John, Bandonbridge — 1691. W. Cork
,, John, Cork, innkeeper — 1714. W. Cork
,, John, Cork, gent. — 1734. W. Cork
,, Joseph, Dunkerren — 1790. F.2.
,, Joshua, Cork, cooper — 1731. W. Cork
,, Judith, widow of Robert T., of Ballynort — 1725. W.P.
,, Joseph, Dunkerren — 1790. F.2.
,, Lovelace, Noan, Co. Tipperary — 1767. S.1.P.
,, Peter, Dublin, merchant — 1742. S.1.P.
,, Rebecca, Dublin, widow — 1803. F.A.
,, Robert, Dublin, gent. — 1705. F.2.
,, Sir Thomas, Bart. — 1736. S.1.P.
,, Thomas, Dublin, alderman — 1764. Swan. P.
,, Thomas, Glasnevin, Co. Dublin, Esq. — 1789. F.2.
,, William, London, innholder Dated 1650. W. Ferns
,, William, Boyerstown, Co. Meath — 1741. F.A. and W.P.
Telford, Michael, Mount Temple, Co. Westmeath — 1785. B.
Temple, Gustavus Handcock, Waterstown, Esq. — 1792. F.A.
,, Robert, Mt. Temple, Co. Westmeath, Esq. — 1741. F.A.
,, Robert, Allentown, Co. Dublin, Esq. — 1782. F.A. and F.2.
Tench, John, Mullenderry, Co. Wexford, Esq. — 1684. F.2.
,, Margaret, Mullenderry, Co. Wexford, widow — 1717. F.2.
,, Samuel, Mullenderry, Co. Wexford — 1713. F.2.
Tennison, Richard, Bishop of Meath — 1705. B.
Terry, Sarah, Dublin, spinster — 1746. W.P.
,, William — 1793. S.4. (H.BM.)
Terrye, Richard, Cork — 1692. W.P.
Tew, Mark, Culmullen, Co. Meath — 1736. S.1.P. and Swan. P.
Thinkild, Sarah, Dundalk, widow — 1722. Swan. P.
Thomas, Amy, Oldcourt, parish of Ringrone, Co. Cork, widow — 1680. W. Cork
,, Arthur, Dublin — 1803. C.D.B.

IN THE GENEALOGICAL OFFICE, DUBLIN 267

Thomas, Rev. Bartholomew, Johnstown, Co.
Wexford, clerk   1775. F.2.
" Benjamin, Dublin, gent.   1694. F.2.
" Caleb, Dublin, merchant   Admon. 1715. F.2.
" Daniel, Bellamoe, Co. Galway, gent.
    Dated 1657. F.2.
" Edmond, Ballynasarny, Co. Meath   1739. F.2.
" Edwin, Dublin, Esq.   1771. F.2.
" Elizabeth, Kilkenny   1799. F.2.
" Francis, Hacketstown, Co. Carlow   1813. C.D.B.
" Henry, Rathcormuck, Co. Cork,
tanner   1741. F.2.
" John, Waterford, saddler   1750. F.2.
" John, Quartermaster in Doughlas'
Regt.   1764. F.2.
" John, Castletown   1771. F.2.
" Jonathan, Thomas Court and Donore   1744. F.2.
" Luke, Galway, merchant   1796. F.2.
" Mark, Queen Street, Dublin   1772. F.2.
" als. Williams, Maria, wife of Edwin
T., of Athlone   Admon. 1717. F.2.
" Mary, widow of Edwin T., of Athlone   1737. F.2.
" als. Lea, als. Roe, Mary   1752. F.2.
" als. Knott, Mary   1765. F.2.
" Richard Baldwin, Dublin, gent.   1789. F.2.
" William, Athlone, Co. Westmeath,
farmer   1722. F.2.
" William, Cork, gent.   1783. F.2.
" William, Barrowmount, Co. Kilkenny,
Esq.   1799. F.A.

Thompson, Alexander, Paymaster 53rd Foot   1812. C.D.B.
" Edward, Lisnaskea   1778. Swan. Clogher
" Francis, Vicar of Drumcree, Dio.
Meath   1780. Swan. P.
" George, Camden St., Dublin   1813. C.D.B.
" George, Ely Place, Dublin, merchant   1831. S.4. P.
" James, Enniskillen, Co. Fermanagh,
gent.   1773. Swan. Clogher
" John, Killebandrick, Co. Cavan   1731. S.2.P.
" John, Dungannon, Co. Waterford   1812. C.D.B.
" Martha, Dublin   1813. C.D.B.
" Rev. Nicholas, Greek St., Dublin   1801. C.D.B.
" Norris, Legakelly, Co. Cavan   1768. S.2.P.
" Parr, Cork, merchant   Dated 1741. F.2.
" Theophilus, Dublin, Esq.   1791. Swan. P.

Thompson, Thomas, Richhill, Co. Armagh, merchant   1721. F.2.
„   Thomas, Greenmount, Co. Antrim   1802. C.D.B.
„   William, Cork, merchant   1746. F.2.
Thomson, Eliza., Tattybrack, Co. Monaghan   1824. Swan. Clogher
„   Humphrey, Tullybrack, Co. Monaghan   1822. Swan.
„   Jonas A. T. Corry, Co. Monaghan, merchant   1741. Swan. P.
„   Margaret, Tattybrack, Co. Monaghan, widow   1832. Swan. Clogher
„   Patrick, G.P.O., Dublin   1814. Swan. P.
Thorn, Richard, Rush, Co. Dublin   1803. C.D.B.
Thornhill, James Badham, Thornhill Lawn, Co. Limerick   1813. F.A.
Tighe, Richard, Dublin, gent.   1699. F.2.
„   William, Gartlandstown, Co. Westmeath   1801. S.4.
Tilson, Thomas, the elder, Dublin   1722. S.1.
„   Thomas, Dublin   1744. S.1.P.
Tinte (? Tuite), James, junr.   1734. Swan.
Tirry, Wm., Macrompe   1732. W. Cloyne
Tisdall, Elinor, widow   1743. Swan. P.
„   James, Bawn, Co. Louth   1748. Swan.
„   James, Bawn   1797. Swan. P.
„   Mary, Dublin, spinster   1775. Swan.
„   Michael, Dublin, Esq.   1681. F.2.
„   William, Dublin   1796. Swan.
Todd, Mary, Dublin, widow   1754. Swan.
Todderick, Thomas, College Green, Dublin   1812. C.D.B.
Toler, Charles, Graigue, Co. Tipperary   1741. B.
„   Daniel, Graigue, Co. Tipperary   1756. B.
„   Dorothy, Dublin, widow   1732. B.
„   Elizabeth, Clara, Co. Kilkenny   1686. B.
„   Capt. Henry   1654. B.
„   John, Tiermoyle, Co. Tipperary   1768. B.
„   Nicholas, Graigue, Co. Tipperary   1732. B.
„   Richard, Ballytore, Co. Kildare   1758. B.
Tomkins, Elizabeth, Dublin, widow   1780. Mol. P.
„   Francis   1718. Mol. Limerick
„   John, Killian, Co. Clare   1678. Mol. P.
Tompkins (Tomkins), Francis, Galway   1761. Mol. Tuam
Tonge, Edward, Shallon, Co. Meath   1812. C.D.B.
Tooker, William, Lisnagree, S. Liberties of Cork, gent.   1702. W. Cork
Toole, Elizabeth. *See* **Divin.**

IN THE GENEALOGICAL OFFICE, DUBLIN 269

Toole, Hugh, Kilmeoney, Co. Wicklow — 1803. C.D.B.
„ Patrick, Sheds of Clontarf — 1802. C.D.B.
Toone, Sir William, K.C.B. — 1830. S.4. (H.I.)
Topham, Sir John — 1700. F.
Toplady, Francis, Enniscorthy, Co. Wexford, Esq. — 1732. F.2.
Tounly, Dorcas, Dromrousk, Co. Cavan, widow — 1703/4. Swan. Kilmore
Towgood, Audrey, widow — 1717. F.
„ George, Cork — 1720. F.
Townley, Henry, Clare, Co. Louth — 1691. B.
„ Samuel, Drumrusk, Co. Cavan — 1699. B. and F.2.
Townly, Charles, Co. Cavan — 1717. Swan. Kilmore
Townsend, Brian, Castletownsend — 1727. F. and Davis
„ John, Shepperton, Co. Cork, Esq. — 1810. F.E.
„ Philip, Cork, clk. — 1734. F.
„ Richard, Castletown, Esq. — 1692. F. and Davis
„ Thomas, the younger, Parish of Morrogh, Co. Cork — Dated 1636. F. and Davis
„ William, Castletown, Co. Cork, gent. — 1711. F. and Davis
Tracton, Lord (James Dennis), Tracton Abbey — 1782. F.2.
Traill, Hans, Drumticonnor, Co. Down — 1692. Swan. Down
Trant, Clara, Listowel — 1790. F.2.
„ Dominick, Dingle, Kerry — 1759. F.2.
„ Dominick, Dunkettle, Co. Cork — Dated 1790. F.2.
„ Garrett, Dingle, Esq. — Admon. 1705. F.2.
„ Garrett, Grantia [Gransha], Co. Kerry, gent. — 1798. F.2.
„ James, Dublin, Esq. — 1775. F.2.
„ Philip, Cork, merchant — 1755. F.2.
„ Richard, Dingle, Esq. — 1750. F.2.
„ Susanna, widow of James T., of Dublin — 1796. F.2.
„ Thomas, Aghamanta, Co. Cork, Esq. — 1794. F.2.
„ William, Cork, merchant — 1725. F.2.
Travers, Anna Maria, Bandon — 1753. F.
„ Anthony, Ballinbroky — 1727. F. and Davis
„ Boyle, Dublin, merchant — Admon. 1742. F.A. and F.2.
„ Boyle, Bandon — 1754. F.
„ Rev. Boyle, D.D. — 1759. F.
„ Boyle, Cork, Esq. — Admon. 1767. F.A.
„ Boyle, Ballymcowen, Co. Cork — 1826. F.A.
„ Cassandra, Dublin, widow — 1745. F. and W.P.
„ Charlotte, Dublin, widow — Admon. 1758. F.A.
„ Daniel, Dublin, merchant — 1726. W.P.

INDEX OF WILL ABSTRACTS

Travers, Elizabeth, widow of Robert T., of
   Kilgolinch   1824. F.A.
„   Francis   Admon. 1771. F.A.
„   Hannah, widow of Jonas T., of Cork   1824. F.A.
„   Isabella, Dublin, widow   Admon. 1790. F.A.
„   James, Dublin, grocer   Admon. 1776. F.A.
„   John, Cork, Esq.   1712. F. and W.P.
„   John, Bandon   1727. Swan and W.P.
„   Rev. John, D.D., Dublin   1727. F. and W.P.
„   Jonas, Cregane, Co. Cork, gent.
           Admon. 1725. F.2.
„   Jonas, Butlerstown, Co. Cork   1787. F.A.
„   Jonas, Butlerstown, Co. Cork, Esq.   1789. F.2.
„   Joseph, Archdeacon of Kildare
            Dated 1664. F.
„   Mary Anne, Kill (or Bandon), spinster   1839. F.A.
„   Michael, Dublin, Esq.   1748. S.4.
„   Richard, Rochfordstown, Cork, Esq.
           Admon. 1700. F.A.
„   Robert, Ballynerokie, Cork, gent.
            Dated 1699. W. Cork
„   Robert, Coolconorthy   1728. F. and W. Cork
„   Robert, Coolconoritty, Barony of East
   Carbery, gent.   1728. Davis
„   Robert, Ballycurreen, South Liberties
   of Cork, gent.   1781. F.A.
„   Robert, Cork, Attorney   Admon. 1798. F.2.
„   Robert, Kilgobenet, Co. Cork, Esq.   1818. F.A.
„   Robert, Clonakilty   1824. F.A.
„   Sir Robert, of the Mardyke, formerly
   of Gortigrenan, Co. Cork   1835. F.A.
Trench, Anne, Birr   1809. S.1. Killaloe
„   Mary, Portarlington, widow   1819. S.1.P.
Tresilian, Catherine   1787. F.2.
Trewman, Thomas, Brackly, Co. Armagh   1762. Swan. P.
Trotter, Rev. Edward, Downpatrick, D.D.   1778. S.4.P.
„   George, Dublin, gent.   1723. S.4.P.
„   John, Downpatrick, Co. Down, Esq.   1772. S.4.P.
„   Ringan, Dublin, merchant   1730. S.4.P.
„   Stephen, Duleek, Co. Meath Esq.   1764. S.4.P.
„   Stephen, Duleek, Co. Meath, Esq.   1766. S.4.
„   Thomas, Magherafelt, Co. Derry   1744. S.4.P.
„   Thomas, Dublin, Esq.,LL.D.   1745. S.4.P.
„   Thomas, Duleek, Co. Meath, Esq.   1802. S.4.P. and
                Swan. P.
„   Thomas, Youghall, Co. Cork, merchant 1810. S.4.P.

IN THE GENEALOGICAL OFFICE, DUBLIN 271

Troy, James William — 1797. S.4. (H.BM.)
Tuam, John Vesey, Archbishop of — 1716. F.E.
„ Edward Synge, Archbishop of — 1741. W.P.
Tucker, Andrew, the Hospital, Co. Limerick
    Dated 1638. W.P.
„ Edward, Cork, merchant — 1695. W. Cork
„ John — 1642. W. Cork
Tuite (?), James. *See* Tinte.
Tuite, Philip, Newcastle, Co. Meath — 1778. Swan. P.
Tunnadine, Rev. John, Park; Lib. of Limerick, clk. — 1768. F.2.
Turner, Edward, Balligobane, Co. Cork, merchant — 1633. W. Cork
„ Henry, Bandonbridge, Co. Cork, burgess — 1648. W. Cork
„ Henry, Bandonbridge, Co. Cork — 1653. W. Cork
„ Henry, Dublin, Esq. — 1707. F.2.
„ Mary, widow — 1643. W. Cork
„ Sarah, Youghal, widow — 1679. W. Cork
„ William, Limerick — 1715. W. Limerick
„ William, Limerick, burgess — 1741. W.P.
Tuthill, Christopher, Kilmore, Co. Limerick — 1712. F.
Tweedy, Thomas, [? Dublin] — 1747. W.
Tydd, Daniel, Clyduff (Annegrove), King's Co. — 1802. S.1.P.
„ Francis, Ballybritt, King's Co.
    Dated 1718. S.1.P.
„ Francis, Creighton's Grove, Co. Tipperary
    Dated 1738. S.1. Killaloe
„ Mary, widow [? King's Co.] — 1743. S.1.P.
„ Thomas, Knockearly, King's Co. — 1733. S.1.P.
Tymens, John, Riverston, Co. Clare — 1803. Mol.
Tynte, Henry, Ballycrenan — 1692. M.
Tyrry, Dominick, Macroom — Dated 1746. W. Cloyne
„ George Fitzwilliam — 1669. W. Cork
„ Patrick — 1678. W. Cork

Unak (or Unake), James, Youghal, burgess — 1578. W. Cork
Uniacke, James, Dublin, gent. — 1682. W.P.
„ James, Mount Uniacke, Co. Cork, Esq. — 1733. W.P.
„ John, Curreheen, Co. Cork, gent. — 1730. W.P.
„ Mary, Dublin, widow — 1691. W.P.
„ Mary, Youghal, Co. Cork, spinster — 1734. W.P.
„ Norman, Curraheen, Co. Cork, gent. — 1727. W.P.
„ Thomas, Youghal, Esq. — 1734. W.P.
Upton, Ambrose, Dublin — Dated 1801. C.D.B.

Upton, Henry, Dublin 1812. C.D.B.
„ John Dated 1779. S.4. (H.I.)
Usher, Susan. *See* Clearke.
Ussker, Frances, Dublin, widow 1803. C.D.B.
Uvedale, Edmond, Lieut. in Brown's Regt. 1745. W.P.

Van Cruyskercken, Henry, Limerick 1728. Mol. P.
Vandeleur, Giles, Rathlahine, Co. Clare Circa 1701. [1701]. F.2.
Van Homrigh, B., Drogheda, atty. at law 1804. Swan. P.
„ Bartholomew, Drogheda 1809. Swan. P.
Vaughan, Hector, Knocknamcase, King's Co. 1711. F.
„ John, Youghal, merchant 1683. F.2.
„ Sophia, [King's Co.], spinster 1816. Sadleir Deeds
„ William, Youghal 1738. F.
„ William Peisley, Golden Grove, King's Co. 1843. Sadleir Deeds
Veaitch, Josias, Island Bridge, Dublin Admon. 1811. Swan.
„ Rev. Wm., Newtownbutler, Co. Fermanagh 1788. Swan.
Veatch, Charles, Gortanardress, Co. Cavan 1814. Swan.
Veitch, John, Roscul, Co. Cavan 1841. Swan.
Venables, Jane. *See* Wiseman.
Vepy, Jane. *See* Dodson.
Verling, Rev. Richard Dated 1725. F.
Vernon, George, Clontarf, Co. Dublin Dated 1792. C.D.B.
Vero, Alles, widow of Thomas V. 1692. Ir.
„ Neptune, Dublin 1772. Ir.
„ Thomas Admon. 1685. Ir.
„ Thomas, Loughrea, Co. Galway, apothecary 1757. Ir.
„ Rev. Thomas, Dublin, late of Loughrea 1767. Ir.
Verow, Nicholas, Loughrea, Co. Galway 1704. Ir.
Vesey, John, Archbishop of Tuam 1716. F.E.
Vicars, Daniel, Balledmond, Queen's Co., gent. 1788. F.2.
„ Elizabeth, Clotaney, King's Co. 1798. F.2.
„ Richard, Garran McConly, Queen's Co., Esq. 1707. F.2.
„ Richard Warneford, Levally, Queen's Co. 1812. C.D.B.
Vickers (or Vicars), Jane 1760. F.2.
Vincent, John, Limerick, alderman 1735. S.I.P.
„ John, Limerick, Esq. 1780. S.I.P.
„ Richard, Rector of Monaghan 1764. Swan. P.
„ Thomas, Irishtown, Co. Dublin 1666. Swan. P.
„ Thomas, Ballysimon, Co. Limerick 1731. S.I.P.

IN THE GENEALOGICAL OFFICE, DUBLIN 273

Vincent, Thomas, Enniskillen — 1763. Swan. P.
Vivors, Eliz., Crosstown, Co. Wexford, widow — 1685. S.1.
Vowell, Christopher — Dated 1709. F.2.
„ Christopher, Garynegrang, Co. Cork — 1709. F. and W.P.
„ Christopher, Ballyorane, Co. Cork, gent. — 1724. F.2., Swan. and W.P.
„ John, Springfort, Co. Cork, Esq. — 1735. Mol. and W. Cloyne
„ Richard, Castlelyons — 1681. Swan., Mol. and W. Cloyne

Wade, Rev. Nicholas, — 1822. S.4. (H.BM.)
„ Rev. William. [Notes from Exch. Bill, 15 Feb., 1800. No Will] — Swan.
Waight, Bernard, Dublin, gent. — 1695. S.1.P.
Waite, Lucy, Rutland Sq., Dublin — 1802. C.D.B.
Wakeham, John, Aghada, Co. Cork — 1715. W. Cork
„ Richard, Ballylegan, Co. Cork — 1710. F. and W. Cork
„ William, Little Island, Co. Cork — 1718. Swan. and W.P.
Walcott, Jane, Limerick, widow — 1693. F.P. and F.2.
„ John, Croagh, Limerick — 1736. F.
Wale, William, Cuilnemurky, Co. Waterford — 1636. F.2.
Walker, Elizabeth, Dublin, widow — 1738. Swan. P.
„ James, [? Armintha], Co. Roscommon, gent. — Admon. 1756. Ir.
„ John, Borough of Wexford, cooper — 1660 F.2.
„ John, Dublin, alderman — 1750. Swan. P.
„ Joseph, Dublin, brewer — 1716/17. Swan. Dublin
„ Mary, Athboy, Co. Meath, widow — 1771. S.2.P.
„ Mathew, Castlereagh, Co. Roscommon — 1719. Ir.
„ Richard, Dublin, merchant — 1760. Swan. P.
„ Thomas, [Glassdargan] — 1685. W. Cork
„ Thomas, Lislicky, Co. Roscommon — 1700. Ir.
„ Thomas, Portlester, Co. Meath — 1799. S.2.P.
„ William, Dublin, alderman — 1750. Swan. P.
Wall, Garrett, Pallis, Co. Limerick, junr. — 1817. S.2.
„ James W., Kirmingham Hall, Cheshire — 1819. S.1.P.
Wallace, Major Samuel — 1805. S.4. (H.BM.)
„ Solomon, Francis St., Dublin — 1804. C.D.B.
Waller, Richard, Cully, Co. Tipperary — 1702. S.1.P.
Wallis, Audry, Shannagaree, Co. Cork, widow — 1685. F.2.
„ George, Youghal — 1823. Swan. P.
„ Henry, Drishane, Co. Cork — 1734. F.
„ James, Cork — 1800. Swan.

Walsh, Charles, Derrylahan, Co. Tipperary
                                    Dated 1727. S.1.P.
    "   Charles, Walsh Park, Co. Tipperary 1801. S.1.P.
    "   Rev. Charles, Etna Lodge, Monaghan,
         clerk   1863. Swan.
    "   Edmond, Ballybricken, Waterford
                                    Dated 1797. C.D.B.
    "   John, Killifargon, Co. Monaghan, gent. 1766. Swan. P.
    "   John Adams, Derrylahan, Co. Tipperary   1783. S.1. Killaloe
    "   Joseph Irwin, Ballyshannon   1860. Swan.
    "   Rev. Joseph, Killaghtee   1860. Swan.
    "   John West   1854. Swan. P.
    "   Rev. Ralph Dawson, Pomeroy   1869. Swan.
Walter, Thomas, gent.   Dated 1687. F.2.
    "   Thomas, Youghal, alderman   1698. F.2.
Warburton, George, Dublin, Esq.   1731. Swan. P.
    "   John, Dublin, Esq.   1703/4. Swan. P.
    "   Mary, Dublin, widow   1729. Swan. P.
Ward, John, Whitestown, Co. Dublin   1801. C.D.B.
    "   Peter, Dublin, merchant   Dated 1722. Swan.
Warden, William, Burres [? parish], Co. Kilkenny, Esq.   1667. F.2.
Wardlaw, Rev. John, Glebe, Co. Limerick 1802. Swan.
Waring, Elizabeth, Maralin, Co. Down, widow 1804. C.D.B.
Warner, Anne, Cork, spinster   1743. F. and F.B.
    "   Elizabeth, Bandonbridge, widow 1678. W. Cork
    "   Lieut.-Col. Henry   1682. S. 4.P.
    "   Mary, Cork, widow   1748. W. Cork
    "   Randall   1661. W. Cork
    "   Randall, Lissecrimeen   1725. W. Cork
    "   William, Ballymodan, Co. Cork   1697. W. Cork
Warren, Alice. *See* Baldwin.
    "   Michael, Warrenstown, Co. Meath 1712. Ir.
    "   Robert, Kilbarry, Co. Cork, Esq. 1743. F.A.
    "   William, Grangebeg, Co. Kildare, Esq. 1667. F.2.
    "   William, Dublin, gent.   1719. Ir.
    "   William, Cork, Esq.   1793. F.A.
Watkins, Abraham, Cork, Esq.   1715. W. Cork
    "   Edward, Ballymodan, gent.   1642. W. Cork
    "   John, Kilbolane   Dated 1659. W. Cork
    "   John, Bandonbridge, Co. Cork, gent. 1687. W. Cork
    "   John, Ballymee, Co. Cork, gent. 1700. W. Cloyne
    "   John, Pallastown, Co. Cork
                                    Dated 1765. F.
    "   John, Derrylusk, Co. Fermanagh 1803. C.D.B.

IN THE GENEALOGICAL OFFICE, DUBLIN 275

Watkins, Margaret, Bandonbridge, Co. Cork 1699. W. Cork
„ Mary, Cork, widow 1729. W. Cork
„ Thomas, Somerset, Co. Tipperary 1802. C.D.B.
„ Westrop 1783. F.
„ William, Derrybrusk, Co. Fermanagh
    Dated 1768. Swan. Clogher
Watson, Christopher, Garrancurragh, Co. Tipperary 1711. S.1. Killaloe
„ Feltham, Garrykennedy, Co. Tipperary Dated 1745. S.1. Killaloe
„ Feltham, Brookwatson, Co. Tipperary
    Dated 1853. S.1. Killaloe
„ Hannah, Killester, Co. Dublin, widow 1728. F.D.
„ Jane, Rarush, Co. Carlow 1786. F.D.
„ John, Rathrush, Co. Carlow 1752. F.D.
„ John, Carlow 1757. F.D.
„ John, the elder, Clonmel, Co. Tipperary 1783. F.A.
„ John, Kilcommer, Co. Carlow 1783. F.D.
„ John, Clonbrogan, Co. Tipperary 1789. S.1. **Cashel**
„ Samuel, Dublin, linen draper 1731. F.D.
„ Samuel, Kilconnor, Co. Carlow, gent. 1764. F.D.
„ Samuel, the elder, Lisgarvan, Co. Carlow 1784. F.D.
„ Thomas, Caherhurly, Co. Clare 1822. S.1. Killaloe
„ Thomas Colclough 1834. S.4. (H.I.)
„ Thomas, Capuanane, Co. Clare
    Not dated   S.1.
„ William, Ballynamallagh, Co. Kildare 1728. F.D.
Way, John 1683. W. Cork
Wayes, Peter, Cork, carpenter 1741. W. Cork
Webb, Abraham, Ballybeg, Co. Cork, gent.
    Dated 1718. Davis
„ James, Ballynehenry, Co. Limerick 1712. F. and F.E.
„ James, Cork, merchant 1724. F.E.
„ James, Dublin, gent. 1730. F.D.
„ John, Cloheenmelcon, Co. Cork, gent. 1728. F.E.
„ John, Cork, alderman 1796. Swan. P.
„ Noah, Dean of Leighlin 1695. F. Leighlin
Webber, Edward, Cork, alderman 1695. W. Cork
„ Edward, Cork, Esq. 1730. F.A. and W.P.
„ Elizabeth, Cork, spinster 1780. F.A.
„ George, Cork, merchant Dated 1674. W.P.
„ George, Cork, merchant 1679. F.2.
„ George, Clonmell, skinner 1680. W. Waterford
„ George, Cork 1772. F.A.

Webber, Martha, Cork, widow — 1675. W. Cork
„ Michael, Cork, mariner — 1666. F.A. and W. Cork
„ Michael — 1669. F.A. and W. Cork
„ Michael, Cork, gent. — 1749. F.A. and W. Cork
„ Rev. Samuel, Baldoyle, Co. Dublin, clk. — 1742. W.P.
„ Samuel, Kilmurry, Co. Wexford — 1764. F.A.
Weekes, John, St. Kevan Street, Dublin — 1678. W.P.
„ John, Bride Street, Dublin — 1802. C.D.B.
„ Mark — 1681. Ir. and W.P.
„ Mary, Dublin, widow — 1724. S.2. Dublin
„ Nicholas, Ballynanty, Co. Limerick, Esq. — 1739. W. Limerick
„ Richard, Dublin, gent. — 1685. S.2. Dublin
„ Thomas, Kilmullum, Co. Dublin — 1768. S.2. Dublin
„ William, Glonegar, Co. Limerick, gent. — 1670. W.P.
„ William, Loughgur — 1667. W. Cashel
Welsh, John, Dean of Connor, Co. Antrim — 1754. Swan. P.
Welstead, John, Kilburne, Co. Cork, gent. — 1708. W. Cork
Wemys, Sarah. *See* Mansergh.
Wentworth, Sir George, Wentworth Woodhouse, Co. York, knt. — 1666. F.D.
„ Thomas, Clone Court, Isle of Thanet, Kent, Esq. — 1685. F.D.
Wesley, Garrett, Dangan, Co. Meath — 1682. F.2.
„ Garrett, Earl of Mornington — 1781. S.2.
West, Mary, Dublin, spinster — 1813. C.D.B.
„ William, Boyle, Co. Roscommon — 1812. C.D.B.
Westby, Nicholas, Dublin, Esq. — 1716. F. and F.A.
Westray, Henry, James Street, Dublin — 1802. C.D.B.
Westropp, Elizabeth, widow of Mountifort W. — 1768. F.E.
„ Mountifort, Attiflin, Co. Limerick, Esq. — 1726. F.D.
„ Mountyfort, Bunratty, Co. Clare — 1698. F. and F.D.
„ Ralph, Carduggan, Co. Cork — 1741. F.D.
„ Ralph, Cork, Esq. M.D. — 1772. F.D.
„ Thomas, Melon, als. Mullan, Co. Limerick — 1744. F.D.
Wetenhall, Edward, Cork, Doctor of Physick — Admon. 1745. F.A.
Wetherby, Anne, widow — 1749. Swan. P.
„ John, D.D., Dean of Cashel — 1749. Swan. P.
„ Smyth — 1742. Swan. P.

Wetherelt, Sewell, Castletown, King's Co.		1790. S.I.P.
,, Thomas, Dublin		1750. S.I.P.
Wharton, Philip, Duke of		1736. S.I.P.
Wheddon, Thomas		1710. W. Cork
Whelpley, Matthew, par. of Desert Serges, Co. Cork	Admon.	1638. W.
Whitby, Helen, Kilterman, Co. Tyrone	Dated	1689. W. Clogher
,, Marcus, Fermoy, Co. Cork	Dated	1656. W.P.
,, Robert, Whitfieldtowne, gent.		1684. W.P.
,, Robert, Kilcregan, Co. Kilkenny gent.		1745. W.P.
White, Geo., Fortchester, Co. Wexford		1758. Swan. P.
,, Frances. *See* Foukes.		
,, Hamilton, Bantry, Co. Cork, Esq.		1789. F.A.
,, John, Ballyellis, Co. Wexford, gent.	Dated	1685. F.2. and M.
,, John, Ballenbracke, Co. Cork, gent.		1688. W. Cork
,, John, Mallow, Co. Cork		1727. W. Cloyne
,, John, Ballinahinch		1813. C.D.B.
,, Joseph, Cork, blacksmith		1740. W. Cork
,, Richard		1733. F.A.
,, Richard, Bantry, Co. Cork		1776. F.A.
,, Swithin, junr., Rochfordstown, gent.		1737. W. Cork
,, Symour, Knockcentry, Co. Limerick	Dated	1704. S.4.
,, William, Cork, dyer		1744. W. Cork
Whiting, Anne, junr., Cork		1729. W. Cork
,, John, Cork, alderman		1719. W. Cork
Whitton, Edward, Crow Street, Dublin	Dated	1786. F.D.
Whitty, Rev. John, Killinellick		1847. S.4.
,, Thomas Ravenscroft, Baltinglass, Co. Wicklow		1861. S.4.
Widenham, Rev. Daniel, Milford, Limerick		1791. S.1. Limerick
,, Henry, Court, Co. Limerick		1719. F. Swan and W.P.
,, John, Castletown, Co. Cork, Esq.		1679. F.2. and W.P.
,, John, Castletownroche, Co. Cork, gent.		1709. F. Swan. and W.P.
,, Mary, Court, Co. Limerick, widow	Dated	1736. W.P.
Wigans, Thos., Corneyherne		1696/7. Swan. Clogher
Wiggins, John, Cluncara, Co. Fermanagh		1750. Swan. Clogher
Wight, Rice, St. Finbarrys near Cork		1637. W. Cork

INDEX OF WILL ABSTRACTS

Wight, Thomas, Cork, clothier — 1725. W. Cork
Wildman, George, Drummumery, Clones — 1809. Swan. Clogher
Wileman, Margaret. *See* Scoals.
" Thomas, Skeagh, Co. Monaghan — Dated 1721. Swan. P.
" Thomas, Skeagh, Co. Monaghan — 1722. Swan.
Wilkinson, Cuthbert, Sarsfield's Court, Co. Cork, Esq. — 1728. W. Cork
" John, Collinstowne, Co. Kildare — 1716. S.2.P.
" John, Ringlestown, Co. Meath — 1837. S.2.P.
" Mathew, Collinstown, Co. Kildare — 1722. S.2.P.
" Mary, Golden Lane, Dublin, widow — 1768. S.2.P.
" Peter, Balsom — 1778. S.2.
" Peter, Clanbrazzil Place, Dublin — 1808. S.2.P.
" Robert, Limerick, gent. — 1676. F.2.
" Capt. William, Dublin — 1733. S.2.
" Zachariah, Co. Antrim — 1729. S.2.
Willerd, Lovegrove, Ringrabow — 1685. F. Cork
Williams, Elizabeth, widow — 1737. W.P.
" Hanna, widow — 1708. F.
" als. Looby, Margaret, Cork, widow — 1710. W. Cork
" Maria. *See* Thomas.
" Oliver, Bealabahalla, Co. Cork, gent. — 1745. W. Cloyne
" Owen, Newmarket, Co. Cork — 1640. F. and W. Cloyne
" Williams, Mahonstown, Co. Cork — 1710. F.
Willington, Charles, Ballymoney, King's Co. — 1721. B. and S.1.
" Charles, Dublin — 1760. B.
" Charles, Eccles St., Dublin. Dated 1800. M.
" Elizabeth, Lisnacody, Co. Galway — Dated 1769. S.1.
" James, Killaskehan, Co. Tipperary — 1730. B.
" James, Newhouse, Co. Tipperary — 1781. B.
" John, Killeen, Queen's Co. — 1658. B.
" King, Tentower, Queen's Co. — 1729. B. and S.1.
" Mary, Ballymoney, King's Co. — 1758. B. and S.1.
" Palliser, Tentower, Queen's Co. — 1730. B. and S.1.
" Priscilla, Waterford — 1790. B.
" Thomas, Ballymoney, King's Co. — 1752. B. and S.1.
" Williamite, Ballymoney, King's Co. — 1724. B. and S.1.
Wills, Hannah, widow — 1708. F.
" Hannah, Anagh, Co. Cork, widow of Thos. W. — 1710. F. and W.P.
" Thomas, Cork, gent. Dated 1739. W.P.
Willson, Hill, Purdysburn, Co. Down — 1773. S.1.P.
" Robert, Archdeacon of Kilmore — 1684. F.2.

Wilmer, Capt. Nathaniel, Cashell, Co. Tipperary 1655. W.P.
Wilmot, Lt.-Col. Edward E., R.H.A., Island Bridge, Co. Dublin 1834. S.4. P.
„ Henry, Gardiner's St., Dublin 1826. S.1.P.
Wilson, Andrew, Piersefield, Co. Westmeath 1725. Ir. and F.2.
„ Francis, Tully, Co. Longford 1737/8. Swan.
„ Hugh, Collinstown, Co. Dublin, Barr.-at-law 1805. Swan.
„ als. Johnston, Jane, Tully, Co. Longford 1754. Swan. P.
„ James, Augher, Co. Tyrone, gent. 1732. Swan. P.
„ James, Cairncastle, Co. Antrim 1812. C.D.B.
„ John, Glanmore, Co. Longford 1725. Ir.
„ John, Proudstown, Co. Meath, gent. 1792. Swan. P.
„ Joseph, student at Glasgow Univ. 1746. Swan. P.
„ Katherine, Mullingar, Co. Westmeath, widow 1709. Ir.
„ Nicholas, St. Thomas St., Dublin, schoolmaster 1660. F.2.
„ Sir Ralph, Cahirconlish, Co. Limerick, Knt. Dated 1668. W.
„ Robert 1785. S.4. (H.BM.)
„ Robert, Archdeacon of Kilmore 1684. Ir.
„ Rowland, Westmeath 1671. Ir.
„ Rowland, Dublin, Esq. 1671. F.2.
„ Thomas, Dublin 1754. Swan.
„ Thomas, Proudstown, Co. Meath 1812. Swan. P.
„ Rev. William, Shinglas, Westmeath 1743. Ir.
Wilton, Roger, Anna, Co. Cavan 1797. Swan. Kilmore
Winsloe, Thomas, Parsonstown, King's Co. 1720. F.
Winter, Hugh, Kinsale, Co. Cork 1758. S.1. Cork
Wiseman, John 1737. W. Cork
„ Joseph, Carrigadrohid, Co. Cork 1804. C.D.B.
„ als. Venables, Mary, widow of Edward W., Wexford 1683. W.P.
„ Ruth, Dublin, widow Dated 1662. W. Dublin
„ William, Bandon, Esq. Dated 1635. F.E. and W. Dublin
„ William [uncle to Edmund Spenser] 1635. B.
Witherington, [Mrs.] Catherine 1797. Swan. P.
Withers, Elizabeth, Cork, spinster 1798. F.A.
Wogan, John, Rathcoffy 1743. Cav.
Wolfe, Major Walter, Dublin 1771. S.4.P.

Wolsely [Wolsesley], Col. Robert, Camolin, Co.
        Wexford   1702. F.2.
Wood, Alex., Calledon, Co. Tyrone   1697. S.2.P.
    „   Edward, Londonderry   Dated 1702. S.2. Derry
    „   John, Geilstown   ? 1620. S.2. Derry
    „   John, Menmurry   1729. S.2. Clogher
    „   Robert   1781. S.4. (H.BM.)
Woodley, Anthony, par. of Kinneih, Co.
        Cork   1666. Swan. Cork
    „   Elizabeth, Cork, widow   Not dated [1773.] Swan. Cork
    „   John, Cork   1684. Swan. Cork
Woodliffe, Thomas, Cork, alderman   1665. W. Cork
Woodruffe, Clement, Bandonbridge   1662. W. Cork
    „   Samuel, Cork, gent.   1734. W. Cork
Woods, Andrew, Ardcanna, Co. Tyrone   1774. S.2.P.
    „   Arthur S., Market Hill, Co. Armagh,
          now of Clifton   1756. S.2.P.
    „   Catherine   1802. C.D.B.
    „   David, Ballydown, Co. Down   1755. S.2.P.
    „   Edward, Glasslough, Co. Monaghan   1736/7. S.2. Clogher
    „   Jas., Milliknock, Co. Monaghan
                                  Dated 1757. S.2. Clogher
    „   John, Cavanreagh   1702. S.2. Clogher
    „   John, Figlish, Co. Tyrone   1736. S.2. Clogher
    „   Robert, Lettergees, Co. Tyrone   1678. S.2. Clogher
    „   Robert, Ardkonne, Co. Tyrone   1791. S.2. Derry
    „   Thomas, Dromeen, Londonderry
                                  Dated 1737. S.2. Derry
    „   William, Legfrashin, Co. Tyrone
                                  Dated 1682. S.2. Derry
    „   William Lyon, par. of Urney, Co.
          Tyrone   1778. S.2. Derry
Woodward, William, Burrisakane   1816. S.1. Killaloe
Workman, Meredith, Mahan, Co. Armagh   1726. W.P.
    „   Meredith, Mahan, Co. Armagh   1742. Swan. P.
    „   Meredith, Mahan, Co. Armagh   1795. Swan. P.
Worth, Edward, Bishop of Killaloe   1670. F.2.
Wray, Mrs. Angel, Fore   1737. S.4.
    „   Jackson, Birr, King's Co.   1800. S.1.P.
    „   Jackson, Bentfield, Co. Antrim   1802. S.1.P.
    „   Henry, Castle Wray, Co. Donegal   1666. S.4. P.
    „   Henry, Castle Wray   1737. S.4.
    „   Henry   D. 1809. S.4. (H.BM.)
    „   als. Babington, Rebecca. *See* Dunkin.
    „   William, Fore (Ards), Co. Donegal   1710. S.4.
Wright, Christopher, Drumloo, Co. Monaghan 1766. Swan. P.

IN THE GENEALOGICAL OFFICE, DUBLIN

Wright, William, Cork — 1813. C.D.B.
Wrightson, Anne, Dublin, widow — 1803. C.D.B.
Wrixon, Henry, Ballygiblin, Co. Cork, gent. — 1714. F.A., F.B. and W.P.
„ Henry, Glinfield, Co. Cork, Esq. — 1732. F.A. and W.P.
„ Henry, Blossomfort, Co. Cork, gent. — 1778. F.A.
„ Henry, Assollas, Co. Cork, Esq. — 1794. F.A.
„ John, Blossomfort, Co. Cork, gent. — 1744. F.A. and W.P.
„ Mary — 1744. F. Cork and F.B.
„ Mary — 1745. F. Cork
„ Nicholas, Ballygiblin, Co. Cork, gent. — 1740. F.A.
„ Robert, Kilroe, Co. Cork — 1750. F.A. and W.P.
„ Robert, Woodpark, Co. Cork, gent. — 1753. F.A.
„ Robert, Cork, Esq. — 1768. F.A.
Wybrants, Rev. Peter, Ballymackey, Co. Tipperary — 1755. Swan.
„ Stephen, Dublin, Esq. — 1810. Swan. P.
Wynne, Anne, Portarlington, Queen's Co. — 1801. C.D.B.
„ Rev. John, D.D., Prec. St. Patrick's — 1762. Swan.
„ Rev. John, junr. — 1782. Swan.

Yarner, Mary. *See* Eccles.
Yeadan, John, The Abbey, Boyle, Co. Roscommon — 1681. Ir.
„ John, The Abbey, Boyle, Co. Roscommon — 1682. Ir.
„ John, The Abbey, Boyle, Co. Roscommon — 1691. Ir.
Yeamans, Edmond, Lisfuntion, Co. Tipperary, Esq. — 1734. F.A.
„ Francis, Limerick, merchant — 1757. F.A.
„ Mary, Rathkeale, Co. Limerick, widow — 1780. F.A.
Yeates, Robert, Dublin, gent. — 1699. W.P.
Yeedon, Mathew, Liserlogh, Co. Sligo — Dated 1730. Ir.
„ Thomas, Castlereagh, Co. Roscommon — 1710. Ir.
„ Thomas, junr. — 1716. Ir.
Yelverton, William, Lackafinna, Co. Galway — Dated 1744. W. Clonfert
Yielding, James, Tralee, Co. Kerry, gent. — 1725. W. Ardfert
„ John, Tralee, gent. — Dated 1745. W. Ardfert
Young, Cosby, Lahard, Co. Cavan — 1825. Swan. P.
„ Francis, Rockfield, Co. Cavan — 1777. Swan. Kilmore
„ James, the elder, Lahard — Not dated [1798.] Swan. P.

INDEX OF WILL ABSTRACTS
IN THE GENEALOGICAL OFFICE, DUBLIN

Young,	John, Drumgoon, Co. Cavan, gent.	1779. Swan.	Kilmore
,,	John, Corlismore, Co. Cavan, Esq.	1791. Swan.	P.
,,	John, Drummore, Co. Cavan, gent.	1793. Swan.	Kilmore
,,	John, Philpotstown, Co. Meath	1823. Swan.	P.
,,	Mathew, Coolban, Co. Cavan	1697. Swan.	P.
,,	Rachel, Cootehill	1757. Swan.	Kilmore
,,	Richard, Lahard, Co. Cavan	1749. Swan.	P.
,,	Richard, Creeny, Co. Cavan	1769. Swan.	Kilmore
,,	Richard, Drumgood, Co. Cavan	1795. Swan.	P.
,,	Thomas, Corlismore, Co. Cavan	1791. Swan.	P.
,,	Rev. William Not dated	Swan.	